Language Center
Handbook
2021

Language Center Handbook 2021

Elizabeth Lavolette
and
Angelika Kraemer, Editors

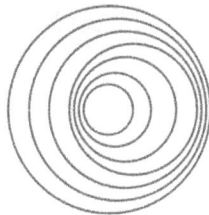

A publication of the International Association for Language Learning Technology

First Printing: 2021

ISBN: 9-781946-123053

International Association for Language Learning Technology

Liberal Arts – Admin

302 Tichenor Hall

Auburn University, AL 36849

United States

https://iallt.org

Designed by Robert Terry using Adobe® InDesign CC®. Typefaces used in this book are Minion Pro, Myriad Pro, and Tahoma.

Table of Contents

Introduction

Elizabeth Lavolette, Kyoto Sangyo University, Japan
Angelika Kraemer, Cornell University, USA

The International Association for Language Learning Technology (IALLT) aspires to be an international organization but has sometimes fallen short of that goal. However, our leadership has made efforts to live up to the "international" label, especially recently. Starting in 2019, the IALLT survey has reached a wider global audience (see Lavolette & Kraemer, this volume) and forged partnerships with organizations in Germany (Arbeitskreis der Sprachenzentren; AKS) and Japan (Japan Association for Self-Access Learning; JASAL). In parallel with these achievements, the editors of the current volume have also made an effort to internationalize the *Language Center Handbook 2021*. While the authors of the original *Language Center Handbook* (Lavolette & Simon, 2018) were mainly based in the US, the authors of the current volume live and work in Canada, Germany, Hong Kong, Japan, Mexico, and the US, and several chapters represent international collaborations.

Given the international character of this volume, defining the subjects of our work takes on new importance to avoid misunderstandings. First, certain chapters (e.g., Sebastian, Gopalakrishnan, & Hendricks; Lavolette & Kraemer) refer to "language labs," particularly with reference to history. As Sebastian et al. (this volume) explain, the first language labs were "installations of mechanical and electronic equipment" (Johnston & Seerley, 1958, p. 1). However, a contemporary language lab can be pictured as "a room filled with desks or cubicles, each of which has a computer for individual use" (Lavolette, 2019, p. 12).

Moving forward in history, many chapters in this volume concern "language centers." Lavolette and Kraemer (2017) defined a language center in the US context as "a physical and/or virtual space that supports foreign and/or second language learning and/or teaching within a larger educational institution" (p. 149). These language centers, or LCs, often maintain language labs as drop-in spaces for students or as classrooms.

Outside of the US, language education spaces are often conceptualized somewhat differently. In name, they are referred to as self-access centers (SACs), self-access learning centers (SALCs), or similar. They have been defined in ways that do not differ greatly from US LCs: A self-access center is "any purpose-designed facility in which learning resources are made directly available to learners" (Benson, 2001, p. 114). However, note that no mention is made of language teaching, making such centers unlikely to provide professional development support to language teachers (Lavolette, 2019; see also Lavolette & Kraemer, this volume). Another important difference from US LCs is that SALCs are intended to promote self-directed learning (or self-access learning). This approach encourages learner autonomy (Garner & Miller, 1999), which is a defining focus of SALCs (e.g., Benson, 2001; Little, 2017; Mach, 2015; Mynard, 2016).

We have divided the chapters in this volume thematically into three sections: The Origins and Fundamentals of Language Spaces, Designing and Redesigning Language Spaces, and Technologies for Language Spaces.

The Origins and Fundamentals of Language Spaces

Five chapters cover big-picture issues for language spaces, including their history, related professional organizations, and important services. Sebastian, Gopalakrishnan, and Hendricks begin this section by tracing the history of US LCs and global SALCs from their beginnings as language laboratories in the early 20th century. Although they show that the golden age of language labs is long past, they offer hope for the future of language education spaces that innovate and reinvent themselves.

One way that US LCs could reinvent themselves is by learning from SALCs, that is, by cultivating a focus on developing learner autonomy and offering learning advising services. In the next chapter, Thornton, Taylor, Tweed, and Yamashita provide an introduction to SACs in Japan, as social learning spaces that foster learner autonomy. They also introduce JASAL, the Japanese organization that supports SACs and became an official partner organization of IALLT in 2020. Naturally, SACs are also facing challenges in keeping self-access language learning relevant, including the push to move services online, which was accelerated due to the COVID-19 pandemic.

Some hints for rising to these challenges may be found in the following chapter, in which Giupponi, Heidrich Uebel, and Van Gorp offer strategies for LCs to advance online language instruction, including two case studies of the strategies in action.

Change is the only constant in many language spaces, as Baumann shows in her chapter focused on four categories of change at the University of Chicago Language Center. She explores how LCs can function in various institutional contexts and provides ideas for initiatives and programs that are applicable to a wide variety of LCs.

Completing this section, Lavolette and Kraemer provide a different perspective on the history of (mostly US) LCs through an overview of IALLT surveys, starting in 1975, and focusing on the four most recent IALLT surveys (2013, 2015, 2017, and 2019). They paint a picture of the "typical" LC director, including employment conditions, educational background, and perceived challenges, and the "typical" LC, including its staffing, physical spaces, and services. They conclude with predictions for the future of LCs.

Designing and Redesigning Language Spaces

In this section, four chapters report on approaches to designing and redesigning language spaces around the world. In the first chapter, Li and Ching describe a research project around the redesign of a SALC in Hong Kong in which they successfully transformed the physical space, materials available to students, and services on offer.

Next, Lalovic offers insights into the bilingual context at the University of Ottawa and the creation and evolution of the Official Languages and Bilingualism

Institute that promotes cultural understanding and linguistic competence in both of Canada's official languages. His chapter concludes with challenges related to transitioning from a resource center to a social hub and suggestions for potential partnerships beyond the university context.

Kirchmeyer examines co-adaptation occurring in and around a LC at a university in Japan as the center was rebuilt after a series of devastating earthquakes and was redesigned again in response to the COVID-19 pandemic. Rooted in complex dynamic systems theory, his chapter illustrates how new and existing technologies can be leveraged to adapt to drastic changes in one LC's environment.

In their chapter, Kronenberg and Schwienhorst take an innovative approach by introducing their evolutionary model for LC design and showing how they used it in case studies of co-design processes at one institution in the US and one in Germany.

Technologies for Language Spaces

The four chapters in this section describe innovative projects undertaken at language centers that required technological expertise and support from LC staff. First, Majors, Hugo, and Aoki argue for the continuing need for LCs to provide media conversion, curation, preservation, and creation. In particular, they provide examples of how LCs can support Indigenous communities and language faculty projects.

Next, Brinckwirth, Hernández Alvarado, Hidalgo Avilés, Espinosa Butrón, and Alfaro Flores report on numerous telecollaboration projects that connected students at universities in the US and Mexico and that LC staff were instrumental in facilitating.

In the following chapter, Fitzgerald introduces immersive language learning technologies, considers the role of LCs in supporting the use of this technology, identifies affordances and persistent challenges, and offers preliminary conclusions on the role of LCs in facilitating immersive learning applications.

Finally, Enkin and Kirschling explain their concept of a "smart language lab" and the expertise needed to build one. They describe immersive VR-based projects that were made possible by their smart language lab.

We hope you will find this volume to be thought-provoking and inspiring. We would be remiss if we did not thank everybody who made this volume possible. Thank you to the IALLT Board for entrusting us with this project. Particular gratitude goes to all authors, who gave their time to write and rewrite manuscripts, and to the many reviewers, who completed double-blind reviews. Finally, special thanks go to Bob Terry for his meticulous and swift work as graphic and page layout designer.

References

Benson, P. (2001). *Teaching and researching autonomy in language learning*. Essex, UK: Longman.

Gardner, D., & Miller, L. (1999). *Establishing self-access*. Cambridge, UK: Cambridge University Press.

Johnston, M. C., & Seerley C. C. (1958). *Survey of foreign language laboratories in secondary schools and institutions of higher education*. Washington, DC: U.S. Department of Health, Education, Welfare.

Lavolette, E. (2019). A very brief introduction to US language centers. In L. Xethakis & C. Taylor (Eds.), *JASAL 2018 x SUTLF 5: Selected papers from the Sojo University Teaching and Learning Forum 2018: Making connections* (pp. 4–25). Kumamoto, Japan: NanKyu JALT. https://www.nankyujalt.org/publications#h.p_twJDnQsJDWmj

Lavolette, E., & Kraemer, A. (2017). The language center evaluation toolkit: Context, development, and usage. In F. A. Kronenberg (Ed.), *From language lab to language center and beyond: The past, present, and future of the language center* (pp. 147–160). Auburn, AL: International Association for Language Learning Technology.

Lavolette, E., & Simon, E. F. (Eds.). (2018). *Language center handbook*. Auburn, AL: International Association for Language Learning Technology.

Little, D. (2017). University language centres, self-access learning and learner autonomy. *Researching and Teaching Languages for Specific Purposes, 34*(1), 13–26. https://doi.org/10.4000/apliut.5008

Mach, T. (2015). Promoting learner autonomy through a self-access center at Konan University: From theory to proposal. *The Journal of the Institute for Language and Culture, 19*, 3–29.

Mynard, J. (2016). Self-access in Japan: Introduction. *Studies in Self-Access Learning Journal, 7*(4), 331–340. https://doi.org/10.37237/070401

Cultivating International Connections in Language Spaces

Elizabeth Lavolette, Kyoto Sangyo University, Japan

As I was preparing to move to Japan in early 2018, I became very interested in discovering the language education spaces in my new country. I had heard of self-access learning centers (SALCs) (often also called self-access centers or SACs) but did not know much about them. A web search brought me to the Japan Association for Self-Access Learning (JASAL), and I immediately joined. Thanks to the interactions I had with JASAL members and my own explorations, I soon understood that the language centers (LCs) I was familiar with in the US and those in Japan had some important differences. My eyes were opened to the world of self-access and its focus on learner autonomy, which is found not only in Japan, but in much of the rest of the world. I also came to understand that professional development events would not be offered at the SALC at my university—or at those of other universities in Japan, for the most part.

Despite these differences, I found that SALCs and LCs were actually the same in many important ways. Both types of centers aim to support language learners. Both place a high value on social learning. Both provide materials and technology to learners in physical and virtual spaces.

Given the similarities of these spaces, why did I know so little about SALCs? The main reason is that I was immersed in the American LC literature, which rarely cited the SALC literature. I imagined that this might be due to American insular attitudes, and perhaps that is part of the reason. However, as I delved into the SALC literature, I found that it also rarely cited the US literature on LCs. The underlying reasons for this are still not clear to me, but I speculate that historical differences between the types of centers may have resulted in both sides dismissing ideas originating from the other type of center.

In the two bodies of literature and the two groups of scholars surrounding them, I saw a great potential for mutual learning that could be realized simply by encouraging communication between the two groups. Thus, in addition to their scholarly merit, the chapters for this book were deliberately selected to facilitate that international conversation. This volume is the most international that IALLT has yet published, with more than half of the chapters (7 of 13) including at least one author who does not live in the US. It is a great honor to include chapters from authors in Canada, Germany, Hong Kong, Japan, and Mexico, in addition to authors based in the US.

I have learned a great deal from the privilege of working with these authors. I invite you to do the same, whether you approach this book from the perspective of someone who is new to language spaces, a US language center specialist, a SALC specialist, or (dare I imagine it!) someone with a deep knowledge of both.

The Origins and Fundamentals

of Language Spaces

Chapter 1
Language Laboratories and Centers: Looking to History and Anticipating the Future

Paul Sebastian, Appalachian State University, USA
Sangeetha Gopalakrishnan, Wayne State University, USA
Harold H. Hendricks, Brigham Young University, USA

Abstract

Language laboratories and their successors, language centers (LCs), have been in a continual state of flux for over a decade. Major shifts in both educational technology and second language teaching methods have contributed strongly to the evolution of these support units. This chapter examines how language laboratories came to be, how they transformed into language centers, and what the future of the LC might be.

The chapter begins with a broad overview of the history of language labs and how they eventually evolved into LCs. It concludes with some forward-looking suggestions for how LCs might rise to meet the future technological and pedagogical needs of language teachers and students. Throughout the chapter, the authors have enriched the narrative with their own personal accounts from their time as former LC administrators. The chapter's ultimate conclusion is that although the future will likely test the inherent adaptability of LCs, those who manage to keep their doors open will find themselves well-positioned to assist language teachers and students as they navigate a radically transformed hybrid and online learning landscape.

For about 100 years, language laboratories and their successors, language centers (LCs), have been in a continual state of adaptation (Clarke, 1918; Roby, 2004). Although much of this chapter refers to language labs and centers in the context of the United States, it is important to note that their history extends beyond US borders. Radical and rapid shifts in both technology and second language teaching methods have contributed strongly to the evolution of these dynamic spaces and their functions. Any attempt to understand the future direction of language labs and centers must take into account how they came to be and how they have changed over time. In this chapter, we provide an updated history of these dynamic support units, with a particular focus on how they have been shaped by broader technological and methodological advancements.

A handful of historical summaries have emerged over the past few decades. Kronenberg's (2017) edited volume provided a platform for multiple voices to comment on the past, present, and future directions of LCs. More than a decade before that, Roby (2004) compiled a detailed account of the history of LCs and their 20th century counterparts, language laboratories. Written during the golden age of the audio-lingual-era language laboratory, Hocking's (1964) book explored the role of these spaces within their respective technological and methodological contexts.

These historical accounts are separated by periods of intense technological and methodological fluctuations in the field of language education. Over the years, the language learning and technology community has concerned itself with questions about the future of the language laboratory and, more recently, the language center, in all of their various forms. Numerous conference sessions and publications have been devoted to this very topic, many of which have been sponsored by the International Association for Language Learning Technology (IALLT) and other organizations that have emerged in similar professional circles. For instance, at the Teachers of English to Speakers of Other Languages (currently known as TESOL International Association) convention in March 1994, a panel of experienced language laboratory directors deliberated this topic at a session titled "Whither the Language Lab?" (Dvorak et al., 1995). During the session, Trish Dvorak, the then director of the Language Resource Center at the University of Michigan and President of the International Association for Learning Labs, asked the panelists to discuss the future of language labs and centers:

> Some schools have actually done away with language labs altogether. Others are expanding, remodeling, renovating, and adding new equipment, while other schools are trying to figure out if any of this matters anymore. What's happening to language labs around the country, and who cares? What role can they play in communicative language programs and in supporting faculty and curriculum development? Who are the next generation of language lab directors and what knowledge and skills must they bring to their task? What attitudes do students have about language labs and how does this affect their experiences as learners? (p. 14)

The questions posed to that 1994 panel centered around core issues for language laboratories including their perceived status in broader educational contexts, their role in facilitating the prevalent pedagogies of the time, the role of the language lab directors and their competencies, and students' perceptions of the usefulness of language labs. These very issues continue to resurface and are especially present in IALLT's handbooks, manuals, and other publications. Such topics reflect the dynamic and ever-evolving identities of these complex support units and their role in the world language curriculum.

Even in the midst of accelerated technological and pedagogical change, language centers continue to respond with great institutional agility. In many ways, technology is now predominantly place-free, allowing students to access online workbooks, game-based language applications, and high-quality authentic resources without having to visit a centralized physical location. Furthermore, language teaching methods, although mostly unified by the common goal of real-world communication, are numerous and highly variable. Complicating this new technological and methodological context, the emergence of the coronavirus in 2020 has caused a massive reevaluation of traditional teaching and learning paradigms. For these reasons, the contemporary LC, a facility that has historically existed as a physical, technology-enhanced teaching and learning space, finds itself in yet another phase of adaptation. Thus, at this moment of heightened uncertainty, it is paramount that the historical roots of the LC be retraced. Both the technological and methodological contexts have changed drastically since both the Roby (2004) and Hocking (1964) historical overviews. Furthermore, although Kronenberg's (2017) edited volume revisited this important conversation, the mostly anecdotal accounts generated even more questions regarding what is happening to LCs and where they will end up 10 or even 50 years down the road. And so, we take up this narrative once again, if not because there is more story to tell, then because hearing it from new perspectives may provide answers as to where LCs are headed in the future. To accomplish this goal, our synthesis draws on many historical fragments, some published through official academic channels, others shared by generous colleagues or taken from our own personal and professional experiences as former LC directors who are at the beginning, midpoint, and end of their careers.

As a point of departure, it is important to clarify some key terms used in this chapter. First, when referring to language centers, we have in mind the definition set forth by Lavolette and Kraemer (2017), who described them as a "physical and/or virtual space that supports foreign and/or second language learning and/or teaching within a larger educational institution" (p. 149). However, because our analysis is mostly restricted to the technological and methodological roots of LCs, its relevance may not extend to centers which are now completely void of any technological tools or that exist more as general libraries or study halls. As for the term "language laboratory," we have in mind the description of Johnston and Seerley (1958), who referred to such support units as "installations of mechanical and electronic equipment to facilitate language learning by groups or by individuals" (p. 1). The two definitions overlap only in their reference to language learning. In the latter, the principal emphasis is on the role of technological installations and in the former, technology is not mentioned at all. Instead, Lavolette and

Kraemer focused on the supportive role of the language center while leaving room for the many variations of form and function found in contemporary centers. Interestingly, this idea of institutional variation was also noted in Johnston and Seerley's survey of 261 language laboratories in the United States, whose results showed "a great variety of facilities and a wide divergence of opinion concerning what constitutes a language laboratory" (p. 2). Beyond the US context, the task of reaching any uniform consensus as to what these facilities are and how they serve the efforts of second language teaching and learning becomes drastically more difficult. Lavolette's (2019) article represents one such attempt to broaden the discussion by weaving together the literature involving US-style language centers with self-access learning centers (SALCs). In defining the latter, she highlighted the importance given to learner autonomy of SALCs and pointed to Swanson and Yahiro's (2012) explanation that they "can range from simple resource libraries of materials that students can self-access to full blown physical spaces with large amounts of resources, staffing, and equipment" (p. 115). Although the definition captures both the idea of learner support and the potential role of technology, second language teaching and learning are not explicitly mentioned.

We have chosen to divide the history of these facilities into four distinct periods, each marked by certain important historical events. Broadly speaking, we begin with a discussion of the phonetics lab and the subsequent rise of the language laboratory during the early 1900s. Following, we comment on what has been referred to as the golden era of language labs (Roby, 2004), a period ranging from 1958 to 1970. The third period spans the last three decades of the century and focuses on the gradual and somewhat messy transition from language laboratory to language center. Although it is particularly challenging to write about the historical period in which one is currently living, we attempt to round out the analysis by discussing how language centers have fared from 2000 to 2020. Finally, we offer some predictions about where LCs are headed next and what they might look like in the future. In each of the sections of the chapter, we explain the period's dominant technologies and methods in their respective chronological contexts. Lastly, we have woven into the analysis a number of vignettes that highlight our own encounters with various historical artifacts, tools, and practices to illustrate the broader trends and patterns that we discuss in our narrative.

1. The Rise of the Language Laboratory: 1877–1958

With technological roots in Thomas Edison's 1877 invention of the phonograph, language laboratories slowly emerged during the first few decades of the 20th century and existed as technology-enhanced physical spaces dedicated primarily to the teaching and learning of phonetics (Clarke, 1918; Waltz, 1930). Archived on a website hosted by the US National Park Service, an audio clip contains the earliest known recording of Thomas Edison's own voice. The clip, recorded in 1888, begins with a garbled mix of white noise that quickly gives way to Edison's discernible voice saying, "I'll take you around the world on the phonograph" (Edison, 1888). For some language educators, the short clip could very well have been their first time hearing any audio recording at all. For the field of language education, the phonograph was the spark that kicked off a century of pedagogical, philosophical, and technological change. Still, wide adoption of the device was slow (Keating, 1936; Roby, 2004), and it was not until 1908 that a dedicated phonetics laboratory was established at the University of Grenoble in France (Roby, 2004). Roby described this first lab as a "dedicated facility for foreign-language study" (p. 524). Frank C. Chalfant, after visiting the pioneering center in France, later returned to the United States to create the first language laboratory at Washington State College in Pullman in 1911. Chalfant's lab used a version of Edison's phonograph to record student language production, and listening was facilitated through networked headphones (Roby, 2004). At about this same time, the US Military and Naval Academy had begun to set aside rooms for listening to foreign language records (Clarke, 1918). Not too long after, Ralph Waltz established a phonetics lab at the University of Utah in 1919 and then another at Ohio State University in 1925 (Waltz, 1930). In spite of Chalfant and Waltz's pioneering efforts, wider adoption was slow. As Roby (2004) pointed out, this delay may have been due to broader economic challenges of the time. However, another potential reason for the slow proliferation of labs was because of the mismatch between the technological affordances of the phonograph and the dominant language teaching methods at that time.

Prior to World War I, one of the primary goals of language education was to facilitate the reading of classical literature in the languages in which each piece was written. Accordingly, the dominant pedagogical approach at the time was the grammar-translation method, which "focused on translation of printed texts, learning of grammatical rules, and memorization of bilingual word lists" (Shrum & Glisan, 2015, p. 44). With World War II came an increased need for students who could not only read and write in a foreign language, but who could also speak and understand the language in an increasing number of contexts. This development coincided chronologically with the parallel developments of increasingly sophisticated versions of Edison's phonograph and magnetic tape-recording technology. What unfolded, then, was a period in which technology existed as an ideal complement to the needs and demands of language teaching methods. The increased focus on language for communication ultimately resulted in the transition from the literary-focused grammar-translation method to the mass adoption of the fluency-focused audio-lingual method of language instruction. This method's heavy orientation to the listening and speaking modalities was reinforced by the technological tools of the time. In this manner, teaching methods and technology worked in tandem to define the next several decades of second language teaching and learning. This relationship was further strengthened by developments in the field of behavioral psychology that suggested that learning occurred through conditioning responses by repeating the appropriate combination of stimuli and reinforcements (Driscoll, 2005). Thus, the political, methodological, technological, and broader educational contexts of the 1940s and 1950s provided the ideal conditions for the subsequent mass proliferation of language laboratories. During these two decades, language labs began to transform from a small collection of mostly experimental phonetics labs to an increasingly technologically and methodologically homogenous group of support units. Koekkoek (1959) described the transition in this way:

> The language laboratory and its spread is a postwar [World War II] development, fostered by a climate of experimentation which was stimulated by the Army language teaching program during the war. Of tangible importance for the emergence of the language laboratory were the increasing number of commercial machines which could be adapted for language teaching, the willingness of language teachers to work with such machines, and the receptivity of school administrators to buy them. (p. 4)

As evidence of this transitional period, Whitehouse (1945) described what he referred to as a language "Work Shop" which, although technologically similar to earlier phonetics labs, provided a laboratory-like space to enhance the teaching and learning of languages. Whitehouse's language Work Shop, located at Birmingham-Southern College, was part of a language curriculum that called for "one day a week in the Work Shop, that is, one-fifth of the time allotted to each class is spent in the Work Shop under the supervision and direction of the instructor regularly in charge of the class" (p. 88). Just a few years, later in 1947 Wayne State University opened the doors to one of the first language laboratories documented during this era. An annotated bibliography compiled by José Sánchez in 1959 contains additional clues as to the existence of these postwar laboratories. The document shows that early language laboratories were in place as early as 1948 at Mount Holyoke College and 1949 at Cornell University, Georgetown University, Iowa State University, and Yale University. Another US lab was opened in 1951 at the University of Nebraska, the same year that the first language lab opened in Japan at the Kyoto Liberal Arts College (Kakita, 1973). About this time, Pierre Capretz at the University of Florida was experimenting with magnetic tape recorders and developed an audio lab of his own design. By 1952, labs were in place at Purdue University and the University of Tennessee, and by 1954, at the University of Kansas and the University of Miami (Sánchez, 1959). Almost all of these language labs were created, administered, and often maintained by individual pioneering and innovative faculty to enhance the teaching of their own students. There were, no doubt, other laboratories that emerged during this time, but these stories have largely faded from the collective memory of our institutional past. Then, in 1958, due to the shockwave felt from the 1957 launch of Russia's Sputnik satellite, the US government passed the National Defense Education Act, a major milestone in the evolution of language labs and centers.

2. The Golden Era of the Language Laboratory: 1958–1970

Largely in reaction to the October 1957 launch of Sputnik, the United States Government passed the National Defense Education Act (NDEA) in 1958. Title III of the bill allotted 70 million dollars per year for four years to be used for the "acquisition of equipment (suitable for use in providing education in science, mathematics, or modern foreign language)" (National Defense Education Act, 1958, p. 1588). To access the funds, states were encouraged to submit proposals

Wayne State University: The Origins of the Language Lab, circa 1940s

The evolution of the "Language Lab" to the "Language Laboratory Center" and then to the "Foreign Language Technology Center (FLTC)" at Wayne State University (WSU) is illustrative of the progression that occurred in the field over the years. In 2009 I had the opportunity to deliver the Henderson plenary at the International Association for Language Learning Technology (IALLT) conference in Atlanta. The talk, "The evolution of teaching language, culture and literature with technology: Has the role of technology changed?", got me digging into the history of the language laboratory at Wayne. Until I began preparing for this talk, I would have asserted that the story of technology integration in foreign language instruction at WSU began in the 1960s. Because some of the photos and artifacts that I had found at the FLTC pointed to the 1960s, I had come to that conclusion. However, it turned out that I was wrong. Doing the research for my IALLT talk brought much of my own institution's history in this regard to light. I chanced upon an article published in 1959 in The Modern Language Journal (MLJ) by Koekkoek about the dominance of the phonograph and the onset of the new language laboratory movement. While reading this article, I came across a section which almost knocked me right off my chair! The passage read: "The first MLJ description of the use of a language laboratory, specifically called by that term, is that of the one at Wayne State University from 1948" (p. 5). The modern language laboratory movement is considered to have begun after WWII in 1946 (Hocking, 1967; Koekkoek, 1959). Little did I know that WSU, my institution, had joined the language laboratory movement as early as the 1940s!

Eager to know more about this pioneering use of technology, I attempted to find the earlier MLJ article. After some digging, I found the article published in 1948 by John Ebelke. I discovered that the language laboratory had indeed been established at my institution in 1947! John Ebelke (1948) described the language laboratory at Wayne as an "experiment" (p. 590). Wanting to know more about the 1940s language laboratory at WSU, I searched the university archives and asked some of the senior faculty members. Unfortunately, other than this article, I found little documentation about this pioneering early lab at WSU. A lot of the historical information has been scattered and, perhaps, even lost entirely. Reconstructing the history of the language laboratory at Wayne for my IALLT talk turned out to be a walk down discovery lane.

—*Sangeetha Gopalakrishnan, Wayne State University*

demonstrating their plans for the "acquisition of laboratory and other special equipment, including audio-visual materials and equipment and printed materials (other than textbooks)" (National Defense Education Act, 1958, p. 1589). Although the Title III funds were made available specifically to elementary and secondary schools, Titles VI and VII of the bill earmarked millions of dollars more over the next four years to institutions of higher education, incentivizing renewed efforts in the area of language education research, professional development for current and future language educators, and the further expansion of programs for languages and cultures deemed of critical importance to national security. Further coupling the funds to the development of educational technologies, Title VII outlined the formation of a new committee charged to:

> Conduct, assist, and foster research and experimentation in the development and evaluation of projects involving television, radio, motion pictures, and related media of communication which may prove of value to State or local educational agencies in the operation of their public elementary or secondary schools, and to institutions of higher education, including the development of new and more effective techniques and methods. (p. 1595)

The committee would also oversee advancements in the educational use of "motion pictures, video tapes and other audio-visual aids, film strips, slides and other visual aids, recordings (including magnetic tapes) and other auditory aids, and radio or television program scripts" (p. 1595). Thus, by allocating massive amounts of money, and by restricting those funds to very specific uses, the NDEA of 1958 ushered in what Roby (2004) referred to as the golden era of language laboratories.

By the beginning of the new decade, the number of language laboratories skyrocketed thanks to both the infusion of federal funds and the aggressive marketing of educational technology companies. Figure 1 has been generated using data from reports by Hocking (1964), Johnston and Seerley (1958), and Locke (1965) and represents the growth of language laboratories in the United States.

Figure 1

Number of Language Laboratories in the United States: 1957–1965

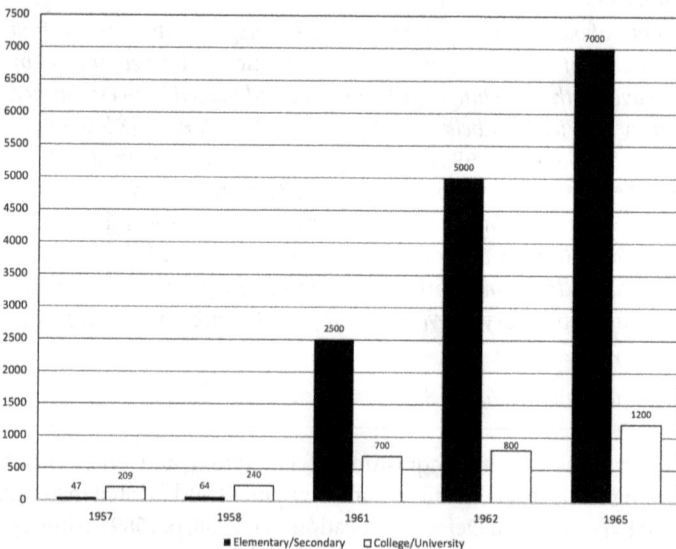

The expansion was exponential. Reflecting on this growth in 1962, Gaudin wrote: "Today a school, college or university without a language laboratory is almost as inconceivable as one without a library" (p. 79). The extensive installation of language laboratories was received with a mix of almost nationalistic optimism and cautious concern. A video highlighting innovative programs at Claremont Colleges, circa 1963, shows video and images of a newly installed laboratory. The clip, narrated by the man who would become the 40th President of the United States, Ronald Reagan, shows a scene of a language professor making use of the language laboratory to carry out a lesson in Russian using recordable phonograph disks. Reagan explains that by "combining both personal instruction and modern techniques, the language laboratory is important in the race to communicate our ideas" (Claremont Colleges, 1963).

Throughout this period, the main function of both the lab facilities and the technology in the classroom was first and foremost to bring authentic spoken language to the ears of students who were often being taught by non-native instructors. Another important function was to aid in the memorization and repetition of dialogs and pattern drills. Additionally, the language lab allowed for the recording of student speech, both as repetition from master-track modelling and free-form conversation. Consequently, the early 1960s saw an increase of commercially available lab systems from a variety of manufacturers based on reel-to-reel tape players that offered scheduled listening of publisher-developed tapes, workbook exercises, and the ability to record both individual and class oral production. Many of these manufacturers were based in Europe and Japan, and the language lab continued to be adopted in more countries. Attempting to understand the state of language laboratories on a more global scale, Locke (1965) reported estimates of language laboratories in countries outside the United States. The estimations were acquired through a combination of Locke's research and personal correspondence with colleagues knowledgeable about each of the countries listed in Figure 2.

Figure 2

Estimated Number of Language Laboratories Outside of the US as of 1965

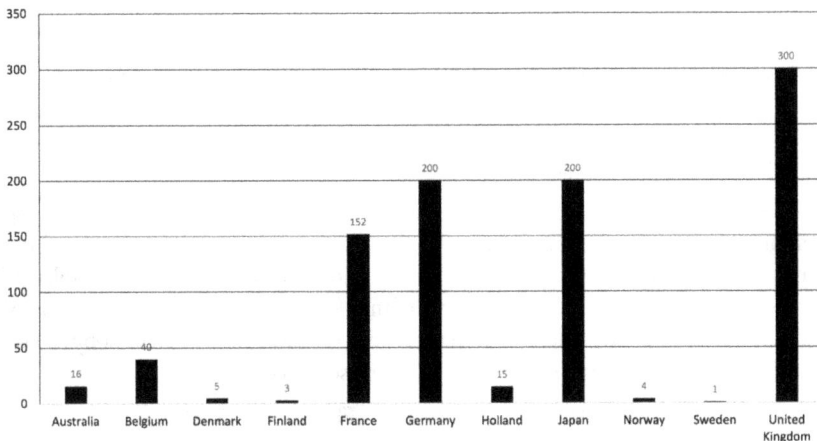

As the popularity of these somewhat standardized language laboratories continued to spread, language educators around the world began to organize, and in July of 1961, the Language Laboratory Association of Japan (LLA) was founded with about 700 members throughout Japan (Kuroda, 1981). Four years later, in December of 1965, another group of language professionals, whose duties now included the supervision and management of these labs, gathered in Chicago, IL, to hold the inaugural meeting of the National Association of Language Lab Directors (NALLD), which took place concurrently with the Modern Language Association Convention (NALLD Newsletter, 1966). NALLD and LLA became strong partners over the following years, and in 1981, the two organizations would cosponsor the Foreign Language Education and Technology (FLEAT) international conference in Tokyo, Japan (Kuroda, Kohmoto, & Sheehan, 1981).

Still, even during the golden era of language laboratories, there were signs of growing pains. Zeldner's (1963) fictional dialog between a language teacher and her department chair is telling. After expressing frustrations about the time-intensive task of dealing with broken machines, loose plugs, and wrong tapes, the teacher warns, "and if the Board will put in a laboratory, it will be a nightmare" (p. 246). Cioffari (1961) cautioned:

> The danger in the use of *laboratory* comes from a false feeling of security. In and of itself the laboratory cannot teach complete language because it cannot teach people to think, and language is the expression of thought. The laboratory cannot perform miracles nor produce a new generation of speakers who have been spared the weary hours of training previously required. School systems which install language laboratories with the expectation of relegating teaching to tape recorders are misleading themselves and the public. (p. 9)

By the end of the decade, both the newly installed technologies and the methodological premises that supported their use had begun to lose their shine. Sherrow's (1970) sentiments capture this particular period of waning popularity:

> Let's install a lab! Nothing can go wrong! It was the decade of the sixties: a golden era. Language institutes flourished, electronic labs sprouted, magnetic tapes proliferated, and Candide-like optimism prevailed throughout the land. Surely, labs could help solve many of the problems facing language educators. The sixties, however, often proved to be a golden error. Language labs caused at least as many problems as they solved, and teachers discovered, contrary to expectations, that almost nothing could go right in lab. (p. 28)

Sherrow's report ends, however, on a hopeful note for language laboratories, calling for an increased use of the spaces as centers for individualized instruction, something Sherrow believed to be quite achievable given the particular advances in the flexibility of the new audio cassette tape. The golden days of the 1960s lasted only till about the end of the decade, by which time federal funding had been drastically withdrawn. Roby (2004) noted, "language laboratories ended the 1960s on a sour note" (p. 527).

3. Language Laboratories in Flux: 1970–2000

3.1 Growing Pains: 1970–1991

By the 1970s, language labs started to change yet again. "The 1970s and early 1980s," as noted by Roby (2004), "were a period of malaise for the language laboratory" (p. 527). The loss of federal funding contributed significantly to the end of the golden era of the language laboratory, and beliefs about language learning were shifting yet again. Stone (1991) explained: "For the most part, the rejection of the language lab in the 1980s was the result of its integral relation to the audio-lingual methodologies, which labs were originally intended to support" (p. 2). Emphasizing this relationship between methods and technology, Stone (1991) explained that:

> Language acquisition theories, however, have changed significantly from the days when the language labs ruled as the pre-eminent technology in language instruction. On the whole, the primary objective now is communicative fluency rather than linguistic accuracy. As a result of this change, the language lab came to be seen as a relic with no merit in today's language learning environment. (p. 2)

Until the 1980s, language laboratories relied mostly on audio technologies. Until this point, the technological options of the audio-lingual labs were comparatively limited, and language teaching methods were similarly monotone in nature. However, during the last two decades of the century, this started to change. Major advances were being made in computer-assisted language learning (CALL), specifically in the areas of video media (Lawrason, 1990; Otto, 1989) and network-based language teaching (Warschauer & Kern, 2000). Thus, although the audio-lingual language lab could still be found in various states of declining use, beginning around the 1970s, the previously cohesive story of language labs begins to branch out, forming a collection of stories united by a common history. This particular period in the history of language labs and centers is especially difficult to summarize because these spaces ceased to evolve in a cohesive fashion and started to change in very different and unique ways. In one of the first accounts of this change in terms of nomenclature, Rallo (1970) described the transition of his school's traditional lab in 1968 to what he called a language resource center:

> It was hoped that the laboratory, when properly used, would supplement the classroom work by relegating tedious, repetitive exercises to taped, authentic voices. This hope, however, was to be only partially fulfilled. The agony suffered by many a teacher who was thrust into a technological venture for which he had neither love nor adequate preparation brought

about serious negative results. Today, [many] laboratories are being ill-used, discarded, routinized or dismantled. Darien High School, too, was faced with this dilemma: to abandon the laboratory, to deemphasize its importance or to give it a new dimension. We opted for the latter. (p. 15)

Rallo went on to describe how the room holding the traditional rows of carrels with a master control console was redesigned to look more like a library reading room with collections of books, newspapers, magazines, records, slides, and filmstrips. His renovated lab design can still be found in many small language centers today, minus the console, and with computers in the carrells instead of just headsets. Additionally, his objectives for the center and his suggestions for its use, supervision, and management would be relevant for at least the next 40 years.

Figure 3

Rallo's Transition of Darien High School Laboratory to Language Resource Center

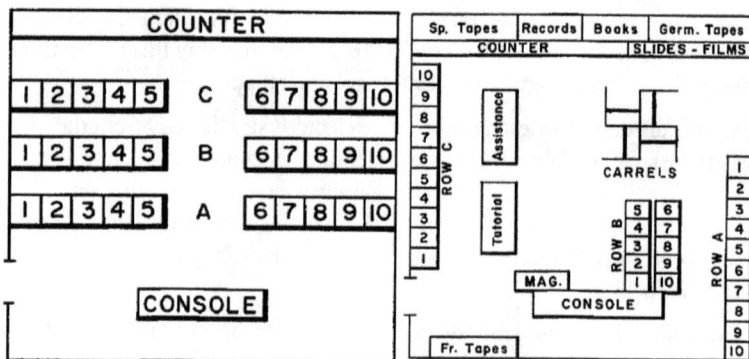

Original Language Lab

Foreign Language Resource Center

Part of the reason for this shift was the emergence of educational and consumer electronics like the portable audio cassette recorder and the audio cassette-driven slide and filmstrip viewer. Some labs began incorporating shortwave radio transmissions, both live and recorded. By the mid 70s, the invention of Betamax and VHS quickly brought authentic video into the mix. By the end of the decade, C-band satellite broadcasts from around the world were available for viewing and recording. All these together created collections of language media, equipment, and materials that were all "resources" that could be used individually or checked out. Soon, the language lab began to resemble a specialized library, and many institutions would follow Rallo's lead in redesigning and redefining their facilities.

For those institutions that chose to continue to upgrade or install new traditional labs, the new audio cassette format reduced the size of the master control consoles. Furthermore, cassette recorders could be automated, and the sound had higher fidelity. The functions of pairing and grouping students, along with the consolidation of all student responses to a single tape for ease of instructor grading, were now common among all the manufacturers. These functions added the extra dimension of group oral testing to the list of lab services. Around this time, textbook publishers began releasing their ancillary audio on cassettes, and some saw this as a revenue stream. The difficult issue of copyright and the fear of unauthorized reproduction of audio material led to discussions between publishers and language lab directors which, in turn, resulted in new protocols for copying and reproducing audio materials in the lab. One specific byproduct was that language students would be required to visit the language lab to have the tapes erased and to have new lessons recorded on them. This required a facility and staff to create these copies, and thus, another function was added to the language lab.

Wayne State University: From Language Lab to Language Center: 1970–2000

Surprisingly, from all that I could gather, the Language Laboratory at Wayne State University was in no way languishing during this period of "malaise," as Roby (2004, p. 527) called it. In sharp contrast to what was happening elsewhere, the 70s were a period of growth for the Language Laboratory at WSU, which moved from the State Hall building to the newly constructed Speech and Language Building, which was dedicated in 1971. It was renamed the "Language Laboratory Center." It occupied most of the third floor in the new building and was considered extraordinary, one of the best in the country. In addition to the language laboratory being featured in university publications, I also found documents indicating tours of the new language laboratory by its director were included in the itinerary of important institutional visitors. Undoubtedly, the new language laboratory had been a source of great pride for the institution.

—Sangeetha Gopalakrishnan, Wayne State University

In their discussion of second language acquisition theory, Shrum and Glisan (2015) explained how, starting around the mid 1960s, the methodological pendulum started to move away from behaviorist ideas and toward the notion that language learning was more than a complex set of conditioned responses. Researchers began to argue that language acquisition occurred not only from listening to massive amounts of input over and over again but also from being exposed to it in a way that was comprehensible to the language learner (Krashen, 1982). Long (1983) emphasized the importance of interaction in the language learning process, an idea that stood in stark contrast to the physical isolation of the individual carrels of the golden-age language laboratory. Finally, Swain (1995) stressed the necessity of providing opportunities for students to speak the target language in ways that went beyond repetitive mimicry. Thus, at the same time that technological advances were causing language centers to become increasingly diverse in form and function, language teaching methods were being transformed from a mostly homogenous enterprise to a rather eclectic set of techniques, tools, and approaches, all of which were rooted in the idea that the goal of learning a second language was for the purpose of real-world communication.

A key technological advancement of this era that facilitated real-world communication was the personal computer. The affordances of the personal computer, although initially unfamiliar and cumbersome, eventually enabled language educators to provide opportunities for students to interact with the target language and target culture in new and meaningful ways. Speaking to these affordances, Blake (1998) wrote:

Throughout the 1960s, 1970s, and early 1980s computer practitioners talked about creating computer-assisted instruction (CAI) for foreign languages. The focus was more on the program than on the learner. CAI programs typically guided learners through a series of tutorials with exercises, tutorials embellished by branching routines that responded to the students' success or difficulty with the lesson. (p. 212)

Addressing the transition from technology-focused programming to a more student-centered model of technology-enhanced pedagogy, Blake (1998) explained that software developers shifted from a focus on linear programming to designing technology that allowed for more user autonomy. Thus, late 20th-century technology became more of a medium for communication than a bank of digitized preprogrammed knowledge.

3.2 Language Laboratories and the Analog-to-Digital Transition: 1991–2000

Developments in technology and teaching methods accelerated quickly throughout the last decade of the millennium. Of particular interest was the year 1991, when the International Association for Learning Laboratories (IALL) changed its name to the International Association for Language Learning Technology, dropping the reference to laboratories and shifting the organizational focus toward broader applications of language technologies (IALLT, 2019). The name change turned out to be more than just a semantic pivot, as remaining language laboratories entered into their final days of audio-lingual relevance.

By the beginning of the 1990s, language centers within US universities were likely to be a combination of old and new technologies. This was an era in which a console-controlled laboratory could be found at one institution and a row of desktop computers at the next. Rewritable CDs and DVDs could be found in the same drawers as audio cassette and VHS tapes. Soundproof recording booths were being converted into video production studios, as large camcorders were replaced by video recorders that fit in the palm of your hand. In-house dedicated servers offered one set of programs while others were offered via networked computing. Walking into a typical classroom, one could often find an LCD overhead projector along with an old 35-mm slide projector off in the corner. Digital document cameras were rolled in and often kept on top of desks whose drawers still contained transparency sheets with remnants of partially conjugated verb trees scrawled in erasable marker. Computer monitors got thinner, telephones became smaller and more mobile, and the cost of almost every piece of consumer technology finally started to be within reach of the general public. Just as their centers were changing around them, language center administrators began taking on the roles of tutoring schedulers, professional development facilitators, and backup IT support for language-specific problems such as television standards, audio formats, computer fonts, and non-roman keyboard inputs.

Introduced in 1991, the World Wide Web suddenly revolutionized access to quotidian information of life and culture in almost every corner of the globe. Within a few years, language teaching and learning was transformed by the internet boom. By the end of the century, teachers and students found themselves in a world that was hyperlinked, networked, and full of global possibilities. Roby (2004) noted that the presence of computers in the language laboratory in the 1980s "was bound to increase in the 1990s" (p. 529). Expounding on this idea, he wrote, "[t]hat computers were to occupy center stage in the language laboratory is not surprising. After all, computers are omnibus machines that can provide audio, video, text, and interactive written exercises" (p. 529). Further expansion of the internet cemented the role of computers in the language laboratory during this time period and precipitated yet another identity shift.

Wayne State University Language Laboratory: From Analog to Digital

As unique and extraordinary as the Language Laboratory Center was in the 1970s, it became outdated as we moved into another era, the Digital Era. The transitions described by Roby (2004) as happening to language laboratories elsewhere happened at WSU too. Not only were technologies replaced but there was the rechristening alluded to by Otto (1989) and Lawrason (1990), namely from Language Laboratory Center to Foreign Language Technology Center. By the end of the 1990s, the Language Laboratory Center at my institution, with the reel-to-reel tapes and all the paraphernalia that surrounded them, was completely renovated. The carrels were all torn down and sleek new computer tables were installed in their place.

The center was renamed the Foreign Language Technology Center, and in November 2000, the new $1.8 million facility was opened with great fanfare. There was a change in the leadership of the center and its staff. The center contained 6 multimedia instructional labs with about 300 computer stations, a new Satellite TV System with 13 international channels, a new videoconferencing system, and CAN8, The Virtual Language Lab. Audio and video material relating to the course textbooks were put on CAN8, and some were beginning to be put online. Some audio material on cassette tapes was still being duplicated for students.

In the early 2000s, soon after the FLTC moved into the digital era, I arrived. With a fresh degree in Educational Technology and teaching experience in German language, I began my new job as Instructional Technology Coordinator. I was impressed by the FLTC's modern technology infrastructure. Wandering around our facility, trying to familiarize myself with it, I saw equipment, clearly from another era, no longer being used. Many machines were stacked on unreachable top-shelves in back rooms. Clearly, this equipment had seen better times. I wondered how it might have been used in language learning in times bygone. A link to not only the immediate, but also the distant, past was our electronics technician. Thinking back to the decades of change that he had witnessed, he often reminisced with fondness about the reel-to-reel tapes and the carrels that had been torn down during the "big renovation."

During the early years of my tenure, although we had this terrific infrastructure, I found the FLTC to be often empty and underused, reminiscent of "electronic digital graveyards" (Turner, 1969, p. 1). During my initial years, I approached faculty to discuss ways they could leverage technology to enhance language,

---

literature, and culture instruction. I worked on making our center's resources and services useful to faculty and students in ways that were aligned with the teaching paradigms of the day and addressed the needs of the hour. As technology advanced and the educational landscape shifted, some aspects of lab usage started changing as well. Looking back, I now see those shifts to be reflective of what was unfolding in the larger foreign language education arena.

—Sangeetha Gopalakrishnan, Wayne State University

From the late 1990s to the early technologies began to impact teaching and learning in powerful ways. They altered the educational landscape by increasing the capabilities for creating multimodal learning environments. In the late 1990s, Blake observed, "language teaching, assisted by technology is entering a new paradigm" (1998, p. 210). Technology was being used for content generation, community building, and evaluation. It was increasingly at the center of communicative activities and was used to automate repetitive practice exercises.

The technologies of this period enabled world language educators to address many pedagogical needs that were prevalent at the time. One of these new trends was the identification and incorporation of authentic materials. Speaking to this particular issue, Blake (1998) stated that "perhaps the greatest excitement of the hypermedia approach comes from its potential to bring authentic materials into the classroom, home, and lab" (p. 213). Blake argued that "network-based communication has the potential to open up the traditional classroom to learners from remote sites around the nation and the world, a prospect that should be explored and exploited by language professionals" (1998, p. 210). Still, access to the technological tools that afforded these benefits was not yet ubiquitous. Thus, at the end of the 20th century, most language centers enjoyed high levels of relevance as physical places that provided teachers and learners access to sophisticated technologies that were otherwise financially out of reach for individual purchase.

4. Early 21st-Century Language Centers: 2000–2020

By the start of the 21st century, technology was evolving at an unprecedented pace, and research on its effective application in the language classroom continued to lag behind. Before anyone could tease out the nuanced advantages and disadvantages of things like WebQuests, online grammar workbooks, and e-pals, along came blogs, wikis, and a myriad of social media platforms. Online dictionaries could now translate a verb at the click of a button, show you how the word had been used in actual written contexts, and provide you with a completed conjugation chart for reference. Efforts to understand, critique, and explain these developments have and continue to be made by organizations like the Computer Assisted Language Instruction Consortium (CALICO), the European Association for Computer Assisted Language Learning (EUROCALL), and of course, the International Association for Language Learning Technology (IALLT). Still, much of early 21st-century language teaching was a hodgepodge of technologies, applications, and hybrid methods (Liddell & Garrett, 2004; Omaggio Hadley, 2001).

By the early 2000s, language centers at many universities did not look anything like the language laboratories of the 1960s. Some continued to resemble traditionally oriented computer labs while others transitioned toward materials libraries. More often than not, language centers performed all of these functions while also taking on new responsibilities. One increasingly popular trend was to call upon language center directors and staff to provide professional development for the myriad of emerging technologies and methods. During this time, a powerful cultural gap was felt between digital-native students (Prensky, 2001) and language faculty who had not been trained in the use of computer-assisted language learning tools and techniques. Desperate to find guidance on how to better connect with their technologically savvy students, language faculty and administrators turned to language center professionals who had, at that point, decades of experience in using technology to enhance the teaching and learning of world languages. The problem, however, was that language centers, which were already feeling the strain of being asked to do too much with too little, were called upon to do even more with even less.

Brigham Young University 2000–2015: Caught Between the Analog and Digital Divide

At the beginning of the new millennium, a new humanities building was being planned for 2005 that would triple the space used by the current Humanities Learning Resource Center (HLRC) at Brigham Young University. At the time, the HLRC operated a 40-carrel Tandberg IS-10 system with audio, video, and computer signals controlled by a master console that could serve two separate classes. There were also 36 carrels for independent study, each equipped with an audio cassette recorder and a networked Macintosh computer with video input from a multi-standard VCR, a laser disc player, and cable and satellite television. Students listened and recorded to both cassette and computer software and worked with home-grown and internet-based CALL lessons and interactive video discs. Students sometimes had to wait for a carrel to be free. The service counter was still very busy duplicating hundreds of audio cassettes per day, and the HLRC had recently purchased a robot CD duplicator. Conversion of PAL and SECAM video happened almost every day, and new audio material was being recorded or digitized regularly in a fully equipped sound studio. All this, plus the checkout of books, media, sound and video equipment, and myriad types of cables, kept two lab attendants busy. In spite of this activity, certain trends were occurring that signaled big changes ahead. Textbook audio was moving both to CD and digital formats, including internet access. Consequently, the Tandberg lab saw very few classes and was almost entirely used for out-of-class testing. By 2002, students were asking how to get their audio on mobile devices. How could we plan for a new building in the midst of rapidly changing technologies? Unfortunately, we could see that the change of technologies would not be rapid enough to build a completely digital learning environment in our new building. After all, there were still faculty checking out overhead transparencies. In the end, we had to design a new space that would accommodate the dying technologies as well. With our new building barely completed in time for the 2005 FLEAT V conference, we offered attendees a view of a state-of-the-art center that still held large pockets of the past. After 15 years of using the center, here is what we observed:

- *The dedicated "language lab" was not reinstalled, much to the chagrin of the two professors who were still using it. Apparently, they got along fine without it before retiring soon after. Instead, a dedicated testing center with 72 computer stations was soon filled to near capacity with out-of-class, computer-based language testing and continued to grow over the next decade.*
- *Audio cassette usage dropped dramatically within the first year, and audio CD use for textbook audio only saw about two years of use.*
- *There was a three-year burst of activity on our iPod Filling Station, but that too quickly died out as publishers began offering internet-based audio accessible through mobile phones.*
- *All those multi-standard VCRs were hardly used as DVDs rapidly overtook VHS.*
- *The 41 computer carrels saw heavy use for about six years and then declined. By 2015, students were moving the monitors to the side to make room for their laptops.*
- *Satellite television viewing and recording grew at the beginning and then rapidly declined as the internet provided access to both live and recorded video.*
- *Small group study/video viewing rooms transformed into videoconferencing rooms.*
- *Our biggest success was building a room equipped with a kitchen where classes could cook and hold cultural activities. This, along with our student lounge area, was quite popular for group conversations, tutoring, and socializing, and were the most frequently used spaces.*
- *By 2015, all analog and print collections were obsolete, unused, and forgotten. Even our DVDs were underused. Most computer carrels sat empty, and many language students and new faculty were unaware of our existence. With rare exceptions, any technology they needed was either already in the classroom or in their pockets.*

—Harold Hendricks, Brigham Young University

During the first decade of the 21st century, mobile technologies and devices became increasingly popular, undermining the importance of desktop computers. By the second decade, wireless communication technologies and smartphones were being used to create audio, video, and text-based content. In the language classroom, instructors no longer needed to bring their classes to a centralized physical location to provide access to authentic materials, native speakers, and multimodal experiences. Instead, there was a growing interest in place-free pedagogies including virtual exchanges (O'Dowd & O'Rourke, 2019), collaborative online writing (Elola & Oskoz, 2010), and game-based virtual learning environments (Godwin-Jones, 2014). Instructors and researchers were curious about how popular social media sites could be used to connect students with language and culture communities that had previously been inaccessible (Lin, Warschauer, & Blake, 2016). For many language centers, this untethering of technology from the physical spaces demanded additional reimagining of form and function. Thus, by the end of the second decade of the 21st century, the transformation from the relatively homogenous language lab to the increasingly heterogenous language center was complete (Kronenberg, 2017).

Appalachian State University, 2017

In 2017, I was hired as the Director of the Language Acquisition Resource Center at Appalachian State University. My primary charge was to convert the aging language laboratory into a contemporary, 21st -century language center. This endeavor was to be accomplished while also carrying a teaching load of two courses per semester, providing institutional and extra-institutional service, and maintaining a rigorous and active research agenda.

My first impression of the physical space of the center was that it was a cross between a computer lab and a lost-and-found storage room. Large iMac computers were arranged in a horseshoe-shaped perimeter of desks, and in the center of the room, an additional six computers made up a small island. The sole computer which was connected to the main overhead projector for the room was the second iMac on the right side of the island, but apart from the cable attached to the back, there was no indication that this was the case. There was a large desk between the island and a single whiteboard, which was sandwiched between two entrances located at either side of the front of the classroom.

Through another door near the front of the room, next to a small makeshift printing station, was a storage closet. The closet was long and lined on either side by narrow shelves which, presumably, were the home of no-longer-present audio and video cassette tapes. Boxes and storage bins dotted the floor and were filled with all sorts of things, including unidentifiable cables and plugs, and in the corner stood a fully decorated and pre-lit artificial Christmas tree. With all the energy and optimism of a newly hired assistant professor, I went to the office of the department chair to discuss matters of finance to perform the daunting makeover. "Oh, there's no dedicated budget for the center" was the direct reply, followed by "and our attempts to establish a standing lab fee in hopes of generating some income have been dismissed altogether." Thus began my first year as a newly appointed language center director.

—Paul Sebastian, Appalachian State University

5. The Future of Language Centers

What does the third decade of the 21st century hold for language centers? Technology trends for the 2020s include 5G networks, autonomous driving, (big) data analysis, human augmentation, artificial intelligence products, and increased automation through robotics (Harari, 2017). How these innovations will affect the language classroom is yet unknown, but as we saw with Edison's phonograph, it may only be a matter of time until they start to change the ways we teach and learn languages. It seems increasingly clear that language centers will not only be called upon to recommend specific technologies for specific purposes, but that they will be asked to clarify the pedagogical reasons for their use and then to facilitate professional development for their proper implementation. This responsibility creep is in keeping with the historical trend of asking language centers to do more with less, to swiftly adapt to new and unforeseen circumstances, and to justify their very existence whether in conversation with a colleague in the hallway or in a 20-page report to a suspicious administrator.

While we cannot be entirely sure of which technological advancements will find their way into the world language classroom, we can be relatively sure that language professionals will continue to explore, experiment, modify, and adapt to further the field of teaching and learning languages. With the outbreak of the coronavirus in 2020, these skills have become all the more necessary. Many educators who were previously suspect of trends toward online and hybrid teaching models now find themselves forcefully immersed in this new reality. Our physical teaching and learning spaces have changed radically because of the COVID-19 worldwide pandemic and will continue to change in ways we cannot yet foresee. At present, information technology departments and teaching support centers are overworked and understaffed. As of Spring 2021, a number of language centers have closed down due to extreme financial strains in higher education and elsewhere. Roles and responsibilities that had previously been tied to language centers are being reassigned, redistributed, and, in some cases, eliminated altogether.

The reality is that, at present, technology is not only evolving at a blistering pace, it is evolving in hundreds of different directions. New and improved technologies continue to change the way we work, shop, learn, and socialize. It seems like every month we are prompted to update programs, drivers, and operating systems. We no longer see changes over the span of years or decades, we see them day to day, and in some cases, from one moment to another. These technological complexities are reflected in the language classroom as teachers struggle to keep pace and students become more engaged by tweet-length monologs than by sustained engagement with target language input. Multiple methods and techniques are often employed by the same faculty member and often even within a single class period. This fragmentation of tools and methods is not inherently a bad thing, but it does force LCs to continually demonstrate high levels of flexibility in their roles as technological and pedagogical support units. Although we are confident that some language centers will overcome these challenges, it cannot be denied that others, for whatever reason, will cease to exist.

Appalachian State University: *The Death of a Language Center*

In the fall of 2018, I was asked to serve on a committee that would oversee a multimillion-dollar renovation project to the building which housed both the English Department and the Languages Department where I, along with the Language Acquisition Resource Center, was housed. I was excited to take part in the process and spent many hours alongside my fellow committee members pouring over architecture firm applications and proposals. Once we had selected the firm, we went on to spend many more hours discussing potential layouts for the five-story building. One of the central focal points for the renovation would be a newly envisioned Language Acquisition Resource Center, one that would take the shape of a technologically enhanced active learning environment. Colleagues and administrators showed a renewed curiosity about what contemporary language centers looked like and what functions they typically performed.

Then, soon after the start of the spring term, we received the news that due to limitations in overall space, and to allow room for both departments to grow, the Languages Department was, after all our planning and hard work, to be permanently relocated to a neighboring building. In that building, many rooms were in a terrible state of disrepair and had been left empty for some time. It was unclear whether there would be enough office spaces for our faculty members, and the number of classroom spaces was insufficient for our needs. Needless to say, there was simply no room for a language center. Thus, we were left in what was originally to be a temporary swing space with no guarantee of an improved situation for at least 5–10 years.

Not only was this a crushing blow for those of us working in the area of languages, literatures, and cultures, it was a death knell to the Language Acquisition Resource Center. In a matter of weeks, a facility that had started in 1967 as a 32-booth audio-lingual era language lab had been snuffed out, traded in for bigger offices and comfy reading nooks furnished with bright moveable furniture.

—Paul Sebastian, Appalachian State University

Brigham Young University: Looking to the Future

In 2018, BYU surveyed both faculty and students in an effort to reinvent and redesign the language center. The survey showed that the need for out-of-class computing stations had disappeared due to the increasing abundance of affordable personal devices. What surprised us most was that many faculty members were de-emphasizing the use of technology both in class and in assignments. The greatest need voiced by the faculty and by many students was a place to provide individual tutoring in conversation and in writing. In fact, most of the language departments were creating writing centers to assist students with their writing assignments. Based on surveys and interviews, most of the computers were removed from the language center and space was provided for these writing tutors to meet with students. Comfortable furniture was ordered, and designs were considered to increase areas where food and social activities could take place in spaces that could be quickly reconfigured to meet various individual and group needs. There was very little mention of technology except for the need to prepare media for streaming or enhancing videoconferencing. Other comments focused on the practical use of language and ways of facilitating remote communications with native speakers without the need to simulate or mediate it. With the ability to communicate instantly with anyone, anywhere now normalized by personal technology, the original purpose of the pioneering phonetics labs, hearing and speaking a foreign language, has not only been achieved, it has been surpassed.

—Harold Hendricks, Brigham Young University

> **Wayne State University: Is it the Final Act for the Language Laboratory?**
>
> *As I crossed the middle of my second decade at the Foreign Language Technology Center, I worried about its future. After about a decade of high usage, we were feeling underutilized. We opened up our facilities, resources, and services to the broader campus, not just the language faculty and students, in an effort to keep them coming. There was a variety of reasons for this change in usage which had to do with shifts in the larger landscape of language education, institutional factors, and of course, the inevitable, unstoppable, technological evolution chronicled in this chapter. For example, the untethering of technology from physical spaces meant that FLTC's four large 60-station computer labs were no longer as needed as they used to be for students to access computers during classes because students had their own laptops, with connectivity, in their classrooms. The large computer labs were still needed when specialized software was to be accessed that was available only on the lab computers or for administering proctored online tests, but these situations were not that frequent.*
>
> *Technology is no longer bound to the physical location of a language laboratory. It is online and mobile, omnipresent, omnipotent, and omniscient. Because of these massive changes in the language teaching and learning environment, it is increasingly challenging to make the technology resources of the FLTC as relevant as they used to be even a decade ago.*
>
> —*Sangeetha Gopalakrishnan, Wayne State University*

What does more than 100 years of history tell us about the future of language centers? For one thing, language labs and centers have survived worldwide wars, volatile financial fluctuations, the rise and fall of multiple learning theories, methodological practices, theoretical frameworks, new findings, old findings, institutional reorganization, and intense technological evolution. If we think the language laboratories and language centers are in a precarious state now, their situation is hardly new. Those involved in foreign language education have been writing about the evolution, and demise, of language labs for very many decades. While some foreign language educators have strongly advocated for them, their role in foreign language instruction has never been unilaterally accepted in foreign language education, leading to the continued need to justify their relevance. The identities of language laboratories and language centers have been ever evolving in their efforts to remain in existence. In some ways, they started as an experiment and in many ways, have remained so. This history suggests that, rather than ask whether language centers will survive, a more suitable question is how they will do it.

Some centers will weather the storm and find themselves uniquely situated to lend much needed technological and pedagogical support. This ongoing work can be seen in language centers that have distinguished themselves as intercultural and social hubs (Jeanneau, 2017), institutional research partners (Sun, 2017), community outreach advocates (Schenker & Kraemer, 2018) and interdisciplinary champions (Yaden, 2018). As the coronavirus continues to force schools to rethink and redesign traditional teaching and learning spaces, language centers will be called upon to share what they have learned from decades of experience of working at the crossroads between digital and analog technologies and multiple pedagogies. One phenomenon that is happening already, and that is likely to become stronger in the future, is that students will prefer, and even demand, learning environments that are compatible with their learning preferences. Whereas instructors in the past tended to use technology to create controlled, teacher-mediated learning environments, future trends suggest that technology is being used to liberate the student and teacher from these overly rigid physical spaces (Cottrell, 2020; Simon, 2019). These new environments are increasingly student-centered, interactive, and social. Still, these changes come with challenges. The need for support, guidance, and professional development in these areas is greater than ever, and many language centers will continue to be called upon to provide these much-needed services.

The untethering of technology from the physical space and the financial and pedagogical repercussions of the ongoing worldwide pandemic will also, inevitably, result in the closure of some LCs. In some cases, these centers will be replaced by increasingly centralized academic support centers that serve the needs of the broader teaching and learning community. Such units often consist of teams of professional development experts, many of whom have advanced skills in the use of educational technologies. At the same time, they often work in generalities and are not equipped to address the nuances of teaching language and culture in online and hybrid spaces. Thus, content experts must be involved in the work of connecting these general practices to disciplinary traditions and customs. Whether they work as consultants housed within a separate language center or are pulled in to more general support centers as full-time staff, the involvement of praxis-minded language professionals will be absolutely necessary to present and post-pandemic contexts.

Though some language centers may be discontinued, others will find themselves well positioned as critical support units. LCs that successfully weather the storm will be called upon to offer technological and pedagogically support at a time when demand for such guidance is high and access to such expertise is limited. What these future LCs will look like, it is hard to say. However, what we can and do strongly affirm, is the fact that the human resources housed by labs and centers will always be relevant. Even if the cords and monitors are boxed up and stowed, if the blinds are pulled shut, and the doors are closed, language center professionals can and must remain. Language center directors and their staff have extensive knowledge of tools and practices. They are masters at bridging research and praxis and adept at demystifying the new and the intimidating. These uniquely human skills are, have always been, and will continue to be the legacy of language labs and centers.

For over one hundred years, the language lab helped to infuse foreign language education with pedagogical innovation through technology. About two decades ago, Roby (2004) wrote:

Within the field of education, the language laboratory must be seen as a singular phenomenon. By virtue of its unique equipment and its specific pedagogy, it stands alone. There is nothing quite like it in any other discipline. (p. 538)

We further affirm Roby's description of the language laboratory's uniqueness. As we look ahead to a post-pandemic world, what will become of the language center? Although our individual stories are not particularly hopeful examples, we believe that other LCs will find themselves in a post-pandemic state of renewed relevance. These successful centers will be called upon to help teachers and students navigate newly created online and hybrid learning environments, develop virtual conversation exchanges, curate high quality online tools and resources, and provide professional development for an increasingly complex set of instructional techniques. These resilient language centers will accomplish this by doing what they have always done, by innovating, evolving, and adapting to the technological and pedagogical contexts around them.

References

Blake, R. (1998). The role of technology in second language learning. In H. Byrnes (Ed.), *Learning foreign and second languages: Perspectives in research and scholarship* (pp. 209–237). New York, NY: Modern Language Association.

Cioffari, V. (1961). What can we expect from the language laboratory? *The Modern Language Journal, 45*(1), 3–9. https://doi.org/10.2307/320666

Claremont Colleges. (Producer). (1963). *Claremont Colleges promotional video.* https://voices.pomona.edu/2012/10/pomona-college-circa-1963/

Clarke, C. C. (1918). The phonograph in modern language teaching. *The Modern Language Journal, 3*(3), 116–122. https://doi.org/10.1111/j.1540-4781.1918.tb03384.x

Cottrell, B. (2020). Google arts and culture in world language classrooms. *FLTMAG.* https://fltmag.com/google-arts-and-culture-in-world-language-classrooms/

Driscoll, M. P. (2005). *Psychology of learning for instruction.* Boston, MA: Pearson Allyn and Bacon.

Dvorak, T., Charlotteaux, B., Gilgen, R., Herren, D., Jones, C., & Trometer, R. (1995). Whither the language lab? *IALL Journal, 28*(2), 13–45. https://doi.org/10.17161/iallt.v28i2.9591

Ebelke, J. F. (1948). An experiment with recording and playback machines in academic foreign language teaching. *The Modern Language Journal, 32*(8), 589–595. https://doi.org/10.1111/j.1540-4781.1948.tb05930.x

Edison, T. (Producer). (1888, October). *Around the world on the phonograph.* https://www.nps.gov/edis/learn/photosmultimedia/very-early-recorded-sound.htm

Elola, I., & Oskoz, A. (2010). Collaborative writing: Fostering foreign language and writing conventions development. *Language Learning & Technology, 14*(3), 51–71.

Gaudin, L. S. (1962). The language laboratory and advanced work. *The Modern Language Journal, 46*(2), 79–81. https://doi.org/10.1111/j.1540-4781.1962.tb00804.x

Godwin-Jones, R. (2014). Games in language learning: Opportunities and challenges. *Language Learning & Technology, 18*(2), 9–19.

Harari, Y. N. (2017). *Homo deus: A brief history of tomorrow*. New York, NY: Harper Collins.

Hocking, E. (1964). *Language laboratory and language learning*. Washington, DC: Department of Audiovisual Instruction National Education Association of the United States.

IALLT. (2019). *About*. https://iallt.org/about/

Jeanneau, C. (2017). Redefining language centres as intercultural hubs for social and collaborative learning. In F. A. Kronenberg (Ed.), *From language lab to language center and beyond: The past, present, and future of the language center* (pp. 61–82). Auburn, AL: International Association for Language Learning Technology.

Johnston, M. C., & Seerley C. C. (1958). *Survey of foreign language laboratories in secondary schools and institutions of higher education*. Washington, DC: U.S. Department of Health, Education, Welfare.

Kakita, N. (1973). The language laboratory situation in Japan. *NALLD Journal, 7*(4), 13–24. https://doi.org/10.17161/iallt.v7i4.8874

Keating, L. C. (1936). Modern inventions in the language program. *School and Society, 44*, 677–679.

Koekkoek, B. J. (1959). The advent of the language laboratory. *The Modern Language Journal, 43*(1), 4–5. https://doi.org/10.1111/j.1540-4781.1959.tb04333.x

Krashen, S. (1982). *Principles and practice in second language acquisition*. Oxford, UK: Pergamon Press.

Kronenberg, F. A. (Ed.). (2017). *From language lab to language center and beyond: The past, present, and future of language center design*. Auburn, AL: International Association for Language Learning Technology.

Kuroda, T. (1981). Spotlight on—Language Laboratory Association of Japan. *NALLD Journal, 15*(3/4), 9–11. https://doi.org/10.17161/iallt.v15i3-4.9096

Kuroda, T., Kohmoto, S., & Sheehan, J. H. (1981). Expectations of the International Conference *NALLD Journal, 15*(3/4), 5–8. https://doi.org/10.17161/iallt.v15i3-4.9095

Lavolette, E. (2019). A very brief introduction to US language centers. In L. Xethakis & C. Taylor (Eds.), *JASAL 2018 x SUTLF 5: Selected papers from the Sojo University Teaching and Learning Forum 2018: Making connections* (pp. 4–25). Kumamoto, Japan: NanKyu JALT. https://www.nankyujalt.org/publications#h.p_twJDnQsJDWmj

Lavolette, E., & Kraemer, A. (2017). The language center evaluation toolkit: Context, development, and usage. In F. A. Kronenberg (Ed.), *From language lab to language center and beyond: The past, present, and future of the language center* (pp. 147–160). Auburn, AL: International Association for Language Learning Technology.

Lawrason, R. E. (1990). The changing state of the language lab: Results of 1988 IALL member survey. *IALL Journal, 23*(2), 19–24. https://doi.org/10.17161/iallt.v23i2.9387

Liddell, P., & Garrett, N. (2004). The new language centers and the role of technology: New mandates, new horizons. In S. Fotos and C. M. Browne (Eds.), *New Perspectives on CALL for Second Language Classrooms* (pp. 27–40). Mahwah, NJ: Lawrence Erlbaum.

Lin, C.-H., Warschauer, M., & Blake, R. (2016). Language learning through social networks: Perceptions and reality. *Language Learning & Technology, 20*(1), 124–147.

Locke, W. N. (1965). The future of language laboratories. *The Modern Language Journal, 49*(5), 294–304. https://doi.org/10.1111/j.1540-4781.1965.tb00872.x

Long, M. H. (1983). Native speaker/non-native speaker conversation in the second language classroom. In M. A. Clarke & J. Handscomb (Eds.), *On TESOL '82: Pacific perspectives on language learning and teaching* (pp. 207–255). Washington, DC: TESOL.

National Association of Language Laboratory Directors (NALLD) Newsletter. (1966). *NALLD Newsletter, 1*(1), 1–7.

National Defense Education Act of 1958, Pub. L. No. 85–864, 72 Stat. (1958). https://www.govinfo.gov/content/pkg/STATUTE-72/pdf/STATUTE-72-Pg1580.pdf

O'Dowd, R., & O'Rourke, B. (2019). New developments in virtual exchange for foreign language education. *Language Learning & Technology, 23*(3), 1–7.

Omaggio Hadley, A. (2001). *Teaching language in context.* Boston, MA: Heinle & Heinle.

Otto, S. E. K. (1989). The language laboratory in the computer age. In W. F. Smith (Ed.), *Modern technology in foreign language education: Applications and projects* (pp. 13–41). Lincolnwood, IL: National Textbook Company.

Prensky, M. (2001). Digital natives, digital immigrants: Part 2: Do they really think differently? *On The Horizon—The Strategic Planning Resource for Education Professionals, 9*(6), 1–6.

Rallo, J. A. (1970). Foreign language resource center. *NALLD Journal, 4*(3), 14–22. https://doi.org/10.17161/iallt.v4i3.8760

Roby, W. B. (2004). Technology in the service of foreign language learning: The case of the language laboratory. In D. H. Jonassen (Ed.), *Handbook of research on educational communications and technology* (pp. 523–541). Mahwah, NJ: Lawrence Erlbaum.

Sánchez, J. (1959). Twenty years of modern language laboratory: An annotated bibliography. *The Modern Language Journal, 43*(5), 228–232. https://doi.org/10.1111/j.1540-4781.1959.tb04387.x

Schenker, T., & Kraemer, A. (2018). The role of the language center in community outreach: Developing language enrichment programs for children. In E. Lavolette & E. F. Simon (Eds.), *Language center handbook* (pp. 71–88). Auburn, AL: International Association for Language Learning Technology.

Sherrow, R. (1970, March). *Software for the seventies.* Paper presented at the Northeast Conference on Teaching, Boston.

Shrum, J. L., & Glisan, E. W. (2015). *Teacher's handbook: Contextualized language instruction.* Boston, MA: Cengage.

Simon, E. F. (2019). An overview of blended language learning. *FLTMAG*. https://fltmag.com/category/articles/page/4/

Stone, L. (1991). *Task-based activities: Making the language laboratory interactive.* ERIC Digest. 1–6. https://files.eric.ed.gov/fulltext/ED343407.pdf

Sun, M. (2017). Fostering a language center-based research community. In F. A. Kronenberg (Ed.), *From language lab to language center and beyond: The past, present, and future of the language center* (pp. 99–110). Auburn, AL: International Association for Language Learning Technology.

Swain, M. (1995). Three functions of output in second language learning. In G. Cook & B. Seidlhofer (Eds.), *Principle and practice in applied linguistics: Studies in honour of H. G. Widdowson* (pp. 125–144). Oxford, UK: Oxford University Press.

Swanson, M., & Yahiro, H. (2012). Attributes of successful self-access learning centres. *Bulletin of Seinan Jo Gakuin University, 16*, 113–122.

Turner, E. D. (1969). *Correlation of language class and language laboratory.* ERIC Focus Report on the Teaching of Foreign Languages. https://files.eric.ed.gov/fulltext/ED034451.pdf

Waltz, R. H. (1930). The laboratory as an aid to modern language teaching. *The Modern Language Journal, 15*(1), 27–29. https://doi.org/10.1111/j.1540-4781.1930.tb01285.x

Warschauer, M., & Kern, R. (2000). *Network-based language teaching: Concepts and practice.* Cambridge, UK: Cambridge University Press.

Whitehouse, R. S. (1945). The Work Shop: A language laboratory. *Hispania, 28*(1), 88–90. https://doi.org/10.2307/333964

Yaden, B. E. (2018). Supporting the LRC mission through collaborative partnerships across campus and beyond. In E. Lavolette & E. F. Simon (Eds.), *Language center handbook* (pp. 91–103). Auburn, AL: International Association for Language Learning Technology.

Zeldner, M. (1963). The bewildered modern language teacher. *The Modern Language Journal, 47*(6), 245–253. https://doi.org/10.1111/j.1540-4781.1963.tb06663.x

Author Notes

Paul Sebastian holds an EdD in Curriculum and Instruction with a specialization in bilingual and ESL education and an MA in Spanish with a specialization in second language pedagogy. He is Assistant Professor of Spanish and TESL/Applied Linguistics at Appalachian State University where he teaches courses in language methodology, second language acquisition, computer-assisted language learning, and Spanish as a second language. His research deals with the relationship between language and the constructed environment whether that be physical, hybrid, or online. He is the former Director of the Language Acquisition Resource Center at Appalachian State University.

Sangeetha Gopalakrishnan was Director of the Foreign Language Technology Center (FLTC) at Wayne State University (WSU). She joined the FLTC in 2002 as

Instructional Technology Coordinator and became its Director two years later. In that role she worked with faculty on the integration of innovative technologies in language, literature, and culture courses and oversaw the center's services and its technology infrastructure. After 18 years at the FLTC, she left in 2020 to become Director of Online Programs for the College of Education at the University of Illinois at Urbana-Champaign. She has a background in foreign language teaching, having taught German at the Goethe Institut in Chennai, India for several years. She holds a certificate for teaching German and advanced German language proficiency from the Goethe Institut, Germany, and received a PhD in Instructional Technology from WSU. She served as President of IALLT from 2015–2017.

Harold H. Hendricks began working with language technology in 1973 as a member of the Brigham Young University (BYU) Time-Shared, Interactive, Computer-Controlled, Information Television system team. He managed the Department of Computer Teaching Services from 1978–1989 and supervised the Humanities Learning Resource Center at BYU from 1989 until his retirement in 2018. During his over 40-year career he oversaw the development of multiple language programs and interactive video applications. He served as President of IALLT from 2013–2015.

Correspondence concerning this chapter should be addressed to Paul Sebastian (sebastianpl@appstate.edu).

Chapter 2

JASAL and the Self-Access Learning Center Movement in Japan

Katherine Thornton, Otemon Gakuin University, Japan
Clair Taylor, Gifu Shotoku Gakuen University, Japan
Andrew D. Tweed, Soka University, Japan
Hisako Yamashita, Kobe Shoin Women's University, Japan

Abstract

Self-access centers (SACs), social learning spaces which combine support for language learning with a strong focus on fostering learner autonomy, are becoming popular in tertiary institutions in Japan. While they have much in common with language centers (LCs) in the US, the two fields have, until recently, remained largely unaware of each other. This chapter introduces SACs, specifically explaining how they have evolved in the Japanese context, and the organization which has been established to support SACs, the Japan Association for Self-Access Learning (JASAL). Firstly, the origins of self-access language learning (SALL) and characteristics of SACs are explained, with a comparison to US-based LCs. Particular attention is given to the ways in which SACs support learners in developing both their language skills and their capacity as autonomous learners, often through professional learning advisory services. This is followed by an introduction to JASAL and a discussion of the ways in which JASAL has supported SALL in Japan over the last 15 years. Drawing on data from a survey of JASAL members, the authors then explain the extent to which JASAL has been able to achieve its aims and identify the challenges it still faces to keep SALL relevant to Japanese learners in the 21st century.

In an article that appeared in a collection of papers from a recent Japan Association for Self-Access Learning (JASAL) conference in Japan, Lavolette highlighted the need for the until recently largely separate language center (LC) movement in the US and the field of self-access language learning (SALL) in Japan to learn more about each other (Lavolette, 2019). Her article provided a very useful introduction to US-based language centers for a Japanese audience. The present chapter, written by the 2016–2019 JASAL board, aims to respond to her call in the same article to introduce Japanese self-access centers (SACs) (often also called self-access learning centers or SALCs) to US-based colleagues and International Association for Language Learning Technology (IALLT) members.

This chapter will first outline the origins of SALL, as part of the larger learner autonomy movement which has developed since the 1980s, and discuss the influence that the first self-access center, the CRAPEL at University de Nancy, France, has had on the subsequent growth of the self-access movement. It will discuss how this movement spread to Japan (among other places) from Europe in the late 1990s, and the other more recent factors that have driven the growth of SACs in Japan. As the vast majority of SACs in Japan are at tertiary institutions, the chapter will focus on the university context. The driving forces behind the proliferation of SACs and the influence these forces have had on the common characteristics of SACs in Japan will be illuminated. These distinguishing features will be highlighted: autonomy support through professional learning advisory services, the strong focus on target language interaction and the prominence of English, and, more recently, the move toward conceptualizing SACs as social learning spaces. In detailing the variety of different SAC models that can be found in Japan and what they focus on, parallels will be drawn between SACs and language centers in the US. Next, the chapter will chart the origins and growth of JASAL and how it has supported SALL in Japan. Finally, the results of a survey of JASAL members to investigate the extent to which JASAL is meeting its members' needs will be presented.

1. The SAC Movement in Japan and Its Origins

1.1 The Role of Learner Autonomy in SAC Development

Cotterall and Reinders (2001) defined SACs as follows:

> A Self Access Centre consists of a number of resources (in the form of materials, activities and support) usually located in one place, and is designed to accommodate learners of different levels, styles, goals and interests. It aims to develop learner autonomy among its users. (p. 24)

Lavolette (2019) stated that one of the main ways SACs in the Japanese context differ from US LCs is this focus on learner autonomy, noting that this is actually a "defining focus" (p. 7). We agree and maintain that a feature of many Japanese SACs is not simply that they focus on fostering learner autonomy, but that they consider it their driving philosophy around which all their functions are organized. This chapter will attempt to explain this connection, and how, from its origins in Europe, the field of learner autonomy has influenced the development of SALL and SACs in Japan.

SALL, and the physical and virtual spaces that support it, finds its origins in the larger learner autonomy movement that has developed since the 1980s, in particular with the work of Henri Holec (1981) and David Little (1989) in the Council of Europe. The first recognized self-access center, the CRAPEL, which was set up by Yves Chalon in 1969 and run by Henri Holec from 1972 to 1998 at University de Nancy, France, greatly influenced the subsequent growth of SALL in places as diverse as the UK, Mexico, Hong Kong, and Japan (Mynard, 2019a; Thornton, 2020; see also Li & Ching, this volume). In a world before the mobile and communication technologies we now take for granted, proponents of fostering autonomy recognized that students needed physical spaces outside the classroom in which to access the language learning materials, particularly audio-visual materials, and that they needed to achieve their personalized learning goals. Thus, the CRAPEL was envisaged as a place for learners to exercise their autonomy (Gremmo & Riley, 1995). To support this, from the very beginning, dedicated learning advisors were seen as essential to the successful promotion of autonomy among SAC users (Gremmo & Riley, 1995; Holec, 2000). Learning advisory services became core components of SACs across the world, notably in the UK (Mozzon-McPherson, 1997), Hong Kong (Gardner & Miller, 1999), and Mexico (Clemente & Rubin 2008) throughout the 1990s.

1.2 The Origins of SACs in Japan

Learner autonomy and self-access have been embraced by educators and researchers in Japan since the 1990s, with the founding of the Learner Development Special Interest Group of the Japan Association for Language Teaching (JALT) in 1993. According to JASAL's Language Learning Spaces (LLS) Registry, the earliest SACs include Soka University (1996), Nagoya University of Commerce and Business (1999), and Kanda University of International Studies (2001), although it is not clear from the registry alone the extent to which these centers followed an autonomy model from the outset. While practitioners in Japan were active in self-access throughout the early 2000s, early papers on self-access, advising, and self-directed learning courses in Japan did not emerge in any great quantity until toward the end of the decade and focused on work done at Akita International University (Cotterall & Murray, 2009; Murray, 2009) and Kanda University of International Studies (Cooker, 2008; Cooker & Cutting, 2002; Cooker & Torpey, 2004). However, despite a recent upsurge in the number of SACs in Japan (26 of the 51 facilities registered on JASAL's LLS Registry have been founded since 2009), the number of facilities remains low and appears to be largely confined to private institutions. Mynard (2019a) suggested that the relative scarcity of SACs in Japan is due to the beliefs held about languages in Japan, which have been seen as a subject of study rather than as a means of communication, leading to more emphasis on one's body of knowledge of the language (and ability to reproduce this on a standardized test) rather than the ability to use the language. Additionally, the emphasis on teaching over learning, which places importance on the role of a teacher in a classroom, means that less institutional attention is given to non-classroom learning.

According to Mynard (2019b), the recent trend to introduce SACs has two origins. The first is the need for universities to attract students in a competitive environment due to the low birth rate, resulting in the building of attractive and marketable facilities that can help one institution stand out from the crowd. This may be one reason why the proliferation of SACs is centered on private universities; public and national institutions are generally seen as very prestigious and have less trouble in attracting applications. The second is the promotion of practical English skills by the Ministry of Education, Culture, Sports, Science and Technology (MEXT). Since the 1980s, MEXT has set guidelines for promoting English education in elementary and secondary education through the publication of several Courses of Study, which all schools are expected to follow, and in 2002 announced a strategic plan to cultivate Japanese with English abilities (MEXT, 2002; Tanabe, 2004). This was followed in 2011 by a further document: *Five Proposals and Specific Measures in Developing Proficiency in English for International Communication* (MEXT, 2011).

To the two origins Mynard (2019b) mentioned, we add a third, closely connected to the second: The pressure from MEXT for educational institutions to embrace and promote internationalization. In 2010, MEXT started promoting inter-university exchanges between institutions in Japan, East Asia, and the United States (MEXT, 2010), and in 2012, the ministry launched a *Project for Promotion of Global Human Resource Development* (MEXT, 2012), a funding project which provided support to 42 tertiary institutions to facilitate the globalization of whole universities or certain faculties or departments within those institutions. The MEXT (n.d.) website currently lists four globalization projects: *Top Global University Project, Inter-University Exchange Project, Project for Promotion of Global Human Resource Development*, and *Global 30 Project - Establishing University Network for Internationalization*. These projects focus on areas such as making Japanese universities more competitive on the world stage, promoting exchange programs and attracting high quality international students and faculty to study and work at Japanese universities, and developing "Global Human Resources," or Japanese who can function successfully in a globalized world. Establishing physical spaces like SACs where students from different backgrounds can interact is one way that some institutions have sought to visibly globalize their campuses.

This trend for more social and informal spaces on campus has also been influenced by the wider Learning Commons movement (Somerville & Harlan, 2008), which originated in North America, then spread to the UK, and is now also being seen in Japan. It aims to support learners by making campuses more social, attracting students, and reducing dropout rates by offering more academic support for students and providing comfortable spaces for students to interact outside of traditional class structures (Taylor, 2014). This has been accompanied by a growing emphasis on project-based learning and active learning in curricula, which require such social spaces for students to collaborate and complete assignments, as opposed to traditionally silent library spaces.

The result of these influences from pedagogy and research on one side and national policy on the other can be seen in the different kinds of SACs that have emerged in Japan. They are often multi-functional and may be designed to fulfill several missions:

1. to promote language learner autonomy (autonomy focus),
2. to provide opportunities for students to use the languages they are learning, often but not exclusively English (communication and language focus), and
3. to promote interaction between international students and domestic students, and to develop intercultural understanding and the internationalization of the majority Japanese student body (international exchange focus).

How these different missions are balanced is determined by local conditions: the beliefs of the institution's management team and other major stakeholders and how they have been influenced by national policy initiatives, the nature of the student body (fields of study, presence, and number of international students), and the beliefs and backgrounds of those who work in SACs.

The different emphasis placed on each of these missions by each SAC results in different kinds of service provision and staffing patterns. An autonomy focus SAC is likely to have self-directed learning programs that promote reflection and workshops that focus on strategies for language learning, developed and run by professional learning advisors and/or teaching faculty with training in learner autonomy. Communication and language focus SACs may place more emphasis on target language use and employ faculty to provide sessions and workshops on academic language skills and test preparation. Communication in the target language is often encouraged through explicit language policies determining the language(s) of interaction in the physical space, and more structured interaction may be facilitated through group or individual sessions run by international students or teachers fluent in English, who may or may not be faculty members. International exchange focused SACs may be more multilingual in nature, due to the variety of international students encouraged to use the space, and focus more on social events and cultural exchange activities, bringing domestic and international students together, than on academic language skill development. They may employ staff and students from a variety of countries to organize these events.

Mynard (2019a) suggested another way to categorize Japanese SACs—according to the level and kind of support they receive from their institutions—identifying the following types of SACs:

1. Social-supportive SACs, which are purpose-built facilities with strong institutional backing and a mission to promote language learner autonomy, dedicated staff, and support for research and professional development.
2. Developing SACs, which are driven by individual faculty or students passionate about language learning or autonomy, often using unused classrooms or other makeshift spaces on campus, but which may have little institutional backing or formal staffing arrangements, preventing them from offering full learner support programs.
3. Administrative centers, which may resemble social-supportive SACs at first glance, as they are often purpose-built and well-funded spaces, but lack an infrastructure which supports autonomy, in terms of properly trained staff and self-directed learning programs, and may have been established more for marketing purposes than with a sound pedagogical foundation.

This categorization emphasizes the primary importance of learner autonomy in SALL and suggests how SACs in Japan that focus on communication and language or international exchange can develop an accompanying autonomy focus to better serve their student body. Mynard emphasized that Type 2 and 3 SACs can be turned into Type 1 SACs if they are supported to do so by institutions that recognize the importance of learner autonomy and research. For this to happen, universities must be willing to invest in creating an autonomy-supportive environment, with trained staff and learner support programs, resources that promote autonomy, and well-designed spaces that are attractive to users and facilitate communication and community building.

1.3 A Comparison with Language Centers in the US

This picture of SACs in Japan differs somewhat from the situation in the US. Based on a literature review and a survey of IALLT members conducted in 2015, Lavolette (2018) suggested that US LCs have the following mandates:

- Awareness and advocacy
- Providing an intellectual home for language teaching
- Professional development
- Administration and support of programs
- Assessment and evaluation
- Learner support
- Grant writing
- Physical space
- Language learning and teaching resources
- Teaching
- Online spaces (p. 3)

From our own experience of working in the field of SALL in Japan, we would say that SACs in Japan are less likely to fulfill all these roles, but this has not yet been empirically investigated. They are often small, stand-alone facilities, attached to one department or faculty, or possibly the international affairs office in charge of internationalization and study abroad programs. As such, with some notable exceptions, they are less likely to have control of or influence over language programs for students or faculty development programs, and they tend to focus very strongly on the student user experience. From the above list, the following mandates would be familiar to many SAC directors in Japan:

- Awareness and advocacy
- Learner support (including advising services)
- Physical space
- Language learning, and to some extent teaching, resources
- Teaching (usually in the form of non-credit bearing workshops and courses)
- Online spaces

Less common are:

- Providing an intellectual home for language teaching (in that SACs are often isolated from teaching staff who may actually see them as a threat to the classroom model of language learning rather than a form of support)

- Professional development (with the exception of advising, see below)
- Administration and support of programs (apart from those directly run by and in the SAC, which are often non-credit bearing)
- Assessment and evaluation
- Grant writing

The following section details some of the trends evident in the SALL movement in Japan.

1.4 Features of SACs in Japan

1.4.1 Learner Autonomy, Advising, and Self-Directed Learning Programs

As may be expected from a movement which grew out of the field of learner autonomy, SACs in Japan often have a strong emphasis on advising in language learning (ALL). Mynard (2019a) defined ALL as "the intentional use of one-to-one dialogue to promote deeper thought with the aim of promoting language learning autonomy" (p. 188).

In the US, there is some evidence of LCs offering self-directed learning programs, but little sign that learner autonomy is an explicit driving principle of these initiatives. There is a whole organization dedicated to supporting institutions providing self-instructional programs for languages, the National Association of Self-Instructional Language Programs, but their emphasis is on supporting institutions who want to provide opportunities for the learning of less commonly taught languages in a way that is financially viable, a laudable goal but without a visible emphasis on learner autonomy. The previous volume of the *Language Center Handbook* featured a chapter that included a profile of a Directed Independent Language Studies program at the University of Denver (Gonzales, 2018). While the role of a "coach" who requires specific training is mentioned (p. 165), the terms "advisor" and "advising" are not used, and no information is given on the kind of training that should be provided. It seems that ALL has not yet taken hold as a regular feature of LCs in the US.

In contrast, the SAC at Kanda University of International Studies, the leading institution in the field of advising not only in Japan but also worldwide, currently has 10 full-time learning advisors. The literature on self-access in Japan features several books dedicated to ALL (Kato & Mynard, 2015; Ludwig & Mynard, 2019; Mynard & Carson, 2012), special issues of the Japan-based international journal *SiSAL Journal* (Studies in Self-Access Learning) (Thornton, 2012; Yamashita & Mynard, 2015), and numerous articles, focusing on such aspects as the transition from teaching to advising and approaches to advising (Lammons, 2011; Morrison & Navarro, 2012; Yasuda, 2018), professional development for advisors (Kato, 2012), spoken and written reflective dialog between learners and advisors (Mynard & Navarro, 2010; Rutson-Griffiths & Porter, 2016; Thornton & Mynard, 2012), and the development of advisor-supported curricula and reform programs (Cotterall & Murray, 2009; Curry et al., 2017; Thornton, 2013).

1.4.2 Target Language Use

A type of SAC that focuses on communication and language use was identified above, which suggests that providing opportunities for students to use the languages they are learning is a major function of Japanese SACs, and many students have few chances for English or other language communication in their everyday lives. While LCs in the US tend to support the learning of multiple languages, data from a survey in a recent study into language policy in SACs by one of the authors of this paper (Thornton, 2018) revealed that, of the 23 Japanese SACs featured in the survey, 14 focused solely or mainly on English, with six of these also catering to Japanese as a second language, and only two of 23 catered to more than four languages. In addition to promoting language study through advising, workshops, and materials, SACs in Japan often focus on providing opportunities for using and even requiring students to use the languages they are learning through explicit language policies. Eleven of the 23 Japanese SACs in the study had some form of English-only language policy, and a further eight reported that use of the target language for interaction in the space (such as book-borrowing and informal conversation between users) was deliberately encouraged.

1.4.3 Emphasis on Social Learning

With the growth in understanding the importance of the social dimensions of learning in both language learning in general and learner autonomy in particular (Murray & Fujishima, 2016), SACs in Japan are increasingly designed and self-identify as social learning spaces (Murray & Fujishima, 2013). These social spaces support learner autonomy and language learning through developing and encouraging communities of practice, which provide an environment for learners to make friends, share their learning experiences, and work together. In social learning spaces, relationships between space users are vital components to their success and explain why students choose to spend time in those spaces (Hughes, Krug, & Vye, 2011). A similar shift in emphasis from resources and technology to social learning and communities of practice has been observed in LCs in the US (Lavolette, 2019; see also Lavolette & Kraemer, this volume), sometimes with a focus on internationalization (Frances, 2018).

The next section will focus on the growth of an organization that has emerged to support SALL in Japan.

2. Introduction to JASAL

The Japan Association for Self-Access Learning (JASAL) is an academic association devoted to promoting self-access language learning in Japan. The unincorporated organization aims to

> provide a forum for its members to disseminate knowledge and share ideas about self-access language learning, running self-access centers and developing learner autonomy. JASAL offers opportunities for professional development and networking, as well as offering its members practical help and support for self-access related projects. (JASAL, n.d.)

In this section, we will detail how the organization started and has grown over the years and describe the various resources and opportunities that JASAL provides to its members.

2.1 How JASAL Started

In early 2005, there were only a few institutions in Japan that had SACs, and the concept of self-access learning and learner autonomy was a rather new approach to language education in Japan. The idea to open a SAC was often initiated by individual faculty members with a strong passion to provide a self-access learning environment for their learners. As mentioned above, Mynard (2019b) called this type of SAC a developing SAC. The dedicated faculty members who instigated these kinds of SACs needed to communicate with their colleagues and the upper management of their institution to get approval for opening such a facility. However, especially in the early 2000s, providing a SAC was not an option for most institutions, as with few publications and little work done yet in Japan in this field, it was not easy to get support from institutions or even colleagues in the same department. These faculty members faced difficulties that often prevented them from putting into action what they thought would be a wonderful learning opportunity for their students.

When faculty members were able to get their ideas accepted by their institution, the next hurdle was a low budget, if any was received at all. In addition, many of these faculty members now responsible for directing a SAC were new to management work, and in most cases, training was not available for them to become managers of resources, people, and budgets (Gardner, 2017); this is not unlike the challenges faced by LC directors in the US (see Lavolette & Kraemer, this volume). The most pressing issue was the lack of information necessary to start a SAC specifically in the Japanese context, including guidance on purchasing resources, recruiting and training staff, furniture and educational programs, or ways to promote the SAC. Because each SAC is unique, it can be challenging for managers to deal with issues that are not shared by others.

JASAL was founded in the face of such challenges. Garold Murray and Lucy Cooker, faculty members who were in the process of establishing centers at Akita International University and Kanda University of International Studies, respectively, founded JASAL. One of the authors of this chapter, Hisako Yamashita, served as the third founding board member of JASAL. The organization goes through an election process every term (originally set as a five-year term but changed to a three-year term in 2016). Currently, JASAL is run by its fourth executive board, and the number of board members has increased from three to eight: president, publicity chair, membership chair, publications chair (a role currently shared by two people), events coordinator, treasurer, and student involvement coordinator. JASAL started with 15 members (June 2005) and currently has 200 members (January 2021).

Murray and Cooker felt the need to create a community where members could share their struggles, exchange ideas, and encourage and support each other as they started their respective SACs. The founders hoped that JASAL would become a welcoming and helpful space for faculty members to ask questions and to get in touch with someone more experienced to get practical help. From 2005 to 2010, during JASAL's first executive board term, JASAL focused on building its infrastructure as an organization, including starting up regular forums at conferences, recruiting members, and building a website. During the second term of the executive board, the JASAL logo was created (Figure 1).

Figure 1
JASAL Logo

The logo represents our hope that one day, the seeds of self-access learning will grow and sprout in Japan. The growing green leaf shows our hope that self-access learning and SACs become part of language education in Japan.

Since its inception, JASAL has encouraged anyone interested in self-access learning to visit another JASAL member's SAC individually to find out useful information, such as what kind of furniture is being used, the layout of the physical space, and their stories of success and failure, so that they can use the information when they plan their own SAC or SALL program. During the second executive board term (2011–2016), this idea developed into our official SAC Tours program (see Section 2.2.5), which is now one of the most popular JASAL events.

2.2 JASAL Resources and Opportunities

2.2.1 Japan Language Learning Spaces (LLS) Registry

In addition to reaching out extensively to recruit new members, in its second executive board term, JASAL launched many new resources and opportunities for people to meet and share. In 2013, JASAL set up a registry of self-access centers in Japan, which aims to be a central database with basic information about the centers in Japan, to facilitate communication and research activities between centers. Our aim is to have every SAC in Japan represented. As of January 2021, we have 51 SACs registered. Information includes the name of the center, the name of the institution, the contact person, and features of the center, including facilities, resources, and services offered. The registry can be accessed through the JASAL website (JASAL, n.d.).

2.2.2 JASAL Forums and National Conferences

From 2006 to 2014, JASAL organized a forum devoted to self-access, language advising, and learner autonomy each year at the JALT Annual International Conference. By 2015, JASAL had grown into an organization large enough to organize a stand-alone conference, the JASAL 10th Anniversary Conference, which had 50 attendees and was a big step forward for the organization.

In the third executive board term (2016–2019), JASAL members realized that having administrative staff and Japanese teachers understand our field is crucial in advancing the construction and development of SALL programs in Japanese institutions. Therefore, JASAL put energy into continuing to reach out and expand our membership to administrators and Japanese educators. Also, having successfully held our first stand-alone conference in 2015, JASAL became confident enough to organize an annual conference, in Kobe (2016), Chiba (2017),

Kumamoto (2018), Osaka (2019), and then, due to the coronavirus pandemic, online in 2020. As Table 1 shows, as a general trend, the number of presentations and participants at JASAL forums/conferences have been increasing almost every year.

Table 1

Number of Presentations and Participants at JASAL Forums/National Conferences (2009–2020)

Year	No. of presentations	No. of student presentations	No. of participants
2009	8	0	10
2010	8	0	?
2011	8	0	32
2012	7	0	?
2013	6	0	?
2014	4	0	?
2015	13	1	50
2016	32	2	95
2017	42	4	149
2018	44	6	110
2019	53	9	150
2020	21	1	approx. 100

Note. Participant numbers for 2020 are approximate, as numbers of participants registered and those actually attending online are different and were not possible to track on the day of the conference.

During JASAL's third executive term, the organization also conducted workshops and forums at other national and international conferences (such as the JALT PanSIG 2017 Conference and the Independent Learning Association

2018 Conference). JASAL also started regional self-access related social get-togethers. Moreover, in this period, JASAL began to increase opportunities for its members to publish. Since the 2009 forum, members have written a report after each annual forum or conference, and these have been published in a number of places, including *AILA RenLA*, *JALT Proceedings*, and the *SiSAL Journal* (Bigelow, 2019; Kodate, 2012; Lin, 2017; Mynard & Navarro, 2010; Okamoto, 2015; Reinbold, 2018; Shibata, 2013; Tweed, 2016). Papers from the 2017 annual conference were published in a special issue of the *SiSAL Journal* (Yamashita, Taylor, & Tweed, 2018), and papers from the 2018 conference (held jointly with the NanKyu Chapter of JALT) were published by the JALT chapter (Taylor & Xethakis, 2019).

2.2.3 Formalizing the JASAL Board Structure

With the current fourth executive board term (2019–2022), we have increased the number of board members to eight, with the aim of formalizing and further professionalizing the organization. For the first 13 years, JASAL had been run in a somewhat informal manner. There was no written constitution and no financial reporting. Members were added to the membership list and remained there indefinitely (unless they contacted JASAL to ask to be removed). As a result, the list contained "ghost members" who had long since left the country or the field, and many email addresses which were no longer in use. By 2018, it was clear that these practices needed improvement.

There were several reasons why this structural formalization became necessary. First, the organization had continued to grow, and the annual income (from conferences; JASAL has never charged membership fees) and expenses were rising; it was time to move on from a cash-only payment system. Next, the European Union (EU) General Data Protection Regulation, which was implemented in May 2018, required all organizations with members from EU countries to manage personal information more carefully, obtaining consent from members periodically to store their data. Moreover, with the rise of predatory conferences, some universities were beginning to restrict funding for conference participation to those run by academic organizations with a constitution on their website, preventing potential delegates from attending JASAL conferences and events. Additionally, the board became aware that because the organization was not listed in the Kyouryoku Gakujutsu Kenkyū Dankai, the list of "Cooperative Science and Research Bodies" maintained by the Science Council of Japan (n.d.), members may be given little or no recognition for their JASAL-related activities when being considered for new positions or promotion. To apply to be listed with the Science Council of Japan, JASAL would need to meet certain criteria, including stronger administrative practices and producing an in-house journal.

The current board is taking steps to meet these standards and to build secure foundations for future growth. It has asked all members to reregister and set up a bank account for cashless payment of conference fees. It held its first Annual General Meeting during the JASAL 2019 annual conference at which the organization's constitution and bylaws were approved. Annual finance reports are now provided to members and there is an auditing process. The current board has also set up the *JASAL Journal*, an online, open-access, peer-reviewed journal in which members can publish their self-access related research papers in English or Japanese, publishing the inaugural issue in June 2020 and the second issue in December 2020. JASAL has also established partnerships with several related organizations both in Japan and beyond (including signing a Memorandum of Understanding with IALLT in 2020) and is in talks with others to build a stronger network of organizations that can help serve the needs of those working in the field of self-access in Japan and help JASAL achieve recognition as an academic organization.

2.2.4 JASAL Student Events

JASAL believes that students are the center of SACs. Since 2013, JASAL has been actively creating opportunities for students involved in or who work at SACs to share and learn from each other. In 2013, the Student Involvement in Self-Access Centers Conference was held at Nanzan Kenkyu Center in Nagoya, organized by Umida Ashurova, Vick Ssali, and a student committee led by then fourth-year undergraduate student, Lisa Hayashi. This conference was run by students with student conference chairs and featured nine presentations from students at universities across Japan. Following the success of this event, in 2015, JASAL organized a JASAL Student Show and Tell event at Okayama University in Okayama with 13 student presentations representing seven institutions. In 2016, JASAL supported the Empowering Students in Self-Access Conference, which was organized by Jo Mynard and Kie Yamamoto at Kanda University of International Studies in Chiba. Since 2016, JASAL has offered undergraduate student staff presentation slots at our annual conference. Every year since 2016, we have given opportunities to undergraduate students who work in SACs to present about their staff work and projects/activities they plan and conduct in their facilities. We also include student staff get-together time during our annual conference so that student staff can have time to meet and share their challenges and their ideas with students from other university SACs.

As JASAL expanded its executive board in 2019, we added a new position, student involvement coordinator. With this launch, we hosted a larger-scale student conference, JASAL SAC Student Conference 2019, at Konan Women's University in Kobe. Forty-six students from 13 university SACs in 10 prefectures in Japan came together and presented about their respective SACs and their projects, engaged in active Q&A sessions and discussed action plans for their respective centers, and shared and discussed further with students from other universities. A total of 72 participants attended this student conference full of students' passion and energy. Student presentations represent student voices. Hearing students' presentations allows SAC faculty members, including directors, administrative staff, and learning advisors, to see their operations and the workings of SACs from perspectives that differ from their own and provides many insights. The survey at the end of the SAC Student Conference 2019 showed how much this student conference inspired both students and faculty members with new ideas and motivated them to improve their SACs.

2.2.5 Self-Access Center Tours (SAC Tours)

One of JASAL's popular events is its SAC tours, where members can visit and see the actual workings of a self-access center. At JASAL, we have been organizing SAC tours since 2013. A SAC tour usually includes a guided tour of the SAC, followed by discussion sessions. Participants see a wide variety of SACs operating at different institutions in different contexts. For the host institution, it is an opportunity to receive feedback from their JASAL colleagues. During the tour, participants are free to ask any questions they have about SAC-related issues. So far, we have had SAC tours at Soka University (2013), Kanda Institute of Foreign Languages (2014, 2015), Sojo University, Kumamoto (2015, 2018), Tokoha University (2015), Chiba University (2016), Meijo University (2016), Akita International University (2017), Konan Women's University (2016, 2019), Konan University Nishinomiya Campus (2019), Konan University Okamoto Campus (2019), Otemon Gakuin University (2019), and Ritsumeikan University Osaka Ibaraki Campus (2019).

2.2.6 JASAL Website

The JASAL website (JASAL, n.d. is a hub of information for members and non-members alike. We provide information about JASAL, links to publications and resources, and details about upcoming events organized by JASAL. Through our Conference pages we also provide information, including abstracts, summaries, and slides/pdfs of previous JASAL presentations and events.

2.2.7 JASAL Online Discussion Group and Social Media

JASAL also has a members-only email discussion group (run through Yahoo Groups) designed to facilitate communication on self-access issues. In previous posts, people have asked questions about orientation activities and staff payment and posted job opening announcements and calls for proposals or other announcements from related organizations. Additionally, we have a Facebook Page and Twitter and Instagram accounts.

2.3 The JASAL Membership

JASAL started with only 15 people, but the membership has increased steadily. At the time the survey of the membership discussed in Section 3 was carried out (late 2019), data from our membership records (provided when members join and updated regularly) showed that there were 173 members, with 160 based in Japan in areas covering all four main islands from Hokkaido to Kyushu, and 13 members based overseas. There was a good gender balance, with 74 women, 97 males, and two members who preferred not to say. Fifty-one members were Japanese and 122 non-Japanese. More recent records show that as of January 2021 the total number of members has increased to 200.

The majority of JASAL's members work in the tertiary sector (see Table 2). The records show that over two-thirds have academic titles ranging from Assistant Professor/ Research Associate (the lowest rank in Japan) and Lecturer/Instructor (the next rank, in the table combined with Senior/Principal Lecturer, a slightly higher rank) through to Associate Professor (second highest) and Professor (the highest). These roles typically include teaching, research, and administrative duties, but in practice, the responsibilities of these members may also involve advising or language tutoring in a SAC, facilitating in a conversation lounge, or management of SAC spaces, including design, purchasing, hiring staff, or promoting SAC services. Some JASAL members hold a position which indicates that their primary or only work is SAC-based, such as Learning Advisor or Center Director. These roles are also likely to include research, and these members may also teach several courses. The fact that these positions exist demonstrates that in the

Japanese tertiary context, language advising is beginning to establish itself as a distinct role, requiring a skillset different from classroom language teaching.

One unusual and important segment of JASAL's membership is administrators. Fourteen members (just over 8% of the membership) have administrative roles related to university SACs. In Japan, university administrators and clerical staff typically receive no research funding and rarely join academic associations or take part in conferences alongside educators. JASAL's free membership policy and affordable conferences help to support a fruitful dialog between classroom educators, language learning advisors, and administrators at different institutions, which is essential for the operation and development of any successful self-access learning center.

JASAL's diverse membership also includes a small number of K–12 teachers, teachers at various kinds of schools, researchers (at companies or research institutes), and several graduate students. The diversity (in terms of gender, nationality, and type of employment) brings richness and breadth to the interactions between members.

Table 2

Positions/Roles Held by JASAL Members (N = 173)

Role	JASAL members	
	n	%
Lecturer/Instructor or Senior/Principal Lecturer	54	31.2%
Professor or Associate Professor	43	24.8%
Assistant Professor/Research Associate	16	9.3%
SAC/LLS Administrator	14	8.1%
Learning Advisor	13	7.5%
Adjunct Lecturer	10	5.8%
Graduate Student	10	5.8%
Researcher (at a company or research institute)	5	2.9%
Teacher (K–12, or at a vocational or cram school)	5	2.9%
Center Director	3	1.7%

3. Survey of JASAL Members

In late 2019, JASAL surveyed its members to establish the extent to which JASAL has been able to achieve its aims thus far: 1) to provide a forum for its members to disseminate knowledge and share ideas about self-access language learning, running self-access centers, and developing learner autonomy, 2) to provide opportunities for professional development and networking, and 3) to provide members with practical help and support for self-access related projects. The survey also aimed to identify the challenges JASAL faces in the years to come to keep SALL relevant to Japanese learners in the 21st century.

The survey, conducted in English, was sent to all JASAL members by email and posted on the JASAL website and Facebook page. There were 38 responses, 35 from members and 3 from prospective members, representing just over 20% of the total membership. In terms of employment roles, the demographics of the respondents closely match the demographics of the JASAL membership as a whole (see Table 3).

Table 3

Roles Held by Survey Respondents (N = 38) in Comparison with the JASAL Membership (N = 173)

Role	Survey respondents		JASAL members	
	n	%	*n*	%
Lecturer/Instructor or Senior/Principal Lecturer	11	28.9%	54	31.2%
Learning Advisor	9	23.7%	13	7.5%
Professor or Associate Professor	8	21%	43	24%
Assistant Professor/Research Associate	3	7.9%	16	9.3%
Center Director	3	7.9%	3	1.7%
Teacher (K–12, or at a vocational or cram school)	1	2.6%	5	2.9%
SAC/LLS Administrator	0	0%	14	8.1%
Researcher (at a company or research institute)	0	0%	5	2.9%
Adjunct Lecturer	2	5.3%	10	5.8%
Graduate Student	0	0%	10	5.8%
No response	1	2.6%	0	0%

The survey had six sections. The first asked for demographic information from members, the second asked respondents about the type of JASAL events and activities they have participated in. In the third section, respondents were asked to evaluate their satisfaction with JASAL in general and in the fourth to evaluate the extent to which JASAL has been meeting its stated objectives. The fifth section posed questions about JASAL's future direction, and the last section provided space for any other comments to be freely expressed. Below we focus on the third, fourth, and fifth sections of the questionnaire.

3.1 Evaluation of JASAL Events and Publications

Part 3 of the questionnaire included questions regarding members' satisfaction with JASAL's events and publications. While not all respondents had had direct experience with each item included in the survey, those who did respond generally indicated that they were satisfied with them.

Figure 2

Participant Satisfaction with Events and Publications & Proceedings

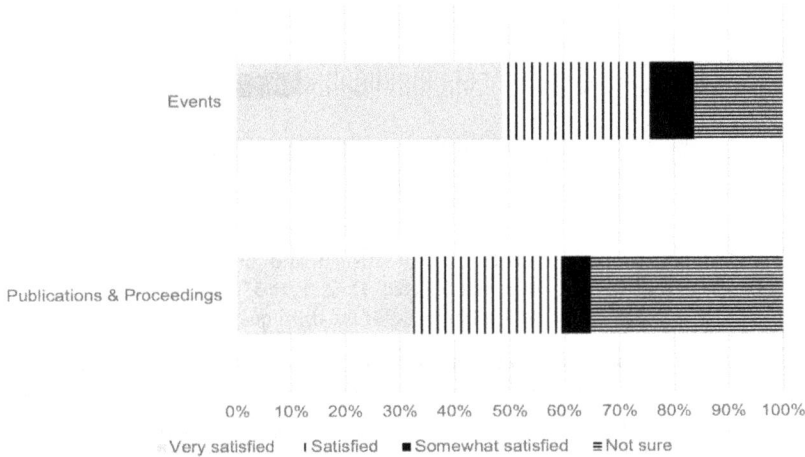

Note. Results are expressed in percentages. "Not satisfied" and "not at all satisfied" were also options for these items, but they were not selected. There were 37 responses for each question (97% response rate).

Figure 2 shows the results of two questions regarding JASAL members' satisfaction with JASAL events (conferences, SAC tours, and forums) and JASAL publications and proceedings. More than three quarters of respondents reported that they were very satisfied or satisfied with JASAL events. In contrast to events, there was a lower rate of satisfaction indicated by respondents for JASAL publications and proceedings, with less than 60% of respondents indicating that they were "very satisfied" or "satisfied." Further, more than a third answered that they were not sure regarding their satisfaction with JASAL publications and proceedings. This relatively high percentage may indicate that a number of JASAL members have not read any JASAL publications. It may also indicate that they were not aware of them. Since the survey was administered in late 2019, we have published two issues of the JASAL Journal, so we hope that any future surveys will show increased awareness of our publications.

More focused results on participants' satisfaction with JASAL conferences, SAC tours, and forums are shown in Figure 3. The majority of survey participants indicated that they were "very satisfied" with conferences, and just over a quarter of them answered that they were "satisfied." While approximately two thirds of respondents expressed that they were "very satisfied" or "satisfied" with the SAC tours, just over a fifth indicated that they were "not sure." In addition, although more than half of participants responded that they were "very satisfied" or "satisfied" with forums, nearly 45% answered that they were "not sure." In response to the comparatively less positive responses regarding SAC tours and forums, we believe that we should do more to promote these events and gather feedback from participants so that we can improve them. It is worth noting that it is possible some members do not know what these events are.

Figure 3

Participant Satisfaction with JASAL Conferences, SAC Tours, and Forums

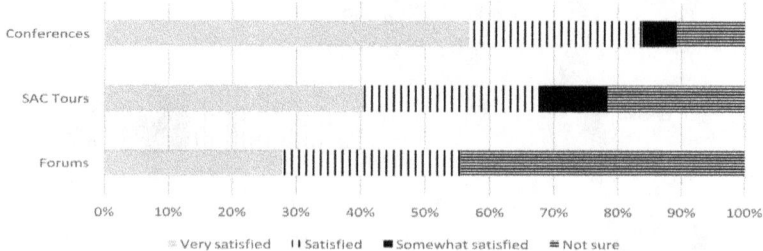

Note. Results are expressed in percentages. "Not satisfied" and "not at all satisfied" were also options for these items but they were not selected. There were 37 responses for the first two questions (97% response rate) and 36 responses for the third question (95% response rate).

Part 3 of the questionnaire also included two open-ended questions related to individuals' experiences with JASAL events and publications. While there were no comments related to the publications, several valuable responses were received regarding different JASAL events.

There were 26 responses to the question "Out of all of the JASAL events you have attended, which have you found the most valuable and why?" (69% response rate). Most of the answers to this question focused on JASAL conferences. Many respondents expressed that they liked JASAL conferences because they could get good ideas there. As one respondent wrote, "I like JASAL conferences. I get interesting ideas every time. They have a friendly, supportive and constructive atmosphere." A few people also commented that JASAL conferences represented good opportunities for networking with like-minded professionals. There was also a specific comment praising JASAL student conferences, where students make up the majority of the presenters: "I liked the Student Conference 2019. It was great to hear about programs and services from the students' perspective and learn about what they are doing at other centers." Finally, there were several comments that expressed positive sentiments about the SAC tours. The following response shows how the unique nature of SAC tours can be helpful for some: "SAC tours have helped me to take back great ideas for the SACs I have worked at. It is hard to explain in a lecture about floor plans and bulletin boards, etc."

One final open-ended question elicited comments about specific experiences with JASAL events and publications. There were 12 responses to this question (32% response rate). While many of these included expressions of appreciation to the JASAL team, a couple of them offered some very helpful suggestions. For instance, one respondent wrote of the need to have JASAL events at smaller, lesser-known SACs:

> This is not really a comment but more of a suggestion. It might be interesting to have JASAL events at institutions with lesser known and/or smaller scale SACs. While it may be difficult to do this, holding events at such places could give participants an opportunity to see how such centers, especially those without a large staff, are run. Consequently, such an event may be informative and useful for both attendees and the host.

We agree with this sentiment and, recently, have been actively talking to those involved with smaller SACs to gauge their interest in holding a future JASAL event. Another helpful comment was about designing events so that there is more fruitful discussion between classroom teachers and advisors: "I think co-operation with events that are about things teachers can do to foster autonomy is a good idea and really every advisor and teacher should understand as much as possible about both roles." This is certainly a helpful reminder because making meaningful connections with teachers and increasing mutual understanding about how to support learner autonomy both are likely to have a positive impact on students.

3.2 Evaluation of JASAL in Relation to its Objectives

Part 4 of the questionnaire asked respondents to evaluate JASAL in relation to its objectives. Specifically, this section included questions about how well JASAL has provided a forum for its members for knowledge sharing, opportunities for professional development and networking, and practical help and support related to self-access.

Figure 4

Participant Evaluation of JASAL in Relation to its Objectives

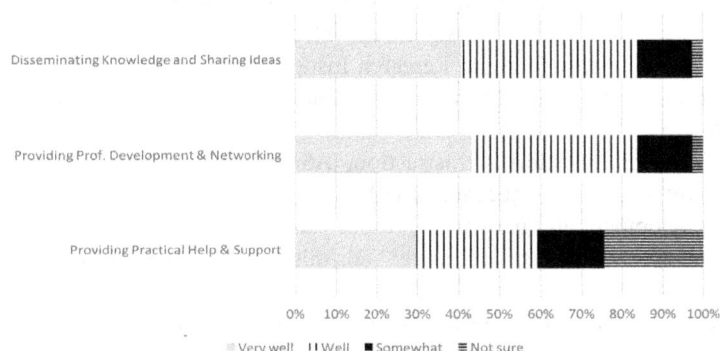

Note. Results are expressed in percentages. "Not very well" and "not well at all" were also options for these items but they were not selected. There were 37 responses for each of these questions (97% response rate).

Participants had the opportunity to respond to both Likert-scale and open-ended questions regarding these three areas. Each Likert-scale question was followed by a corresponding open-ended question.

The responses to the question "JASAL aims to provide a forum for its members to disseminate knowledge and share ideas about self-access language learning, running self-access centers and developing learner autonomy. From your own experience, how well has JASAL been able to meet this objective?" are shown in Figure 4. The answers were overwhelmingly positive, with over 80% answering "very well" or "well."

Twelve respondents (32% response rate) shared a wide range of responses to the open-ended follow-up question about JASAL disseminating knowledge and sharing ideas, including both positive comments and suggestions. Regarding the positive comments, several individuals mentioned that they had benefited from knowledge and practice being shared. One person mentioned sharing JASAL's Language Learning Spaces Registry to talk to their employer about expanding the SAC, and another mentioned visiting SACs as a way to learn about various resources and programs to develop and expand their SAC. Others praised the presentations at conferences. For example, one respondent said that the presentations that included "what each institution has been doing are very interesting," and another explained that they are "invaluable and have helped me to grow as an educator." Survey participants also included several helpful suggestions in their responses. One person recommended that JASAL conduct outreach programs and workshops to help those outside the field of self-access, including administrators. Similarly, another person commented that JASAL could do more to facilitate dialog between self-access practitioners and classroom teachers who are also interested in promoting autonomy to learners. A few others replied with suggestions of how JASAL could provide more practical support, including offering online learning and discussion and workshops on how to set up and run SACs. Finally, there were two recommendations related to promotion. While one respondent commented that JASAL should do more to promote itself so that more people know about the organization, another said that JASAL should actively promote other organizations in the field of self-access, such as the Research Institute for Learning Autonomy Education at Kanda University of International Studies, a step which JASAL has already taken.

Similar to the first question in this section, JASAL members answered with rather positive responses to the question "JASAL aims to provide opportunities for professional development and networking. From your own experience, how well has JASAL been able to meet this objective?" For this item, nearly 85% answered "very well" or "well."

In the follow-up item to this question, we received both positive comments and helpful suggestions, mostly related to networking and professional development opportunities. There was a total of 11 comments (29% response rate). As for comments about networking, two respondents said that they appreciate social events, such as the casual meetups, that involve eating and drinking together. Another said that poster presentations and SAC tours are good places for networking. In addition, one person commented, "It's always a friendly and relaxed environment. I've always felt that people appreciate the diversity of participants." There were also some suggestions, including one that more time should be given at events for socialization and another that social events could be held in more regions throughout the country.

Some respondents also provided comments related to professional development. While one person said "JASAL events offer a range of PD options," another referred to JASAL conferences as "valuable learning opportunities." There were also useful recommendations related to reaching out to those who are less knowledgeable of SALL. One person suggested that offering "a bilingual materials bank explaining self-access learning would be beneficial, and testimonials for the success in varying settings." Another survey participant proposed a peer-buddy system in which more knowledgeable participants could support presenters with less knowledge of SALL. Finally, one respondent suggested that JASAL promote itself more so that more people are aware of JASAL and the diversity of events that it offers.

In contrast to the two closed questions about disseminating knowledge and sharing ideas, and providing professional development and networking opportunities, the responses to the question about providing practical help and support were more mixed. This question read: "JASAL aims to provide members with practical help and support for self-access related projects. From your own experience, how well has JASAL been able to meet this objective?" Less than 60% responded "very well" or "well," and just over 15% answered "somewhat." We will discuss possible reasons that JASAL members responded to this item less positively below.

There was a total of 11 comments (29% response rate) to the follow-up question to this item about JASAL providing practical help and support. A few people commented positively that they gained practical ideas and support from conferences, face-to-face communication, and/or the JASAL email discussion list. Others gave suggestions related to offering practical support. One respondent said that JASAL could be "more deliberate in trying to meet this objective" by providing focused workshops by experts at conferences. More specifically, another recommended that "more practical presentations and info on the website about things like copyright, library systems etc. could be useful." This person also commented that having more information in Japanese would be useful. In contrast to these views, one person questioned whether offering practical workshops is useful because "each institution has their rules and procedures." Finally, a few individuals responded by saying that they were not aware that JASAL offered practical help and support, seemingly implying that such support would be different from that regularly offered at JASAL conferences and other JASAL events, and that it would take the form of more focused and perhaps more prescriptive sessions.

3.3 Meeting JASAL Members' Needs Moving Forward

Part 5 of the survey focused on the direction JASAL needs to be heading and how to best meet JASAL members' needs moving forward. Respondents were asked which content areas they would like to see included at future conferences and were given a number of options to select from. The 37 responses (97% response rate) indicated that many members hope to learn more about current trends in the theory and practice of foreign language education as applied to SALL (70.3%), advising

(67.6%), and the promotion of globalization and the development of intercultural skills in SACs (62.2%), although other areas also scored highly (see Table 4).

Table 4

Content Areas Respondents Would Like to See Included at Future JASAL Conferences

Content area	n	%
Current trends in the theory and practice of foreign language education as applied to SALL	26	70.3%
Advising in language learning	25	67.6%
The promotion of globalization/provision of "international experiences" and development of intercultural skills in SACs	23	62.2%
Resources for SALL	21	56.8%
Management of SACs	18	48.6%
Space and furniture design in SACs	18	48.6%
Incorporating technology into SALL	17	45.9%
Issues related to copyright	12	32.4%

Note. This was a multiple-select item, so adding up individual percentages exceeds 100%.

Comments by 16 respondents (42% response rate) indicated the challenges that members face in developing SALL at their institutions and identified areas that JASAL as an organization could explore so that solutions can be developed and support provided. Several comments raised concerns about a lack of clarity in copyright laws as they apply to SACs, for example, and the need for sessions led by experts in this field. Another comment mentioned resistance to setting up a SAC from over-burdened colleagues. This highlights a significant issue in Japan, as declining student numbers cause institutions to place greater demands on faculty to be involved in recruiting students, on top of teaching, research, and administrative duties.

Technology was an area that respondents felt is likely to become more important over time: "I believe technology will occupy an increasing role in SALL in the future. As people might see SACs as old-fashioned, it is important to consider ways that technology can enhance SACs and SALL." Another wrote, "I am interested in learning about digital learning resources for students and technology to improve advertisements of our activities & events." The marketing or promotion of SACs and

SAC services to students and difficulty attracting students to use the SAC is an issue for many institutions in Japan and was mentioned in several comments, such as this one, which someone shared in response to a different item on the questionnaire:

> We are trying to find ways to have students use the facilities. We've integrated its use with course work, but most students will not use the SAC "voluntarily." Unfortunately, perhaps, since the LC is part of the library, students tend to associate the LC with studies [rather] than a place to have fun.

JASAL could offer workshops both on tools that support learning and on tools that support staff in managing and promoting their SACs.

Another area of interest was the understanding of SACs as human-centered spaces that support the development and overall well-being of the students. One respondent stated that their interest in SACs stemmed from the following understanding: "I feel like it is more closely related to learning, life, health, and development as a person than a traditional classroom." Another commented, "I'm interested in developing theory and understanding of mechanics and systems related to regulation in learning, human development, and health." The health and well-being of students is a growing concern in Japan, as universities are now accepting more students with disabilities, including those with developmental disorders and mental health issues, who are likely to need more support.

The survey data also indicated that JASAL members are aware of the need to develop the field of SALL by making stronger links with related fields. One suggestion was that drawing on "design principles research" when looking at space, furniture, and equipment would make SALL "a more rigorous academic field." Another stated goal was "furthering the field of self-access learning to fields outside language learning." As this suggestion implies, there is potential for the expertise which we have developed in building learning communities and providing learning advising services to be used in other disciplines.

4. Conclusions: Future Directions for JASAL

JASAL was originally set up in response to the rapid growth of the self-access movement in Japan around the turn of the century, and since then we have both evolved with the movement and, we hope, played a valuable role in furthering its development. Self-access environments need to be carefully designed to provide learners with flexibility to explore resources and opportunities for learning. We have a great variety of self-access environments across Japan and many factors have influenced these: the learner population and their needs, the availability of financial and human resources, the goals of the institution, and the beliefs of administrators, staff, learning advisors, and teachers. By sharing experiences and expertise, we can grow together even more as a field.

We are rightly proud of the supportive community that JASAL has become. The organization has changed significantly since the early years, growing into an association with a well-attended annual conference, numerous smaller events, and its own journal. JASAL is at the center of the self-access movement in Japan, and we are connected with organizations that have similar goals through the partnerships we have made, in particular in Japan, with the Research Institute for Learner Autonomy Education, the Writing Centers Association of Japan, and more recently The Japan Association for Language Teaching. Based on the results of the survey of members and reflections of the JASAL board, and through learning more about similar organizations such as IALLT, we can identify a number of possible future directions for the association.

Our current priority is to complete the registration process for the Cooperative Science and Research Bodies of the Science Council of Japan, which will enhance our status in Japan and bring many benefits for members, as explained above. As part of this initiative, the newly launched *JASAL Journal* can help disseminate SAC-related research and practice to a wider audience. The LLS Registry of SACs is an ongoing project, and we intend to continue contacting institutions and informing them of the benefits that registration will bring in terms of recognition and possibilities for collaborative research. Where bureaucratic suspicion from administrators has at times prevented academic directors from being able to register their centers, the enhanced status that membership in the Cooperative Science and Research Bodies brings will surely help in this regard.

The coronavirus pandemic that has shaken the world since early 2020 has profound implications for a movement such as self-access, which by its very definition aims to bring people together, just when the public health crisis requires us to keep our distance. The move into emergency remote teaching has affected SACs in Japan, which are supporting students who may feel isolated and overwhelmed, with advising, conversation sessions, and opportunities for interaction with peers via online tools. JASAL is also embracing the opportunities presented by the sudden popularity of conference software to support our community with online events for both academics and students. Physical distancing requirements have significant implications for center layout and the format of any student interactions that do happen in physical centers. JASAL will continue sharing best practices and providing opportunities for communication and collaboration among members as they tackle the inevitable challenges this situation will present.

Student involvement and student-centered events have been an important part of our growth and give JASAL conferences a unique energy, so we are eager to enhance this aspect of the organization and encourage more students to take ownership of their self-access spaces, whether physical or online. Results from the survey indicate that more practical support for members, in the form of workshops on issues such as copyright, learning space design, and technology for language learning, would be appreciated and could draw on related fields of study. These workshops could be held as stand-alone events or as part of our annual conference. Finally, IALLT's impressive record in supporting its members through the Language Center Evaluation Tool Kit (Simon et al., 2017) and the other initiatives featured in previous IALLT publications (Kronenberg & Lahaie, 2011; Lavolette & Simon, 2018; Ross, 2013) also offer possible future directions for JASAL.

References

Bigelow, B. (2019). Review of the JASAL 2018 x SUTLF 5 conference. *Studies in Self-Access Learning Journal, 10*(2), 205–211. https://doi.org/10.37237/100206

Clemente, A., & Rubin, J. (2008). Past, present and future of a Mexican self-access center: The case of the SAC at UABJO. *MEXTESOL Journal, 32*(2), 23–37.

Cooker, L. (2008). Some self access principles. *Independence, 43*, 20–21.

Cooker, L., & Cutting, M. (2002). The SALC—from theory to practice. *Gengokyouikukenkyu, 13*, 1–13.

Cooker, L., & Torpey, M. (2004). From the classroom to the self-access centre: A chronicle of learner-centred curriculum development. *The Language Teacher, 28*(6), 11–16.

Cotterall, S., & Murray, G. (2009). Enhancing metacognitive knowledge: Structure, affordances and self. *System, 37*(1), 34–45. https://doi.org/10.1016/j.system.2008.08.003

Cotterall, S., & Reinders, H. (2001) Fortress or bridge? Learners' perceptions and practice in self access language learning. *Tesolanz, 8*, 23–38.

Curry, N., Mynard, J., Noguchi, J., & Watkins, S. (2017) Evaluating a self-directed language learning course in a Japanese university. *International Journal of Self-Directed Learning, 14*(1), 17–36.

Frances, C. (2018). The language center: A hub for global communities of practice. In E. Lavolette & E. F. Simon (Eds.), *Language center handbook* (pp. 295–317). Auburn University, AL: International Association for Language Learning and Technology.

Gardner, D. (2017). The evolution and devolution of management and training needs for self-access centre staff. *Studies in Self-Access Learning Journal, 8*(2), 147–156. https://doi.org/10.37237/080207

Gardner, D., & Miller, L. (1999). *Establishing self-access.* Cambridge, UK: Cambridge University Press.

Gonzales, A. (2018) Cultures and languages across the curriculum and directed independent language studies. In E. Lavolette & E. F. Simon (Eds.), *Language center handbook* (pp. 153–172). Auburn, AL: International Association for Language Learning and Technology.

Gremmo, M. J., & Riley, P. (1995). Autonomy, self-direction and self-access in language teaching and learning: The history of an idea. *System, 23*(2), 151–164. https://doi.org/10.1016/0346-251x(95)00002-2

Holec, H. (1981). *Autonomy and foreign language learning.* Oxford, UK: Pergamon. (Original work published 1979)

Holec, H. (2000). Le CRAPEL à travers les ages [CRAPEL through the ages]. *Mélanges Pédagogiques, 25*, 5–12.

Hughes, L. S., Krug, N. P., & Vye, S. (2011). The growth of an out-of-class learning community through autonomous socialization at a self-access center. *Studies in Self-Access Learning Journal, 2*(4), 281–291. https://doi.org/10.37237/020405

JASAL. (n.d.) *The Japan Association for Self-Access Learning.* https://jasalorg.com/

Kato, S. (2012). Professional development for learning advisors: Facilitating the intentional reflective dialogue. *Studies in Self-Access Learning, 3*(1), 74–92. https://doi.org/10.37237/030106

Kato, S., & Mynard, J. (2015). *Reflective dialogue: Advising in language learning.* New York, NY: Routledge.

Kodate, A. (2012). The JASAL Forum 2011: Growing trends in self-access learning. *Studies in Self-Access Learning Journal, 3*(1), 122–132. https://doi.org/10.37237/030109

Kronenberg, F. A., & Lahaie, U. (Eds.). (2011). *Language center design.* Auburn, AL: International Association for Language Learning Technology.

Lammons, E. (2011). Transitioning from teaching to advising. *Independence, 53,* 27-31.

Lavolette, E. (2018). Language center mandates and realities. In E. Lavolette & E. F. Simon (Eds.), *Language center handbook* (pp. 3–33). Auburn, AL: International Association for Language Learning and Technology.

Lavolette, E. (2019). A very brief introduction to US language centers. In L. Xethakis & C. Taylor (Eds.), *JASAL 2018 x SUTLF 5: Selected papers from the Sojo University Teaching and Learning Forum 2018: Making connections* (pp. 4–25). Kumamoto, Japan: NanKyu JALT. https://www.nankyujalt.org/publications#h.p_twJDnQsJDWmj

Lavolette, E., & Simon, E. F. (Eds.). (2018). *Language center handbook.* Auburn, AL: International Association for Language Learning and Technology.

Lin, M. (2017). Report on the Japan Association of Self-Access Learning (JASAL) 2016 annual conference. *Studies in Self-Access Learning Journal, 7(*4), 383–393. https://doi.org/10.37237/070406

Little, D. (Ed.). (1989). *Self-access systems for language learning.* Dublin, Ireland: Authentik.

Ludwig, C., & Mynard, J. (2019). *Autonomy in language learning: Advising in action.* Canterbury, UK: International Association for Teaching English as a Foreign Language.

Ministry of Education, Culture, Sports, Science and Technology (MEXT). (n.d). *Support for internationalization of universities.* https://www.mext.go.jp/en/policy/education/highered/title02/detail02/1373875.htm

Ministry of Education, Culture, Sports, Science, and Technology (MEXT). (2002). *Developing a strategic plan to cultivate "Japanese with English abilities."* https://www.mext.go.jp/english/news/2002/07/020901.htm

Ministry of Education, Culture, Sports, Science and Technology (MEXT). (2010). *The concept of global human resource development focusing on the East Asian region. Importance of promoting interuniversity exchanges with quality assurance.* https://www.mext.go.jp/en/policy/education/highered/title02/detail02/sdetail02/1373900.htm

Ministry of Education, Culture, Sports, Science and Technology (MEXT). (2011). *Five proposals and specific measures in developing proficiency in English for international communication.* https://www.mext.go.jp/component/english/icsFiles/afieldfile/2012/07/09/1319707_1.pdf

Ministry of Education, Culture, Sports, Science and Technology (MEXT). (2012). *Project for the promotion of global human resource development: Application guidelines in FY2012.* http://www.jsps.go.jp/jgjinzai/data/download/01_gjinzai_kouboyouryou.pdf

Morrison, B. R., & Navarro, D. (2012). Shifting roles: From language teachers to learning advisors. *System*, *40*(3), 349–359. https://doi.org/10.1016/j.system.2012.07.004

Mozzon-McPherson, M. (1997). The language adviser: A new type of teacher. An analysis of an emerging role. In D. Little & B. Voss (Eds.), *Language centres: Planning for the new millennium* (pp. 97–109). Plymouth, UK: CercleS.

Murray, G. (2009). Self-access language learning: Structure, control and responsibility. In F. Kjisik, P. Voller, N. Aoki, & Y. Nakata (Eds.), *Mapping the terrain of learner autonomy: Learning environments, learning communities and identities* (pp. 118–144). Tampere, Finland: Tampere University Press.

Murray, G., & Fujishima, N. (2013). Social language learning spaces: Affordances in a community of learners. *Chinese Journal of Applied Linguistics*, *36*(1), 141–157. https://doi.org/10.1515/cjal-2013-0009

Murray, G. & Fujishima, N. (2016). *Social spaces for language learning:* Stories from the L-café. Basingstoke, UK: Palgrave Macmillan.

Mynard, J. (2019a). Advising and self-access learning: Promoting language learner autonomy beyond the classroom. In H. Reinders, S. Ryan, & S. Nakamura (Eds.), *Innovations in language learning and teaching: The case of Japan* (pp. 185–220). Cham, Switzerland: Palgrave Macmillan.

Mynard, J. (2019b). Perspectives on self-access in Japan: Are we simply catching up with the rest of the world? *Mélanges CRAPEL*, *40*(1), 13–27.

Mynard, J., & Carson, L. (2012). *Advising in language learning: Dialogue, tools and context*. Harlow, UK: Pearson Education.

Mynard, J., & Navarro, D. (2010). Report on the Japan Association of Self-Access Learning (JASAL) Forum, at the Japan Association for Language Teaching (JALT) 2009 Conference in Shizuoka. *Studies in Self-Access Learning Journal*, *1*(1), 65–67. https://doi.org/10.37237/010108

Okamoto, E. (2015). JASAL 2014 Forum. Self-access conversations: Beyond classroom borders. *Studies in Self-Access Learning Journal*, *6*(1), 142–155. https://doi.org/10.37237/060112

Reinbold, L. (2018). Self-access centers and autonomous learning: Report on the Japan Association for Self-Access Learning (JASAL) conference 2017. *Studies in Self-Access Learning Journal*, *9*(2), 90–99. https://doi.org/10.37237/090202

Ross, A. F. (2013). (Ed.) *IALLT language center management*. Auburn, AL: International Association for Language Learning and Technology.

Rutson-Griffiths, Y., & Porter, M. (2016). Advising in language learning: Confirmation requests for successful advice giving. *Studies in Self-Access Learning Journal*, *7*(3), 260–286. https://doi.org/10.37237/070303

Science Council of Japan. (n.d.) *Kyouryoku gakujutsu kenkyū dankai* [(List of) Cooperative Science and Research Bodies]. http://www.scj.go.jp/ja/group/dantai/index.html

Shibata, S. (2013). JASAL Forum 2012: Making a difference through self access. *Studies in Self-Access Learning Journal*, *4*(1), 62–69. https://doi.org/10.37237/040106

Simon, E. F., Kraemer, A., Kronenberg, F. A., Lavolette, E., & Sartiaux, A. (2017). *Language center evaluation toolkit*. International Association for Language Learning Technology. https://v.gd/toolkit

Somerville, M., & Harlan, S. (2008). From information commons to learning commons and learning spaces: An evolutionary context. In B. Schader (Ed.), *Learning commons: Evolution and collaborative essentials* (pp. 1–36). Oxford, UK: Chandos.

Tanabe, Y. (2004). What the 2003 MEXT action plan proposes to teachers of English. *The Language Teacher, 28*(3), 3–8. https://jalt-publications.org/tlt/articles/730-what-2003-mext-action-plan-proposes-teachers-english

Taylor, C. (2014). The transformation of a foreign language conversation lounge: An action research project. *The Annals of Gifu Shotoku Gakuen University. Faculty of Foreign Languages, 53*, 1–16. http://ci.nii.ac.jp/els/contentscinii_20170928130927.pdf?id=ART0010253310

Taylor, C., & Xethakis, L. (Eds.). (2019). *JASAL2018 x SUTLF 5. Selected papers from the Sojo University Teaching and Learning Forum 2018: Making connections.* Kumamoto, Japan: Japan Association for Language Teaching NanKyu Chapter.

Thornton, K. (2012). Editorial. *Studies in Self-Access Learning Journal, 3*(1), 2–5. https://doi.org/10.37237/030101

Thornton, K. (2013). A framework for curriculum reform: Re-designing a curriculum for self-directed language learning. *Studies in Self-Access Learning Journal, 4*(2), 142–153. https://doi.org/10.37237/040207

Thornton, K. (2018). Language policy in non-classroom language learning spaces. *Studies in Self-Access Learning Journal, 9*(2), 156–178. https://doi.org/10.37237/090208

Thornton, K. (2020). The changing role of self-access in fostering learner autonomy. In M. Jiménez Raya & F. Vieira (Eds.) *Autonomy in language education: Present and future avenues* (pp. 157–174). London, UK: Routledge.

Thornton, K., & Mynard, J. (2012). Investigating the focus of advisor comments in a written advising dialogue. In C. Ludwig & J. Mynard (Eds.), *Autonomy in language learning: Advising in action* (pp. 137–153). Canterbury, UK: International Association for Teaching English as a Foreign Language.

Tweed, A. D. (2016). Report on the JASAL 10th anniversary conference, 2015. *Studies in Self-Access Learning Journal, 7*(1), 60–68. https://doi.org/10.37237/070107

Yamashita, H., & Mynard, J. (2015). Dialogue and advising in self-access learning: Introduction to the special issue. *Studies in Self-Access Learning Journal, 6*(1), 1–12. https://doi.org/10.37237/060101

Yamashita, H., Taylor, C., & Tweed, A. D. (2018). Introduction: Papers from JASAL 2017. *Studies in Self-Access Learning Journal, 9*(2), 86–89. https://doi.org/10.37237/090201

Yasuda, T. (2018). Psychological expertise required for advising in language learning: Theories and practical skills for Japanese EFL learners' trait anxiety and perfectionism. *Studies in Self-Access Learning Journal, 9*(1), 11–32. https://doi.org/10.37237/090103

Author Notes

Katherine Thornton has an MA in TESOL from the University of Leeds, UK, and is associate professor at Otemon Gakuin University in Osaka, Japan, where she works as a learning advisor. She is the director of E-CO (English Café at Otemon), the university's self-access center, and a former president of the Japan Association of Self-Access Learning, currently serving as its events coordinator. Her research focuses on policy and practice in self-access language learning.

Clair Taylor is an associate professor at Gifu Shotoku Gakuen University, Japan, where she manages "Lounge MELT" (a social language learning space for university students). She is currently the president of the Japan Association for Self-Access Learning.

Andrew D. Tweed is a lecturer in the World Language Center and coordinator of the self-access center at Soka University in Tokyo, Japan. He was formerly the events coordinator for the Japan Association for Self-Access Learning (2016–2019). Andrew's research interests include learning beyond the classroom, motivation, and teacher education. He holds an MA TESOL from the University of Washington and an EdD in TESOL from Anaheim University.

Hisako Yamashita is an associate professor at Kobe Shoin Women's University in Kobe, Japan. Hisako has worked in four different self-access learning centers over the past 15 years as a learning advisor. She has been serving on the Japan Association for Self-Access Learning board since its inauguration in 2005 as membership chair (2005–2011, 2011–2016), president (2016–2019), and student involvement coordinator (current). She specializes in learning advisor training and in developing SAC and classroom activities to foster learner autonomy. She holds an MA in Teaching Foreign Languages from the Monterey Institute of International Studies.

Correspondence concerning this chapter should be addressed to Katherine Thornton (thornton.katherine@gmail.com).

Chapter 3
Strategies for Language Centers to Support Online Language Instruction

Luca Giupponi, Emily Heidrich Uebel, and Koen Van Gorp,
Michigan State University, USA

Abstract

As online education continues to become more integral to the mission of post-secondary institutions, and as growth in online language courses follows a similar pattern, language centers find themselves in the unique position of being able to provide strategic guidance and support to innovative online language teaching initiatives. Depending on the size, mission, resources, and priorities of each language center, various strategies may be employed to that end. This chapter describes seven strategies to advance online language instruction and offers two detailed case studies to illustrate those strategies in action.

Online education continues to become more integral to the mission of post-secondary institutions in the United States. Almost two-thirds of college administrators say that distance learning is an essential part of their institution's strategic plan (Xu & Xu, 2019), and a third of post-secondary students are enrolled in at least one online course each semester (Seaman, Allen, & Seaman, 2018). Additionally, while virtually all public institutions and a majority of private institutions offer at least one online course, in 2016, 72% of public institutions and 50% of private institutions in the United States offered at least one fully online degree program (Xu & Xu, 2019). This points to a growing commitment to online education, as demonstrated by the effort involved in ensuring that cross-departmental requirements and electives are available to online students. The increased flexibility, affordability, and access make online courses and programs more attractive to students whose circumstances may prevent them from enrolling in traditional programs (Li & Irby, 2008; Xu & Xu, 2019).

Language centers (LCs) have transitioned from the traditional language labs of the mid- to later-1900s to language centers. Until more recent years, language centers often continued to focus on technology, perhaps left over from the legacy of "computer labs" (Kronenberg, 2017; Roby, 2004; see also Sebastian, Gopalakrishnan, & Hendricks in this volume). The changes in the labs and the possibilities of future language centers have been the subject of broader discussion (see various chapters in Kronenberg, 2017, and Lavolette & Simon, 2018). For example, Yaden and Evans (2017) claimed that

> [l]anguage centers based solely on providing technology may become increasingly challenged to maintain their uniqueness as more of our resources are online and widely available across the campus. The raison d'être for the language center must be organic to the pedagogical mission of the language programs. (p. 97)

The growing popularity of online language courses provides one excellent opportunity for LCs to partner with language programs to advance their mission.

In this chapter, we first provide an overview of online language learning in the United States, and we argue that LCs have a unique opportunity to function as hubs for supporting online language programs. We offer readers seven strategies LCs can use to advance online language instruction at their institutions and beyond, and we describe in detail two case studies illustrating a number of those strategies.

1. Online Language Learning in the United States

Available demographic data for online language instruction are not as comprehensive as those for higher education in general. Yet, we can say that language programs in the United States have seen a growth in distance offerings similar to that experienced in post-secondary instruction more generally, with first- and second-year level courses being more prevalent than upper-division courses (Murphy-Judy & Johnshoy, 2017). As expected, online language enrollment data reflect that of traditional, face-to-face (F2F) offerings (Modern Language Association, 2019), with Spanish offering the largest number of online sections and accounting for more than half of the total enrollment. However, as of 2015, 17 different languages were taught online at US institutions, indicating that demand for online language offerings is continuing to grow, and that departments are responding to this demand (Murphy-Judy & Johnshoy, 2017).

Another indication of this growth is that literature investigating aspects of online language instruction has been proliferating in recent years. One important question is whether students enrolled in online language courses achieve outcomes that are comparable to those achieved by students enrolled in F2F courses. While a number of studies argued that this is indeed the case (Blake et al., 2008; Enkin & Mejías-Bikandi, 2017; Goertler & Gacs, 2018; Grgurović, Chapelle, & Shelley, 2013; Isenberg, 2010), Blake (2015) and Lin and Warschauer (2015) rightly pointed out that not enough studies have been conducted investigating outcomes from a proficiency point of view. Moving away from learning outcomes, numerous articles describe theoretical approaches or best practices for online language instruction, generally focusing on the specifics of course and task design, instructor competencies, principled technology selection, and assessment (Association of Departments of Foreign Languages, 2014; Baralt & Morcillo Gomez, 2017; Blake, 2011; Blake & Guillén, 2014; Compton, 2009; Goertler, 2019; Sun, 2011). Finally, Sun (2014) looked at online language learning from a learner perspective to identify common challenges that students face and strategies for overcoming those challenges. If online language instruction is here to stay, instructors need to be prepared to engage with this format of instruction, and institutions, including language centers, need to think critically about how to best support their instructors.

2. The Role of Language Centers in Supporting Distance Education

The literature is brimming with arguments for the need of support at all life stages of online programs, including conceptualization, instructor development, and instructional design and media support (Adnan, 2017; Compton, 2009; Lederman, 2019; Meyer, 2014; Puzziferro & Shelton, 2009). Additionally, the transition to remote teaching due to the COVID-19 pandemic in Spring 2020 has demonstrated once and for all that principled, carefully designed online education is sharply different from unsupported, crisis-prompted remote instruction (Gacs, Goertler, & Spasova, 2020), pointing to the need for substantial, pervasive support for online language education.

While many institutions offer centralized support, instructional technologists may not have the relevant pedagogical background to support the interaction-heavy instruction needed for online language courses (Steadman & Kraut, 2018). As we show in this chapter, language centers can serve as the ideal hub for supporting and helping scale online language courses and programs at their institutions and beyond. As Kronenberg (2017) pointed out, language centers are evolving to be "understood not so much as a physical place for everything, but rather as a not necessarily centralized connecting hub that nourishes a community of practitioners and learners... [making] possible what individual instructors cannot provide on their own" (pp. 160–161). Language centers are a natural hub to share the necessary resources to support online language instruction and provide incentives to support innovation in online language instruction. What follows are several strategies that can be implemented by LCs to support online initiatives, listed from the least to the most resource intensive. These strategies address all stages of online language education: planning, development, teaching, and maintenance. We must acknowledge that this is written from the perspective of employees of a medium/large LC that is focused more on faculty than student services, and, as such, some of these strategies may not be readily applicable to all LCs or may need to be adapted to fit additional stakeholders. Administrators should view these strategies as steps on a support ladder: As LCs successfully implement strategies on the lower rungs, they can begin to make the case for implementing and requesting resources for the strategies that follow (Figure 1). After describing the seven strategies to advance online language instruction, Section 3 will showcase two case studies to illustrate how some of these strategies can be implemented in a LC.

Figure 1
Strategies to Support Online Language Instruction, From Least to Most Resource Intensive

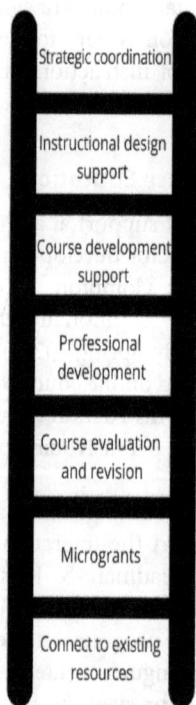

2.1 Connecting to Existing Resources

One easy place to start developing capacity for distance learning support is to collaborate with individuals, offices, and departments that already provide support. Many universities provide instructional design support and resources, usually housed within an academic support center or the institution's central information technology (IT) department (Lieberman, 2018). Depending on these departments' missions and scopes, their expertise may be more limited to technical support, but often individuals in these roles will have at least a limited pedagogical background and will be able to support faculty who desire to develop their online teaching skills.

Once a relationship with these individuals is built, LC staff can serve as a liaison between language faculty, administrators, and the academic support center staff. Depending on what level of support is offered, LC staff can help pair faculty with instructional designers or IT support staff or can serve as a project manager to see a project, such as the onboarding of faculty or the development of a specific online course, to the end. These collaborations will foster mutual understanding and respect between the various sides and can often lead to fruitful curricular collaborations (Yaden, 2018).

What is more, developing a collaborative relationship with such individuals will put the LC "on the map" for institutional online learning leaders, which will ensure the LC has a voice at the table whenever institutional-level strategic, financial, or curricular decisions have to be made.

2.2 Microgrants

A LC can support and motivate language instructors to innovate in their online teaching practices by providing microgrants or fellowships as an incentive. Language programs and departments desiring to initiate online courses and programs should take charge of helping language teachers in this transition, but LCs can complement their efforts by focusing on initiatives that foster the emergence of innovative and transformative practices. By providing small financial incentives, LCs can encourage successful online language instructors to keep experimenting, try out new technologies, participate in professional development, and develop best practices or proofs-of-concept. The LC can support these "fellows" in disseminating such practices across language programs and departments and even beyond their institution.

For example, the Center for Language Teaching Advancement (CeLTA) at Michigan State University (MSU) has awarded fellowships ranging from $500 to $2,000 to faculty to develop novel pedagogical applications, including online content, and promote the use of the technology underlying these applications across language programs. One fellowship project paired a tech-savvy instructor with an instructor who developed a pedagogical technique to help students of Russian build up and expand their vocabulary, enabling them to read authentic literary texts in Russian. The tech-savvy instructor helped convert the F2F materials to online materials using Adobe Captivate, allowing them to be used in a flipped classroom format, thus creating a more efficient hybrid program accommodating the differing needs of a wide range of students. The fellowship incentivized the instructors to work together over the course of one academic year, creating and piloting reading materials for beginning and intermediate students and engaging in a larger conversation through professional development opportunities about how technology can contribute to a more efficient use of actual classroom time by moving certain activities to the flipped classroom. While this example did not directly lead to a fully online course, it is a good illustration of how supporting small-scale innovations can lead to the development of new expertise and innovative practices among the faculty.

We acknowledge that a number of LCs may not be able to readily provide this kind of support because of budgetary constraints. As we discuss below in Section 2.5, underfunded LCs may want to seek funding for these kinds of initiatives both within their institution and externally. We feel there is value in the LC administering these microgrants as opposed to the individual college or university. These small microgrants can help strengthen the relationship between the LC and language faculty, both encouraging greater faculty participation in the center activities and establishing the LC as an important stakeholder in the innovation and improvement of language teaching.

2.3 Course Evaluation and Revision

Online courses tend to require more regular revision and maintenance than F2F courses (Warren & Robinson, 2018). Various factors contribute to this need: technology tools used in the course become outdated or unsupported; learning activities are found to not be as effective as originally assumed; content requires updating; videos need to be redone due to quality or staffing considerations; a new textbook is chosen; or new institutional, departmental, or curricular decisions require changes in course content or design. Whatever the reason(s), it is safe to assume that revision and maintenance will be needed in any online course and should therefore be planned for. Warren and Robinson (2018) refer to this process as the course life-cycle. There is no recommended timeline to which the revision process should adhere; rather, a course life-cycle is dependent on contextual factors and therefore varies. The point here is that departments should plan and budget for a course revision cycle at the onset and experiment with various revision timelines to see which is most appropriate.

LC staff can and should help departments identify appropriate life-cycle routines and can serve as independent course reviewers. There are several research-based and practitioner-vetted rubrics for measuring course quality. The most widely used rubrics are Quality Matters (http://qualitymatters.org, requires institutional membership), OSCQR (https://oscqr.org, open access), and the OLC Scorecard (https://onlinelearningconsortium.org/consult/olc-quality-scorecard-suite, open access). These rubrics are helpful both as a development guide and an evaluation tool to consider what elements may be missing from an online or blended course. LC staff can pursue training opportunities offered by these organizations, seek to become certified auditors, and/or stay updated on the most recent developments in the field. As independent auditors, they can help ensure the quality of online language courses across all language departments or programs. In addition, LC staff can help guide instructors through these steps with an eye toward encouraging faculty to critically self-reflect on their courses throughout each step of development, evaluation, and revision. This ensures that departments do not solely rely on LC staff to evaluate their courses but work in partnership in the process.

For small LCs that do not have resources for conducting actual course reviews, the focus needs to be on advocating for quality assurance processes at the department head, program head, and faculty level. LCs can encourage a closer relationship between instructors and institutional resources (see Strategy 2.1) and identify and encourage faculty champions to develop expertise in this area, apply it to their own practice, and share what they learned in an LC-sponsored professional development event (see Strategy 2.4).

2.4 Professional Development

Arguably, one of the biggest obstacles for language faculty who want to start teaching online is the fact that many of them may not have experienced online learning first-hand. As a result, they lack a conceptual framework for carrying out their instruction in a different medium, and their competence may be limited to transposing their F2F teaching strategies and techniques to the online medium, which will lead to less than optimal results. As Suvorov, Carrillo Cabello, and Janssen Sanchez (2018) argued, LCs are optimally positioned to provide content-aware pedagogical support to language instructors, not only due to the staff's "unique set of expertise," but also because of the "close relationship with departments of world languages (and sometimes with libraries and/or information technology centers)" (p. 194). In the following sections, we will provide an overview of the competencies that successful online language instructors need and discuss ways in which LCs can support the development of those competencies at various levels.

2.4.1 Online Language Teaching Competencies

Compton (2009) proposed a framework for online language teaching skills intended to guide the professional development (PD) of language teachers. She provided a critique of existing computer-assisted language learning frameworks and proposed to divide online teaching competencies in three major skill domains:

> The first set, *technological skills*, relates to knowledge and ability to handle hardware and software issues. Next, the *pedagogical skills* refer to knowledge and ability to conduct and facilitate teaching and learning activities. Lastly, the *evaluative skills* refer to the analytical ability to assess the tasks and overall course and make necessary modifications to ensure language learning objectives are met. (Compton, 2009, p. 81)

In her framework, instructors move along a continuum of expertise from novice to proficient to expert. Compton indicated a range of skills that should get primary focus in language teacher PD and acknowledges that other skills can and should be added to the framework. Together with scholars at the University of Chicago, we drew from a range of current literature to update and reconceptualize Compton's framework (Van Gorp et al., 2019). We argue that both frameworks are a great starting place for organizing a PD agenda for online language teaching, but that competencies in each area need further definition before these frameworks can be used to guide PD initiatives. Drawing from current literature and our own experience working with online faculty, we identify the following list of topics for PD programming. Note that the list is not meant to be comprehensive, but rather is used to exemplify the kind of topics that could be addressed.

- Habits and practices of successful online instructors (Dixson, Kuhlhorst, & Reiff, 2019; Rovai, 2007; Savery, 2010)
- Fostering teaching, cognitive, and social presence (Akyol & Garrison, 2008)
- Research-supported measures of quality (e.g., Quality Matters)
- Accessibility in online environments (Burgstahler, 2017; McAlvage & Rice, 2018)
- Developing effective media (Guo, Kim, & Rubin, 2014)
- Task-based online language teaching (Baralt & Morcillo Gomez, 2017)
- Assessing proficiency online (Blake, 2015; Blake et al., 2008)
- Practical issues in online learning, such as time management and workload
- Iterative course development and backward design

2.4.2 Implementing PD at Different Levels

Suvorov et al. (2018) helpfully differentiated the implementation of PD at three different levels:

- At the micro-level, PD is tailored to a specific local setting and context. PD at this level can be characterized as one-time, on-demand, and language specific.
- At the meso-level, PD is still tailored to the local context but has a broader appeal than micro-level interventions. PD at this level can be non-language-specific and offered at a regular cadence.
- At the macro-level, PD covers topics that have a broad appeal to a large audience. The scope of these offerings goes beyond the local context and can draw audiences from outside the institution.

LCs can and should offer PD at all three levels (Suvorov et al., 2018), which helps them meet the needs of individual instructors and departments as a whole and share best practices on a wider scale without trying to meet all of those needs at once with the same PD event. Table 1 provides a few examples of what PD at each level could look like.

Table 1

Examples of Online Language Teaching PD Events

Level	Example of online language teaching PD
Micro	A half-day workshop for the Portuguese faculty titled "Effectively engage your online students using Flipgrid."
Meso	A faculty learning community on assessing proficiency using institutionally available web tools.
Macro	A series of webinars on principles of effective online language course development.

Determining at which level to focus PD efforts can be tricky. At the onset, LC staff should identify their stakeholders and their interventional capacity. Then, they should perform a needs assessment (Suvorov et al., 2018) to determine what kind of intervention will be most beneficial to their stakeholders. Along with performing a needs analysis and a thoughtful implementation plan, LCs should frequently evaluate the effectiveness of their efforts by soliciting stakeholder feedback and, when appropriate, measuring the effect of PD interventions. Furthermore, strategic coordination of PD interventions between LCs might be desirable to prevent overlap and make more efficient use of available resources (see Section 2.7). A LC wishing to coordinate PD with other LCs could start by reaching out to other LCs in the region, preferably at institutions with similar institutional contexts, and engaging in conversations to determine whether strategic coordination of PD resources and offerings would be mutually beneficial. Not every offering will be suitable for sharing with other institutions, depending on its goals and context, so careful planning is advised. We recommend focusing on one specific type of PD offerings at the beginning, for example, developing a shared series of one-hour workshops to be streamed live at regular intervals. Once a working relationship is established and language faculty have come to expect and appreciate these coordinated offerings, this collaboration can be expanded to include additional institutions and/or additional types of offerings.

2.5 Course Development Support

While microgrants (discussed in Section 2.2) are, by nature, relatively low on the scale of monetary investment, the possibilities for support expand with increased levels of funding. In this section, we focus specifically on the range of funding that can pay for the development of an individual course up to an entire online program. The strategy for both securing and allocating this kind of funding, however, will completely depend on the goals of the institution, the goals of the center, its staffing size, and its expertise (Facer & Stein, 2018). The few ideas we highlight here are by no means a comprehensive list but are intended as a start toward brainstorming possibilities that are in alignment with the individual LC goals.

There are two broad funding sources that many LCs use: institutional funding and "soft money" such as grants. Administrators may be willing to offer funding for a course release to be used to develop a new online course, especially if the product (online language instruction) is one that can possibly increase enrollment or visibility of the language programs. Keeping an open channel of communication with administrators and decision-makers about the opportunities and developments in online language instruction can put these ideas at the forefront of their minds as they consider budgetary requests. LCs with independent sources of revenue can also decide to devote a portion of that revenue toward these more strategic goals. In addition, LCs can devote some staff time to securing soft funding, such as grants, to launch initiatives and prove concepts before more stable and/or renewable funding can be secured.

Expectations for the materials developed within the course release time should be negotiated depending on the practices of the department or institution and the experience level of the instructor. For example, some institutions expect that for each course release given, at least one full course should be developed. Note that developing sound, engaging pedagogy for the online environment is a time-consuming process even when the developer possesses some technical expertise.

2.6 Instructional Design Support

When the LC is embedded in a language department with demonstrated and ongoing need for online learning support, the LC director, in consultation with other stakeholders as needed, should consider hiring a part-time or full-time instructional designer (ID). The job description of IDs varies by institution, but generally, they are academic staff skilled in supporting the design, development, teaching, and evaluation of curriculum. IDs possess a strong background in pedagogy and andragogy, have technical and design skills, can serve as both project managers and consultants, and often have teaching experience and/or content knowledge (Beirne & Romanoski, 2018; Berrett, 2016). The added benefit of hiring an ID within the LC is the ability to screen for professionals who may have a language teaching background and/or are familiar with second language acquisition principles and language learning practices.

According to Milosh (2019), "the easiest way of defining roles in the online course development process is to view the faculty member as a subject-matter expert and the instructional designer as a learning technology expert" (para. 6). The collaborative relationship between the faculty member and the ID is one in which the faculty member brings his or her expertise in teaching the course content, and the ID works to ensure that course design and technology are used in ways that promote the achievement of learning goals. IDs, therefore, play a large role in suggesting learning activities, ensuring students engage in an appropriate amount of interaction, and designing assessments. Based on the number of online courses in an ID's portfolio, he or she may participate in the actual course design or provide more of a consulting role, with the faculty member doing most of the design work (Reid, 2018).

In addition to course development and design, IDs can serve as project managers to coordinate the work of other specialists (educational technologists, videographers, accessibility experts, etc.) to ensure deadlines are met and production stays on track. By doing so, the ID acts as a liaison between language faculty and college-wide support centers and underscores the LC's position as a hub. Lastly, IDs are well positioned to manage course refresh and revision timetables as part of their portfolios.

Do IDs make a difference? Data from a recent survey suggest requiring faculty members to work with IDs can lead to the development of better learning materials (Legon, Fredericksen, & Garrett, 2019). When programs do not require any instructional design support for online courses, for the most part, students engage alone with learning materials. Programs that require instructional design input or rely on course design teams (Puzziferro & Shelton, 2008) see greater student engagement with faculty and other students.

Note that the terms "educational technologist" and "instructional designer" are not synonymous. While the former is focused on selecting and supporting educational technologies (e.g., learning management systems, classroom tools, educational software) to serve the various academic purposes of an institution, the latter is much more focused on pedagogy and the design of learning experiences, with a heavy emphasis on ensuring alignment of learning activities with assessments and learning objectives (Reid, 2018). The two roles will also vary widely in training and experience. While the two overlap, and both types of professionals can and should be on staff at an LC, the roles should not be conflated.

2.7 Strategic Coordination

Innovations implemented at an institutional level can certainly be effective for departments and individual instructors, but with the trend of declining F2F enrollment in language classes, it behooves language programs, individual instructors, and LCs to start thinking more broadly than their own institution, that is, developing strategic coordination. This can take many forms, from coordinating professional development to the highest level of coordinating curricula between institutions. As an example, at a recent conference, a group of LC directors formed the Language Center Alliance (LCA), which "provides a forum for leaders of North American centers/units at postsecondary institutions that are involved in teaching and learning, research, advocacy, and/or outreach in world languages to share ideas, practices and concerns, and to look for areas of collaboration" (Language Center Alliance, n.d., para. 1). The LCA differs from professional organizations such as CALICO and IALLT in that it focused on LC leadership, and it is limited to one LC leader per institution. The hope is that this agility will allow the LCA to make strategic initiatives happen more quickly. At their founding meeting, LC leaders discussed coordinating PD opportunities across campuses, including both in-person collaborative opportunities for those institutions geographically near each other and online opportunities for those distant from each other. Singular PD events are relatively low stakes to coordinate, despite their potential to have a great impact on the individual instructors.

Some of the other rungs of the "support ladder" (Figure 1) could also be considered, including financial and instructional support. As an example, in Section 3.2, we focus on the case of the strategic coordination efforts of the Less Commonly Taught and Indigenous Languages Partnership, which include several rungs of the support ladder and coordination of curricula.

3. Case Studies

In this section, we expand on several of the strategies above by illustrating two case studies implemented by the authors. What follows is a narrative of two projects currently taking place at CeLTA at MSU.

3.1 Fundamentals of Online Language Teaching (Professional Development)

The first case study illustrates in detail an example of macro-level online language teaching PD (Strategy 2.4). *Fundamentals of Online Language Teaching* (OLT) is a fully online course designed to empower experienced language instructors to transition to online teaching. This course was initiated and is currently led by CeLTA staff.

3.1.1 Course Overview

OLT is a six-week, fully online course taught by a team of CeLTA staff members and MSU language instructors with experience and expertise in online pedagogy.

The course is offered regularly to internal and external stakeholder groups (Table 2). The course has been offered for free to instructors of less commonly taught languages (LCTLs) within the Big Ten Academic Alliance (BTAA) during spring semesters. During the summer or the fall semester, any language instructor from any institution can enroll in a paid version of the course. Participation is capped at 12 instructors, and multiple sections of the course are offered each semester. Participants gain an understanding of conceptual frameworks used to describe online pedagogy and develop expertise in the areas of course/task quality and design, accessibility, and media. The course gives instructors an immersive online student experience. Far from being simply a set of materials or online videos, the course exposes participants to many affordances and constraints of online environments, including deadlines, grades, and a variety of collaborative and individual tasks.

At a time when a lot of free and paid resources (many of which are strong, rigorous, and effective) are available to help those who want to transition to an online environment, we believe that this course adds to the available resources and offers something unique for the following reasons:

- It has a specific focus on language teaching and learning.
- It has a small, seminar-style cohort-focused curriculum similar to that in a graduate course.
- It offers extensive and personalized instructor feedback and interaction.

Table 2

OLT Schedule and Stakeholders

Semester	Target audience	Details
Spring	BTAA LCTL instructors	Top applicants selected based on strength of application Free for accepted applicants
Summer and/ or Fall	Any language instructor	First-come, first-served Fee-based enrollment

3.1.2 Course History

The course content came out of a learning community led by the first author with faculty of MSU's English Language Center (ELC) in Fall 2016. The goal of the learning community was to form a core group of English as a Second Language instructors with online development and teaching expertise. As online offerings at the ELC grew, the need for trained instructors also grew. At the same time, CeLTA was looking for ways to train LCTL instructors in online course development and pedagogy as part of the Less Commonly Taught and Indigenous Languages Partnership initiative. The first author drew on expertise developed in that initial learning community to develop a first prototype of OLT, which at the time lasted eight weeks. The course was offered to internal stakeholders in that form for three semesters.

As we began discussing the course with colleagues at professional conferences, it became clear that other institutions were interested in participating in this project. We decided to give the course a major revision, expanding the scope of the content, integrating more hands-on tasks, and reducing the length to six weeks. The course was offered to all BTAA LCTL instructors for the first time in Spring 2019 and was opened to any college or university language instructor in Fall 2019.

3.1.3 Learning Objectives and Content

OLT is designed for experienced language instructors who want to make the transition to teaching languages online. As such, principles of second language acquisition are not discussed in the course, as familiarity with language pedagogy is presupposed. While each participant will bring his or her own pedagogical background, the course also assumes a task-based, proficiency-oriented view of language instruction. By the end of the course, participants are able to:

- Differentiate between F2F and online language instruction
- Identify and demonstrate key competencies of effective online language instructors
- Identify and describe strategies for effective communication and presence
- Identify strategies for ensuring courses meet an acceptable level of quality and accessibility
- Develop effective media based on established criteria
- Identify appropriate tools for online language learning tasks and assessments
- Develop online language activities using different communication modes
- Draft an online language course snapshot

Appendix A describes the course content and learning goals in more detail.

3.1.4 Course Dynamics, Tasks, and Tools

From the very beginning, we conceptualized this course as an important opportunity for participants not only to learn about principles of online pedagogy, but also to directly experience what online learning can and should look like. In line with common practices for fee-based adult professional development and certification practices, and to allow them to participate in an authentic online experience, participants in the course adhere to deadlines and receive grades for each of their assignments. These grades are not reported to anyone outside of the course, but participants only receive a certificate of completion if they achieve a final grade of 80% or more.

Tasks are designed to encourage participants to reflect on their own experiences, apply principles to their own context, and practice real-world skills such as course evaluation and task design. Several scaffolding tools are provided to help participants manage their investigations, engage in sense-making, and articulate their thinking (Hmelo-Silver, Duncan, & Chinn, 2007). For example, before developing their own interpersonal language tasks, participants are encouraged to take part in one example meant to illustrate the principles they encounter in their readings. Task development criteria and evaluation rubrics further scaffold the development process for them. Appendix B contains three example tasks (including the one just described), showcased here to further illustrate the task-based nature of the course.

Because one of our goals was to expose participants to a variety of modes and types of tasks that they could then replicate in their own teaching, the course uses several technology tools and task designs; it also relies heavily on participant interaction and task-based instruction to achieve its goals. What follows is an overview of the tools used in the course, all of which work seamlessly across different types of devices (computer, tablet, and mobile) and platforms (Windows, Android, Mac):

- Learning management system (LMS): The institutionally-supported LMS is used to deliver content such as readings and videos. Content and activities are organized chronologically and are released one week at a time to ensure that the cohort moves through the course at the same time. Text-based discussions are hosted using the LMS's forum tool. The LMS is also used for administrative functions such as announcements, grades and feedback, and the calendar.
- Padlet (https://padlet.com): This bulletin-board-like tool is free to use and easily embedded in LMS pages. It is used in this course for collaborative writing tasks.
- Flipgrid (https://flipgrid.com): This asynchronous video board is used for video discussions. Like Padlet, it is free to use and easily embedded in LMS pages.
- Zoom (https://zoom.us): This teleconferencing software is institutionally supported at MSU, but any teleconferencing software can be used. Participants other than the instructors do not need accounts and can join a live session simply by downloading and running the client on their devices. Zoom is used in this course for pair, group, and whole-class live meetings.
- Remind (https://www.remind.com): This text-messaging app is used to deliver reminders and announcements to course participants.

3.1.5 Participant Perceptions

At the end of the course, we collect participant feedback to measure their perceptions of the program and improve it where necessary. At the time of writing, we are able to report feedback from Spring 2019 (n = 10), Fall 2019 (n = 8), Spring 2020 (n = 20), Summer 2020 Session 1 (n = 17), and Summer 2020 Session 2 (n = 52) participants (total N = 107; note that these are the number of participants who completed the end-of-course survey, not the total number of course participants).

Overall, participants showed positive attitudes toward the course, with their responses largely indicating a strong agreement that the course was beneficial to them. For questions that asked participants to rate how much they had improved regarding particular aspects of online language teaching, their ratings largely indicated a "huge improvement."

As shown in Table 3, respondents agreed that the online course was easy to navigate and use, that there was ample opportunity to communicate with the instructor, and that they feel ready to develop and teach an online course. Overall, participants were glad that they had signed up for this course.

Table 3

Participants' Overall Evaluation of the OLT Course

Statement	Strongly disagree	Disagree	Agree	Strongly agree
1. The online course was easy to navigate and use.	0	0	32	75
2. There was ample opportunity to communicate with the instructor whenever I had a need.	0	0	1	106
3. Thanks to this course, I feel more ready to develop and teach an online course.	0	3	23	81
4. I am glad I signed up for this class.	0	1	8	98

Participants also rated how much their skills had improved in specific aspects of online language teaching. Their ratings generally indicated a "huge improvement" as a result of taking this course. The specific aspects of the course and the ratings are presented in Table 4. Often, participants indicated that their skills had improved to a great extent. For instance, many noted that they currently possessed skills related to online language teaching that they did not possess before this course, for example, their understanding of accessibility issues in online courses. Others indicated major improvement or changes in attitudes from negative to positive toward online teaching after taking the course. Also, the course led to improved confidence in online teaching.

Table 4

Participants' Perceived Improvement

Statement	No improvement	Slight improvement	Huge improvement
1. Proficiency with LMS and educational applications	7	62	38
2. Understanding of accessibility principles	3	23	81
3. Ability to communicate with others remotely	3	48	56
4. Understanding of presence strategies	2	16	89
5. Ability to design online language learning tasks	2	44	61

6.	Understanding of online instruction dynamics	2	23	82
7.	Ability to use course evaluation rubrics and frameworks	14	47	46
8.	Confidence using online learning technologies	5	46	56
9.	Confidence in online language teaching and learning	2	36	69

Qualitative feedback captured participant impressions at a more nuanced level. We report a few participant quotes here that capture the empowering nature of the course:

> This [course] was essential for me to learn pedagogical approaches to online teaching as well as being able to feel the impact of online learning as a student. I see many possibilities for teaching my future online courses now.

> This course was exactly what I hoped it would be: a comprehensive introduction to OLT. The fact that it was specifically for language instructors was helpful because we were on the same page about the needs we might have.

> I was very hesitant about teaching online because for me creating a sense of community is very important in a language class; however, after taking this course I have first hand experience that it is possible to do that. At the end of the course I felt I knew most of my classmates. I am now more confident that an online language class can work.

3.1.6 Outcomes and Future Initiatives

Before the Spring 2020 transition to remote teaching, the course had been offered both internally and within the BTAA to about 40 instructors and had already led to the proposal, development, and teaching of several new online courses:

- At MSU, OLT alumni developed four online language courses and an online TESOL Certificate.
- Within the BTAA, 15 new online courses were either in development or were being offered.

The transition to remote teaching caused by the COVID-19 pandemic has skyrocketed interest in the course, leading to the enrollment of 88 instructors from various US higher education institutions in Summer 2020 alone. We are currently working on plans to expand this initiative in various ways. Some of the ideas we are currently discussing are:

- Developing and offering a sequence of more advanced courses to follow OLT, which could eventually constitute a certificate. In Fall 2020, we launched two advanced courses (*Creating Engaging Materials* and *Oral Communicative Tasks*), and additional future topics could include teaching Languages for Specific Purposes online and managing online language programs. More up-to-date information can be found on the OLT website (https://olt.cal.msu.edu).

- Incorporating a version of the course within CeLTA's online Master of Arts in Foreign Language Teaching program (https://maflt.cal.msu.edu) as an elective course.
- Developing specific sections of the course for specific audiences, such as Indigenous language instructors (in development at the time of writing) or K–12 instructors.

3.2 Less Commonly Taught and Indigenous Languages Partnership (Strategic Coordination)

The highest rung on our ladder of strategies to support online language instruction is the most resource-intensive: strategic coordination (Strategy 2.7). Not only does it require significant time investment and partners with the spirit of collaboration and coordination, but in our experience, it also requires resources available to hold F2F meetings and experiment with some of the less resource-intensive strategies to prove concepts. As the second case study, we feature the Less Commonly Taught and Indigenous Languages Partnership, a project funded by the Andrew W. Mellon Foundation. The project involves institutions from across the BTAA and aims to create sustainable models for language instruction, emphasizing online collaboration and instruction. We first give some history of the activities of the Less commonly Taught and Indigenous Languages Partnership for contextualization, then explain how we have tested some new strategies within the CourseShare structure, and then discuss how strategic coordination efforts are present throughout the project.

3.2.1 History of the Less Commonly Taught and Indigenous Languages Partnership

The Less Commonly Taught and Indigenous Languages Partnership hopes to transform the way LCTLs have been traditionally taught by introducing proficiency-based teaching materials following a backward design and task-/project-based language teaching approach so that more students, across more institutions, achieve at least Intermediate High proficiency (on the ACTFL proficiency scale) in a greater number of LCTLs.

During the first cycle of the grant (2016–2019), three working groups in Swahili, Hindi, and Hebrew, with members from seven BTAA institutions, developed a range of open educational resources from flexible modules designed for instruction ranging from a few weeks to a complete online asynchronous course. Initially, the grant also focused on examining the interinstitutional collaboration via the language working groups. We were interested to see how we could promote collaboration across institutions with instructors who were often isolated as the only or one of very few instructors of their language. Through our experiences in working with the working groups and in conversations with our colleagues, we noted that the issues that many languages face (low enrollment, articulation issues) are amplified in LCTL programs.

Initiatives such as the established CourseShare structure within the BTAA address some of the articulation issues that LCTL students face. If a student cannot enroll in a particular language and/or language level at their home institution, they can work with their CourseShare coordinator to connect with another institution teaching the particular language course they need. Students will then use videoconferencing software to virtually attend that class, but they earn credits as if they were attending the class on their home campus. However, the CourseShare system is reactive by nature: a student requests a course, and then the CourseShare coordinator finds a partner institution that can offer this course to the student. One aim of the Less Commonly Taught and Indigenous Languages Partnership is to expand the scope and refine the focus of the CourseShare initiative within the BTAA. Our Hebrew working group's course, discussed in more detail in the following, was our first attempt to work outside the normal CourseShare pattern.

3.2.2 A Different Approach to CourseShare

In the traditional CourseShare approach, students must adhere to the sending institution's academic calendar and class timetable, which has created some issues, especially when start/end dates and break periods of the semester do not align, or if the time of the class period means a student cannot enroll in several course slots on their home campus due to the CourseShare course overlapping with them. Even though CourseShare continued to grow throughout the years, there were few ways to overcome some of these obstacles without moving instruction online and removing a set class meeting time. Therefore, the Hebrew working group developed an online, asynchronous course focused on Israeli innovation and entrepreneurship. The students interacted in the LMS and used tools such as Flipgrid to practice skills in modalities other than reading and writing. The asynchronous course format does not mean that there were no synchronous moments; students scheduled times to meet (often virtually) with each other and with the instructor for assessment, but students in different time zones and with otherwise demanding schedules could participate.

In addition, we proactively advertised the course across the BTAA to all Jewish Studies centers, Hebrew programs, and CourseShare coordinators instead of waiting for students to seek out upper-level Hebrew courses. This proactive promotion of courses is a reversal from the reactive model and has, so far, been successful in enrolling students from multiple campuses, which encourages us as we look forward to building upon this success.

3.2.3 Strategic Coordination Efforts and Goals: Looking Ahead

To build up to our conversations surrounding strategic coordination, our LC began co-coordinating the Shared LCTL Symposium (SLCTLS) with the University of Chicago in 2016. The annual symposium explores experiences and best practices in the sharing of LCTL instruction across institutions through established consortia and between individual institutions. By understanding what is currently being done at a variety of institutions, we can incorporate those examples into our models of best practices we share within the network. SLCTLS provides a unique environment where instructors of LCTLs and administrators can dialog about these issues. At this conference, the Language Center Alliance mentioned in Section 2.7 was formed. Based on the feedback from the first years of SLCTLS, we know that there is a need to bring together administrators from various levels to address the issues that may prevent coordination at a higher level in the individual institutions. In addition, someone needs to be the driving force gathering the stakeholders and moving the conversation forward. During the second cycle of the Less Commonly Taught and Indigenous Languages Partnership grant (2019–2023), our LC hopes to be that driving force by focusing conversations within and beyond the BTAA to explore options in strategically coordinating curricula.

SLCTLS has proven to be a good place to initiate conversations and discuss ideas that could help foster strategic coordination and create sustainable offerings of LCTLs. One idea is to create suites of online courses in a particular language to create a minor that can be shared between institutions that may otherwise not be able to support the necessary courses. This would require securing commitments from institutions to run the courses on a regular basis and promoting the opportunity to enroll in the courses.

Another idea is to guarantee the offerings of languages by having institutions commit to sharing particular languages and/or levels, even if enrollment might be low or non-existing at one institution one academic year. While the initial drive for this strategy is a part of the grant project, we must emphasize that this particular strategy would not be limited to LCs that can secure grant funding. Many approaches are possible for BTAA institutions. First, for example, the first two years of Vietnamese are currently offered by MSU online (synchronous course sessions) and are received by several institutions through CourseShare. There is stable demand for these courses and even interest in upper-level courses. If a different cost-sharing mechanism were put in place for these courses, for example, different institutions contributing to the salary of a Vietnamese instructor, MSU might be able to develop and offer higher levels of Vietnamese. Second, institutions could do direct exchanges. For example, MSU might wish to offer certain languages but cannot afford the personnel to do so. In this scenario, an agreement could be created in which MSU agrees to offer Vietnamese to another institution for a certain number of years in exchange for their desired language, which then would be guaranteed by the other institution. A third approach is to work between institutions to guarantee full articulation of a language curriculum. For example, institutions could work together to guarantee that a variety of levels of a language are consistently offered across institutions, which would mean coordinating which levels are taught by which institution. This would mean that a student in search of second-year courses of a language would always be able to access that level through CourseShare.

None of these approaches are easy or can be implemented by one institution alone. They require a strong level of strategic coordination and commitment in which institutions develop strong interdependent relationships and manage their LCTL offerings (and budgets) as if they were one big campus rather than separate institutions. Through strategic coordination, the aim would be to develop stable positions for LCTL instructors across institutions. We also hope that by incorporating the online offerings of shared curricula and stabilizing the course offerings in other LCTLs, we can attract and retain more students and help them achieve higher proficiency in those languages.

4. Conclusion

In this chapter, we argued that LCs are uniquely positioned to take on a range of responsibilities that are essential for the support and flourishing of online language programs. Given the skepticism still surrounding online language instruction, these efforts must be accompanied by pervasive advocacy efforts to educate skeptics, demonstrate the value and effectiveness of online education, and challenge outdated or uninformed beliefs that ultimately damage our students, who are the main beneficiaries of the increased access to language instruction offered by online education. While advocacy goes beyond the scope of this chapter, we underscore its importance and note that it is an integral component of each of the seven strategies outlined above.

To support and inform our advocacy efforts, we must ground all our support and advancement efforts in research. Data on the effectiveness of online practices on student retention and proficiency are the most effective form of advocacy, targeting skeptics and, most crucially, targeting the administrators we call upon to support our efforts financially and strategically. Research can also help LCs refine their support efforts and design the initiatives of the future. As McKenney and Reeves (2014) suggested, we should work to solve educational problems in our contexts but at the same time seek to "discover new knowledge that can inform the work of others facing similar problems" (p. 131).

Not all strategies will be applicable to all LCs depending on their size, resources, and center-specific goals. While the strategies described in this chapter are by no means exhaustive, we hope we have provided readers with a solid starting place for engaging with online education efforts in their context. Future research efforts will inform these strategies and refine the approaches that work best in serving our students and colleagues.

References

Adnan, M. (2017). Professional development in the transition to online teaching: The voice of entrant online instructors. *ReCALL, 30*(1), 1–24. https://doi.org/10.1017/S0958344017000106

Akyol, Z., & Garrison, D. R. (2008). The development of a community of inquiry over time in an online course: Understanding the progression and integration of social, cognitive and teaching presence. *Journal of Asynchronous Learning Network, 12*, (2–3), 3–22.

Association of Departments of Foreign Languages. (2014). *Suggested best practices and resources for the implementation of hybrid and online language courses.* https://www.adfl.mla.org/Resources/Policy-Statements/Suggested-Best-Practices-and-Resources-for-the-Implementation-of-Hybrid-and-Online-Language-Courses

Baralt, M., & Morcillo Gomez, J. (2017). Task-based language teaching online: A guide for teachers. *Language Learning & Technology, 21*(3), 28–43. http://llt.msu.edu/issues/october2017/baraltmorcillogomez.pdf

Beirne, E., & Romanoski, M. P. (2018). *Instructional design in higher education: Defining an evolving field.* https://intentionalfutures.com/instructional_design/%0Ahttp://files/9/instructional_design.html

Berrett, D. (2016, February 29). Instructional design: Demand grows for a new breed of academic. *The Chronicle of Higher Education.* https://www.chronicle.com/article/Instructional-Design/235425

Blake, R. J. (2011). Current trends in online language learning. *Annual Review of Applied Linguistics, 31*, 19–35. https://doi.org/10.1017/S026719051100002X

Blake, R. J. (2015). The messy task of evaluating proficiency in online language courses. *The Modern Language Journal, 99*(2), 408–412. https://doi.org/10.1111/modl.12234_5

Blake, R. J., & Guillén, G. A. (2014). Best practices for an online Spanish course. *FLTMAG.* https://fltmag.com/best-practices-for-an-online-spanish-course-2/

Blake, R. J., Wilson, N. L., Cetto, M., & Pardo-Ballester, C. (2008). Measuring oral proficiency in distance, face-to-face, and blended classrooms. *Language Learning and Technology, 12*(3), 114–127.

Burgstahler, S. (2017). ADA compliance for online course design. *Educause.* https://er.educause.edu/articles/2017/1/ada-compliance-for-online-course-design

Compton, L. K. L. (2009). Preparing language teachers to teach language online: A look at skills, roles, and responsibilities. *Computer Assisted Language Learning, 22*(1), 73–99. https://doi.org/10.1080/09588220802613831

Dixson, M., Kuhlhorst, M., & Reiff, A. (2019). Creating effective online discussions: Optimal instructor and student roles. *Online Learning, 10*(4), 15–28. https://doi.org/10.24059/olj.v10i4.1743

Enkin, E., & Mejías-Bikandi, E. (2017). The effectiveness of online teaching in an advanced Spanish language course. *International Journal of Applied Linguistics, 27*(1), 176–197. https://doi.org/10.1111/ijal.12112

Facer, B. R., & Stein, J. (2018). The fundamentals of grants for world language education. In E. Lavolette & E. F. Simon (Eds.), *Language center handbook* (pp. 129–152). Auburn, AL: International Association for Language Learning Technology.

Gacs, A., Goertler, S., & Spasova, S. (2020). Planned online language education versus crisis-prompted online language teaching: Lessons for the future. *Foreign Language Annals, 53*(2), 380–392. https://doi.org/10.1111/flan.12460

Goertler, S. (2019). Normalizing online learning: Adapting to a changing world of language teaching. In N. Arnold & L. Ducate (Eds.), *Engaging language learners through CALL* (pp. 51–92). Sheffield, UK: Equinox.

Goertler, S., & Gacs, A. (2018). Assessment in online German: Assessment methods and results. *Die Unterrichtspraxis/Teaching German, 51*(2), 156–174. https://doi.org/10.1111/tger.12071

Grgurović, M., Chapelle, C. A., & Shelley, M. C. (2013). A meta-analysis of effectiveness studies on computer technology-supported language learning. *ReCALL, 25*(2), 165–198. https://doi.org/10.1017/S0958344013000013

Guo, P. J., Kim, J., & Rubin, R. (2014). How video production affects student engagement: An empirical study of MOOC videos. *Proceedings of the First ACM Conference on Learning @ Scale Conference, 1*(1), 41–50. https://doi.org/10.1145/2556325.2566239

Hmelo-Silver, C. E., Duncan, R. G., & Chinn, C. A. (2007). Scaffolding and achievement in problem-based and inquiry learning. *Educational Psychologist, 42*(2), 99–107. https://doi.org/10.1080/01421599979743

Isenberg, N. A. (2010). *A comparative study of developmental outcomes in Web-based and classroom-based German language education at the post-secondary level: Vocabulary, grammar, language processing, and oral proficiency development* [Doctoral Dissertation, The Pennsylvania State University]. PSU Electronic Theses and Dissertations. https://etda.libraries.psu.edu/catalog/10339

Kronenberg, F. A. (Ed.). (2017). *From language lab to language center and beyond: The past, present, and future of language center design.* Auburn, AL: International Association for Language Learning Technology.

Language Center Alliance. (n.d.). *Language Center Alliance.* http://www.languagecenteralliance.org/

Lavolette, E., & Simon, E. F. (Eds.). (2018). *Language center handbook.* Auburn, AL: International Association for Language Learning Technology.

Lederman, D. (2019, February 13). Too little help for professors teaching online. *Inside Higher Ed.* https://www.insidehighered.com/digital-learning/article/2019/02/13/assessing-faculty-role-online-learning-public-comprehensive

Legon, R., Fredericksen, E. E., & Garrett, R. (2019). *CHLOE 3 behind the numbers: The changing landscape of online education 2019.* http://qualitymatters.org/qa-resources/resource-center/articles-resources/CHLOE-3-report-2019

Li, C.-S., & Irby, B. (2008). An overview of online education: Attractiveness, benefits, challenges, concerns and recommendations. *College Student Journal, 42*(2), 449–459. https://link.galegroup.com/apps/doc/A179348426/AONE

Lieberman, M. (2018, February 28). Centers of the pedagogical universe. *Inside Higher Ed.* https://www.insidehighered.com/digital-learning/article/2018/02/28/centers-teaching-and-learning-serve-hub-improving-teaching

Lin, C.-H., & Warschauer, M. (2015). Online foreign language education: What are the proficiency outcomes? *The Modern Language Journal, 99*(2), 394–397. https://doi.org/10.1111/modl.12234_1

McAlvage, K., & Rice, M. (2018). *Access and accessibility in online learning: Issues in higher education and K–12 contexts.* https://files.eric.ed.gov/fulltext/ED593920.pdf

McKenney, S., & Reeves, T. C. (2014). Educational design research. In J. M. Spector, M. D. Merrill, J. Elen, & M. J. Bishop (Eds.), *Handbook of research on educational communications and technology* (4th ed., pp. 131–140). New York, NY: Springer. https://doi.org/10.1007/978-1-4614-3185-5

Meyer, K. A. (2014). An analysis of the research on faculty development for online teaching and identification of new directions. *Journal of Asynchronous Learning Networks, 17*(4), 1–20.

Milosh, T. (2019, January 17). Building a collaborative instructor-instructional designer relationship. *Insider Higher Ed.* https://www.insidehighered.com/digital-learning/views/2018/01/17/building-collaborative-instructor-instructional-designer

Modern Language Association. (2019). *Language enrollment database, 1958–2016.* https://apps.mla.org/flsurvey_search

Murphy-Judy, K., & Johnshoy, M. (2017). Who's teaching which languages online? A report based on national surveys. *IALLT Journal, 47*(1), 137–167.

Puzziferro, M., & Shelton, K. (2008). A model for developing high-quality online courses: Integrating a systems approach with learning theory. *Online Learning, 12*(3), 119–136. https://doi.org/10.24059/olj.v12i3.58

Puzziferro, M., & Shelton, K. (2009). Supporting online faculty: Revisiting the seven principles (a few years later). *Online Journal of Distance Learning Administration, XII*(III), 1–11.

Reid, P. (2018). EdTechs and instructional designers—What's the difference? *Educause.* https://er.educause.edu/articles/2018/12/edtechs-and-instructional-designers-whats-the-difference

Roby, W. B. (2004). Technology in the service of foreign language learning: The case of the language laboratory. In D. H. Jonassen (Ed.), *Handbook of research on educational communications and technology* (pp. 523–541). Mahwah, NJ: Lawrence Erlbaum.

Rovai, A. P. (2007). Facilitating online discussions effectively. *Internet and Higher Education, 10*(1), 77–88. https://doi.org/10.1016/j.iheduc.2006.10.001

Savery, J. R. (2010). BE VOCAL: Characteristics of successful online instructors. *Journal of Interactive Online Learning, 9*(2), 141–152. http://www.ncolr.org/jiol/issues/pdf/4.2.6.pdf

Seaman, J. E., Allen, I. E., & Seaman, J. (2018). *Grade increase: Tracking distance education in the United States.* https://onlinelearningsurvey.com/reports/gradeincrease.pdf

Steadman, A., & Kraut, R. (2018). Preparing the online language program administrator: A needs analysis of intensive English programs in the United States. *CALICO Journal, 35*(3), 274–293. https://doi.org/10.1558/cj.34636

Sun, S. Y. H. (2011). Online language teaching: The pedagogical challenge. *Knowledge Management & E-Learning, 3*(3), 428–447.

Sun, S. Y. H. (2014). Learner perspectives on fully online language learning. *Distance Education, 35*(1), 18–42. https://doi.org/10.1080/01587919.2014.891428

Suvorov, R., Carrillo Cabello, A., & Janssen Sanchez, B. (2018). Professional development in language learning centers: Approaches and guidelines for design and implementation. In E. Lavolette & E. F. Simon (Eds.), *Language center handbook* (pp. 193–216). Auburn, AL: International Association for Language Learning Technology.

Van Gorp. K., Giupponi, L., Heidrich Uebel, E., Dursun, A., & Swinehart, N. (2019). Defining teachers' readiness for online language teaching: Toward a unified framework. In F. Meunier, J. Van de Vyver, L. Bradley, & S. Thouësny (Eds), *CALL and complexity – short papers from EUROCALL 2019* (pp. 373–378). Research-publishing.net. https://doi.org/10.14705/rpnet.2019.38.9782490057542

Warren, S. J., & Robinson, H. A. (2018). The product life-cycle of online courses and student engagement. *American Journal of Distance Education, 32*(3), 161–176. https://doi.org/10.1080/08923647.2018.1475937

Xu, D., & Xu, Y. (2019). *The promises and limits of online higher education: Understanding how distance education affects access, cost, and quality.* American Enterprise Institute. https://www.aei.org/research-products/report/the-promises-and-limits-of-online-higher-education/

Yaden, B. E. (2018). Supporting the LRC mission through collaborative partnerships across campus and beyond. In E. Lavolette & E. F. Simon (Eds.), *Language center handbook* (pp. 91–103). Auburn, AL: International Association for Language Learning Technology.

Yaden, B. E., & Evans, C. (2017). Envisioning new spaces. The human element. In F. A. Kronenberg (Ed.), *From language lab to language center and beyond: The past, present, and future of the language center* (pp. 83–98). Auburn, AL: International Association for Language Learning Technology.

Appendix A

Fundamentals of Online Language Teaching Course Content and Goals

Unit	Topic	Goals
Unit 1	Introduction: So, you want to start teaching online?	· Introduce yourself to the rest of the class · Self-evaluate your Online Language Teaching readiness
Unit 2	Basics of course design; Presence and Communication	· Identify course objectives and structure · Identify, differentiate, and apply social, cognitive, and teaching presence strategies · Identify, differentiate, and apply communication strategies
Unit 3	Quality and Accessibility	· Describe the concept of course quality and explain its importance · Identify and differentiate different course quality rubrics · Describe the concept of accessibility and explain its importance · Identify accessibility strategies to meet minimum institutional requirements
Unit 4	Media and Language Learning Tasks	· Identify and apply effective media production principles and strategies · Investigate and evaluate existing online interpretive, presentational, and interpersonal tasks · Design and produce an online task
Unit 5	Learning Environment Design and Workload Management	· Identify and differentiate usability, visual design, and findability principles and strategies in an OLT context · Evaluate course homepages and design your own course homepage · Identify, categorize, and apply online workload management principles and strategies
Unit 6	Your Course Snapshot	· Synthesize acquired knowledge by developing a detailed course development proposal

Appendix B

Fundamentals of Online Language Teaching Sample Tasks

Sample Task 1: Introductions and Beliefs about OLT (Week 1)

Welcome to your first learning activity! The goals of this video discussion are twofold:

1. Introduce yourself to the rest of the class, and
2. Share previous experiences as well as your motivation for joining this course.

Part 1: Your initial post (due Tuesday at 1pm)

For this task, we will use Flipgrid. Please post a video answering the following questions:

- Tell us a little bit about you, including one fun fact.
- Do you have any experience teaching or learning in an online format?
- Have you had a positive experience with remote teaching so far during the COVID-19 pandemic? (if applicable)
- What are your goals for this course?

If you would like to use your smartphone to record your contribution (recommended), the grid code for this assignment is (code). You can download the Flipgrid student app here (link).

Your message should be somewhat prepared, but not scripted. Aim for your video to have a conversational, friendly "feel" and please limit your response to 1–2 minutes (the program will cut you off after two minutes). Consider how variables like lighting, location, pacing, and tone of voice affect your video.

Part 2: Respond to your colleagues (due Tuesday at 5pm)

After watching your colleagues' videos, please respond to 1–2 posts in a constructive way. Aim to move the conversation forward!

Sample Task 2: Learning Environment Design (Week 5)

For this assignment, you will design a **Homepage** for an online course you would like to teach and showcase it to the rest of the class via a walkthrough video.

STEP 1: Design your course Homepage. You can choose one of the following options:

- Use the actual course shell for the course you are teaching
- Use a "sandbox" or development course within your institution's LMS
- Get a free Canvas teacher account (link with instructions and guidance)
- Create a Google Sites website (only recommended if you do not have access to an LMS)

At a minimum, we would like you to create a Homepage, but it will be beneficial for you to try creating a basic course structure with modules and pages as well, if you're up to it. Refer to the principles you learned in this module for guidance. Here is one example from a student in a previous section of this course: (link)

STEP 2: Record a video of your Homepage. This can be a walkthrough video (with your OLT instructor and classmates as the audience) or a navigation video (with your future students as the audience). You can use a variety of tools for this step, but we encourage you to choose whatever your institutional tool of choice is (for MSU, it would be Zoom or Kaltura Capture). Here is a list of tools that can be used for screen recording:

- Loom
- Zoom
- Kaltura Capture
- Panopto
- Camtasia
- Screencast-o-matic

As you record this video, remember you are now an expert in media production principles! This will be a great opportunity for you to reinforce what you learned in Week 4. Here is an example video from a student in a previous section of this course: (link)

STEP 3: In the forum below, start a new thread, post a link to your video, and reflect on the following questions:

1. Do you find the usability, findability, and design guidelines restricting, daunting, freeing, helpful, something else? Why?
2. Comment on your homepage and course outline. Why did you make the decisions you made? What principles did you try to implement? How easy or intuitive was to follow these principles?

Sample Task 3: Interpersonal Tasks (Week 7)

Step 1: Complete this interpersonal task

Task Overview

Can-Do Statement / Learning Objective: I can describe preference and make plans about everyday activities.

Communicative Mode: Interpretive/presentational, reading/writing (individual); Interpersonal, Speaking

Delivery Mode: Asynchronous (no synchronous component for the instructor)

Estimated Time: 60 minutes

Assessment: Delayed formative feedback

Technology Used: LMS; Video-conferencing tool; Computer and/or smartphone; Web browser

Directions

You are going to New York City! Your proposal was accepted at a big-time conference taking place in Chelsea, and your budget is plush. You discover that one of your former colleagues is going to the conference, too, and so you call them to make plans to get dinner together. Before the call, you do some research.

Step 1 (individual): Do some background research to determine where you want to go eat. You can use Google Maps, Zagat, Eater, Yelp, or whatever your go-to resource is! You should identify at least 3–4 restaurants. If happy hour is your thing, do some research for that, too.

Step 2 (together): Call your colleague and make plans. Share the restaurants you found and make your case. Listen to your colleague as they make their case, too. If you can't settle on a restaurant, do some more searching together. **Make sure to record the call** if the tool you are using allows you to do so.

Step 3 (individual): Write a short paragraph to your instructor and answer the following questions:

· Who was your partner? What tool did you use?
· Where did you decide to go? Why?
· What did you learn about your partner?
· Comment on the logistics of the task. Was it easy to schedule a time to talk? Did the technology pose a challenge to you?

Submit your paragraph along with a link to the recording (if you have it) to your instructor using the link below.

Step 2: Design original interpersonal task

After exploring the tasks and resources above, you will create your own interpersonal task! Feel free to adapt a task you already use with your students, or go ahead and create a completely new one. Your task will have three components, following models you have seen in this course:

1. A Task Overview like the one below
2. A detailed set of instructions
3. The actual task, developed using any of the tools listed in the Favorite Tools page or a different one of your choice

Task Overview

· Can-Do Statement / Learning Objective:
· Communicative Mode:
· Delivery Mode:
· Estimated Time:
· Assessment:
· Technology Used:

Author Notes

Luca Giupponi (MA, Iowa State University) is an Academic Specialist in the Center for Language Teaching Advancement (CeLTA) at Michigan State University, where he supports the design and development of online language courses and programs. He is a doctoral student in the Instructional Systems Technology program at Indiana University, and he is interested in investigating issues of online faculty development and quality in online instruction.

Emily Heidrich Uebel (PhD, University of Wisconsin-Madison) is an Academic Specialist in the Center for Language Teaching Advancement at Michigan State University. She serves as the Project Manager for the Less Commonly Taught and Indigenous Languages Partnership, an Andrew W. Mellon Foundation grant project focused on enhancing instruction in less commonly taught and Indigenous languages. Her work on topics including language proficiency and technology has been published in several journals and edited volumes. Her research interests include language proficiency, educational technology and online instruction, curriculum design, and education abroad topics.

Koen Van Gorp (PhD, KU Leuven) is Head of Foreign Language Assessment in the Center for Language Teaching Advancement, core faculty in the Second Language Studies PhD Program, and affiliated faculty in the MA TESOL Program at Michigan State University. He also serves as a Research Fellow at the Centre for Language and Education (KU Leuven). His research interests are task-based language teaching and assessment, language-in-education policy, critical multilingual awareness, and multilingualism. On those topics, he has published various book chapters and articles in international journals. In addition, he co-edited volumes for De Gruyter Mouton (2018, *Language Awareness in Multilingual Classrooms in Europe: From Theory to Practice*) and Palgrave (2018, *The Multilingual Edge of Education*). He is founding Co-Editor (together with Kris Van den Branden) of *TASK. Journal on Task-Based Language Teaching and Learning* and Treasurer of the International Association for Task-Based Language Teaching and learning (IATBLT).

Correspondence concerning this chapter should be addressed to Luca Giupponi (giupponi@msu.edu).

Chapter 4

Within and Across Languages: Language Center Community, Expertise, and Visibility

Catherine C. Baumann, University of Chicago, USA

Abstract

In 2005, a committee was charged to reexamine the facilities of the University of Chicago's Language Faculty Resource Center and Language Labs and Archives and make recommendations for their further use. In the ensuing years and up until the present day, the renamed University of Chicago Language Center has undergone changes in its physical facility, its leadership, and the roles it plays in the institution and the language-teaching community. This chapter describes four trajectories of change, exploring how different language centers can function in different institutional ecosystems, and providing multiple ideas for initiatives and programs that are possible on a variety of campuses.

Language centers (LCs) often serve the needs of diverse groups of instructors strewn across different departments, programs, and divisions, as well as equally complex populations of learners. Not only does establishing community, developing expertise, and creating programming meet the needs of these instructors and learners, but when done strategically, seemingly disparate initiatives can also raise the visibility of the LC institutionally, including its work and its mission, and further center the role of language learning in 21st-century higher education.

This chapter describes the evolution of the University of Chicago Language Center (CLC) from its origins as an equipment resource center and language lab to a vital hub for professional development, supporting everyone teaching language, and thereby meaningfully impacting all language learners. Four key trajectories illustrate opportunities that LCs can adapt and expand. Some involve larger funding initiatives, both internal and external, and some involve no funding at all. It is possible that, in reading this chapter, one might note initiatives that could be undertaken on one's own campus, or conversely, initiatives beyond reach because of institutional aspects of structure or governance or limitations in funding or political will. One might also see a way forward by altering or shifting an initiative. All of these considerations reflect the particular ecosystem in which every LC finds itself. A parallel goal of this chapter is to invite reflection about the ecosystem, that is, the particular academic setting within which a LC has evolved. Whether you are establishing a new LC, reimagining an existing language lab or resource center, or looking for new ways to serve the needs of your users, this chapter will provide you with ideas for concrete initiatives and longer-term strategies.

1. Language Centers, Then and Now

After the Russians put Sputnik, the first man-made satellite, into orbit in 1957, the ensuing educational crisis revealed language education as one area where the United States lagged behind the Soviet Union. Money poured into both higher education and public-school systems to support the teaching of languages (see Sebastian et al., this volume). This event coincided with Skinnerian behaviorism, Chomskyan linguistics, and linguistically derived and driven language learning approaches such as audiolingualism (Richards & Rogers, 1986). Furthermore, linguistics as a field, wishing to gain credibility as a *science*, found a resonating home in the language lab, where equipment, carrels, and step-by-step instructions felt and looked very scientific.

The floor plan of the CLC, debuted in its 2007 renovation, depicts the changing roles of LCs as well as the changing outcomes of language study.

All of the space to the right of the stairwell belongs to the CLC, as well as the multiuse space in rooms 201A-B-C. The central design motif is the circle, representing the primacy of communication and collaborative learning and the role of community. Multiple small "pods" meet the needs of our many less commonly taught languages (LCTLs) (rooms 206, 207, 215, 216), whose classes may number fewer than six students. Other rooms are equipped to accommodate remote students joining synchronously through video conference (208, 210). The CLC's central work area (adjacent to offices G, H, I) provides a large space for its many constituents, over 100 instructional professionals and graduate students teaching languages, many of whom do not have an individual office or access to other workspaces. On the far end of the hall, a large classroom space (201A-B-C) can be configured as three small classrooms holding 8–12 people, or two classrooms of different sizes, or one large theatre-style room that can accommodate up to 75 individuals. Flexibility is key in meeting the needs of the large and varied offerings of the CLC, just as flexibility in instruction is now needed for our multiple audiences learning languages: undergraduates, graduate students, heritage learners, those headed toward the major study of texts, those interested in reading or translating, and those studying languages for specific purposes.

Figure 1
University of Chicago Language Center Floorplan Upon its Reopening in January 2007

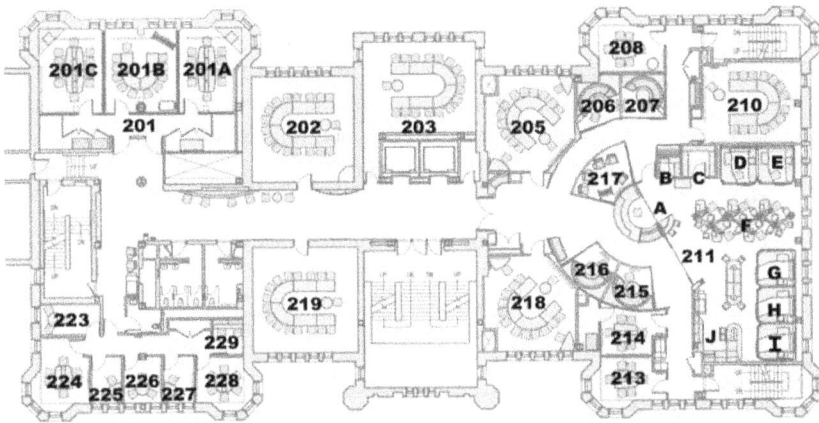

The CLC is not unique in the physical and other changes it has undergone to meet the changing needs of its users. Its history, both in terms of the changes to the physical facility and the mission of the center, echoes the transitions described in Askildson (2011) and further explored by Kronenberg (2017). In his list of questions to consider as part of a needs assessment, Kronenberg (2013) highlighted the identification of a LC's mission as an essential—and often overlooked—step when establishing a new LC or shifting the role or purpose of an existing center. That task was partially accomplished for the CLC when the dean of the Humanities Division assessed all of the "centers" under her purview (including Title VI, arts, and research centers, among others) and made the decision to hire a full-time director for the CLC. Until that point, it had been directed by an instructional professor with a course release. Since 2006, an instructional professor with expertise in testing (as an American Council on the Teaching of Foreign Languages (ACTFL)-certified Oral Proficiency Interview tester and trainer) had, under the aegis of the CLC, overseen and centralized many of the testing procedures across campus (e.g., placement testing, language competency testing related to a new language requirement). This individual became the CLC's new director, and, in a fashion similar to that described by Gopalakrishnan, Yaden, and Franz (2013), seized the opportunity to focus on leadership along with management. Because of her background in testing, a driving organizational principle emerged: assessment-driven reverse design. (Also known as "backward design," I prefer the term "reverse," especially in the sense of "reverse engineering.")

The mission of the CLC is described on its website:

> The University of Chicago Language Center is a hub of professional development and services for the hundreds of instructors and graduate students that teach the 60+ languages spread across various departments within the university. We also promote language study and increase the visibility of our language offerings, helping students navigate and go beyond the university's language requirements. (languages.uchicago.edu)

The next four sections will illustrate how the CLC realizes its mission by describing four trajectories that detail evolutions in programming, practices, and strategies. These are meant to serve as points of departure in considering one's own LC, whether one is designing, rethinking, expanding, or reviewing what is in place. Although we have been fortunate to have adequate funding (and have successfully won internal and external grant funds), suggestions will be made for each trajectory for similar efforts with limited (or no) funding or minimal personnel.

2. From Lender of Equipment to Technology-Enhanced Language Instruction

From its founding in 1985 until its reopening in 2007, the CLC was called the "Language Faculty Resource Center" (LFRC), and its chief roles were to lend equipment to instructors and provide space and equipment for individuals working on locally funded pedagogical projects. Lent equipment ranged from tape and video players to monitors and the tapes and videos themselves. In 2005, just as a committee was appointed to reexamine the LFRC's facilities and roles, many classrooms on the University of Chicago's campus were being updated as "smart classrooms," with built-in units comprising all of the hardware one needed to teach at that time. This eliminated the need to store and lend equipment, but not the need to teach users how to use it effectively. Around the same time, publishers and other providers were moving or creating materials online, and video and audio texts could be designed and/ or edited on one's desktop or laptop. The need to provide project-development space diminished. However, in the ensuing years through the present moment, the enormous proliferation of platforms, apps, online resources, and materials has created an almost too varied array of technological possibilities for teaching and learning language. Now the role of the CLC vis-à-vis technology is best described as a resource and support center. Lage-Otero (2013) argued that the support, and ultimately, professional development provided by experts in LCs is "more important than ever" (p. 133) as instructors are confronted with ever more possibilities for using technology when they deliver instruction. The impact of the COVID-19 pandemic and swift movement of instruction online have further heightened the needs of instructors in this realm.

Across the wide array of languages taught at the University of Chicago is an equally diverse population of instructors, all of whom possess greatly varying expertise and experience in integrating technology into their teaching. Except for the fairly generalized use of Canvas as a learning management system (LMS), no use of technology has been mandated until very recently. Additionally, a more rigorous process for the evaluation of instructors was put in place as a result of the implementation of a union contract finalized in March of 2018. "Effective use of technology" is listed among the criteria on a generalized form used for in-class observations of language instructors (although that criterion is interpreted broadly). Nevertheless, many instructors want and need help understanding and implementing technology. Back in its days as the LRFC, the center offered very occasional workshops for using technology. When its current director was appointed in 2013, she was able to leverage the appointment of a full-time multimedia pedagogy specialist (MMPS) because she did not have a knowledge base in instructional technology and wanted to focus on strategic planning and design of new programs. The role of the MMPS is to "provide innovative direction for the integration of multimedia and language instruction" (from the position description posted in the autumn of 2014).

The choice of the MMPS was informed by an approach to technology use where it *serves* language instruction, instead of *driving* it, which is also compatible with reverse design practices. (Reverse design is discussed in detail in Section 4, as it plays a key role in our Language Pedagogy Innovation Initiative.) For the purposes of thinking about making choices around technology use, suffice it to say that in reverse design, we start by identifying proficiency outcomes at the end of longer instructional sequences (usually one or two years), then design valid assessments to measure student achievement of the outcomes. Decisions about curriculum come only after we have decided what our learners will know and be able to do and how we will assess them. Technology is just one aspect of curriculum, and decisions about using it can be made most effectively when one has the outcomes and assessments in place, just like the decisions we make about textbooks and other materials, work done in and outside of classroom face-to-face time, and balancing the four skills, along with grammar and vocabulary.

In the CLC and in terms of pedagogical support, the MMPS provides direction for the integration of multimedia in language instruction, including coordination of workshops, one-on-one assistance, decision-making about purchasing multimedia (in all of its forms), and supporting course-sharing (i.e., remote students joining face-to-face instruction). When the MMPS first arrived, he did a lot of outreach, meeting with individuals or programs to talk about current technology use, needs, and aspirations. Those conversations gave him a sense of how much and what types of technology were being used and a starting point to choose topics for workshops or other events. As mentioned above, now that instructional professors must demonstrate effective use of technology in their evaluations, they are more likely to seek out help to integrate it. When they have had successes, they also give their own workshops, sharing what works (and does not).

In many LCs, it is not possible to hire both a center director and an individual responsible for technology and pedagogy. Thus, the director might very well be the only source of expertise for implementing technology effectively, and if that is the case, knowledge and experience in instructional technology should be foregrounded in the description of the director's position. Another option is to call upon the expertise of and collaborate with specialists available in campus centers for teaching or IT departments to enhance offerings (Lage-Otero, 2013). Furthermore, just as the identification of language learning outcomes helps us make choices about curriculum, so does having an identified mission or purpose help us to focus on what tasks or priorities a LC might tackle. If you are an under- or minimally funded one-person-show, you could identify one purpose in a given year or semester and build your programming around it. For example, "This year/semester we will focus on supporting and innovating in the area of listening comprehension." Having a focus will not only make it possible to make necessary choices in using resources, it will also give your constituents a way to concentrate on a manageable chunk of their curricula. You cannot do everything at once, but even within limited offerings, having a focus will deepen the impact of your offerings.

3. From Advising Resource to Assessment Center

By 2011, the duties of the erstwhile language assessment coordinator (who would become the LC director and who is the author of this chapter) had expanded to comprise language placement testing (including the establishment of online testing), competency testing (related to the undergraduate College's language requirement), advanced proficiency testing, graduate reading exams (including test administration and development of tests in new languages), and overseeing the processing and approval of language petitions (used to satisfy the language requirement or to gain additional language course credits). She was serving as a point of contact in all matters related to language testing for advisers, instructional professors, graduate student instructors, students, faculty, chairs, deans, and pertinent administrative offices.

This language assessment coordinator realized that in taking on the additional duties described above, she had earned the role of an "expert" and could now coordinate issues related to language assessment *and communicate them to others*. To say that she played to her strengths would be an over-simplification, but that is, in effect, what happened. In much the same way that Gopalakrishnan (2013) described her own undeliberate pathway to becoming a LC director, the director of the CLC took the "road less travelled" and "learned on the job" (p. 3). When she was appointed as director in 2013, the CLC became a highly visible site for all issues related to language assessment. College advisers had someone to turn to with questions about students; these individual cases often raised policy issues that could be addressed, resulting in clarity across languages. Instructors sometimes brought up issues they encountered, or supplied data to help establish policy, or drove new programming that would benefit their programs. For example, incoming first-year students used to take language placement exams during a week-long orientation on campus and received automatic credit when they placed beyond the first quarter of instruction. The director of the CLC played a key role, along with the College dean's office, College Programming (responsible for the orientation week), the Curriculum Committee, registrar's office, and College advisers to move the language placement tests online, eliminate the automatic credit policy, revise the language requirement process, and create a petition process to meet the needs of some entering students. In time, ladder-faculty and chairs sought clarification of policies or raised new questions. The director became both an ally and source of primary data and documentation for the registrar's office.

A few years later, with language testing expanding and on the eve of the application for two grants designed around assessment-driven reverse design, a case was made to hire a full-time assessment specialist in the CLC. The position was to be partially funded by the grants; the remainder was to be funded by testing revenue, primarily from graduate reading exams. Many language programs do such testing pro bono, or as part of their duties, or as a professional courtesy. In our case, students were paying the registrar to take the exams. Because we assumed the design and administration of the tests, it made sense for that revenue to flow into the CLC account. Ultimately, this focus on assessment evolved into the CLC's Office for Language Assessment (OLA, https://languageassessment.uchicago.edu) and the centralization of all language testing on campus (including English language testing, another revenue source) into one office. The OLA can be seen as the continuing evolution of assessment as a key focus in the CLC as well as the initiative and tremendous work of the newly appointed director of language assessment, but the institutional ecosystem within which the OLA grew also played a key role. Internally, the University of Chicago has no college or division of education, and its Linguistics Department's focus is largely historical. Thus, no other program or division is "doing" language pedagogy or possesses pedagogical expertise related to language learning. Until 2015, there was no campus-wide English as a second language program. The English Language Institute (ELI) was the result of multiple conversations by the director of the CLC with the provost's office about other issues related to language learning and testing. It was decided to locate the ELI in the CLC because that is where language pedagogy was "living," and cross-pollination of expertise seemed likely and desirable. The testing of nonnative speakers of English subsequently fell to the OLA. The assessment specialist and his OLA would ultimately play a key role in the two professional development grant initiatives, which are driven by assessment and reverse design (see Section 4).

New assessments developed under the two grants are now part of a Language Proficiency Certification Program. By identifying ACTFL levels as end-of-sequence outcomes and designing four-skills tests to measure student progress, the OLA offers students the possibility to "show the world what they can do with language," as OLA advertisements state. Students receive certifications that document their proficiency and describe their abilities in speaking, writing, reading, and listening. (While we use ACTFL levels in reverse design as valid descriptions of outcomes, the OLA does not use ACTFL levels or ACTFL Guidelines descriptions in its certifications because it does not administer official ACTFL tests.) Tests given to

College undergraduates and graduate students in the Humanities Division are free, and the OLA and CLC are now in the process of marketing these assessments across the entire university, including to groups that would pay for their proficiency tests: business students, computer science students, and medical students. Because our testing is moving into areas in the social sciences and professional units such as medicine and law, designing language for specific purposes (LSP) proficiency assessments is also underway in the OLA. LSP courses will be developed through reverse design. All of this programming is designed to raise the visibility of the value of language proficiency within *and* beyond the Humanities Division and the undergraduate College.

Discovering the best way to establish or expand a LC within an ecosystem sometimes happens capriciously, but ideally, it should be deliberate. The direction taken by the CLC is firmly rooted in its stance on pedagogy defined by assessment and reverse design, originating with its director's expertise. That does not mean that this particular stance would work (or should work) at another institution under a different director. What it does mean is that in a given LC, the ecosystem of the institution and the expertise of the center's director should be considered as strengths with which to inform eventual programs and initiatives. What programming is needed, and what can be provided? (Look for the low-hanging fruit.) In what areas does the LC director have expertise, or, inversely, what expertise will be sought when searching for a director? How can the needs of language (and literature/culture) programs be anticipated? How can the needs of other programs be anticipated? Is there programming or are there services that can bring in revenue, no matter how modest?

For a one-person LC, playing to one's strengths can be a way to kick-start programming and get it established. Being able to demonstrate vital work done in the LC that is also visible to the larger institution can be one argument when trying to expand programming and, when possible, receive additional funding. Showing that the LC is collaborating with other centers on campus, avoiding reinventing the wheel, and now needing only a small investment to do more tells the administration that you have worked to tap existing sources. For example, the CLC collaborates closely with Title VI centers on campus. We meet during each application cycle to brainstorm roles the CLC can play in terms of the targeted priorities. Two cycles ago, outreach to community colleges was a priority. We began to invite community and city college faculty to our workshops, especially those focused on assessment. It did not cost us anything extra, it paved the way for the Title VI centers to contribute to our funding, and it proved to the administration that we are working together to maximize our resources.

4. From Ad Hoc Workshops to Professional Development Hub

Most US LCs are invested in providing professional development workshops for their constituencies. At the CLC we, like so many others, have turned from serving learners and teachers by lending CDs or equipment to serving instructors in professionalizing the use of a wide array of equipment and technologies. Multiple workshop topics are offered to meet the broad, often disparate needs of instructors. But this variety can feel ad hoc and disconnected. Workshops should and can provide professional development, but the term "professional development" can connote that instructors need assistance in developing their teaching skills (Lage-Otero, 2013). There is a delicate balance between offering workshops you believe your colleagues need and giving them the impression they do not know what they are doing. Van Deusen-Scholl and Young's (2017) comprehensive chapter about the role of LCs in professional development, especially of non-ladder faculty, suggested dual roles of advocate and facilitator in working with language instructors. The LC becomes a space—we would call ours a hub—for everyone engaged in language instruction to engage in professional development, guided by LC staff, but informed by the instructors themselves. We took an assessment-driven, reverse design approach in this as well and tried to design and offer meaningful professional development while instilling a sense of agency in our colleagues.

The University of Chicago recently adopted a "budget allocation" model to inform some decisions around funding departments and divisions. The bottom line is that revenue from undergraduate tuition is allocated in direct proportion to the number of undergraduates enrolled in the courses taught by the faculty. The University of Chicago had heretofore been an institution primarily focused on graduate education (founded on Humboldt's model of the German university). In the summer of 2018, as a result of this shift to a focus on undergraduate education, funding became available for faculty to redesign or create courses that would appeal to undergraduates. The director of the CLC was asked (by a strategically astute dean) to create a professional development program targeting language instruction that would not only support instructors in the reflection of their teaching practices, but also shift them away from traditional pedagogies. The Language Pedagogy Innovation Initiative (LPII) was born with reverse design as an operating principle. Instructors first identify proficiency outcomes for the end of a given sequence (e.g., first-year German), then develop four-skills proficiency assessments. These assessments are designed in close collaboration with CLC staff, including required participation in workshops and the creation of a test design document identifying levels and task types for each skill. The next step is the full development of the assessment: finding or creating reading and listening input, finalizing test tasks, and creating a scoring rubric. Throughout design and development, instructors receive input and feedback from CLC staff, who position themselves as experts. That is a critical point. In our experience, many language instructors, even those with years of experience or with strong backgrounds in applied linguistics, have little training in assessment design. Everyone gives "tests," but these new assessments are specifically designed to measure the proficiency outcomes the instructors have themselves identified. Using LPII funding, we are able to give the instructors an "incentive payment." Participation in all assessment-related aspects of the LPII also "count" as part of the unionization-mandated professional development quota.

Once these assessments have been approved and are in place, the process of realigning instruction begins. It is here in our work with our colleagues that we have witnessed a meaningful transition. Instructors opt-in to participate in the LPII. They themselves have identified the outcomes and designed the tests. Not only does this mean that neither of those are imposed from outside, but we also find that in the process of designing proficiency assessment tasks, instructors are already reflecting on their curriculum. Will my students be successful on this test, a test for which I have identified the outcomes (based on my expertise in my language) and test tasks I have created myself as valid measures of the outcomes? At this point, the instructors are ready to realign their curriculum, also with input from the CLC staff, but the CLC staff steps back and cedes the role of expert to the individual language instructors. Curricular development usually takes place over the summer, and LPII funds are available for modest honoraria.

The LPII impacted the CLC's workshop offerings in multiple ways. First of all, its structured (reverse-designed) format provides a beginning, middle, and end of professional development activities. Second, once instructors have participated in our test design and curricular development workshops, they are free to propose new test and curriculum projects and to receive additional incentive payments and honoraria. The CLC also offers a more "ad hoc" workshop series, and participation has increased significantly because instructors are continually seeking ways to use new technology or instructional techniques as they realign their curricula. We have also been able to anticipate topics for workshops (e.g., structuring dynamic class discussions) in response to issues that come up in the curricular design phase. Finally, the LPII has contributed to the development of a community of practice in ways we did not plan for and could not have predicted. Each year we hold a Language Summit to highlight LPII projects and announce workshops for the coming year. We are also expanding into online course development and LSP courses. Instructors have been able to present their assessments and their curricular projects at professional meetings. And, locally, the dean of our College has been both impressed and gratified by curricular work happening across literally dozens of languages.

Most institutions do not have the funding that we have to carry out a program like the LPII, and indeed, we will not have funding forever. But language instructors are revising the curricula they use and creating new materials all the time. Providing instructors with an outcome-focused professional development initiative is a way to attract them to and keep them engaged in professional development programming offered in a LC. The outcome-focused structure is what matters, no the disciplinary strength of the LC director, or the mission of the LC, or the focus of a workshop series in a given academic year or semester. For example, a one-semester focus on listening comprehension might be structured as follows:

- announce the program; participants opt-in
- share 2–3 key articles on teaching or testing listening comprehension; participants read these and share critical feedback about their own materials
- each participant plans to revise or replace materials to be used in the next semester, basing the changes on the secondary literature

- participants meet to share drafts of their new/amended materials and get feedback from LC staff and peers
- in next semester, participants teach using the new materials
- at the end of the semester, participants share feedback about the effectiveness of the materials, ideally based on some data (improved performance on tests, feedback from students around confidence in listening)
- participants share their work with other non-participants
- a new cycle begins.

5. From Social Events to a Community of Practice

At any phase of an evolving LC, there are multiple ways to build community. But before exploring some of those options, it is worth considering why community building is so essential, aside from the longer-term goal of fostering a community of practice. Depending on the structure of a given institution, language instructors usually "live administratively" in different departments. While engaged in academic activities with similar goals and sharing a scholarly field, instructors scattered across a university or college may not know who other language instructors are, much less how different languages are being taught, what policies are in place (for placement, to cite just one example), or how majors and minors are structured. Complicating this is the bifurcation of language and literature departments as described and lamented in the 2007 Modern Language Association Report. In this context, language instruction is carried out by individuals who are not tenure-line faculty, often putting them in a precarious political situation. Furthermore, instructors of LCTLs may be further isolated, as they strive to update teaching materials and chase enrollments. Creating community plays a significant role in bringing these often-marginalized faculty together. Especially in cases where all languages have been reorganized into a single department or a LC, something that often happens under institutional or fiscal duress, establishing and nourishing community is crucial.

Building community can begin by creating a contact list of everyone on campus teaching language. Deceptively simple—or not! Instructors come and go, adjuncts may only work a semester or two, new languages may get funded, seemingly permanent linguistic fixtures may meet their revenue-driven demise. And then there are the graduate students, a population of instructors who should—must!—be included, but who are the most challenging to keep track of. Each autumn, the administrator of the CLC, over multiple days of contacting departments and language program directors, consulting online course lists, and using data from previous years, establishes a contact list of languages and instructors for the coming academic year. This list is used to send announcements for social and academic events, forward job listings, advertise external professional development opportunities and other information, and solicit input for policy questions as they arise—to name a few of the many reasons for circulating information.

Social events occur at the beginning (and sometimes the end) of each academic term. Receptions, potlucks, coffee hours, and cookie summits (a regular December event at the CLC) are easy to set up, inexpensive, and create an informal setting where instructors can get to know each other. Collegiality begins here. The CLC also established an Advisory Council designed to solicit issues from colleagues of general interest to the community, circulate agenda items to colleagues for input, disseminate information from and about the CLC to colleagues, give input to the CLC on various matters, and vet and vote on locally funded proposals (one vote per department). Regular quarterly or semester meetings are also essential for sharing policy changes, updates, new programs, and other issues as they arise. Announcements include job postings, job talks, workshops and workshops series, external professional development opportunities, funding for workshops or projects (internal and external), news items, and reports. Information flows multidirectionally. We are offering these workshops; what other topics are of interest? Here are professional development opportunities; what others do you know of? Are there available funding sources?

Language fairs are another way to establish community while also raising the visibility of languages taught on a campus. At the University of Chicago, an event called "The Universe of Languages" has been held for over a decade during Orientation Week, a strategic moment when incoming undergraduate and graduate students are thinking about registering for the coming year. The event includes not only those programs that teach languages, but others where language learning has an impact: study abroad, fellowships and awards (i.e., Fulbright, Boren), Title VI centers, film studies, even the bookstore. In the lead-up to the event, different programs share information about their offerings, fostering cross-pollination (what is the language requirement for the Fulbright English Teaching Assistantship?) and combining of resources (yes, I'll announce your program to my German classes). Chairs and deans are also invited, along with the vice-provost for globalization. Not only does everyone learn how to strengthen offerings and multiply outreach to students, the fair becomes de facto evidence for deans and provosts that the campus is invested in international initiatives, while also demonstrating the vitality and commitment of those who teach languages. In just the past two years, the CLC and language instructors have been invited to take part in informational fairs offered by other programs, increasing opportunities for language offerings, and more importantly, demonstrating that language study is integral to other campus opportunities.

Having an established process and rhythm for communication has other benefits. When an institutional administration wants to collect information (enrollment trends, volume of petitions, contact hours for different languages), it can turn to the LC. The LC can also poll its constituents to get a read on different issues. Are you (as a group) interested in remotely enrolling students? How do various languages handle nonbinary pronouns? What are pros and cons of different LMSs for languages? How can and should transfer credits be treated for languages? Would it be possible to move language placement tests online, and how will that impact enrollments? All of those queries have been brought to the CLC over the past decade. When administrators in divisions (e.g., Humanities, Physical Sciences), programs (e.g., Study Abroad, Office for Fellowships), departments (e.g., English, History), and other agents on campus know they can tap into an entire disciplinary population, they gladly reach out. This begins to establish the LC and its director as a source for answers to questions about policy or the impact of different programming. The director can speak knowledgeably both to the policy and its impact. The ability to "speak in one voice," whether there is consensus or whether multiple viewpoints need to be accommodated, is critical to the visibility of language learning in the institution.

A caveat: This visibility and "one voice" does not happen overnight. It took the director of the CLC more than a decade to be able to claim these attributes for the LC, first in her role as the part-time assessment coordinator and then as LC director, to earn the recognition from the larger institutional community and, more crucially, the trust of her language-teaching colleagues. On some campuses, speaking in one voice may be neither possible nor desirable. But I argue that being recognized as an important program on campus and making one's own voice and the voices of language teachers heard, no matter how diffuse the opinions, is important. How a LC or its director ultimately leverages this potential can vary as appropriate to a given institution.

Just as Wenger (1998), in her provocative volume about communities of practice, could not remember whether she or her colleague coined the phrase, it is impossible to say when we realized we were establishing a community of practice ourselves. We have done it, and in the CLC we experience the three dimensions of community (Wenger, 1998, pp. 72–85) every day. Because we are all using ACTFL levels to describe learner outcomes and performance on assessments, there is mutual engagement. Across all languages, including American Sign Language and Classics, we discuss and collaborate on the work we are doing. Newly designed assessments and realigned and new courses represent our joint enterprise. We hear our colleagues talking to each other and presenting at meetings speaking expertly about assessment and reverse design, evidence of our shared repertoire. Although the languages live in seven distinct departments, they belong to a community of practice in the CLC.

6. Conclusion

In the trajectories described above, I hope that I have captured the intertwined functions of the role of a LC on its campus and its ability to harness the bottom-up initiatives and talents of its constituencies. The successful collaboration that can ensue can be tailored to maximize the efficacy and impact of the LC in its institutional ecosystem. In a plenary session given at the 2019 American Association of Applied Linguistics conference, the presenters spoke about the importance of trust and respect between researchers and the teachers they endeavor to inform and support (Lightbown & Spada, 2019). In this talk, key terms resonated with the work the CLC tries to accomplish with and for its language instructor colleagues. Those terms were "collaboration" and "goals." Collaboration happens through joint projects and endeavors, yes, but it is enhanced by the dual stance taken in the CLC. The first is one of expert collaborators offering programming to support and inform the work being undertaken by language instructors. The second is advisory, when instructors are the agents of their own change as they realign curricula and the day-to-day work of teaching, advising, and engaging in professional development. Shared goals make it possible for this work to be more effective and to raise the visibility and vitality of everyone engaged in the work of teaching languages on our campus.

References

Askildson, L. (2011). From lab to center: A vision of transforming a language learning resource into a language learning community. In F. A. Kronenberg & U. S. Lahaie (Eds.), *Language center design* (pp. 11–21). Auburn, AL: International Association for Language Learning Technology.

Gopalakrishnan, S., Yaden, B., & Franz, J. (2013). Management and leadership: Roles, styles and philosophies. In A. F. Ross (Ed.), *IALLT language center management* (pp. 1–15). Auburn, AL: International Association for Language Learning Technology.

Kronenberg, F. A. (2013). The LLC and public relations: Promoting the language learning center. In A. F. Ross (Ed.), *IALLT language center management* (pp. 121–132). Auburn, AL: International Association for Language Learning Technology.

Kronenberg, F. A. (2017). Conclusion: From language centers to language learning spaces. In F. A. Kronenberg (Ed.), *From language lab to language center and beyond: The past, present, and future of language center design* (pp. 161–165). Auburn, AL: International Association for Language Learning Technology.

Lage-Otero, E. (2013). The LLC's role in technology training and professional development. In A. F. Ross (Ed.), *IALLT language center management* (pp. 133–157). Auburn, AL: International Association for Language Learning Technology.

Lightbown, P., & Spada, N. (2019, March). *In it together: Teachers, researchers and classroom SLA.* Keynote address presented at the meeting of the American Association of Applied Linguistics conference, Atlanta, GA.

The Modern Language Association. (2007). *Foreign languages and higher education: New structures for a changed world.* New York, NY: MLA Publications.

Richards, J., & Rodgers, T. (1986). *Approaches and methods in language teaching: A description and analysis.* New York, NY: Cambridge University Press.

van Deusen-Scholl, N., & Young, S. (2017). The role of language centers in the professional development of non-tenure track language faculty. In F. A. Kronenberg (Ed.), *From language lab to language center and beyond: The past, present, and future of language center design* (pp. 46–60). Auburn, AL: International Association for Language Learning Technology.

Wenger, E. (1998). *Communities of practice: Learning, meaning, and identity.* Cambridge, UK: Cambridge University Press.

Author Notes

Catherine C. Baumann a Senior Instructional Professor and Director of the University of Chicago Language Center (CLC). She received her PhD in Second Languages and Cultures Education from the University of Minnesota, specializing in reading comprehension and language testing. She is a certified ACTFL tester and trainer and does consulting for language programs in higher education on a variety of curricular and assessment-related issues. She directed the German language program at the University of Chicago from 1999 to 2019 and now oversees all programs in the CLC.

Correspondence concerning this chapter should be addressed to Catherine C. Baumann (ccbauman@uchicago.edu).

Chapter 5

Language Center Trends:
Insights From the IALLT Surveys, 2013–2019

Elizabeth Lavolette, Kyoto Sangyo University, Japan
Angelika Kraemer, Cornell University, USA

Abstract

This chapter reports on insights from the four most recent IALLT surveys of language center (LC) directors. It begins with a brief history of the IALLT survey, followed by a discussion of survey data that were collected in 2013 (Kronenberg), 2015 (Kronenberg & Lavolette), 2017 (Lavolette & Kraemer), and 2019 (Kraemer & Ledgerwood). Results are presented in broad categories, including director employment details (contract type, faculty status, contract length, percentage of time devoted to LC work, salaries, and compensation type), director job duties, director job satisfaction and challenges, LC budgets, employee work hours, center evaluation, and LC users, functions, spaces, and other services provided.

Some of the insights that we report are as follows: Beginning with general job satisfaction, survey responses were consistently high, with a mean of 8 or higher on a 10-point scale for all four years. "Center" was much more common in LC names than "lab," though little change was seen during the years of the survey. Some data that support the suggestion that LCs are evolving from labs to centers, for example, increasing numbers of LCs provide social and event spaces and plan and host events. However, increasing numbers of LCs are also providing physical language lab environments. In addition, more LCs are also providing professional development and increasing numbers of student employee hours. Open-ended survey responses relating to the preparation of LC directors indicate a lack of training in areas such as personnel management, administration, and budgeting. General challenges faced by LCs include declining language enrollments at their institutions, budget cuts, and low awareness of the LC's existence. On a positive note, LC directors generally made positive comments about the independence and flexibility their positions afforded, their colleagues, and their salaries. We hope that this information will be useful in planning for the future of LCs.

Language center (LC) directors and staff in the US context have the near-impossible job of predicting the future of language learning and teaching. (Who could have imagined the effect on education of the COVID-19 pandemic?) They need to accurately predict what technology will be used and useful in the coming semester and future years, and they need to be familiar with trends in teaching methods and be able to evaluate their effectiveness. LC employees must train themselves, faculty, and future faculty for teaching in an uncertain future, and they must be able to prepare language learning spaces, both physical and virtual, for student interactions.

To accomplish this difficult task, LC directors can and should look at the past and present of their institutional context. The current report of recent International Association for Language Learning Technology (IALLT) surveys serves as another source for insights.

Our intention in the current report is to discuss selected results of the four most recent IALLT surveys of LC directors, collected in 2013, 2015, 2017, and 2019. The time is ripe for this comparison because as an organization, we now have collected data over four survey years that are largely consistent, making it much easier to compare than older survey data. Lavolette (2019) provided a preliminary comparison of the 2013, 2015, and 2017 data, and the current chapter both follows up and expands on her analysis. As we move forward as a field, it will be important to continue to monitor ongoing trends so we can not only react to them, but anticipate and prepare for them.

We first provide some historical background on the IALLT surveys since 1976 and discuss why we chose to analyze only the four most recent surveys. Then, we provide details of how the four surveys were conducted, analyzed, and compared. In the main body of this chapter, we examine trends and other potentially interesting and useful results and provide our interpretations, with an eye toward how this information can be useful to LC employees and administrators. We conclude with a summary of the "typical" LC director and LC and our predictions for the future of LCs, particularly given the ongoing COVID-19 pandemic.

1. IALLT Survey History

The first report of an IALLT survey was published in 1976 (Stern, 1976a, 1976b), when the organization was known as the National Association of Language Laboratory Directors (NALLD). Since then, survey reports have been published periodically (see Table 1). The most recent survey was conducted in 2019 (Kraemer & Ledgerwood, 2019), and another survey was underway in spring 2021 (although the results were not yet available at the time of writing).

As Table 1 shows, the targeted respondents for the survey have varied over the years. In fact, presenting all surveys together is somewhat misleading because some surveys were aimed exclusively at IALLT members, with the results intended to guide internal IALLT decision-making, while other surveys were aimed at the broader audience of LC directors and/or staff, with the results intended to be published for a wider readership. However, the intentions of the authors of older survey reports are not always clear, so for the sake of completeness, we have included all known surveys and published survey reports in the table.

Table 1

IALLT Surveys and Published Survey Reports

Date of survey	Date of report	Target survey participants	Responses received	Report author	Report title	Publication venue
circa 1975	1976a	"language and learning laboratories as they exist today in colleges and universities across the United States" (p. 7); 150 institutions	89 responses	Stern	The university language/learning laboratory: A survey of the facilities: Their technologies; disciplines; organizations. Part I	*NALLD Journal*
circa 1975	1976b	See above	See above	Stern	The university language/learning laboratory: A survey of the facilities: Their technologies; disciplines; organizations. Part II	*NALLD Journal*
Unknown	1989	Readers of Journal of Educational Techniques and Technologies (J.E.T.T.)	Unknown	Editors of J.E.T.T.	J.E.T.T. reader profile survey	*Journal of Educational Techniques and Technologies*
1988	1990	All US IALL[a] members; language labs at 1,500 colleges and universities in the US	376 responses	Lawrason	The changing state of the language lab: Results of the 1988 IALL member survey	*IALL Journal of Language Learning Technologies*
2000	None	Unknown	248 total responses; 111 from directors and associate/assistant directors	Dressler	None	None
2005	2006	Unknown	116 responses	Pankratz & Ross	The 2005 IALLT survey of the profession	*IALLT Journal of Language Learning Technologies*
2013	2014	IALLT and regional group members	109 responses; 65 in charge	Kronenberg	Language center design and management in the post-language laboratory era	*The IALLT Journal*
2013	2016	See above	See above	Kronenberg	Curated language learning spaces: Design principles of physical 21st century language centers	*The IALLT Journal*

Table 1 (cont'd.)
IALLT Surveys and Published Survey Reports

2014	NA	IALLT members	59 responses	Kronenberg & Lavolette	NA	NA
2015	2018	IALLT members, CALICO[b] members, LLTI[c] listserv subscribers, via social media; those "in charge" of language center	71 responses; 49 in charge	Lavolette	Language center mandates and realities	Language Center Handbook
2017	NA	IALLT members, CALICO members, LLTI listserv subscribers, via social media	74 responses; 57 in charge	Kraemer & Lavolette	NA	NA
2013, 2015, 2017 (report of trends)	2019	See above	See above	Lavolette	A very brief introduction to US language centers	JASAL[d] 2018 x SUTLF 5: Selected papers from the Sojo University Teaching and Learning Forum 2018
2018	NA	IALLT members	66 responses	Kraemer & Ledgerwood	NA	NA
2019	NA	IALLT members, CALICO members, LLTI listserv subscribers, via social media	111 responses; 61 in charge	Kraemer & Ledgerwood	NA	NA

[a] IALL is the International Association of Learning Laboratories, a precursor to IALLT. In 1981, the organization changed its name from NALLD to IALL, then changed its name to IALLT in 1991.

[b] CALICO is the Computer-Assisted Language Learning Consortium, a professional organization that serves a membership involved in both education and technology.

[c] LLTI is the Language Learning Technology International listserv, maintained by IALLT.

[d] JASAL is the Japan Association for Self-Access Learning, an academic association devoted to promoting self-access language learning in Japan.

Note. Various conference sessions also provided IALLT survey results for some years where no reports had been published (e.g., Kraemer & Lavolette, 2017; Kraemer & Ledgerwood, 2019; Lavolette & Kraemer, 2019). In 2021, IALLT added a page about surveys to its website: https://iallt.org/resources/survey/.

Our original hope in conducting this historical analysis of IALLT survey data was to look at trends from as far back in history as possible. However, examining the older surveys quickly showed that the data are simply not comparable. We do not have access to the raw data for most of the surveys, and some of the reports discussed the data in idiosyncratic ways (e.g., the J.E.T.T. reader profile survey, 1989, reported the data for men and women separately) and did not include any information about the number of respondents. In addition, the questions that have been asked over the years have varied widely.

Given these barriers to comparing older surveys, we focused our attention on the four most recent surveys of language center directors, with data collected in 2013, 2015, 2017, and 2019. Because the 2015 survey was aimed at only those "in charge" of LCs (referred to as LC directors in the current report), we restrict our comparison to LC directors across the surveys. By doing so, we also avoid including data from multiple people at a single institution. Next, we describe the data collection procedures.

2. Method

2.1 2013, 2015, 2017, and 2019 IALLT Survey Data Collection

The survey tool Qualtrics was used to conduct all four surveys via the web. The number of directors who responded to each survey and the maximum number of questions that were asked of directors are shown in Table 2. Because the questions branched based on previous responses, the number of questions that each director saw varied. The 2013 survey was emailed to IALLT members and to members of IALLT-affiliated regional groups (Kronenberg, 2014, 2016). The 2015, 2017, and 2019 surveys were distributed via social media and emailed directly to IALLT members, subscribers to the LLTI listserv (maintained by IALLT), and members of CALICO. Refer to Lavolette (2018a) for more details of the 2015 survey.

Table 2

Details of 2013, 2015, 2017, and 2019 IALLT Surveys

Date of survey	Number of directors who responded	Maximum number of questions
2013	65	53
2015	49	60
2017	57	65
2019	61	76

2.2 Participants

We report here some basic demographics about the participants in the four surveys. Given the differences in the number of respondents each year, we report most results by percentages, rather than raw counts. Data on gender, age, first languages (L1s), and IALLT membership status are shown in Table 3 (questions on these topics were not included on the 2013 survey). A slightly larger percentage of respondents identified themselves as women in 2017 as compared to 2015 (this question was not included in the 2019 survey). About three-quarters of directors indicated that English was a first language in all three years, and other common first languages in the three years were French, German, Mandarin, and Spanish. Nearly three-quarters of directors were IALLT members in all three years.

Table 3

Demographic Data on 2015, 2017, and 2019 IALLT Survey Participants (Directors)

	2015	2017	2019
Gender	Woman: 50%	Woman: 55%	Question was not
	Man: 50%	Man: 45%	included
Age	Range: 34–64	Range: 25–66	Range: 25–69
	Mean: 50	Mean: 46	Mean: 48
Common L1s[a]	English: 76%	English: 77%	English: 74%
	French: 4%	French: 7%	French: 7%
	German: 4%	German: 11%	German: 7%
	Mandarin: 6%	Mandarin: 4%	Mandarin: 3%
	Spanish: 10%	Spanish: 9%	Spanish: 10%
IALLT membership	Member: 73%	Member: 74%	Member: 72%
	Nonmember: 27%	Nonmember: 26%	Nonmember: 28%

[a] Percentages do not necessarily sum to 100 because participants could choose more than one L1 and low-frequency choices are omitted.

Note. Updated and expanded from Lavolette (2019), Table 1.

The age of directors changed slightly from 2015 to the later years. The mean age of 50 in 2015 dropped to 46 in 2017 and moved to 48 in 2019; the age of the youngest director was 34 in 2015, but held steady at 25 in both 2017 and 2019.

Figure 1

Highest Degree

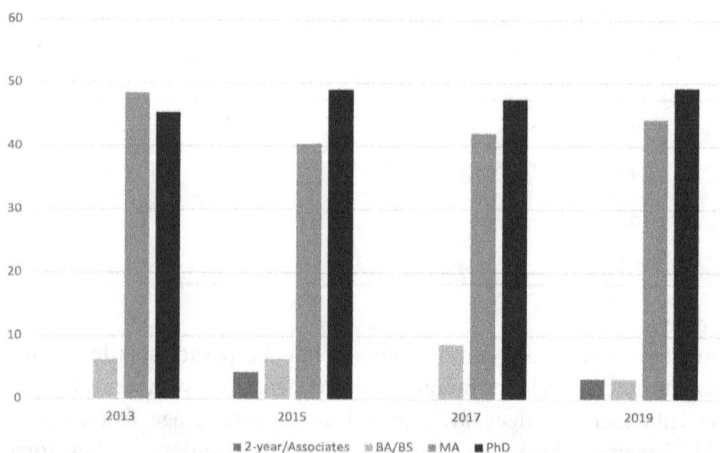

Note. The degrees as indicated or equivalents, presented in percentages.

The distribution of highest degrees remained largely stable throughout the four survey years under investigation (Figure 1). The majority of directors held advanced degrees in all four years. This implies that an MA is the minimum required education for most director jobs, even in cases when it is not an explicit requirement for hiring.

Figure 2
Field of Highest Degree

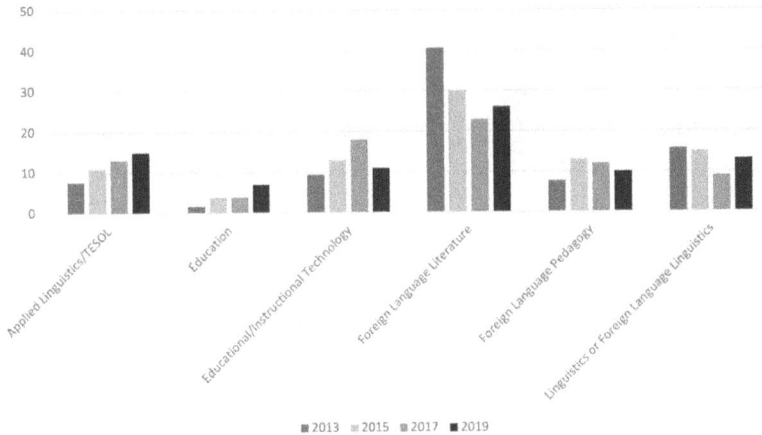

Note. Most common categories only, presented in percentages.

With regard to the field of highest degree (Figure 2), LC directors have heterogeneous backgrounds. Over the four survey years, most LC directors were trained in foreign language literature (ranging from 23–30%), followed by degrees in (foreign language) linguistics (slightly decreasing from 13% to 12% to 10%) and educational/instructional technology (ranging from 11–18%). The data suggest that there is no traditional path to the role of LC director, which is further substantiated by the open-ended responses that indicated a lack of training in areas such as personnel management, administration, and budgeting (see Sections 3.1 and 3.4). The fields of applied linguistics/TESOL (teaching English to speakers of other languages) and education have seen small steady increases over the four years, while the percentage of directors with degrees in foreign language literature decreased.

2.2.1 Participant Institutions
The distribution of institutions at which LC directors were employed also remained stable throughout the four survey years under investigation (Figure 3). The majority of LC directors worked at PhD-granting research universities, followed by liberal arts colleges or universities (emphasizing undergraduate education and awarding at least half of their degrees in liberal arts fields). Few LC directors who responded worked at regional universities or colleges (focusing on undergraduate education, but granting fewer than half of their degrees in liberal arts disciplines), community colleges, and K–12 schools.

Figure 3

Institution Type

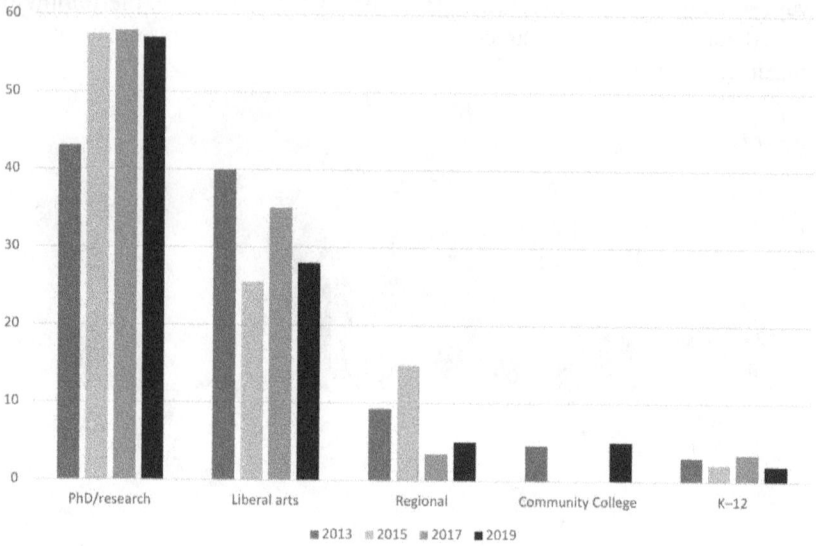

Note. Presented in percentages.

The majority of directors' institutions were public across all survey years. The exception was 2017, when the distribution between public and private was nearly equal (Figure 4).

Figure 4

Public vs. Private Institutions

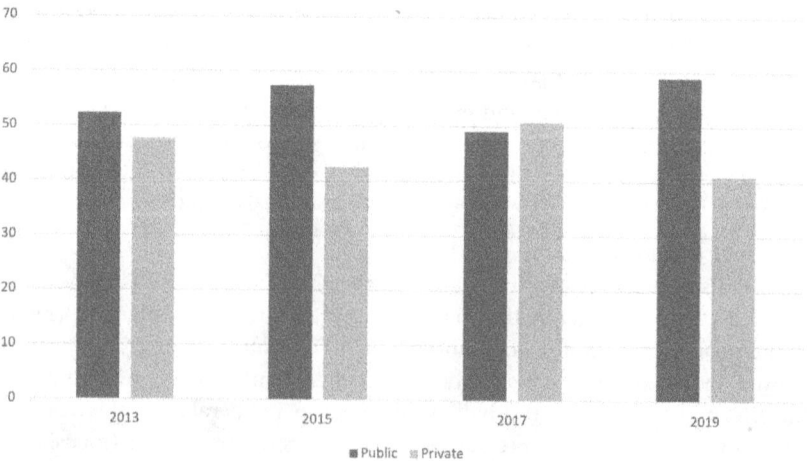

Note. Presented in percentages.

Regarding geographical location, the majority of institutions were in the US: 94% in 2015, 96% in 2017, and 83% in 2019 (this question was not included in the 2013 survey). In 2015, the non-US responses came from Asia, Canada, and South America; in 2017, the non-US responses all came from Europe. 2019 represented the most diverse group with 7% of responses from Asia, 3% each from Canada and Europe, and 2% each from Africa and South America. IALLT's recently forged connections with affiliate organizations like the Japan Association for Self-Access Learning and Arbeitskreis der Sprachzentren an Hochschulen in Germany will hopefully emphasize the I (for "International") in IALLT in years to come, making the survey less US-centric.

Within participant institutions, a plurality of language centers were positioned in a language department or a college (Table 4). The number of independent language centers has somewhat decreased over the four survey years.

Table 4

Positioning of LC Within the Institution

	2013	2015	2017	2019
College/division support unit	9%	36%	31%	35%
Independent	12%	11%	7%	7%
IT	2%	4%	11%	4%
Language department	59%	36%	46%	42%
Library	2%	0%	2%	0%
Teaching/learning center/commons	2%	0%	2%	0%
Other	16%	13%	0%	12%

Note. "Other" included units such as humanities, international affairs, education, student affairs, and global studies.

3. Results and Discussion

We began our analysis by looking for trends that held across the four survey years. We were conservative in our identification of trends; for example, when a given result trended up from 2013 to 2017, then back down in 2019, we do not report a trend. Even so, given the limitations of the data (see Conclusion), these patterns are not necessarily meaningful and should be interpreted with caution. In many cases, we did not find a trend, but decided to report on the results over time because LC employees are likely to find the results interesting and relevant to their work.

3.1 Director Employment Details

This section addresses employment details including contract type, faculty status, contract length, percentage of time devoted to LC work, salaries, and compensation type. Not every iteration of the survey asked each question, and the answer options varied slightly across the years, so the results vary accordingly.

Figure 5
LC Director Contract Type

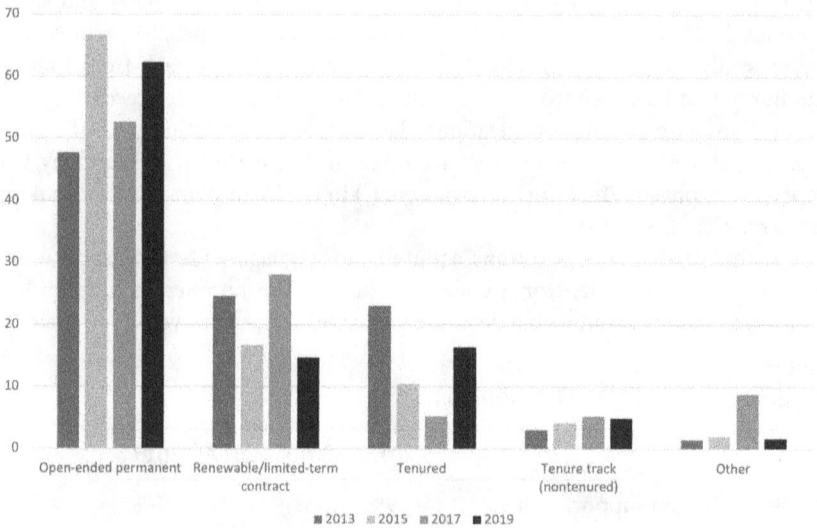

Note. Presented in percentages.

Figure 5 illustrates the contract types that LC directors held. The majority of directors held an open-ended permanent position in all four years under investigation. We can infer that many director positions, while generally not tenured or tenure track, are stable positions. However, as Lavolette (2018b) emphasized, financial problems at institutions may leave language centers and their non-tenured employees vulnerable to cuts.

Figure 6
LC Director Faculty Status

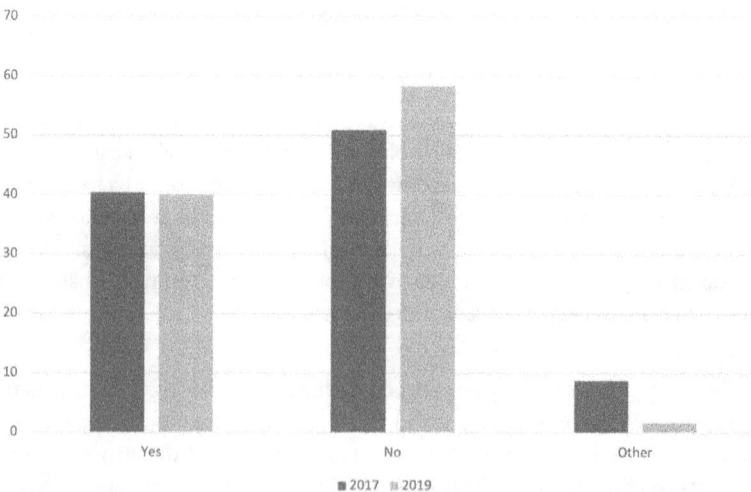

Note. Presented in percentages.

In the 2017 and 2019 surveys, LC directors were asked whether they hold faculty status at their institution (Figure 6). The majority of directors held non-faculty status in both years, and this percentage increased slightly from 2017 to 2019. This may indicate that institutions see the position of a LC director as more administrative than academic. As one director commented in the 2019 survey (in response to the question, "What aspects of your job did your degree NOT prepare you well for?"),

> "My degree trained me to do research, but my job as a Lab Director does not require me to do research. I am in a staff position, and checkout and upkeep equipment, proctor exams, and do room reservations. I have the desire, qualifications, and energy to make this lab something more than a testing center."

Similarly, most LC directors hold a graduate degree, and being classified as staff may be preventing them and their centers from achieving their full potential.

Figure 7
LC Director Contract Length

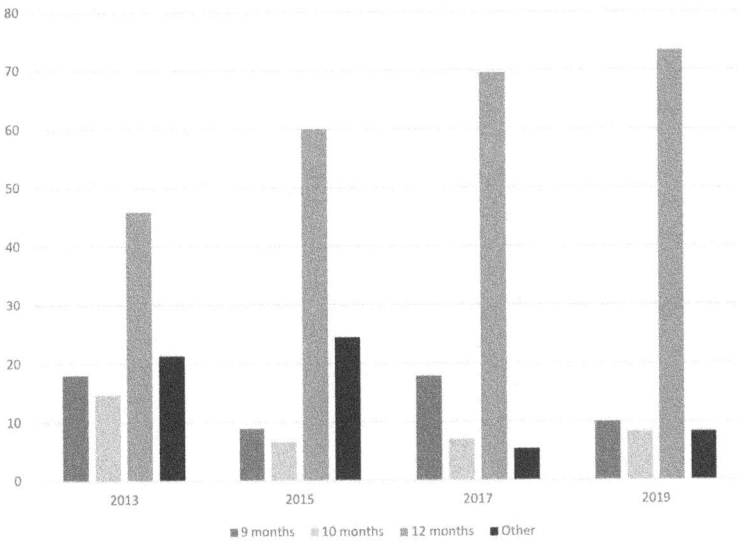

Note. Presented in percentages.

The percentage of positions with 12-month contracts has steadily increased over the four survey years (Figure 7). From a certain perspective, these numbers imply increasing job security for LC directors, more of whom have year-round employment and potentially a higher income than those on 9-month contracts. These numbers also point to the need for providing LC services year-round. However, from another perspective, the change may simply be related to the increase in non-faculty director positions. That is, faculty are more likely to have 9-month contracts, while staff are more likely to have 12-month contracts.

Figure 8

LC Director Percentage of Time Devoted to LC

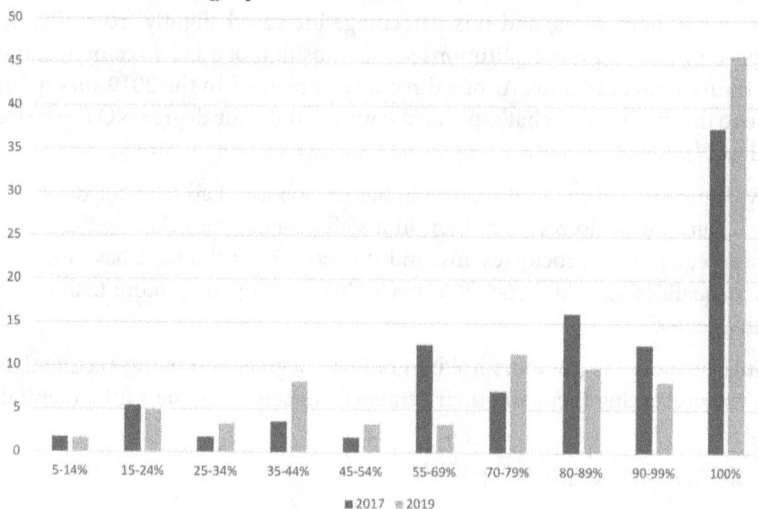

Note. Presented in percentages.

In 2017 and 2019 only, LC directors were asked what percentage of their time was devoted to language center work. As illustrated in Figure 8, most directors spent 90% or more of their work time on LC business (50% in 2017 and 54% in 2019). These numbers indicate that the majority of directors are fully devoted to their centers and not spread across multiple priorities. The range was 5–100% in 2017 and 10–100% in 2019; the mean was 78% in both years, and the mode was 100% in both years.

Figure 9

LC Director Salaries

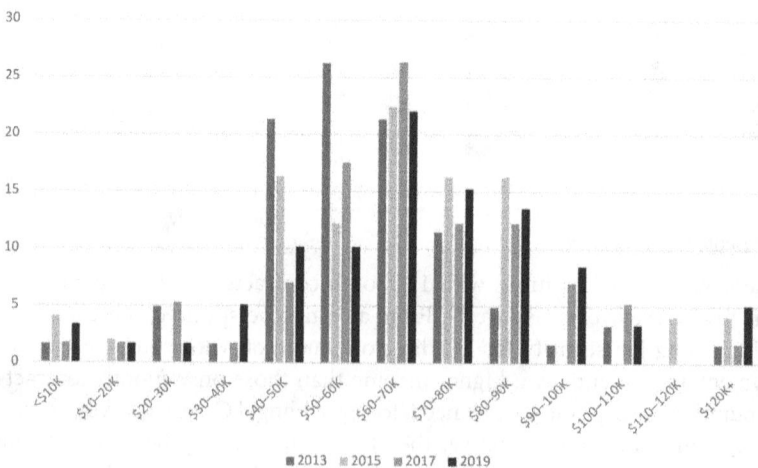

Note. Presented in percentages.

Of particular interest to LC employees is the range of salaries of LC directors. These data are also relevant when centers come under attack or when new hires or new centers are considered. The distribution of director salaries across the four survey years is shown in US dollars in Figure 9. The majority of LC director salaries across the four years clustered around the $40,000–90,000 range. The salary mode was $50,000–60,000 in 2013 and $60,000–70,000 in the following three survey years. Breakdowns by public and private institution status are shown in Figures 10a and 10b. The overall distribution of salaries remains similar when broken down by institution type, indicating little difference in salaries at public versus private institutions, although 2019 was an outlier with 28% of salaries in the $120,000+ range at private institutions (Figure 10b, next page).

Figure 10a
LC Director Salaries, Public Institutions

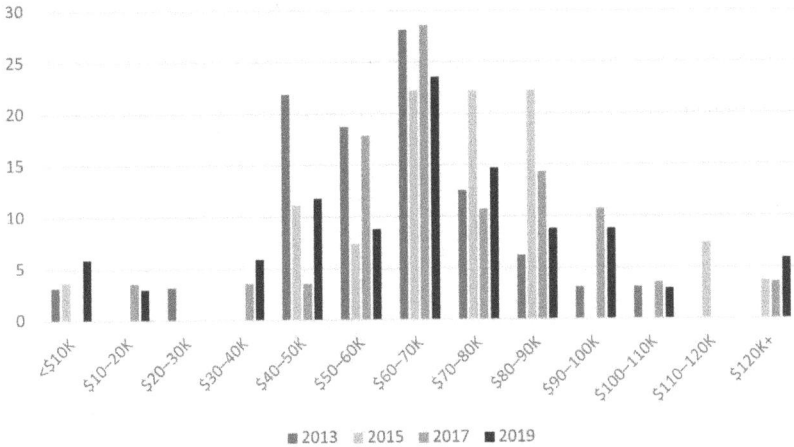

Note. Presented in percentages.

The vast majority of director positions are salaried (Figure 11, next page), supporting the argument that these positions represent stable employment.

3.2 Director Job Duties
The range of job duties varies among LC directors but has not significantly changed over the survey years. As can be seen in Table 5, the majority of directors do not teach (with fewer required to teach each year) and are not required to engage in research or publishing, further substantiating the notion that director positions are seen as more administrative than academic. Of course, this does not mean that LC directors do not engage in scholarly activity (see, e.g., the current volume for evidence of research output by LC staff). The expectation to present at conferences has a more even distribution of nearly half of directors across all survey years.

Figure 10b

LC Director Salaries, Private Institutions

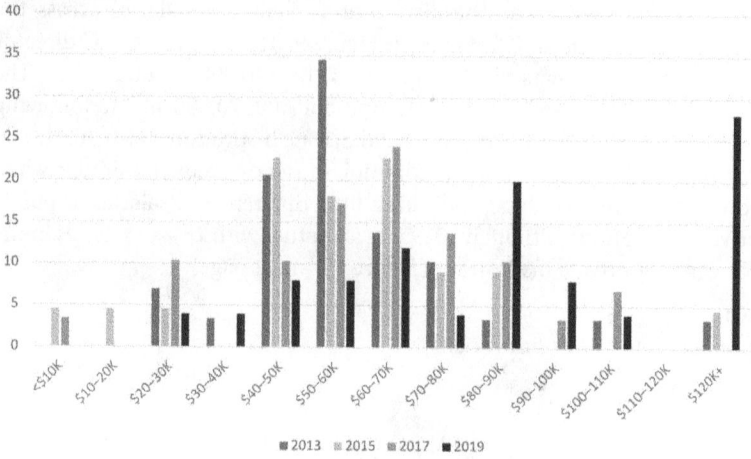

X-axis labels: <$10K, $10–20K, $20–30K, $30–40K, $40–50K, $50–60K, $60–70K, $70–80K, $80–90K, $90–100K, $100–110K, $110–120K, $120K+

■ 2013   ■ 2015   ■ 2017   ■ 2019

Note. Presented in percentages.

Figure 11

LC Director Compensation Type

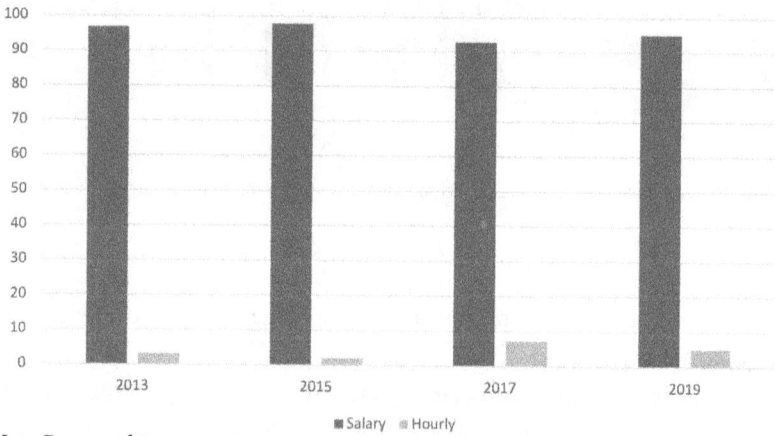

■ Salary   ■ Hourly

Note. Presented in percentages.

Table 5

Job Duties Reported by 2013, 2015, 2017, and 2019 IALLT Survey Participants (Directors)

	2013	2015	2017	2019
Teaching[a]	Question was not included	Yes: 43% No: 57%	Yes: 37% No: 63%	Yes: 28% No: 72%
# of courses per academic year[b]	Question was not included	Range: 4–12 Mean: 5.9 Mode: 5	Range: 1–5 Mean: 2.5 Mode: 1	Range: 1–12+ Mean: 3.6 Mode: 2
Research and publishing[c]	Yes: 28% No: 66% Not sure: 6%	Yes: 22% No: 78% Not sure: 0%	Yes: 25% No: 70% Not sure: 5%	Yes: 25% No: 67% Not sure: 8%
Conference presentations[d]	Yes: 48% No: 48% Not sure: 4%	Yes: 47% No: 41% Not sure: 12%	Yes: 49% No: 37% Not sure: 14%	Yes: 46% No: 47% Not sure: 7%

[a] "Is teaching credit-bearing course(s) a required part of your workload? (Do not consider student/faculty development workshops or instructing students/faculty on technology.)"
[b] This question was asked only of those directors who indicated that teaching was part of their job duties.
[c] "Are research and publishing part of your expected duties?"
[d] "Are you expected to present at conferences?"

3.3 Director Job Satisfaction

Three questions asked LC directors to rate their job satisfaction on a scale from 1 to 10, where 1 indicates low satisfaction and 10 indicates high satisfaction. The questions asked about general satisfaction, satisfaction with salary, and satisfaction with working hours. Although no obvious trends appear in the job satisfaction data, they are of interest because they are consistently high (Table 6).

Table 6

Job Satisfaction Reported by 2013, 2015, 2017, and 2019 IALLT Survey Participants (Directors)

	2013	2015	2017	2019
General satisfaction[a]	Mean: 8.0 Mode: 9	Mean: 8.7 Mode: 9/10	Mean: 8.4 Mode: 9	Mean: 8.2 Mode: 10
Satisfaction with salary[b]	Mean: 8.0 Mode: 8	Mean: 7.0 Mode: 9/10	Mean: 7.2 Mode: 9	Mean: 7.3 Mode: 8
Satisfaction with working hours[c]	Mean: 8.0 Mode: 10	Mean: 8.3 Mode: 9/10	Mean: 8.1 Mode: 8	Mean: 8.2 Mode: 10

[a] "On a scale of 1 (lowest) to 10 (highest), how satisfied are you with your position in general?"
[b] "On a scale of 1 (lowest) to 10 (highest), how satisfied are you with your salary?"
[c] "On a scale of 1 (lowest) to 10 (highest), how satisfied are you with your working hours?"

First, general satisfaction was often the highest of the satisfaction ratings across the four surveys, and the most common response (mode) was at least 9 each year. As a point of comparison, full-time faculty at US universities and colleges were asked in 2012–2014 about their general job satisfaction by rating their level of agreement with the statement "If I had it to do all over, I would again choose to work at this institution" (Webber, 2018, p. 3). When their results (on a 5-point scale, where 1 indicated "strongly agree" and 5 indicated "strongly disagree") are converted to match ours (by multiplying by 2), the results vary from 7.4 to 7.9 on a 10-point scale, depending on institution type. Note that we cannot calculate whether this difference is significant. What we can say is that the general satisfaction of LC directors in 2013, 2015, 2017, and 2019 was consistently higher than Webber's (2018) results for their university colleagues.

LC directors' satisfaction with their salary was also on the higher end of the scale, although a bit lower than their general satisfaction, and the most common response was at least 8. Similarly, LC directors indicated high satisfaction with their working hours, and the modes were very high. Unfortunately, a literature search did not turn up any comparable data on the satisfaction of US academics with their salary or working hours, although Webber (2018) found correlations between reported salary and overall job satisfaction.

In open-ended responses, the most commonly mentioned word related to job satisfaction was "autonomy" across the survey years, referring to the independence and flexibility LC direector positions afforded. In addition, LC directors generally made positive comments about their colleagues and the nature of their positions, as can be seen in the following comments:

"I have a lot of autonomy in my role and I feel supported by the institution." (2019)

"I have a lot of independence, a decent budget, and a talented staff; our center's relationships with faculty and students are quite strong and always an opportunity for new learning." (2019)

"The greatest gig on earth! Running a center for students, teachers and researchers and the ideas and energy that flows through the center is constantly rejuvenating. And they PAY me!" (2017)

"I have a great position with freedom to grow and support from all." (2013)

3.4 Director Job Challenges

Various open-ended survey responses pointed to challenges related to job preparation, type of position, and LC general concerns. Responses relating to the preparation of LC directors indicated a lack of training in areas such as personnel management, administration, and budgeting. Academic degrees provided important grounding in language pedagogy and research, illuminated linkages between theory and practice, and translated into working with students and faculty; however, administrative responsibilities of managing a center were new skills for most LC directors. Particularly, older directors indicated that technology use and integration were not common at the time they obtained their degrees ("Degree was in 1990!" [2017 survey]), and many younger directors also noted that they took a CALL course once but were not intimately familiar with current trends in (educational) technology. The following comment from the 2017 survey best sums up the relation between academic degree and LC director positions: "I'm not sure this is a job for which a degree prepares you." It speaks to the creativity, flexibility, ingenuity, and tenacity of LC directors that they run successful and effective units at their institutions.

Even though LC directors indicated consistently high job satisfaction (Section 3.3), they still had dissatisfaction with aspects of their work. One of the most common complaints was about the lack of upward mobility. Such comments were often connected to lacking tenure status, as illustrated in the following quote:

> "I am increasingly nervous about the future of my position given the downsizing in the humanities and growth in the sciences at my institution. Although I value my position highly, I have been frustrated at the lack of opportunity for promotion or advancement. I am a non-tenure track faculty member without security or possibility of promotion." (2017)

As mentioned in Section 3.1, some institutions may see the position of a LC director as more administrative than academic, as is apparent in this 2019 quote:

> "I have a Ph.D. and I am not satisfied using it to proctor exams and upkeep classroom equipment. I feel a bit overqualified for my job as 'staff.' I miss the rewards of teaching and researching. Nevertheless, I am learning to make this my dream job. This lab is my kingdom, and I'm taking it in a new direction."

General challenges faced by LCs included declining language enrollments at their institutions, budget cuts, and lower relevance as a result of increasing availability of mobile technologies and declining LC usage. The following survey statements are representative of these concerns across the survey years:

> "Dwindling language program enrollments is a major concern, along with a realization that technology cannot be the major focus of the language center going forward, primarily due to cost of maintaining physical computer spaces, especially with the prevalence of mobile devices among the students. Also, our layout is not conducive to hosting large gatherings or events that would attract students. We would like to be a more inviting place for students to gather and use language or collaborate on projects, as well as a location for bringing language instructors together to collaborate on shared projects." (2017)

> "The only concern that I have is the concern that faces all language instructors in the country. There is a movement to undermine the teaching of modern languages with a preference being given to computer science and coding. Modern language departments are no longer seen as money makers and STEM programs seem to see all of the cash these days." (2017)

"Foreign language is not considered a core requirement and is overshadowed by athletic schedules and budget (which bring in money)." (2015)

"The faculty are not as engaged as before, since they now have access to so much personal technology and some feel the language center is not relevant anymore." (2013)

Despite these challenges, LCs continue to fill an important role within institutions of learning and adapt quickly to changing circumstances. This has been particularly noticeable during the COVID-19 pandemic, when LCs pivoted to support remote instruction not only for language education but for other disciplinary areas on their campuses as well.

3.5 LC Budgets

Budgets are an ongoing concern of LC directors, and they provide another relevant data point when discussing the future of language centers with administrators and decision-makers. Questions addressing this were included in the survey starting in 2015. Table 7 shows details related to LC budgets: whether LCs had dedicated budget lines and the size of the budget allocation.

Table 7

LC Budgets in 2015, 2017, and 2019

	2015	2017	2019
Dedicated LC budget	Yes: 83% No: 17%	Yes: 77% No: 23%	Yes: 77% No: 23%
Budget allocation	Range: <$10,000– 120,000+ Mode: $120,000+ Median: $30,000– 39,999	Range: $2,800– 920,000 Mean: $127,965 Median: $64,750	Range: $6,500– 900,000 Mean: $229,160 Median: $93,500

Note. The 2015 survey contained budget ranges for this question, so a mean cannot be calculated; the latter two surveys provided a text field for this question, so only means are reported.

Over three-quarters of LCs had a dedicated budget throughout all survey years. The interpretation of this question and its results are relatively clear. However, the question about the size of the budget is much more difficult, both for directors to answer and for us to interpret. Because LC directors often express interest in knowing budget numbers, we include this information here, along with a breakdown by public and private institution status for 2017 and 2019 in Table 8, but some caveats are necessary. The wording of the question about the size of the budget was, "What is the language center/lab budget in US dollars?", so some of the submitted numbers include salaries, while others do not. (This has been updated for the 2021 survey to explicitly exclude salaries.) The question about budget categories (see Figure 12) shows that this is the case. Further complicating a reliable comparison across the three years is the fact that the 2015 survey provided ranges to select from, while the latter surveys asked directors to enter an amount.

The budget breakdown by public and private institution status (Table 8) shows that the average budget allocation at public institutions was significantly higher than at private institutions. Similarly, the lowest budget allocation was at private institutions in both years, while the highest budget allocation was at public institutions.

Table 8

LC Budget Allocations in 2017 and 2019, Public vs. Private Institutions

	2017		2019	
	Public	Private	Public	Private
Range	$5,000–920,000	$2,800–400,000	$8,000–900,000	$6,500–450,000
Mean	$209,497	$57,296	$184,584	$86,955
Median	$97,172	$19,231	$68,500	$44,000

Figure 12 (next page) shows which major categories were paid for out of the LC budget. The two most commonly chosen categories across all three years were student worker wages and experimental projects (e.g., purchasing software or subscriptions to online services to try them out). There was a steady decrease in the percentage of budgets that allocated funds for student labor from 2015 to 2019, possibly hinting at an increase in the workload for the director and full-time equivalent staff, especially related to more mundane tasks. The percentage of budgets that included funds for experimental projects also decreased from 2017 to 2019. More LCs had funds for professional development for center staff than had room in the budget for computer replacements. The latter could indicate that replacement cycles are funded by units other than the LC, although our data do not directly support this idea.

A clear trend emerged in the availability of travel funds within the LC budget. From 2015 to 2019, budgets that had funds earmarked to support travel fell from 78 to 45%. Note that many "no" responses were accompanied by comments that departmental or college funds were available for university-sponsored travel. In addition, the results from 2015 are not directly comparable to 2017 and 2019 because the 2015 survey only implicitly asked about whether travel support was a part of the budget ("How much travel funding do you have access to per year?"—responses that provided amounts or similar descriptions were coded as "yes," those that indicated no funds as "no"), whereas a specific item was added starting in 2017 ("Is travel funding a part of the center budget, and who is it earmarked for?").

3.6 Employee Work Hours

3.6.1 Full- and Part-Time Employees

LC directors reported the number of hours per week that full-time and part-time employees (excluding student employees) worked. This question was first included in the 2015 survey. We excluded one outlier from analysis (a report of 4,800 employee work hours per week).

Figure 12

LC Budget Categories

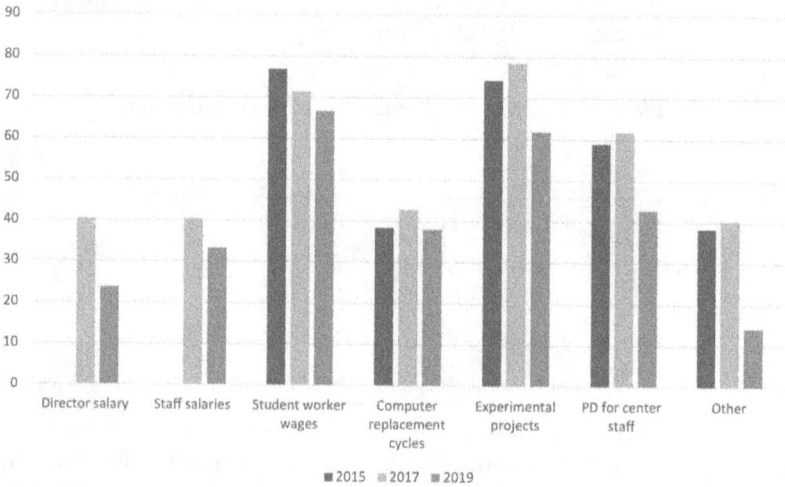

| | Director salary | Staff salaries | Student worker wages | Computer replacement cycles | Experimental projects | PD for center staff | Other |

Legend: ■ 2015 ■ 2017 ■ 2019

Note. Presented in percentages. This was a multiple-select item, so adding up individual percentages may exceed 100%. The options for director and staff salaries were added in 2017.

Figure 13

Availability of Travel Funds Within the LC Budget

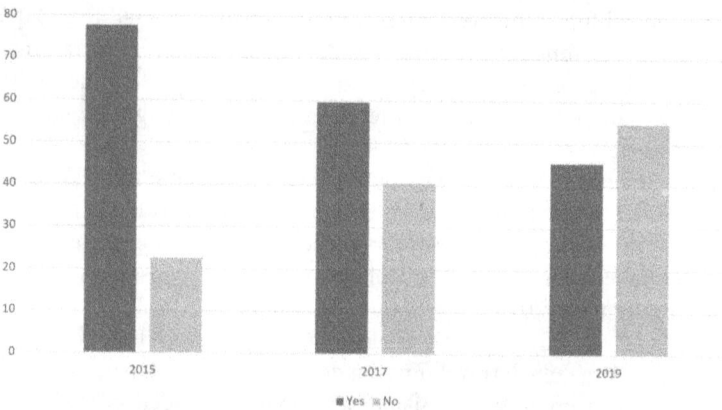

Legend: ■ Yes ■ No

2015   2017   2019

Note. Presented in percentages.

While the mean number of full- and part-time employee work hours per week remained relatively stable from 2015 to 2019 (98, 102, and 97 hours, respectively), the maximum end of the range increased from 400 to 650 to 800 per week, indicating a growing need to staff LCs within some institutions.

3.6.2 Student Employees

LC directors reported the number of hours per week that students worked. While responses from all years were generally in the hundreds of hours or less, two responses from 2013 were an order of magnitude larger (4,512 and 5,000). These responses could be typos, or the director could have understood the question as asking for the number of hours in a semester or year. (The question was updated in 2015 to indicate hours per week.) However, given other responses from the same directors about the number of student workers and the sizes of the centers, the LCs may simply have had unusually large numbers of student worker hours. Regardless of the reason for these responses, they were eliminated as clear outliers before analysis. The analysis showed that the mean number of student worker hours per week steadily increased in the first three survey years (2013–2017) from 63 to 74 to 85 hours. It then fell to the lowest level across survey years in 2019: 57 hours. Potentially, the mean number of student worker hours will continue to decrease in future years, especially given budget crunches related to the COVID-19 pandemic and the fact that many LCs had to close for some duration and make do without any student workers.

3.7 Center Evaluation

The majority of language centers are not formally evaluated (Figure 14). Many survey responses across all four years noted that informal, internal evaluations may take place, but most centers do not undergo a formal, regular evaluation process. Those directors who responded that their centers were formally evaluated indicated that the frequency of these evaluations is sporadic, and over a third noted that evaluations run on a 5- to 10-year cycle.

Figure 14

Language Center Formally Evaluated

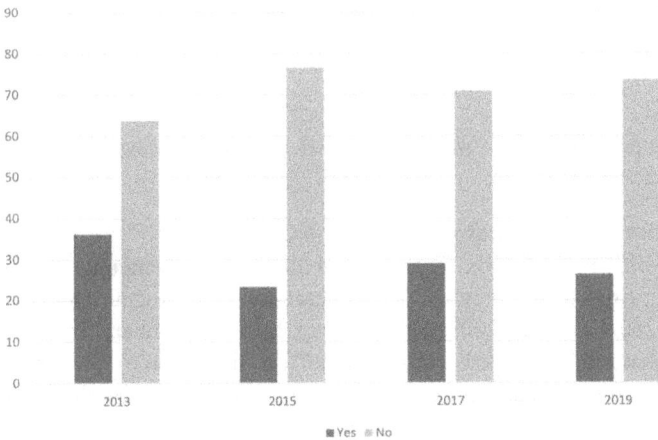

Note. Presented in percentages.

3.8 LC Users

In 2017, two questions were added to the survey to better understand intended stakeholders and actual LC users. While results from only two survey iterations cannot point toward any trends, we think the results may be interesting, especially to those who are not intimately familiar with the field.

The main intended audience for the work of most LCs in both 2017 and 2019 was students (40% and 48%) and faculty and students equally (51% and 43%) (this was a multiple-choice item). Only 7% and 5% of LCs in 2017 and 2019 served faculty only. When asked who actually uses the LC spaces, the responses mirrored the intended audience (Figure 15). Faculty and students were the main patrons of LCs, but the responses also highlighted other users, such as staff and institution-external patrons. The category "other" included high school and summer school students, external workshop attendees, and researchers. Note that in 2017, 100% of responses indicated that students were LC users.

Figure 15
LC Users

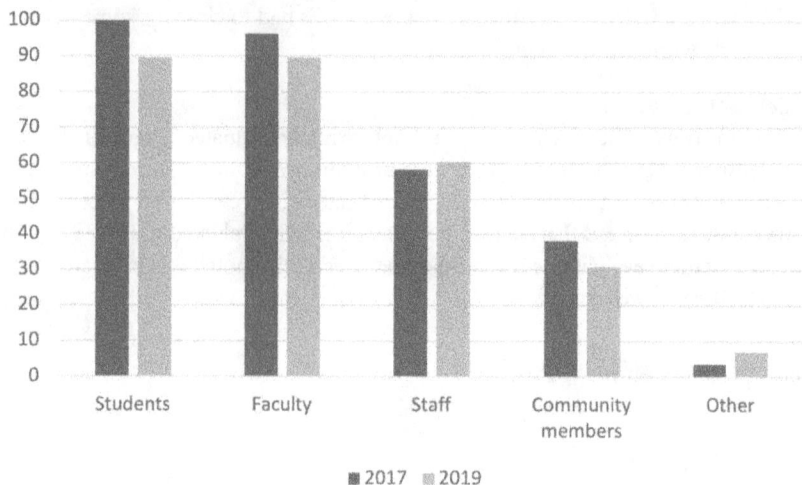

Note. Presented in percentages. This was a multiple-select item, so adding up individual percentages may exceed 100%.

3.9 Evolving From Language Labs to Language Centers

Anecdotal evidence abounds to show that the focus of language centers has been moving from technology to social interaction (e.g., Angell, DuBravac, & Gonglewski, 2007; Garrett, 2003; Kronenberg, 2014; Kronenberg & Lahaie, 2011; see also Sebastian, Gopalakrishnan, & Hendricks, this volume). To examine whether this transition from language lab to language center is taking place more generally, we analyzed the data from the four surveys.

3.9.1 What's in a Name?

First, we considered the likely relationship between LC names and how they are conceptualized by their stakeholders. For example, if the name of a particular LC was changed from "University Language Lab" to "University Language Center," the reason may be because it is intended to function more like a social center than a computer lab. While the data cannot tell us about the name changes of any particular LC, they can tell us about the overall usage of the words "lab" and "center" in LC names. The 2015, 2017, and 2019 surveys asked about this. The results showed that 73% of LCs included the word "center" in both 2015 and 2017, and 67% in 2019. Thus, LCs with "center" in their name are much more common than LCs with "lab" in their names, especially compared to 37% "centers" in 1988 (Lawrason, 1990) and 17% in 1975 (Stern, 1976a). However, these data do not clearly support the idea that labs are continuing to transition to language centers.

3.9.2 LC Functions and Spaces

Beyond the names of LCs, the survey data provide evidence of their functions. If we assume that LCs are transitioning from labs to centers, then we would expect the services and spaces that they provide to be more socially focused. That is, we would expect more LCs to provide social and event spaces and to plan events, and we would expect fewer LCs to provide computer labs.

While the definition of a computer lab is relatively clear, none of the surveys provided a definition of a virtual language lab. However, Lavolette (2018a) stated that "a virtual language center or lab provides language resources that can be used online" (p. 22), based on responses to the 2015 survey. While each participant may have had somewhat different ideas of virtual language labs in mind, this general definition will be adopted here. The impact on these virtual language labs is less clearly linked to the transition from lab to center, but a possible impact is that more virtual labs would be provided to compensate for the loss of physical labs.

We expected that more LCs would provide social and event spaces and plan events from 2013 to 2019, and the data generally confirm this (Figure 16, next page). In 2013, 53% of directors said that their LCs provided social spaces, rising to 70% in 2015, to 85% in 2017, and falling somewhat to 77% in 2019. Similarly, in 2013, 51% of directors said that their LCs provided event spaces, rising to 61% in 2015, to 74% in 2017, and falling slightly to 70% in 2019. Finally, in 2013, only 28% of directors said that their LCs planned events, rising to 54% in 2015, to 64% in 2017, and falling to 60% in 2019. The slight falling trend seen in all three categories in 2019 is likely to accelerate in 2021, given the difficulties in hosting in-person events during the COVID-19 pandemic.

On the other hand, the expected trends were contradicted by the data for physical and virtual lab environments (Figure 17). While we expected that fewer LC directors would report providing a physical language lab environment from 2015 to 2019 (no data were collected in 2013), more than two-thirds of LCs provided them in 2015 (70%), and that ratio rose to include nearly all LCs in 2017 (94%) and 2019 (92%). For virtual language labs, we had expected that more LCs would provide them over time to make up for the lack of physical language labs. Contrary to our expectation, 78% of directors indicated that they provided virtual language labs in 2015, with the percentage falling each year to 47% in 2017 and to 40% in 2019. Thus, in 2019, nearly all LCs still had physical lab spaces, but well under half also provided virtual lab spaces and could claim to be hybrid physical/virtual language laboratories. However, given the effects of the COVID-19 pandemic on education in 2020 and 2021, virtual language labs may be seeing a resurgence that would show up in the 2021 data.

Figure 16

Services Provided by LCs

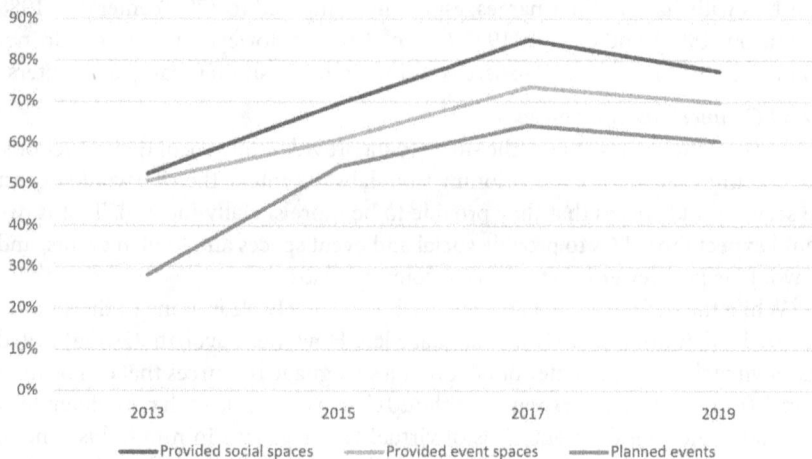

Provided social spaces · Provided event spaces · Planned events

Note. This was a multiple-select item, so adding up individual percentages may exceed 100%.

Figure 17

Physical and Virtual Lab Spaces Provided by LCs

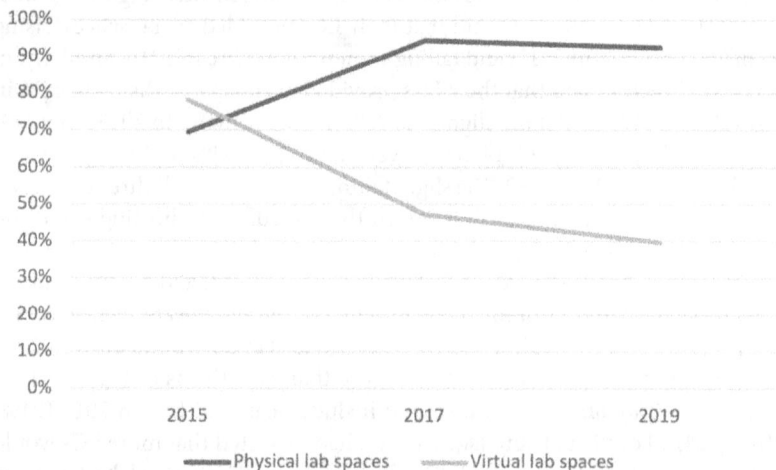

Physical lab spaces · Virtual lab spaces

Note. This was a multiple-select item, so adding up individual percentages may exceed 100%.

3.10 Other Language Center Services

Potentially interesting trends were seen in other services that LCs provide: professional development, offering technology, pedagogy, and computer-assisted language learning (CALL) programs, support for languages not taught at the institution, and lack of support for languages that are taught.

The number of LCs that provided professional development increased from 60% in 2013 to 76% in 2015, 79% in 2017, and fell back to 70% in 2019 (Figure 18, next page). Before the 2019 data were available, Lavolette (2019) reported this as a trend toward more LCs providing professional development. While the 2019 data muddy the waters, we can confidently state that the majority of LCs in the US (given that the majority of our data are from the US) have been providing professional development for language teachers since 2013 or earlier. This contrasts with Japanese self-access centers (SACs; see Thornton, Taylor, Tweed, & Yamashita, this volume), which generally do not provide professional development for language teachers, as Lavolette (2019) pointed out. In addition, Lavolette's evidence for this claim comes from a search of the *SiSAL Journal* (using the terms "professional development" and "faculty development"), which publishes SAC research from not only Japan, but from institutions worldwide, including elsewhere in Asia, the Middle East, Oceania, Europe, and North and South America. Thus, we claim that unlike US-style LCs, SACs in general do not provide PD for language teachers.

Related to professional development, there are fluctuations in the percentages of LCs offering technology, pedagogy, and CALL programs (in the four survey years from 2013 to 2019, 18% to 9% to 44% to 34% of LCs offered such programs). These offerings took many different forms, including workshop series, certificates, individual courses, and graduate degree programs. In some cases, these programs generate revenue for the LC through fees and tuition. This may point to the need for some LCs to think outside the box to support their budgets.

The number of LCs that supported languages not taught at their institution was also reported as a trend from 2013 to 2017 (Lavolette, 2019), although the trend disappeared in 2019. While this support increased from 30% to 35% to 40% in the first three survey years (2013 to 2017), it fell in 2019 to 32% (Figure 18). Support for languages not taught at the institution is common but is provided by well under half of LCs.

On the other hand, roughly 60% of institutions offered languages that the LC did not offer resources or support for (58% in 2015, 64% in 2017, and 59% in 2019). Most common among those non-supported languages were American Sign Language, English as a second language, and ancient and Indigenous languages.

4. Conclusion

While we have made every effort to ensure that our data and analysis are accurate, our interpretations should be treated with caution. First, no comprehensive database of US or global LCs is available, so we cannot state with any certainty what percentage of LCs were reached by the surveys. Thus, we cannot say how representative our results are for the US, and they are certainly not representative of global language spaces. Second, we cannot calculate a response rate because the surveys were distributed via social media, in addition to email. Finally, due to the anonymity of the survey responses, we cannot connect responses from the same participants from one year to another, nor do we know the percentages of new and repeated participants from year to year. Yet, the data provide important snapshots of the landscape of language centers in each survey year.

Figure 18

Support Provided by LCs for Professional Development and Languages Not Taught at the Host Institution

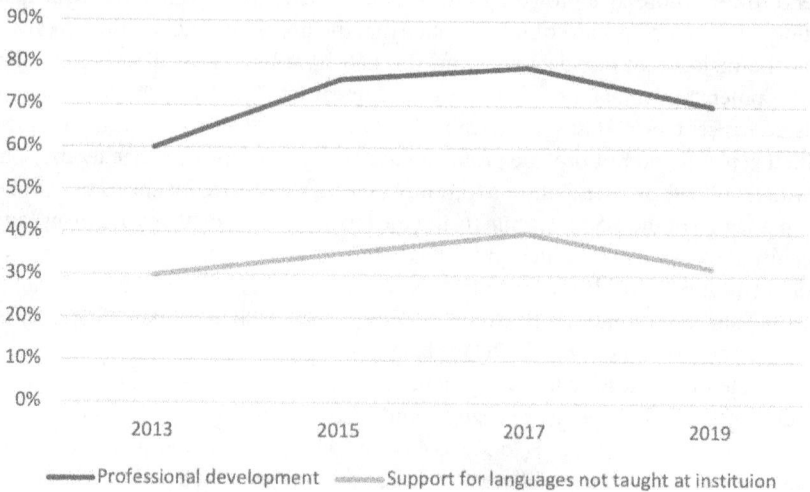

Note. This was a multiple-select item, so adding up individual percentages may exceed 100%.

Below, we describe the typical LC director and the typical language center and offer our interpretations. We conclude with a look to the trends we anticipate in future IALLT surveys.

4.1 The Typical LC Director

During the survey period, the typical director held an open-ended permanent position, with a 12-month non-faculty contract, was salaried at $60,000–70,000, and spent 90% or more of their work time on LC business. They did not teach and were not required to engage in research or publishing, but were expected to present at conferences.

From a certain perspective, 12-month employment and an open-ended permanent contract implies increasing job security for LC directors. That is, more directors have year-round employment and therefore, potentially a higher income than those on 9-month contracts. These numbers also point to the need for providing LC services year-round, making directors in higher demand. However, from another perspective, the change in contract length may simply be related to the increase in non-faculty director positions. That is, faculty are more likely to have 9-month contracts, while staff are more likely to have 12-month contracts.

Despite the indicators of job stability, the fact that the typical director does not teach and is not expected to engage in research implies that director positions are seen as more administrative than academic. If LC directors are not respected as members of the academic community through faculty status, and especially if LC directors are not tenured, they are vulnerable to budget cuts. Particularly in financially lean times, like a global pandemic, non-tenured employees may be seen as dispensable (e.g., Lavolette, 2018b). The forthcoming 2021 survey results may provide more information about how the pandemic has affected employment stability.

While the typical director was highly satisfied with their salary, working hours, and job overall, challenges were related to job preparation, type of position, and general concerns about the LC. Most LC directors felt that their academic degrees did not prepare them for the day-to-day management of a center, including aspects like finance, personnel management, and leadership. Many lamented the lack of upward mobility and a sense of being seen as an administrative staff member rather than as an academic.

4.2 The Typical LC

The main users of the typical LC were students, faculty, and staff. The typical LC had a dedicated budget, although there was no typical budget size. The budget covered student worker wages, experimental projects, and PD for center staff, among other costs. It was increasingly unlikely to include travel funds for LC employees.

The typical LC had full- and part-time employees who worked a combined total of about 100 hours per week. Student workers made a significant contribution to staffing, working a combined total of about 60 to 85 hours per week over the years of the survey.

The typical LC was not formally evaluated, although it was informally evaluated internally. We hope that the creation of the IALLT Language Center Evaluation Toolkit (Simon et al., 2015; see also Lavolette & Kraemer, 2017) can help address this gap and provide an evaluation guide to those who may not be familiar with language centers and their work.

LCs showed some tendencies toward being "centers," starting with the typical LC's name, which contained the word "center" but not the word "lab." In addition, the typical LC provided social spaces and event spaces and planned events from 2013 to 2019. It also provided professional development for language teachers. However, the typical LC still provided physical lab spaces. Somewhat surprisingly, the typical LC did not provide virtual lab spaces.

General challenges faced by the typical LC included declining language enrollments (mirroring the downward trend at US institutions of higher education more generally, see Looney & Lusin, 2019), budget cuts, and lower relevance and use among students and faculty.

4.3 Future

The global pandemic was the dominant force for change in 2020 in all sectors of life, and language education was no exception. It undoubtedly had adverse effects on language centers, prompting the reduction of budgets, reduced part- and full-time staffing, and potentially even the closing of centers at financially weak institutions. However, it also provided opportunities for LCs to shine at what they do best: supporting language learners and teachers, both pedagogically and technologically. We are optimistic that many of them were able to prove their worth to their institutions and communities. Thus, we anticipate that the following areas will show positive changes, particularly in the wake of the pandemic:

- More LCs will provide virtual language lab spaces and other online services, such as language tutoring and conversation hours (see also Sebastian, Gopalakrishnan, & Hendricks, this volume), making these services available to more students.
- More LCs will undertake formal evaluations in an effort to justify their budgets and use of space, for example by using the Language Center Evaluation Toolkit (Simon et al., 2015).
- More LCs will provide online professional development targeting a broader geographical range of language teachers due to ease of providing access to virtual events, even to remote attendees. For example, the annual symposium of the Consortium for Language Teaching and Learning in 2021, held virtually for the first time, attracted more than three times the usual number of participants, including attendees from all over the world.

We believe that LCs have an important role to play in their institutions and communities and have made a particular contribution in maintaining educational continuity during the pandemic. They will also be leading the way as educational institutions recover.

References

Angell, J., DuBravac, S., & Gonglewski, M. (2007). Towards higher ground: Transforming language labs into language centers. *IALLT Journal of Language Learning Technologies, 39*(1), 1–16. https://doi.org/10.17161/iallt.v39i1.8468

Editors of J.E.T.T. (1989). J.E.T.T. reader profile survey. *Journal of Educational Techniques and Technologies, 22*(4), 44–51. https://doi.org/10.17161/iallt.v22i4.9361

Garrett, N. (2003). Language learning centers: An overview. In U. Lahaie (Ed.), *The IALLT management manual* (2nd., pp. 1–9). Wheeling, IL: International Association for Language Learning Technology.

Kraemer, A., & Lavolette, E. (2017, June 22). *Results of the 2017 IALLT survey* [Conference session]. International Association for Language Learning Technology Conference, Moorhead, MN.

Kraemer, A., & Ledgerwood, M. (2019, June 22). *IALLT survey results* [Conference session]. International Association for Language Learning Technology Conference, Eugene, OR.

Kronenberg, F. A. (2014). Language center design and management in the post-language laboratory era. *The IALLT Journal, 44*(1), 1–16. https://doi.org/10.17161/iallt.v44i1.8532

Kronenberg, F. A. (2016). Curated language learning spaces: Design principles of physical 21st century language centers. *The IALLT Journal, 46*(1), 63–91. https://doi.org/10.17161/iallt.v46i1.8554

Kronenberg, F. A., & Lahaie, U. (Eds.). (2011). *Language center design*. Memphis, TN: International Association for Language Learning and Technology.

Lavolette, E. (2018a). Language center mandates and realities. In E. Lavolette & E. F. Simon (Eds.), *Language center handbook* (pp. 3–33). Auburn, AL: International Association for Language Learning Technology.

Lavolette, E. (2018b). The tenuous status of language centers. In E. Lavolette & E. F. Simon (Eds.), *Language center handbook* (p. xv). Auburn, AL: International Association for Language Learning Technology.

Lavolette, E. (2019). A very brief introduction to US language centers. In L. Xethakis & C. Taylor (Eds.), *JASAL 2018 x SUTLF 5: Selected papers from the Sojo University Teaching and Learning Forum 2018: Making connections* (pp. 4–25). Kumamoto, Japan: NanKyu JALT. https://www.nankyujalt.org/publications#h.p_twJDnQsJDWmj

Lavolette, E., & Kraemer, A. (2017). The language center evaluation toolkit: Context, development, and usage. In F. A. Kronenberg (Ed.), *From language lab to language center and beyond: The past, present, and future of the language center* (pp. 147–160). Auburn, AL: International Association for Language Learning Technology.

Lavolette, E., & Kraemer, A. (June 2019). *Predicting the future of IALLT based on the past: IALLT Survey 2013-2017.* [Conference session]. International Association for Language Learning Technology Conference, Eugene, OR.

Lawrason, R. E. (1990). The changing state of the language lab: Results of the 1988 IALL member survey. *IALL Journal of Language Learning Technologies*, 23(2), 19–24. https://doi.org/10.17161/iallt.v23i2.9387

Looney, D., & Lusin, N. (2019). *Enrollments in languages other than English in United States institutions of higher education, Summer 2016 and fall 2016: Final report.* https://www.mla.org/content/download/110154/2406932/2016-Enrollments-Final-Report.pdf

Pankratz, D., & Ross, A. (2006). The 2005 IALLT survey of the profession. *IALLT Journal of Language Learning Technologies*, 38(1), 15–48. https://doi.org/10.17161/iallt.v38i1.8450

Simon, E. F., Kraemer, A., Kronenberg, F. A., Lavolette, E., & Sartiaux, A. (2015). Language Center Evaluation Toolkit. *International Association for Language Learning Technology.* https://v.gd/toolkit

Stern, R. (1976a). The university language/learning laboratory. A survey of the facilities: Their technologies; disciplines; organizations. Part I. *NALLD Journal*, 10(2), 7–24. https://doi.org/10.17161/iallt.v10i2.8954

Stern, R. (1976b). The university language/learning laboratory. A survey of the facilities: Their technologies; disciplines; organizations. Part II. *NALLD Journal*, 10(3–4), 16–39. https://doi.org/10.17161/iallt.v10i3-4.8963

Webber, K. L. (2018). The working environment matters: Faculty member job satisfaction by institution type. *Research Dialogue, 142*, 1–36.

Author Notes

Elizabeth (Betsy) Lavolette is Associate Professor of English at Kyoto Sangyo University. She holds a PhD in Second Language Studies with a focus on CALL from Michigan State University, and she was previously Director of the Language Resource Center at Gettysburg College (Pennsylvania, USA). Her research focuses on language learning and teaching with technology, professional development, language learning spaces, and forging connections between scholars and literatures of such spaces in the US, Japan, and globally.

Angelika Kraemer is the Director of the Language Resource Center at Cornell University. She received her PhD in German Studies from Michigan State University, specializing in second language acquisition and CALL. She currently serves as President of IALLT (2021–2023) and is Co-Editor of the journal *Die Unterrichtspraxis/Teaching German* published by the American Association of Teachers of German. Her research interests include second language acquisition, specifically technology-enhanced language learning, program development, community engagement and service learning, and assessment.

Correspondence concerning this chapter should be addressed to Elizabeth Lavolette (betsy@cc.kyoto-su.ac.jp).

Designing and Redesigning
Language Spaces

Chapter 6

Re-Engineering Self-Access Language Centers: Reaching Out to Students and Promoting Learner Autonomy

Vickie Wai Kei Li and Joe Wai Kin Ching, Hong Kong Polytechnic University, Hong Kong

Abstract

This chapter reports on a research project that aimed to re-engineer the self-access language center (SALC) of a Hong Kong university. With the advancements in technology and an increasingly diverse student population, SALCs need to transform from simply libraries of self-study learning materials to engaging learning spaces that can cultivate independent and autonomous learners. The present project has three main phases. In Phase 1, an online questionnaire survey and focus group interviews were conducted to collect center users' views on the learning materials, facilities, and language support services provided by the center. Center users' feedback informed and shaped the changes made to the center during Phase 2. The re-engineering stage focused on five main areas: i) redesigning the layout of the center, ii) revising and reorganizing the center's existing materials, iii) developing more and varied learning materials, iv) organizing more theme-week workshops, and v) providing regular language support services. Phase 3 focused on the evaluation of the changes made to the center. Feedback was collected from center users through questionnaires and interviews regarding their perceptions of the redesigned center. Center users generally had positive attitudes towards the changes made. They valued the welcoming and motivating learning environment, the variety of learning materials available, and the more regular and frequent consultation services at the center. The strategies adopted in this project to transform a SALC offer insights into the redesign of SALCs of other universities.

Learner autonomy has been a major concern in language education since the 1990s. While helping students develop their language skills is important, language educators have also emphasized supporting students to become autonomous learners. Little (2003) stated that the central role of language educators is to "create and maintain a learning environment in which learners can be autonomous" (para. 5). With an aim to support and facilitate learner autonomy in language learning, many universities have established self-access language centers (SALCs) to complement classroom teaching. Cotterall and Reinders (2000) defined a SALC as a place that "consists of a number of resources (in the form of materials, activities and support)" and is set up to "accommodate learners of different levels, styles, goals and interests [and to] develop autonomy among its users" (p. 24). The design, operation, and management of SALCs across universities vary, yet they share an objective: to provide students opportunities to learn how to learn, using their own styles, at their own pace, so that eventually, students can become autonomous learners.

In Hong Kong, each post-secondary institution has at least one SALC that offers language-enhancement courses or activities to the student body. These SALCs were established in the early 1990s, following a government-funded initiative to enhance the English language proficiency of university students (who mostly speak Cantonese as their first language). All of these SALCs provide support for students' English learning, while some also offer support for students to learn Asian and European languages (Gardner, 2001). During the 1990s, these SALCs were "something along the lines of a hybrid between a small, dedicated library, and an open-access lab" (Gardner, 2017, p. 148). They contained a range of language learning materials, such as books, photocopied materials, and equipment like computers and televisions. These resources were only accessible during the center's open hours.

In Hong Kong, English is taught as a subject from primary to university education. The aim of establishing a SALC is to provide students more exposure to the English language outside the classroom. With the emergence of the concepts of learner autonomy and independent language learning, the SALCs in Hong Kong have started to evolve. Not only do they provide students with more out-of-class English learning opportunities, but these centers also provide support to enable the users to learn how to learn, to help them be more responsible for their learning, and to cater to individual differences (Benson, 2011; Chia, 2007; Dickinson, 1987; Sheerin, 1989). For example, language advisory services like a help desk and one-on-one consultations are provided to help students understand more about their own learning styles and make them aware of the importance of becoming independent language learners.

Over the past 20 years, technology has played an increasingly vital role in the SALCs of the post-secondary institutions in Hong Kong, and several studies have documented this change. Gardner and Miller (2011) noted that hard copies of learning materials have become soft copies and easily accessible online. Various types of technology, such as movable computers on wheels and web-based language learning tools and materials, are also provided at the centers. These technological advances have brought significant impact on language learning. For example, language learners can now remotely access learning resources that were often only available in a library or a SALC. Through web-based learning, language learners can access the internet, searching, selecting, and drawing upon new information to build their knowledge. These activities facilitate personalized learning and learner autonomy.

Technological developments appear to have offered great potential for self-access learning and yet, they may pose some challenges to the operation of SALCS. With the prevalence of mobile technology (such as smartphones and tablets), the internet, and social networking sites, the learning materials at SALCs have become less attractive (Choi, 2017). Learners can now easily access language learning materials through their own mobile devices anytime, anywhere, and they have become less interested in visiting a SALC. SALCs need to transform from simply libraries of self-study learning materials to places that increase students' engagement with the learning materials and other center users, paving learners' way to autonomous learning.

Nevertheless, before any transformation can take place, the effectiveness of a SALC should be evaluated. Gardner (2001) contended that such an evaluation helps indicate "the good and bad practices as well as areas needing further development" (p. 162). This will then facilitate the development of new learning materials and activities at the center. Gardner (2001) also indicated that such an evaluation should involve stakeholders such as the center users, teachers, and center staff members. Center users need to know whether visiting the center is effective for their learning. Teachers need to know if the services they provide at the center are effective in enhancing students' learning. The center staff members need to consider whether they manage and operate the center effectively to facilitate students' learning. Drawing upon Gardner's (2001) ideas on the evaluation of the effectiveness of SALCs, the two-year research project described in this chapter aimed to collect views from the stakeholders of a SALC at Hong Kong Polytechnic University, and based on these stakeholders' views, the authors (the principal investigators of the project) have redesigned the center.

In this chapter, the authors describe and discuss the changes made to the SALC under study. Drawing upon the data from the two-year research project, we discuss the strategies adopted to redesign the center, transforming it from a traditional self-study learning environment to one that is more welcoming and motivating. In the following five sections, we first provide background information on SALCs in Hong Kong, with a particular focus on the center examined in the project and the rationale for the project. In Section 2, we present a brief description of the two-year research project and its findings, which are the basis of the changes made to the center. A detailed discussion of these changes is presented in Section 3 of the chapter. The chapter ends with an evaluation of the changes made to the center (Section 4) and discussion of the insights that those changes may bring to SALCs in other countries (Section 5).

1. The Center for Independent Language Learning Before the Re-Engineering

Most of the universities in Hong Kong use English as the medium of teaching. One way to enhance the English proficiency of Hong Kong students (who mainly speak Cantonese as their first language) is the establishment of a SALC. Self-access learning started to occupy a prominent position in the higher education sector in Hong Kong in the 1990s (Gardner & Miller, 1999, 2011; Morrison, 2008, 2011). All the universities in Hong Kong have dedicated resources to the development of a self-access center for their students. These centers vary in size, but they all function to provide resources to users to enhance the learning of languages. Some centers mainly offer support for students' English learning, while some also offer language courses to support students' learning of other languages, including Putonghua (the official national spoken language in mainland China), French, and Spanish. The support and help provided by these centers are in different formats, ranging from physical learning materials, to seminars and workshops, to face-to-face consultations. Some of these centers are operated as individual academic units, and others are under the governance of the English department at the university.

The Center for Independent Language Learning (CILL) described in this chapter is part of the English Language Center (ELC) of the Hong Kong Polytechnic University (PolyU). The ELC provides English enhancement courses to undergraduate and postgraduate students at PolyU. The CILL was established in 2007, and its major task is to plan and provide out-of-class English learning activities for PolyU students. The center also aims to support and encourage PolyU students to learn English in a self-directed mode and develop as independent language learners. The CILL provides students a self-access learning space and offers a wide range of different types of materials and activities that help students become aware of their language abilities and learning needs. It also provides them guidance to regulate their learning strategies that enable them to construct their own learning. The materials and facilities provided at the CILL before the redesign are briefly described below:

- **The CILL award scheme.** This learning incentive scheme encouraged students to work on a set of English learning tasks designed by the ELC teachers. Students received CILL certificates (bronze, silver, or gold) based on the number of hours spent and learning tasks completed at the CILL.
- **Writing Assistance Program (WAP) and Speaking Assistance Program (SAP).** The WAP and SAP provided one-on-one writing or speaking consultations. These consultations were conducted in two separate rooms located near the reception desk at CILL. Teachers from the ELC provided guidance and suggestions on how students could further improve their English writing and speaking skills. Students had to make an appointment in advance, and each consultation lasted for 50 minutes.
- **Help desk service.** A teacher from the ELC sat at the help desk at a designated time to address students' immediate questions related to their English learning. The help desk service was not provided on a regular and frequent

basis. It rarely met students' needs, especially during the period prior to assignment submission dates.

- **Workshops.** One-time workshops were often offered to students during the semester. These workshops covered a wide range of topics, such as writing a cover letter and a resume and learning English vocabulary through reading.
- **Learning materials.** Language learning books for practice and reference, TVs, VCRs, DVDs, and audio resources were provided.
- **Multimedia computers.** These provided access to language learning software, educational programs, the internet, and video conferencing.
- **A comprehensive set of indexes (computerized).** These provided students information to help them locate the materials relevant to their needs.
- **A range of in-house designed worksheets.** These provided practice in various language areas.
- **Board games.** Students can practice their English skills using these games (e.g., Scrabble). (They remain in the CILL after the redesign.)
- **Fifteen self-study rooms.** Each room can accommodate up to eight people. Students used these study rooms for self-study or group discussion on a first-come, first-served basis. Each room was also equipped with a desktop computer and a TV screen.
- **Book of the month.** A book was recommended each month in line with the university's suggestion of fostering a reading atmosphere on campus. To encourage students to read the selected book and to enhance their reading experience, background information sheets, movie DVDs, and multiple copies of the book were provided at the CILL for students to borrow.

Both before and after the redesign, a center manager, an executive officer, and two supporting staff members are responsible for the daily operation of the CILL. The CILL functions very much like a library. It is open from 9:30 a.m. to 6:30 p.m. from Monday to Friday and 9:00 a.m. to noon on Saturday. During the two-year project, we had a chance to interview the CILL staff members (more information on the interviews is in Section 2.1.2). Based on the data collected from them, students usually used the purchased learning materials at the CILL to prepare for English proficiency examinations such as the International English Language Testing System (IELTS) and the Test of English as a Foreign Language (TOEFL). Many students visited the center in groups and used the self-study rooms to discuss projects and assignments. The CILL was mainly a place that provided language-learning materials, in combination with 15 self-study rooms.

The CILL was set up in 2007, and the layout and design was rather traditional. The old-fashioned chairs and desks were arranged in rows. There was no open space in which interactive activities could be conducted (Figures 1 and 2). The CILL staff members also reported in the interviews that fewer and fewer students used the computers at the CILL. Figure 3 shows a row of workstations with a desktop computer and a monitor placed near the windows. It was common to see an increasing number of students bringing their own laptops and tablets to the CILL. Students can easily access the internet for online learning resources, and this has made the physical copies of the learning materials at the center less attractive. Given the changing and diverse learning needs of students and the growth of electronic resources, we conducted a research project with the goal of transforming the CILL from a self-study space into a welcoming space that enables not only independent but also collaborative and interactive learning. As Little (1994) stated, independent learning can be facilitated through social interaction. We hope that the center can become a more flexible learning space that facilitates and supports more dynamic learning.

Figure 1
Learning Space at the CILL Before the Redesign

Figure 2
Furniture Arranged in Rows Before the Redesign

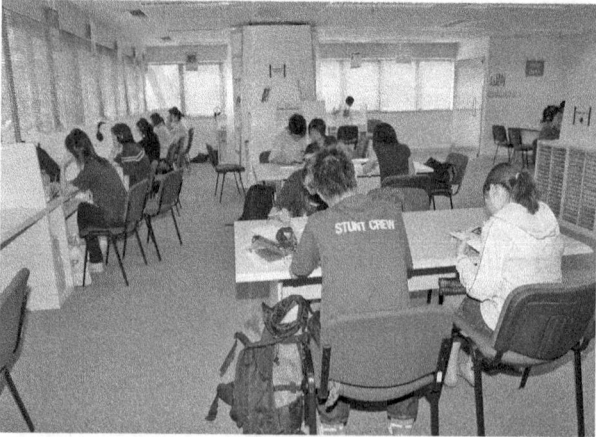

Figure 3

Workstations at the CILL Before the Redesign

2. The Two-Year Project to Redesign the CILL

Funded by a Teaching Development and Language Enhancement Grant from PolyU, the two-year research project aimed to redesign the CILL to create a more supportive and engaging environment for students. We hope that the learning materials and activities at the CILL, after the redesign, enable students to learn to decide for themselves what, when, where, and how to study, based on such factors as their style and pace of study, the level and type of materials they use, and in which activities they participate. The research project was guided by the following objectives:

i.   to redesign the layout of the CILL, making it more lively and student-friendly and providing a more flexible space to facilitate more interactions among students;
ii. to reorganize the existing learning materials at the CILL, making them easier to locate;
iii. to develop more varied English learning materials to support a broader student population;
iv. to introduce theme-week workshops, attracting more students to learn at the CILL; and
v.   to provide a help desk service for students on a more regular and frequent basis.

The project had three main phases. Phase 1 consisted of data collection and analysis. The data were collected through online questionnaires and interviews. These data form the basis of the changes made to the center during Phase 2 of the project. A description of the data collection and analysis process is presented in Section 2.1. Phase 3 of the project was an evaluation of the redesign of the CILL.

2.1 Methods

Before beginning the redesign, we gathered the stakeholders' views to help indicate the good and bad practices at the center and adjustments that could be made. We collected data from students, ELC teachers, and two CILL staff members. Online questionnaire surveys and interviews were conducted during Phases 1 and 3.

2.1.1 Online Questionnaire Surveys

Two questionnaires were used in this study. The first (Appendix A), used during Phase 1, aimed to collect students' views on the materials and facilities provided by the CILL. The way students perceive the importance of English learning and their own learning needs may impact their perception of the effectiveness of the self-access center. Thus, at the beginning of the questionnaire, students were asked to evaluate their proficiency in academic English and describe their use of the CILL to support their English learning. Students were also asked to describe the changes they would like to see at the center. Upon the completion of the questionnaire, students were invited to participate in a post-questionnaire interview during which they could share their learning experiences at the CILL. This first online questionnaire was created using Survey Monkey and was sent to 260 students who took the courses taught at the ELC during the Fall semester of the academic year 2017–18. We chose this group of students in the belief that they would be more likely to respond than other groups. This is because the CILL is part of the ELC, and ELC teachers are required to promote the CILL's activities and services to their students. Altogether, 76 students (29%) completed the questionnaire. Fifteen students agreed to participate in the post-questionnaire interview. A description of the interviews is presented in Section 2.1.2.

Phase 3 of the project focused on evaluating the changes made during the redesign of the CILL. To understand more about what students thought about the "new" CILL, a second questionnaire was developed for CILL users. This second questionnaire aimed to find out about students' use of the facilities and services at the CILL, how often they visited the center, and how much time they spent there (see Appendix B). We emailed this second questionnaire to 628 students who visited the CILL after the redesign, and 76 students emailed their completed questionnaire back to us. Major findings from these questionnaires are presented in Section 2.2 and Section 4.

2.1.2 Interviews

To obtain a holistic and comprehensive picture of what happens in the CILL, individual face-to-face semistructured interviews were conducted with students, ELC teachers, and CILL staff members in English during Phases 1 and 3 of the project. The interviews conducted with students during Phase 1 aimed to provide students a chance to share their perceptions toward and experiences at the CILL. Each interview lasted around 30 to 45 minutes. The questions used in the interviews were:

- Have you visited the CILL? Why or why not?
- What is your general impression of the CILL?
- Which services/facilities at the CILL can help improve your English language skills/meet your learning needs?
- What is your opinion regarding the one-on-one writing and speaking consultation?

- What do you think of the learning materials at the CILL?
- Have you ever asked the help desk teachers for help or used the computers at the center? Why or why not?
- What improvements would you like to see to the learning materials and language support services at the CILL?

Also during Phase 1, interviews were conducted with nine ELC teachers to gain a better understanding of their views on the language support offered at the CILL. These nine teachers have provided help desk consultation services at the CILL. The questions asked in the semistructured interviews with teachers were as follows:

- What is your general impression of the CILL?
- Which services/facilities at the CILL can help improve the English language skills of your students?
- Do you think the learning materials at the CILL can meet students' learning needs?
- Which services or facilities need improvement?
- With the increase in students' use of mobile devices (smart phones, tablets, and laptops), do you think:
  - the learning materials at the CILL are still relevant?
  - the computers are still needed at the CILL?
- Do you prefer conducting English learning activities/workshops in a formal classroom or at the CILL?

The second round of interviews was conducted during Phase 3 of the project. Semistructured interviews were conducted with students and CILL staff members. This round of interviews focused on the interviewees' perceptions of the redesigned CILL and their experiences at the CILL. Students were asked the following questions:

- Have you visited the CILL lately? If yes, did you notice any differences between the CILL now and previous visits?
- What is your general impression of the CILL?
- Which services/facilities at the CILL did you use during your visit(s)? Did you find them useful to improve your English language skills? Did you find that these services/facilities meet your learning needs?
- What do you think of the learning materials at the CILL?
- Have you ever asked the help desk teachers for help? Why or why not?
- What improvements would you like to see to the learning materials and language support services at the CILL?

One challenge that we faced in Phase 3 was students' availability to participate in the interviews. We planned to conduct the Phase 3 interviews during the summer because we thought students would be less busy at the end of the academic year. However, the student participants informed us that they had already made plans for the summer, for example, job placements, internships, and overseas exchange programs. In view of students' busy schedules, we conducted the Phase 3 interviews over the telephone.

During Phase 3, we also collected feedback from the two CILL staff members. We asked the following questions in semistructured interviews in English:

- Based on your observation and the consultation booking system at the CILL, which are the most utilized services/facilities after the redesign?
- How frequently do the CILL users use the noisy zone, the quiet study area, and the 15 self-study rooms?
- How frequently do the CILL users use the computerized index system to locate learning materials?
- Do you think the open hours are too long/too short/about right?
- What is the busiest time period at the CILL?
- Do the CILL users speak in English or their mother tongue in the CILL?

A thematic analysis was conducted on the interview data to highlight the CILL users' perceptions of the role of the CILL in their English learning, the "ideal" CILL in the users' and teachers' mind, and their impressions of the redesigned CILL. Major findings from the interviews are presented in Section 2.3.

2.1.3 Collecting Feedback via Email

To collect feedback from the ELC teachers about the redesigned CILL, we invited the ELC teachers to give us their comments on the changes made to the center. An ELC meeting is conducted at the beginning of each academic year. To introduce the redesigned CILL to the ELC teachers, one author of this chapter provided a short description of the changes that took place at the CILL and invited the ELC teachers to email us their comments about the changes they observed. Five teachers gave us their feedback (summarized in Section 4).

2.1.4 Site Visits to SALCs at Other Universities

During Phase 1 of the project, the authors visited SALCs in five other Hong Kong universities. These SALCs vary in size and the language support they provide to students. Similar to the CILL, these SALCs mainly provide language learning materials, a range of workshops/seminars, and consultations to students. During the site visits, we focused mainly on examining the physical setup of furniture (e.g., fixed vs. mobile chairs, rectangular vs. round tables) and whether the learning space facilitates interaction among students. To understand more about the function and operation of each center, we also had the chance to talk to the staff members or teachers there. We discussed the following questions with these SALC staff members and teachers:

- What is your general impression of the self-access center at your university (the physical layout, the learning materials)?
- Which are the most/least utilized service(s)/facilities at the center?
- Which services or facilities need further improvement?
- With the increase in students' use of mobile devices (smart phones, tablets, and laptops), do you think:
  - the learning materials at your center are still relevant?
  - the computers (if any) are still needed at your center?

The site visits gave us inspirational ideas for the redesign of the CILL layout. We were also able to learn from the other centers how well a particular design has worked out and how it can be adapted to fit the space at and serve the purposes of the CILL.

2.2 Major Findings From the Phase 1 Online Questionnaire

The responses collected through the online questionnaire during Phase 1 of the project reveal that most of the respondents encountered difficulties in writing or speaking academic English. Nearly half of the respondents (48%) expressed that they had difficulties in finding the right academic phrase to express their ideas. The two other major difficulties encountered were "Organizing ideas and connecting them in a logical way" and "Difficult to start writing." Note that students did not tend to seek help from the CILL when they had difficulties in their English writing or speaking. The CILL has promoted the writing and speaking support services across the campus and yet, students preferred to seek help and advice from their own departmental teachers, their classmates, or the university library. Another surprising finding was that more than half of the respondents (57%) reported that they had never used the services or facilities at the CILL before. Some of the respondents (23%) also indicated that they had heard about the center but were not sure how the CILL could help with their English learning.

Most of the respondents who had used the services at the CILL indicated that they visited the center only once each semester. Only a few of them (13%) visited the center more than once each semester. When asked which service or facility they found the most helpful, nearly half of the respondents (48%) indicated that the writing and speaking consultations really helped improve their English skills. While physical learning materials are available at the CILL, many of the respondents (62%) indicated that they would like the center to provide more online materials on the CILL website. 75% of the respondents wanted the center to provide more workshops on a more regular basis.

2.3 Major Findings From the Phase 1 Semistructured Interviews

Semistructured interviews were conducted with 15 students. During the interviews, the students shared their experiences in using the services and facilities at the center. Their general impressions of the learning environment of the CILL were positive. Out of the 15 respondents, eight (53%) indicated that they used the services at the center to help improve their academic writing. In line with the responses from the questionnaire, the interviewees indicated that the writing consultations were the most helpful. During the 50-minute consultations at the CILL, students brought in their own writing and sought advice on how to improve their writing skills. Students valued these one-on-one consultations, which they did not find in their home departments. Regarding the facilities provided at the CILL, 10 students (67%) frequently used the self-study rooms for group discussions on projects and assignments. Eight students (53%) reported that they enjoyed watching English movie DVDs at the center. When asked the reason for choosing to study at the CILL rather than the library, around half (47%) of the respondents expressed that the learning environment at the CILL was quieter than the library, and they were able to seek help from the teacher at the help desk for some quick-fix questions. Note that while some students preferred to study in the quiet environment at the CILL, the other half of the interviewees (53%) wanted to see more interactive spaces at the CILL to support various kinds of learning and social activities. The respondents' idea of creating more interactive learning spaces was in line with the teachers' responses in the interviews during Phase 1. The ELC teachers agreed that the physical space at the CILL could be made flexible to provide spaces for students to conduct discussions. During the site visits to the other SALCs in Hong Kong, the authors noticed that all five centers had designated a particular area for students to hold different types of learning activities. The staff members at these other SALCs indicated that students often gathered in this designated area to conduct their discussions or hold learning activities in a more relaxed manner.

During the interviews with the students, we also asked those who had never visited the CILL about their reasons for not using the services at the center. These students indicated that they would like to use the consultation service, but they experienced difficulties in making appointments because all the available time slots were often fully booked. The number of writing consultation sessions did not seem to meet the growing demand from the students, especially during the middle of the semester when most students need to submit their midterm assessments. The student respondents wanted to have more writing consultation sessions added to the existing schedule. In addition, some of them suggested that more promotion is needed so that they would be informed of the workshops or activities organized at the center. Regarding the learning materials, some students described them as "too general" and said that they would like to see more discipline-specific materials at the CILL. This view is in line with the teachers' responses in the interviews. The ELC teachers who provided assistance to students at the help desk and in the writing consultations also stated that they wished to see more discipline-specific learning materials developed to meet the learning needs of students from different backgrounds.

3. The Redesign of the CILL

The findings from Phase 1 of the project helped inform the redesign of the CILL. The authors considered the views collected from the student and teacher participants and the information obtained during the site visits. A list of the major areas that needed to be revamped was developed. These areas included i) the physical space of the center, ii) the learning materials at the center, and iii) the types of language support provided at the center. The authors then discussed the feasibility of making changes to the three main areas with the CILL manager, the ELC Director, and the facility management office at the university. Because of limited time and resources, it was decided that the redesign would focus on the following areas:

i. Redesigning the learning space at the center by setting up a "noisy zone;"
ii. Reorganizing the existing in-house and purchased learning materials;
iii. Developing more varied learning materials, including discipline-specific materials for students;

iv. Planning and providing theme-week workshops; and

v. Providing regular language support services.

In the sections below, we describe in detail the changes made to the CILL during Phase 2 of the project.

3.1 Redesigning the Learning Space at the Center: Setting up a "Noisy Zone"

The learning space at the CILL, as described by some of the student respondents, was rather traditional. Rectangular desks with immobile chairs were arranged in rows (Figures 1 and 2). The layout was similar to a conventional classroom setting. The old layout of the furniture at the CILL limited the flexibility of the learning space. The physical setup of furniture exerts much influence on students' learning and interaction (Earthman & Lemasters, 2011), and the use of space at a SALC is important to consider to establish a welcoming and motivating learning environment (Barrs, 2010). During the redesign of the learning space at the CILL, we considered flexibility, mobility, and the variety of the furniture. We purchased new furniture and arranged it in a way that makes the learning space more appealing to a larger student body and sufficiently flexible to support the various types of workshops and learning activities organized by the CILL. We hope that the CILL can provide a learning space in which students can work both individually and in groups. It can also be a space for students to relax and mingle with their friends. Extra-curricular activity groups such as the English club can also organize meetings and activities in the CILL.

Based on the site visit observations, the ideas shared by the other learning centers, and the project findings, we noticed that students appeared to prefer more open and flexible collaborative learning spaces. In view of this, some of the existing furniture at the CILL was removed to create more space. The major changes made to the layout of the center are as follows:

- Traditionally styled work tables and high bookshelves were removed to make space for a "noisy zone" to facilitate more interaction among students. The activity area of the noisy zone also allows the ELC teachers to deliver their workshops to students.
- A new set of furniture was purchased and installed to attract students to visit the noisy zone. For example, the center purchased some mobile furniture such as swivel seats and mobile desk-chairs that are well suited to group interactivity at the CILL. This new set of movable furniture provides a versatile and active setting that allows and supports a variety of small and large group activities. Sets of high bar chairs and tables were also placed in the CILL to add a modern touch to the environment (Figure 4).
- A comfortable area was set up for students so that they could wind down and chat with their friends in a more relaxing way. Some colorful bean bag chairs were placed in the area to attract students to gather (Figure 5).
- To facilitate group discussions, the sharing of ideas, and a culture of collaboration among students, a writable wall was installed within the noisy zone. Students can use the writable wall to discuss group projects, or they can simply doodle on the wall to relax (Figure 6).

- Because most students bring their own mobile devices to the CILL and seldom use the computers there, the old computers were removed. Two mobile computers on wheels (MoCoWs) were placed in the noisy zone (Figure 7). Instead of working on their own computers during group discussions, students can now work on the same computer as one group. They can also move the MoCoWs around and rearrange the movable chairs and desks in a way that they deem comfortable.
- The visits to the learning centers at the other universities showed that students feel more welcomed when the center is filled with seasonal decorations. As such, festive decorations were added inside the CILL for Halloween, Thanksgiving, and Christmas to enhance students' sense of belonging and connectedness. Activities related to the holidays were also organized for students. For example, at Halloween, the center asked CILL users to play a treasure hunt game, looking for Halloween-related objects at the center. Book coupons were given to students as prizes.

Figure 4
New Furniture at the CILL

Figure 5
A Comfortable Area

Figure 6
Writable Wall in the Noisy Zone

Figure 7
Mobile Computer on Wheels

While the noisy zone caters to students who prefer working in a more relaxed or informal area, the authors have also considered the needs of those who visit the CILL because of its quiet learning environment. The noisy zone was set up at the far end of the center. It is hoped that the front section of the center, together with the 15 self-study rooms, can still provide students a quiet learning space. Since the redesign of the layout of the CILL, the number of students visiting the center has grown. More information on students' entry records is given in Section 4. Students prefer to gather in the noisy zone for group discussion, and teachers enjoy delivering their workshops there rather than in a classroom (Figure 8). During the evaluation phase of the project, teachers commented that the noisy zone provides an informal learning space, which is more "open" and welcoming. Students who have not registered for a workshop can also join in anytime.

Figure 8

Workshop Being Delivered in the Noisy Zone

3.2 Reorganizing the Learning Materials

The CILL has both in-house and commercially produced English learning materials. The learning materials focus mainly on enhancing students' English abilities in the four main skills: listening, speaking, reading, and writing. The commercially produced materials include self-study examination practice books (e.g., IELTS and TOEFL) and grammar and vocabulary practice. The in-house materials were developed by the ELC teachers to help PolyU students cope with their difficulties encountered in completing assignments from their home departments. For example, guidance materials and learning pathways are provided to help students write their laboratory reports and final year project reports. As stated by Gardner and Miller (1999), students' easy access to the learning materials helps facilitate their effective use of a center. In view of this, the in-house learning materials were reorganized and put near the reception desk at the CILL and in the writing/speaking consultation rooms.

Hoping to make the CILL learning materials more relevant to students' learning needs, the CILL staff members helped check the learning materials and multimedia sources for usefulness and currentness. The materials were reorganized and made more visible to students using color-coded folders. A new set of learning flowcharts and pathways were developed to help students select the appropriate learning materials and direct them to the chosen materials. The set of flowcharts and pathways is now displayed near the help desk area, the writing and speaking consultation rooms, and some of the desks inside the CILL.

A CILL award scheme was set up to develop students' independent language learning skills. This incentive scheme consists of bronze, silver, and gold awards. Students can receive an award based on the number of hours spent and the tasks completed at the CILL. Systematic guidelines are provided for students to meet the requirements of the incentive scheme. For example, students can choose to work on a variety of the CILL learning activities for 15 hours to receive the bronze award. The activities include watching the CILL orientation video and completing a short quiz. Students can also complete a set of worksheets to evaluate their learning needs and set learning goals accordingly. Students who spend a further 15 and 30 hours to complete the in-house learning tasks at the CILL can achieve the silver and gold awards. Students are awarded certificates highlighting their effort and achievement in the award scheme. They also receive book coupons with different dollar values, depending on the award they attain.

The CILL award scheme has always been welcomed by students and yet, few students received the silver and gold awards. During the interview with students in Phase 1, the student interviewees who participated in the award scheme indicated that they had lost patience in working on the learning tasks once they received the bronze award. They were unsure whether they could complete all the remaining tasks and spend the required number of hours at the CILL to attain the silver and gold awards. This is particularly true when students have to complete their course assessments toward the end of the semester.

To attract more students to join the CILL award scheme and to encourage them to attain the silver and gold awards, the learning materials in the incentive scheme were thoroughly revised to meet the needs of the CILL users. The previous set of learning materials in the scheme appeared to be quite general and focused mainly on developing students' basic language skills. Moreover, the materials/task sheets for bronze, silver, and gold awards were placed in three individual portfolios (paper folders). The revised materials for the three awards are reduced in number and are now placed in one set of portfolios to motivate more students to work toward the silver and gold awards. The revised materials focus on not only developing students' English learning skills, but also their critical thinking and independent learning skills. The learning materials in the scheme were revamped and reorganized with a view to encouraging students to receive all three awards and become independent language learners. Since the revamp of the learning materials, the total number of awardees has significantly increased. More information is provided in Section 4.

3.3 Developing More Varied Learning Materials

In general, students visit the CILL to improve their English skills. However, students indicated that at times, they needed help with their applications for exchange programs or postgraduate studies overseas. Both students and teachers wanted to have more materials on this, so the ELC teachers developed a set of sample personal statements for different disciplines.

Most of the academic departments at PolyU require their undergraduate students to conduct a final year project and write a project report to present their findings. Students often find it difficult to write their reports because their home department does not provide any language support services. To help these students, a set of learning materials was prepared by the ELC teachers and is now located in the CILL. These materials provide step-by-step guidance on writing the different sections of a project report, such as writing an effective introduction and a comprehensive review of the literature.

During the interviews with students in Phase 1, some postgraduate students at PolyU indicated their perception that the CILL only provides help and support to undergraduate students. To reach out to the postgraduate student population, the center has also developed a set of learning materials to help the PhD and Masters students write their dissertations and prepare them for their conference/poster presentations. Guidelines on writing the different sections of a research thesis are provided. Some sample research theses/confirmation reports (qualifying papers) are also available at the CILL in the Research Student Corner (Figure 9).

Figure 9

Research Student Corner

The center would like to make the learning materials more relevant to students' learning needs. We purchased more updated learning materials to prepare students for the IELTS and TOEFL. We also bought new learning materials such as Graduate Management Admission Test (GMAT) practice tests. To better prepare students for their applications for Hong Kong government positions, past Common Recruitment Examination (CRE) papers and some new learning materials to help students prepare for their CREs are available at the redesigned CILL. A workshop on how to take the CRE was conducted, and it was well-received and well-attended.

As reflected from the students' responses to the questionnaire during Phase 1, students called for more online materials. During the project period, the ELC has developed a new website for the IELTS, and a link to this website has been added to the CILL online materials site. In Hong Kong, university graduates are expected to achieve an IELTS score of 6.5 to apply for government jobs. Most employers also consider the IELTS score (in particular, the writing score) of their prospective employees during the recruitment process. We hope that the new IELTS website will help students prepare to apply for jobs.

3.4 Planning and Providing Theme-Week Workshops

Workshops with follow-up activities were developed to replace the one-off CILL seminars to further enhance students' independent language learning. These workshops were called "theme-week workshops" because students are expected to complete some follow-up activities on a particular theme for a week after the workshop delivery. These workshops are characterized by facilitators' instruction of the theme-week topic, tasks, and discussion. Unlike the previous CILL seminars, these theme-week workshops include follow-up worksheets or tasks (which last for a week) that aim to reinforce students' out-of-class learning and consolidate what they have learned in the workshops. Most of the follow-up tasks require students to visit the CILL and make use of the learning materials or facilities at the center. As Croker and Ashurova (2012) stated, it is important to provide opportunities for students to develop a strong social bond with other learners so that they can use the target language with others. This makes language learning more interesting and meaningful. Eventually, students may develop independent and autonomous language learning habits. We hope that the theme-work workshops can provide students with more opportunities to visit the center and socialize and learn with their peers while they work on the follow-up activities. We believe that while working on the follow-up tasks, students will become better able to locate the learning materials that meet their needs and eventually, they will become more capable of selecting the appropriate learning materials at the CILL based on their own learning style and pace.

Seven theme-week workshops were conducted throughout the redesign project. The workshop topics were developed based on the ELC teachers' feedback (collected through the interviews during Phase 1) on students' interests and learning needs. The seven workshops covered the following topics:

- "How to think and respond quickly in English for impromptu speech," delivered by a renowned former President of the Hong Kong Toastmaster Club.
- "How to use flexi bar and theraband to reduce body fat and relieve neck and back pain," delivered by a certified health and fitness specialist from PolyU in English. This workshop was conducted to support the PolyU Wellness Center's initiative to promote physical activity on campus to improve the health and wellbeing of the campus community. Students learned how to enhance their physical health while also practicing their English speaking and listening skills (Figure 10, next page).
- "Helpful tips for writing an effective abstract," delivered by the course coordinator of a postgraduate thesis writing course at ELC (Figure 11, next page).
- "How to write a winning curriculum vitae," delivered by two ELC teachers.
- "Effective learning strategies of vocabulary through reading short stories," delivered by an ELC teacher.
- "The top six hottest current affairs for discussion in English," delivered by an ELC teacher.
- "Beyond the classroom: Sharing your writing with the world," delivered by a student journal editor and an ELC teacher.

CILL theme-week workshops primarily aim at boosting students' confidence and core English language competencies. During Phase 3 of the redesign project, online questionnaires and interviews were conducted to solicit feedback from CILL users on the theme-week workshops. The feedback is presented in Section 4.

Figure 10

Theme-Week Workshop on Relieving Neck Pain, Conducted in the Noisy Zone

Figure 11

Theme-Week Workshop on How to Write an Effective Abstract

3.5 Providing Regular Language Support Services

The CILL continues to provide a comfortable and supportive English learning environment in which students are given guidance to improve their English language skills and to develop their independent learning skills and strategies. Two types of face-to-face consultations are provided at the center: the CILL help desk and the Writing/Speaking Assistance Program.

3.5.1 The CILL Help Desk

Before the redesign, the CILL help desk was located at the far end of the center, hidden in a corner. Students were not able to see the help desk unless they walked all the way to the other side of the center. Some students were not aware of its existence. Even though signage was provided at the center, students still found it difficult to locate the help desk. To make it visible to students, it was moved to a spot near the CILL reception counter (located next to the CILL entrance). All center users are now able to see the desk once they enter the center. A weekly schedule of the help desk sessions is also provided within the help desk area and on the CILL website. Students can easily check when a help desk teacher will be available, and they can sign up both on the spot in person and online.

Before the redesign, the help desk schedule was random, depending on the availability and teaching timetable of the teachers. Each ELC teacher is required to teach for a certain number of hours. The help desk schedule was devised only after the ELC general office had allocated all the teaching time slots to the teachers. Teachers who were not assigned to any teaching had to sit at the CILL help desk to meet the required number of teaching hours. It appears that the help desk schedule was a relatively low priority. Sometimes, students were not able to receive any help at the help desk because no teachers were available. To ensure that an ELC teacher would be at the help desk on all weekdays, we consulted the ELC office and sought help from the scheduling team. In the end, we were able to rearrange the help desk schedule. The help desk is now open from Monday to Friday at lunch time (12:30–1:30 p.m.) and after the normal class time (4:30–5:30 p.m.). Lunch time was chosen because the CILL staff members indicated in the Phase 3 interview that more students visited the center during the lunch hour to seek help from the help desk teacher.

3.5.2 The Writing/Speaking Assistance Program

The CILL provides a Writing Assistance Program (WAP) and Speaking Assistance Program (SAP) for PolyU students. Findings from our two-year project revealed that students found these two programs the most useful of the CILL services because they were able to receive ELC teachers' guidance on how to improve their written and spoken assignments. However, students also expressed that the WAP/SAP sessions were usually fully booked and they had to wait for a week for the next available time slot. To meet the increasing demand from students, an online registration system was developed, and an increase in time slots of around 15% was added to both the WAP and SAP during the project period. Moreover, the writing and speaking support services have been expanded to both the research and non-academic staff members to further promote the CILL language support services to the larger university community. These two new services, Writing/Speaking Assistance for Staff, can be booked online. ELC teachers with prior research experience will be assigned to provide such services.

4. An Evaluation of the Changes Made to the CILL

The changes made to the CILL were completed within 12 months. To evaluate the impact of these changes on students' and teachers' usage of the learning space and materials at the center, we conducted a post-redesign questionnaire survey and interviews to collect students', ELC teachers', and CILL staff members' views on the redesign. The questionnaire (Appendix B) was distributed to 628 students via email to collect information about their use of the services and the facilities at the CILL after the redesign. The questionnaire was completed by 76 students (a

12% response rate), and 13 agreed to participate in a post-questionnaire interview. During the evaluation phase, we also received the views of 5 ELC teachers (through email) and 2 CILL staff members (through interviews), regarding their perceptions of the redesigned CILL. The results of the evaluation are summarized in the following sections.

4.1 Student Entry Records

The total number of undergraduate student entries per day to the CILL after the redesign increased by 7.2% in 2018–19 compared to 2017–18 for the first semester (Table 1).

Table 1

Undergraduate Student Entries to the CILL During the First Semester of 2017–18 and 2018–19

	2017–18	2018–19
Sep	158	166
Oct	167	198
Nov	181	190
Dec	80	74
Total	586	628

The number of postgraduate students who visited the CILL before and after the redesign were 149 and 178, respectively, showing an increase of 19.5% (Table 2).

Table 2

Postgraduate Student Entries to the CILL During the First Semester of 2017–18 and 2018–19

	2017–18	2018–19
Sep	39	45
Oct	41	48
Nov	42	46
Dec	27	39
Total	149	178

The most significant increase in undergraduate student entries can be found in October (Table 1). The number of entries increased from 167 to 198 from 2017–18 to 2018–19. One possible reason is that most students need to start working on their assignments in October, and they may visit the CILL for ELC teachers' help with their academic writing and speaking assessments (at the help desk or through the WAP/SAP). Another possible reason is that most of the theme-week workshops began in October, and these workshops attracted more students to visit the center.

4.2 The CILL Award Scheme

The number of participants in the CILL award scheme markedly increased, with 177 awardees in the academic year 2018–19, including bronze (149), silver (22), and gold (6), as compared to 168 awardees in 2017–18 and 122 awardees in 2016–17, 72 awardees in 2015–16, and 15 awardees in 2014–15 (Table 3). The increase in the number of students who have attained the three awards may be due to the revised learning materials in the award scheme. The increase may also be due to the promotion by the ELC teachers, who recommended the scheme to the students, and extensive promotion through posters and the CILL website. As reflected in the drastic increase in the number of awardees over the past years, starting from 2014–2015, it appears that an increasing number of students began to welcome the idea of self-directed learning.

Table 3

The Number of Participants in the CILL Award Scheme From 2014–15 to 2018–19

	Total number of participants
2014–15	15
2015–16	72
2016–17	122
2017–18	168
2018–19	177

To further enhance the effectiveness of the award scheme, the authors plan to place more emphasis on allowing students to choose their own CILL self-study worksheets, rather than asking them to work on the preselected set of worksheets for the three awards. We hope that this will equip students with the necessary skills for independent language learning and enhance their ability to self-assess their language skills. More training and support should also be provided to the CILL staff members so that they can better answer inquiries raised by the award scheme participants.

4.3 Theme-Week Workshops

The theme-week workshops have attracted satisfactory attendance. Before the redesign project, the one-off CILL seminars had 120 participants in two semesters. The new theme-week workshops have attracted 182 participants in two semesters, an increase of 52%. The most popular workshop was the first session on impromptu speech, with 54 participants, which broke the previous record of CILL workshop participants. During the interviews with students in Phase 3, those students who attended the theme-week workshops said that they found the workshops effective and encouraging. They also valued the workshops highly and found the facilitators' advice and suggestions very useful to their language learning.

4.4 Help Desk Consultations

The help desk consultation hours increased from 21.5 to 26.5 hours per week after the redesign. There was also an increase of around 23% in students' usage of the consultations, which are now conducted on a more regular basis. From the feedback solicited using the questionnaire and interviews in Phase 3, students were satisfied with the more regular schedule of the help desk.

4.5 Writing/Speaking Assistance Programs

After the redesign of the CILL, we invited ELC teachers to provide some comments about the changes made to the center. Five teachers responded, and all of their responses are below:

- More resources, such as the MoCoWs and Corner for Research Students, are now available to fulfill different users' needs.
- Pop-up messages have been introduced for online SAP and WAP registration. These messages remind students of the following: a) students should bring their writing, or any instructions/tasks to discuss with the teacher; b) the teacher will not proofread any writing from students (WAP); and c) students will come with a specific topic that they want to talk about with the teacher (SAP).
- More PhD students are attending the consultations. When students bring their research thesis to consecutive consultations, teachers can focus on a particular area (organization, language, etc.) in each session.
- Apart from having the WAP/SAP, more workshops on grammar and academic writing style could be conducted.

To sum up, both the CILL users and teachers were generally satisfied with the changes made at the CILL.

4.6 General Impression of the CILL After the Redesign

The data collected through the questionnaire and interviews in Phase 3 and the CILL usage statistics indicate that students continue to view the CILL in a positive light and anticipate an improvement in their language competence with the help from the CILL. Of the students who responded to the questionnaire, 13% took five or more WAP and SAP sessions during the project period, which indicates that they value the one-on-one consultation service at the center. Below, we directly quote the feedback from students and teachers about the changes made at CILL.

From students:

- A rest place for students to hang out, practice English, prepare for presentations, and so on.
- The writable wall is great.
- The new location of the help desk means that students can now see that there is a help desk teacher.
- The environment is starting to get better.

From teachers:

- The Corner for Research Students is effective.
- The activity space where the help desk area used to be is now the venue for theme-week workshops, so the space is fully utilized.
- The new high bar chairs and the round tables have enhanced the attractiveness of the environment a lot.

5. Conclusion and Future Directions

The prevalence of mobile technology has changed not only the classroom landscape, but also that of SALCs. SALCs need to redefine their role in fostering and facilitating learner autonomy. The present chapter describes and discusses the changes made to one SALC at a Hong Kong university. The changes were informed and shaped by the findings of a research project conducted by the authors. The two-year redesign project set out to transform the center from a traditional self-study learning space to a more welcoming and engaging learning environment for students. The redesign process focused on five main areas: redesigning the layout of the center, revising and reorganizing the center's existing materials, developing more learning materials for different groups of center users, organizing more theme-week workshops, and providing more regular language support services. The project was completed on time and within budget. It appears that the redesigned CILL can meet the learning needs of students and accommodate their different learning styles. This is evidenced by, for example, the increase in student entry records and the theme-week workshop attendance.

The main focus in this chapter is one SALC at a university in Hong Kong, and yet, the changes described can provide useful insights into redesigning SALCs in other settings. The redesign process described in Section 4 offers valuable information on transforming the role of SALCs from merely providing self-directed learning materials to allowing for more student engagement in various learning activities with a view to enhancing learners' independent language learning.

During Phase 2 of the project, we encountered some challenges in the redesign process. Originally, we planned to build a glass sliding door to separate the quiet study area and the noisy zone. We brought forward this idea during the consultation with the facility management office at the university. However, we encountered the following obstacles: i) the cost of the construction work would be over the research budget and ii) the construction work would involve the restructuring of the whole layout of the CILL, which would take a long time and inconvenience the CILL users. After discussing these problems with the CILL manager and the ELC Director, we decided to set up the noisy zone in the far corner of the center. This area is the farthest from the quiet study area. We hope that this arrangement will provide CILL users a quiet place for their study and a flexible learning space for them to socialize and interact with others.

Another issue that needs to be considered is our positionality in the project. The fact that we (the principal project investigators) are ELC teachers who provide the CILL staff members advice and suggestions on the activities and services at

CILL may have had an impact on the research process and the interpretation of the project findings. Being an insider at the CILL could lead to bias and a loss of objectivity, and yet, our insider position gave us greater understanding of the project and the SALC under study. To ensure our own expectations and potential biases were bracketed, we collected our data from various sources (Baxter & Jack, 2008; Ponterotto, 2005). For example, we used questionnaires and interviews to collect data, and interviews were conducted with different stakeholders, including students, ELC teachers, and CILL staff members. We hope that triangulating the data provided views from multiple perspectives.

Here, we suggest a few points that other SALCs can take note of during their redesign process:

- Pay visits to and seek advice from other SALCs with a similar setting. Our site visits to the other learning centers enabled us to visualize possible new physical layouts of the CILL and evaluate the feasibility of making these changes to the CILL.
- Consult the stakeholders of the SALC. We encountered difficulties when setting up the noisy zone, so we consulted the CILL manager, ELC director, and the facility management office at the university to identify the strategy that would work best. In the end, we were able to set up a noisy zone at a minimal cost. Instead of building a glass sliding door as a divider between the noisy zone and quiet study area, the noisy zone was set up at the far end of the center.
- Listen to SALC users' concerns. Collecting feedback from the users can help shape and inform the redesign process. The changes made to the language support services at the center will then make students feel more connected, and they may also develop a sense of belonging.
- Consult and work closely with teachers of other academic departments. By doing this, the center can develop and provide the support and help that the students need when working on the assignments from their home department. For example, a theme-week workshop on how to write final year project reports can be offered in the first two weeks of the semester, during the lunch hour or after normal class hours. The workshops can cover topics such as "Planning your project report," "Presenting and discussing project findings," and "Improving organization and cohesion." After the first two weeks, these CILL theme-week workshops can be rerun so that more students can attend them. Offering multiple time slots at times convenient to students and having content directly related to what they would be doing at the time in their courses could help support their learning and enhance their performance on their assignments.

The redesign process was informed and shaped by a research project on only one SALC in Hong Kong. To provide a clearer picture of how to redesign a SALC, further studies that involve SALC staff members, teachers, and students from other post-secondary institutions could be conducted. A more extensive study could also be conducted to study in greater depth the institutional and contextual constraints that a SALC may encounter during the redesign process. With the increase in students' use of mobile technology, it is also worthwhile to explore and examine the possibilities of using such technology to promote independent language learning at the SALC.

SALCs have played an indispensable role in promoting and supporting learner autonomy across universities. Redesign and continued improvement are needed to ensure that SALCs can i) provide center users a positive learning experience and ii) support and motivate center users to become independent learners.

References

Barrs, K. (2010). What factors encourage high levels of student participation in a self-access center? *Studies in Self-Access Learning Journal, 1*(1), 10–16. https://sisaljournal.org/archives/jun10/barrs/

Baxter, P., & Jack, S. (2008). Qualitative case study methodology: Study design and implementation for novice researchers. *The Qualitative Report, 13*(4), 544–559. http://www.nova.edu/ssss/QR/QR13-4/baxter.pdf

Benson, P. (2011). Language learning and teaching beyond the classroom: An introduction to the field. In P. Benson & H. Reinders (Eds.), *Beyond the language classroom* (pp. 7–16). London, UK: Palgrave Macmillan.

Chia, C. (2007). *Autonomy in language learning: The use of IT and internet resources.* Singapore: McGraw-Hill.

Choi, J. (2017). The metamorphosis of a self-access centre in Hong Kong: From theory to practice (A case study). *Studies in Self-Access Learning Journal, 8*(1), 22–33.

Cotterall, S., & Reinders, H. (2000). Learners' perceptions and practice in self access language learning. *The TESOLANZ Journal 8*, 23–38.

Croker, R. & Ashurova, U. (2012). Scaffolding student' initial self-access language centre experiences. *Studies in Self-Access Learning Journal, 3*(3), 237–253.

Dickinson, L. (1987). *Self-instruction in language learning.* Cambridge, UK: Cambridge University Press.

Earthman, G. I., & Lemasters, L. K. (2011). The influence of school building conditions on students and teachers: A theory-based research program (1993–2011). *The ACEF Journal, 1*(1), 15–36.

Gardner, D., & Miller, L. (1999). *Establishing self-access: From theory to practice.* Cambridge, UK: Cambridge University Press.

Gardner, D. (2001). Making self-access centers more effective. In D. K. Kember, S. Candlin, & L. Yan (Eds.), *Further case studies of improving teaching and learning from the action learning project*, 161–174.

Gardner, D. (2017). The evolution and devolution of management and training needs for self-access center staff. *Studies in Self-Access Learning Journal, 8*(2), 147–156.

Gardner, D., & Miller, L. (2011). Managing self-access language learning: Principles and practice. *System, 39*(1), 78–89.

Little, D. (1994). Learner autonomy: A theoretical construct and its practical application. *Die Neueren Sprachen, 93*(5), 430–442.

Little, D. (2003). *Learner autonomy and second/foreign language learning*. Subject Centre for Languages, Linguistics and Area Studies Guide to Good Practice. https://www.llas.ac.uk/resources/gpg/1409

Morrison, B. (2008). The role of the self-access center in the tertiary language learning process. *System, 36*(2), 123–140.

Morrison, B. (2011). A framework for the evaluation of a self-access language learning center. *Studies in Self-Access Learning Journal, 2*(4), 241–256.

Ponterotto, A. (2005). Qualitative research in social psychology: A primer on research paradigms and philosophy of science. *Journal of Counseling Psychology, 52*(2), 126–136.

Sheerin, S. (1989). *Self-access*. Oxford, UK: Oxford University Press.

Appendix A

English Language Center

Survey on the Roles of the CILL in Improving Students' Academic Writing

This questionnaire is designed to gather information about your perception toward the roles of self-access language learning centers in supporting and improving English academic writing. The self-access language learning center examined in this study is the Center for Independent Language Learning (CILL) at PolyU. Please choose the appropriate option.

Section 1: This section asks for your comments on your own academic writing skills.

1.1 Please indicate the degree you agree with each statement below by choosing the appropriate option ("1" indicating "Strongly disagree" and "5" indicating "Strongly agree").

  A. I have a clear understanding of what academic writing is.
  B. It is easy for me to organize my ideas and present them in a logical way.
  C. It is easy for me to write using an academic style and tone.
  D. It is easy for me to use appropriate vocabulary and word forms to communicate clearly with the readers.
  E. It is easy for me to add citations in my writing using a particular referencing style (e.g., APA and IEEE).

1.2 What are the problems you have encountered when you write academic papers/ thesis? (You can choose more than one option.)

  A. I find it difficult to get started.
  B. It is difficult for me organize my ideas and connect them in a logical way.
  C. It is difficult for me to find the right words to express my ideas.
  D. I find it difficult to write in academic style and tone.
  E. It is difficult for me to summarize or paraphrase ideas from relevant sources.
  F. I have difficulties in citing references (in-text or end-of-text) using a particular referencing system (e.g., APA and IEEE).
  G. No. I have not encountered any difficulties while writing academic papers/ thesis.

Section 2: This section aims to gather information about the assistance you have received that helps improve your academic writing.

2.1 In the past, when you encountered difficulties in academic writing, you sought help from: (you can choose more than one option)

A. Your supervisor(s)
B. Your peers from the same department
C. Your home department
D. The English Language Center (ELC)
E. The teacher from the English writing course (from ELC) you took before
F. The Center for Independent Language Learning (CILL) at A305 and Z213: (circle the services that you used before)
   –The Writing Assistance Program (WAP);
   –The Speaking Assistance Program (SAP);
   –The Help Desk;
   –The Corner for Research Students; or
   –CILL website on academic writing.
G. The PolyU library
H. Online resources: Please indicate some example(s) _____.
I. Other sources: _____
J. I do not need any help with my academic writing.

2.2 Among all the sources of support indicated in Question 2.1, which ONE do you find was the MOST helpful?

A. Your supervisor(s)
B. Your peers from the same department
C. Your home department
D. The English Language Center (ELC)
E. The teacher from the English writing course (from ELC) you took before
F. The Center for Independent Language Learning (CILL) at A305 and Z213
G. The PolyU library
H. Online resources: Please indicate some example(s) _____.
I. Other sources: _____
J. I did not seek any help regarding my academic writing.

2.3 Why do you find the source you indicated in Question 2.2 the most helpful? (You can choose more than one option).

A. It gives me clear instructions on how I should improve my academic writing.
B. It points out my mistakes and provides me with suggestions on how to improve my academic writing.
C. I find it easy to express my difficulties and I received the help which I needed.
D. It provides me with useful resources to further improve my academic writing.
E. It is readily available and easily accessible.
F. I did not seek any help from any of the sources indicated in Question 2.2.

Section 3: This section asks for your comments on the roles of the CILL in supporting your academic writing.

3.1 Have you ever used any one of the English learning resources or activities offered by the CILL?

- A. The Writing Assistance Program (WAP)
- B. The Speaking Assistance Program (SAP)
- C. Theme-week workshops (e.g., How to write an effective abstract?)
- D. Help Desk
- E. The Corner for Research Students
- F. CILL website (e.g., Referencing; Common Error Detector)
- G. Study rooms
- H. Books, DVDs, Magazines
- I. Others: Please specify _____.
- J. No, I have not used any of the English learning resources or activities offered by the CILL.

3.2 How often do you use the resources or activities provided by the CILL in each semester?

- A. Once a week
- B. More than once every week
- C. Once each semester
- D. More than once each semester
- E. Never. Could you tell us the reason why? (You can choose more than one option)
  - I have never heard of the CILL.
  - I can seek help from the other sources.
  - I heard about the CILL but I am not sure what resources or activities it provides to postgraduate students.
  - I thought the CILL only provides help to undergraduate students.
  - The CILL is too far away from my office on campus.
  - Others: Please specify _____.

3.3 If you have used the resources before, how useful do you think they were in helping you with your English learning, in particular academic writing?

Not useful, somehow useful, quite useful, very useful, I have never used the resources before.

3.4 In what ways do you find the resources or activities helpful?

- A. The Writing and Speaking Assistance Programs provide me useful and helpful advice on academic writing.
- B. I found the learning materials at the Corner for Research Students very helpful.
- C. The advice given by the teacher at the Help Desk was helpful.
- D. I attended the theme-week workshop(s) and I found it (them) very helpful.

E. I found the open, flexible, and collaborative learning space at the CILL conducive to my language learning.
F. The learning materials and resources on the CILL website are useful.
G. I have not used any resources and activities provided by the CILL before and I cannot provide any comments on this question.

3.5 What suggestions do you have that could help the CILL improve its resources or activities?

A. I would like the CILL to organize more theme-work workshops to help with my academic writing.
B. I would like the CILL to provide more learning materials on academic writing for postgraduate students.
C. I would like to see more online learning materials on the CILL website.
D. Other suggestions: Please specify _____.
E. The CILL provides sufficient learning materials and facilities. I do not have any suggestions.

THANK YOU

Appendix B
English Language Center
CILL Survey Questions

Dear student,

Thank you for using CILL services this semester. To better meet students' needs, we would like to get your feedback. Can you spare a minute or two to complete this questionnaire and send the completed one to xxxx by xxxx?

Best regards

CILL
English Language Center

Circle the most suitable response.

1. Have you used the CILL services before?

A. Yes
B. No

2. Which of the following CILL services have you used <u>most frequently</u> this semester?

A. Help desk
B. Self-study area
C. Writing Assistance Program/Speaking Assistance Program
D. CILL workshop
E. Others _____ (please specify)

3. How many visits have you made to the CILL this semester?
   A. 1–3 times
   B. 4–6 times
   C. 7–10 times
   D. 10–15 times
   E. more than15 times

4. On average how long do you usually stay in the CILL per visit?
   A. Below 30 min
   B. 30 min to 60 min
   C. 60–90 min
   D. 90–120 min
   E. more than 120 min

5. What is the <u>main</u> reason that attracts you to visit the CILL?
   A. The language support services provided by ELC teachers
   B. The study space
   C. The atmosphere
   D. My teachers' recommendation
   E. Others _____ (please specify)

6. What are the difficulties you encountered in learning?

7. What will you do when you want to seek help for your writing and speaking?

Please indicate your level of agreement for items 8–11.

	Strongly agree	Agree	Disagree	Strongly disagree	NA
8. CILL services have helped me to improve my English.					
9. I will continue to use CILL services.					
10. The CILL provides a pleasant learning environment.					
11. The theme-based activities (e.g., Halloween, Thanksgiving) encourage me to visit the CILL.					

12. What other services or facilities would you like to have in the CILL?

13. Other comments about the CILL monthly theme-based activities (e.g., Photo Competition, Halloween, Thanksgiving)?

Thank you very much for your input!

Author Notes

Vickie Wai Kei Li (PhD, Western University, Canada) is the coordinator of a postgraduate thesis writing course offered by the English Language Center (ELC) at the Hong Kong Polytechnic University (PolyU). She has extensive experience in teaching academic English at both undergraduate and postgraduate levels. Her research interests include English learning experiences, language learning and learner identity, and independent language learning. During her teaching at PolyU, Li participated in research projects on the enhancement of students' academic English skills. She also conducted studies on the major challenges faced by non-English speaking postgraduate students in writing a research thesis in English. The research results were presented at international conferences such as AsiaTEFL (2019) and Canadian Society for the Study of Education annual conference (2016–2019). Her prior studies on the English learning experiences of postsecondary students appeared in the GiST Education and Learning Research and Writing & Pedagogy Journal.

Joe Ching (PhD, Edith Cowan University, Australia) has been the center manager of the Center for Independent Language Learning (CILL) at the Hong Kong Polytechnic University for 12 years. Being a certified health specialist and physical fitness trainer of American College of Sports Medicine, Ching was also fully funded by Hong Kong to join the FINA World Masters Championship swimming contest in South Korea in August of 2019. He is the coordinator of health-related courses and mainly teaches PhD students oral presentation skills. His research focuses on learner autonomy and English language teaching. This includes a research study on the investigation of the factors affecting students' participation in an incentive award scheme to enhance CILL users' independent English language learning skills. The study was presented at the Rethinking ELT in Higher Education: The 11th International Symposium on Teaching English at Tertiary Level.

Correspondence concerning this chapter should be addressed to Vickie Wai Kei Li (vickie.li@polyu.edu.hk).

Chapter 7
Officially Bilingual:
The University of Ottawa Experience

Paco Lalovic, Université d'Ottawa / University of Ottawa, Canada

Abstract

This chapter provides the sociopolitical and historical context within which the Julien Couture Resource Centre (JCRC) at the Official Languages and Bilingualism Institute (OLBI) of the University of Ottawa operates as a central meeting and study space as well as an archive and a library specialized in second language acquisition methodology and tools. The University of Ottawa, as the largest bilingual (French and English) university in the world, has since its foundation welcomed and embraced its mission to advance and maintain the linguistic and cultural rights of its Francophone minority while also promoting the values of bilingualism as inclusion and collaboration between the two founding nations in Canada. The JCRC has an essential role in the structure of OLBI and the University, at the intersection of various programs, courses, and services offered to students, professors, staff members, and the wider community.

The chapter also represents a case study describing the evolution of the JCRC and its various partnerships and collaborations with relevant university services within and beyond the academic environment. Thus, the Centre is presented within the University of Ottawa's complex framework of continuous support to its mission and commitment to institutional bilingualism.

According to the *Times Higher Education* rankings for 2019, the University of Ottawa (uOttawa), at the heart of Canada's national capital, represents the largest bilingual (French and English) university in the world. The university has entrusted its Official Languages and Bilingualism Institute (OLBI) to promote cultural understanding and linguistic competence in both of Canada's official languages.

In keeping with this mission, OLBI's Julien Couture Resource Centre (JCRC) has been, since its inception in 1980, a very particular space, drawing on both French and English cultural traditions to fulfill a multifaceted mandate. Named after Julien Couture, one of the Centre's original founders and a former French as a Second Language (FSL) teacher, it is an academic library, a meeting place for teachers and students alike, a research facility, an archive of pedagogical resources covering many decades of second language acquisition (SLA) methods and tools, and an interactive learning environment. Benefitting from its central location at the Faculty of Arts, the JCRC is a starting point for many students and faculty members looking to improve their French and/or English language skills.

The Centre consists of two complementary sections, the first of which is dedicated to providing services and resources to the university community at large. The other supports the teaching needs of OLBI language teachers and assists graduate students, international scholars, and professors with their research in the fields of language teaching and learning, bilingualism, immersion, language policy, and educational technologies. The Centre functions as a fluid bi-/multilingual environment where the University's bilingual mission is realized through translanguaging (Garcia & Kleyn, 2016; Mazak & Carroll, 2016; Paulsrud et al., 2017) between Canadian Francophone and Anglophone speakers and increasing numbers of international students from a variety of backgrounds.

In a technology-driven context where more and more students are engaging in self-directed work outside the classroom and taking advantage of the various language-related resources and services on campus, "the structure and organisation of language centres in higher education tend to reflect the environment, history and context in which they have evolved" (Ruane, 2003, p. 2). In the case of the JCRC, this is perhaps even more salient due to its core function of supporting a very specific mission of its department and university to preserve, promote, and further advance its students', faculty members', and employees' bi-/multilingualism. As Ruane further pointed out, the very notion of a center "suggests inter-disciplinarity as well as diversity of function, from the purely academic to the practical or applied. It also suggests flexible and adaptable organisational models to support a range and variety of teaching and research functions" (p. 3). As this chapter will show, the JCRC has throughout its history aimed to embody a variety of these functions and adapted to continuously provide resources and assistance to the entire range of its patrons.

Within the OLBI structure (Figure 1), the JCRC represents one of four sectors, along with the Centre for Language Learning (CLL), Language Assessment, and the Canadian Centre for Studies and Research on Bilingualism and Language Planning (CCERBAL). It is very well positioned to thrive and grow beyond its physical location, becoming "a collection of spaces - physical, virtual, hybrid - that has expanded beyond its four walls" (Kronenberg, 2017, p. 161). In a complex organizational structure such as OLBI, the role of its resource center is to support the various courses, programs, and activities that the Institute organizes and offers and to function as a hub for researchers, students, faculty, and employees. The emphasis at the JCRC is thus clearly on the words center, as one space bringing together all physical and human resources, and resource, encompassing a wide range of pedagogical materials (Albero & Poteaux, 2010).

Figure 1
Organizational Structure of OLBI

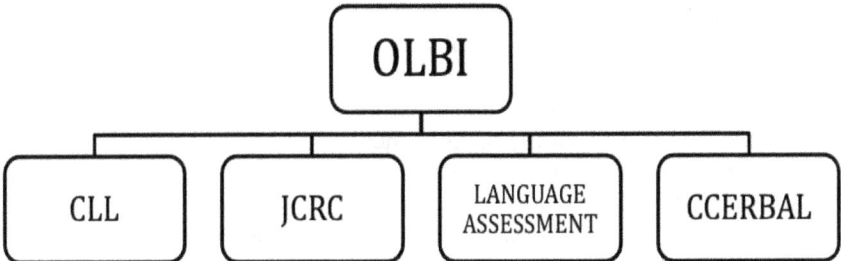

In this chapter, my intention is to trace the JCRC's evolution from its foundation as a Documentation Centre and a Student Resource Centre in the early 1980s (Courchêne et al., 1995) to what it is today. Its creation closely followed the country's commitment to recognizing its bilingual character, and it has gradually evolved into the present-day multifunctional space, supporting a great variety of Canadian and international learners and teachers and fully embracing the University's central mission to advance bilingualism.

I first outline a few crucial moments in Canadian history to provide an overall general context for the development of official bilingualism at the federal level in Canada and its importance in particular for the province of Ontario and the University of Ottawa. It is essential to understand some of these historical developments and the way they led to the eventual creation of the complex institutional body known as OLBI and its resource center. I then describe the Centre's particular collection, the variety of its patrons, the services it offers, its hiring practices, and the partnerships and collaborations it maintains. Finally, I outline some challenges that the JCRC is facing in transitioning from a resource center to a hub (Lavolette & Simon, 2018; see also Sebastian, Gopalakrishnan, & Hendricks, this volume) as it adapts and evolves to keep pace with the development of teaching technologies and the changing needs of our patrons. I conclude by offering some suggestions for potential partnerships that can be explored at other universities and in other contexts.

1. Historical Background: Canada and Bilingualism

The Institute's story starts in the 1970s as the result of some major structural changes taking place primarily at the level of the federal government. In fact, the

1960s were a time of great changes in Canada, when multiple factors contributed to an environment that ultimately strengthened the University of Ottawa's mission of bilingualism and biculturalism. It started with a growing realization of a constitutional crisis resulting from the sociocultural changes taking place in the Francophone province of Quebec. This crisis brought about radical demands for a fuller recognition of the role of the French minorities in the country's sociopolitical life. It was a period known in Quebec as the Quiet Revolution, which ushered in a number of radical transformations in the province's economic, political, and cultural spheres. Throughout this process, however, the underlying tensions and inequality became only more prominent between the two "founding nations," the British and the French (The Canadian Encyclopedia, 2013). It thus exacerbated the growing resentment among the French-Canadian population about their economic, sociocultural, and political status and rights. In response, the federal government proceeded with the creation of a Royal Commission on Bilingualism and Biculturalism (1963–1969). This Commission, in its first preliminary report issued in February 1965, clearly outlined the issue: "Canada, without being fully conscious of the fact, is passing through the greatest crisis in its history" (Clément & Foucher, 2014, p. i).

The Commission's work eventually led to an introduction of a bill enacted in 1969 as the *Official Languages Act*, enshrining the official status of the two languages across Canada. The adoption of this act boosted "a national effort to find more effective ways of teaching French to English speakers" (Burger, Weinberg, & Wesche, 2013, p. 23). The main positive outcomes resulting from this Act "gave Canada's French minorities, who were often particularly mistreated in their respective provinces, both rights and institutions, established real bilingualism in the federal public service and thereby contributed to the bilingualism of many Anglo-Canadians and Franco-Quebecers" (Curzi, 2014, p. 13). However, note that the educational policies and measures in Canada are under the purview of the provincial governments. Universities, as public institutions, depend on the funding and support of their provincial educational authorities. The overall measures instituting bilingualism across the country are therefore only advisory in nature, unless applied to the federal public service, its employees, and other services dependent on the federal government.

The University of Ottawa has strived from its very foundations as the original Bytown College in 1848 to provide an environment promoting the "equitable coexistence" of the two predominant Canadian settler languages, "to cement the most durable bonds, those developed during youth, among men of different cultures and religions, and obliterate the natural but always deplorable antipathies among citizens of the same country" (Guindon, 1998, p. 12). So, while bilingualism has always been at the core of the University's mission, it also remained under the direction of the Catholic order of Oblates until the adoption of the University of Ottawa Act in 1965. With this Act, the university removed its denominational character and became a part of the Ontario higher education network. The Act was also a clear indication of an official government's approval of the institution's values and mission "to further bilingualism and biculturalism and to preserve and develop French culture in Ontario" (Beillard, 2000, p. 471). Just as importantly, it allowed the University to improve its funding sources and to continue expanding the infrastructure necessary to create a greater variety of programs and better meet the increasing needs of its rapidly growing student population.

2. Language Center at the University of Ottawa

It was truly a "spectacular evolution" (Prévost, 2008, p. 86) in the University of Ottawa's infrastructure, funding, and human resources that led to the creation of the Centre for Second Language Learning (CSLL) in 1970 (Figure 2). Its aim was to "provide language teaching and testing services to help students attending the University of Ottawa meet the bilingual requirements of their faculty" (Courchêne et al., 1995, p. xiii). A decade later, in 1980, as the CSLL faculty members started playing more prominent roles in the University's efforts to provide second language (L2) support for a growing number of programs offered in both official languages, a Documentation Centre was added to the overall organizational structure. The purpose was to ensure the CSLL's readiness to take on full responsibility for all second language courses. Quite like some other higher education institutions (see Albero & Poteaux, 2010, for a description of a Language Resource Center experience in Strasbourg, France), the CSLL initially had set up a Documentation Centre as a space reserved for teachers and graduate students. It was equipped with a collection of pedagogical tools and documents (textbooks, curriculum documents, course outlines, etc.) where these teachers could meet and collaborate, as many of them were also pursuing their graduate education. These teachers were developing curricula for a variety of courses focusing not solely on L2 skills, but more specifically targeting learning skills found lacking in their students. These efforts resulted in the creation of a "bank of specialized credit courses such as academic reading, essay writing, technical report writing and grammar that students could take to improve their L2 ability and for which they could receive credit in their program of study" (Courchêne et al., 1995, p. x).

Figure 2

Evolution of the Language Center at uOttawa

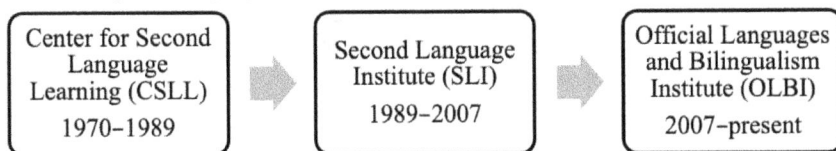

The CSLL was further expanded in 1986 with the addition of a self-directed learning section, called a Student Resource Centre, with the specific purpose to encourage "autonomous L2 learning" (Courchêne et al., 1995, p. xix). The CSLL's evolution had by then reached the stage "where self-directed learning has become an integral part of most L2 courses" (p. xix). Courchêne et al. explained the guiding principle and the main objective of this new center:

> [T]o enable students to assume at least partial control of their learning process, the [CSLL] set up a Student Resource Centre equipped with both traditional

and computer-based approaches to L2 language learning. Students' efforts to improve their L2 ability are strongly supported by counselling provided by full-time staff members and qualified assistants together with a rich variety of language learning materials. (Courchêne et al., 1995, p. xiv)

From that point on then, the CSLL had two different but complementary centers functioning within its structure. One, known as the Documentation Centre, was an archives-like space exclusive to the teachers. The other, the Student Resource Centre, was a meeting space with carefully selected learning materials for the students. The CSLL's collection was partly shared between the two centers, and in the 1980s, when the University of Ottawa started offering a postsecondary French immersion option along with a number of its discipline courses in French, that also meant adding more complexity to its collection through the acquisition and creation of subject-matter-specific materials in French.

This postsecondary French immersion initiative was based upon two factors and was meant to build on the success of the primary and secondary school immersion programs that started in Canada in the 1960s. On the one hand, there was growing interest among students in being able to pursue their university education after completing their primary and secondary schooling in an immersion setting. On the other hand, there was strong interest among professors at the University of Ottawa's CSLL and its School of Psychology to implement and support this initiative at the tertiary level. "This pioneer program was offered in both French and English, taking advantage of the unique bilingual resources of the University" (Burger et al., 2013, p. 22).

There were a few very good reasons for such a tertiary-level French language immersion program to be undertaken at the University of Ottawa. First, as a bilingual French and English institution, it had the resources and expertise in place to implement and sustain it. Second, Ottawa, as Canada's capital, sits on the border between the predominantly Anglophone province of Ontario with a small but vital minority of French speakers, and Quebec, the only Canadian province with French as the single official language. Benefitting from this unique location, the city has a robust number of high schools with a secondary immersion program directly feeding uOttawa. Third, as the largest employer in the public sector, the federal government provides plenty of opportunities for students to gain invaluable preprofessional experiences and upon graduation find gainful employment as proficient English and French speakers.

The university students willing to engage in some of the discipline courses in French as their second language certainly benefited from the additional classroom support from the CSLL's instructors. They were also able to take advantage of the Student Resource Centre, where they had access to supplementary learning resources and could benefit from consulting French language instructors outside of the classroom to further improve their language skills. In 1989, the CSLL officially changed its name to become the Second Language Institute (SLI), as its mission and responsibility expanded beyond English as a Second Language (ESL) and FSL courses and included research in the fields of immersion and bilingualism. The factors playing in favor of the continued importance of the CSLL (and subsequently the SLI) and its two centers largely remained in place throughout the 1980s and 1990s. This was despite the financial constraints and rising class sizes that put increasing pressure on the university budget and in the 1990s temporarily halted the development of its tertiary immersion program. However, early in the 2000s, there was a realization within the University of Ottawa's administration of a growing disparity in numbers between the Francophone and Anglophone students (Table 1).

A closer look at the enrollment numbers by linguistic background for the period 1995–2006 (University of Ottawa, 2007) clearly shows that the growth in numbers of Anglophone students was almost four times faster than that of the Francophone students. Note that the Franco-Ontarian minority represents only 4.3% of the overall population in Ontario (Statistics Canada, 2016). Thus, even with 55% of the Franco-Ontarian population joining the student ranks at the University of Ottawa (Labrie, Lamoureux, & Wilson, 2009), the situation was still clearly endangering the institution's emphasis on bilingualism.

Table 1

Overall University of Ottawa Enrollment by Linguistic Background

Year	Francophone	Anglophone	Francophone %	Anglophone %
1995–96	9,026	14,697	38%	62%
1996–97	8,557	14,471	37%	63%
1997–98	8,292	14,403	36%	64%
1998–99	8,456	14,694	36%	64%
1999–00	8,565	15,327	36%	64%
2000–01	8,817	15,660	36%	64%
2001–02	8,950	16,964	34%	66%
2002–03	8,980	18,481	33%	67%
2003–04	9,711	20,464	32%	68%
2004–05	9,896	21,543	31%	69%
2005–06	10,370	23,206	31%	69%
10-year variation	14.9%	57.9%		

Note. Adapted from University of Ottawa, *Administration and Governance: State of Affairs* (2007).

At the beginning of the 21st century, the University of Ottawa benefitted from yet another joint support project of the federal and provincial governments, and a strategic plan was put in place to reinforce its mission once again. Several new and renewed structures were established, among which features prominently a fresh version of a university-level French Immersion Stream (FIS) program (University of Ottawa, 2021). This iteration of higher education French immersion was offered through an adjunct course model whereby students taking a discipline course offered in French as their second language were provided with additional language support through an added FSL course.

Once again, the primary role in this strategic plan to strengthen the University's focus on bilingualism was assigned to the SLI through its new incarnation as OLBI (University of Ottawa, 2005), whose members started collaborating closely as teachers and advisors with the FIS director and staff. The sustained growth and success of this program since the implementation of the strategic plan has enabled the institution to reduce the growing gap in enrollments between the two linguistic groups.

The specific objective behind the new postsecondary immersion program was to create and maintain a specific group of Anglophone students actively learning French who would represent around 10–15% of the overall student population. If successful, this plan would help reestablish the linguistic balance, and, as stated, "become the standard among Canadian universities in the areas of acquisition, development, evaluation and promotion of the official languages" (Knoerr, Weinberg, & Gohard-Radenkovic, 2016, p. 2). Along with this postsecondary immersion initiative, another one of the outcomes resulting from the University of Ottawa's fresh emphasis on bilingualism has been a sustained effort to invest in outreach and recruiting among Francophone students, internationally and within Canada.

Within this latest incarnation of the Institute (OLBI), the Documentation Centre and the Student Resource Centre kept their roles and purpose. In 2008, the two centers were formally united under its current name to honor one of the centre's original founders and thus became the Julien Couture Resource Centre (JCRC).

3. JCRC Collection: From Archive of Teaching Materials to Specialized Library of SLA Resources

Specialized in the field of SLA, the JCRC holds a unique collection of about 10,000 items. The Centre's primary focus is the preservation, curation, and purchase of pedagogical materials (textbooks and supplementary materials), continuously updated to respond to the needs of French and English as a second language teachers and learners. The collection also includes a variety of scholarly publications relevant to OLBI's own graduate program, a Master of Arts in Bilingualism Studies, concentrated around the areas of bi-/multilingualism, immersion, linguistic policy, and technology in education. A selection of feature films and documentaries, scholarly journals, and popular current affairs magazines as well as board games and reference materials for second language learners are also part of the collection.

In terms of its visibility, the Centre's collection, however, has only in the last few years become accessible online through an integrated library system. In the early 2000s, when the library community underwent the transition from card catalogues to automated systems, the JCRC collection was cataloged through a local database, giving our patrons limited access to the records on site, only with the assistance of the student staff. At several points, various ways of integrating our collection into the central library catalog were considered. However, the collection's very specific emphasis on SLA resources, its relatively small size, and more importantly, its home-grown, language skills-based classification system, makes finding resources straightforward and intuitive. This eliminated the need to adopt or apply a Dewey Decimal or a Library of Congress classification.

In 2017, after extensive consultations with our central library experts and external vendors and consultants, the JCRC committee decided to transition toward Koha (https://koha-community.org/). This open-source library system was already being successfully used worldwide, but more importantly, in the neighboring province of Quebec, where a group of 46 colleges had jointly decided on its adoption (Collecto, 2020). This system has provided the JCRC with a stable platform to display its collection, while also taking part in a global and a local library community. The motivation behind the decision to select an independent platform is therefore quite similar to Brubacher and Evershed's (2018) reasoning behind their language center's decision not to join the central library system, in spite of two completely different contexts.

Note that, due to uOttawa's overall mission and OLBI's specific mandate to "promote excellence and innovation in the fields of bilingualism and language acquisition" (Official Languages and Bilingualism Institute, 2021), the JCRC provides through its collection and its activities various services and spaces to all members of the university community. Every year, an increasing number of international students joins this community wishing to benefit from the unique opportunity to study in an environment where active learning of another language is an added bonus to the academic skills and scientific knowledge they acquire in their disciplinary programs.

4. JCRC Patrons and Staff: The uOttawa Community and Beyond

As an officially bilingual higher education institution, the University of Ottawa continually offers training and tools to its members through programs such as the FIS and structures such as OLBI to prominently feature issues at the core of Canadian identity. The goal of achieving functional official bilingualism thus continues to be a living, growing reality and not merely a lofty ideal.

The JCRC, in that specific context, has a big role to play in embracing that double identity and transforming it from two monolingual constructs into an environment clearly demonstrating that "the bilingual is not two monolinguals in one person" (Grosjean, 1989, p. 4).

Throughout all the changes described above, the JCRC constantly evolved, adapted, and continued providing a vibrant multifunctional space. As a meeting place with multiple study areas, the Centre is open to the entire uOttawa community, whether members are undergraduate or graduate students, Canadian or international, full- or part-time professors, or employees working in a number of front-line positions dealing directly with clients in both English and French across the campus. All of these members find themselves daily in situations on or off campus where they need to interact with individuals belonging to one of the two linguistic communities and are thus frequently looking for additional support in French or English.

4.1 Faculty and Employees

The JCRC has been and remains a place for OLBI faculty to discuss the methodological issues of the day and the development of various methods and pedagogical activities, while also offering resources and tools relevant to all learners in pursuit of their French or English language proficiency. In many ways, all members of the uOttawa community, depending on their status and particular requirements, are considered active learners of one of the two official languages.

For employees and faculty, the official requirement of bilingualism is reflected in the need to reach and maintain a level of proficiency in their other official language, French or English, required for a full-time or a tenure-track position (University of Ottawa, 2016). Depending on their department's or their faculty's specific requirements, the academic staff may be held to a standard of "active" or "passive" bilingualism.

When it comes to the administrative staff, there is also a clear requirement for every member dealing with the public to meet the "active bilingualism" standard (University of Ottawa, 2016).

4.2 Graduate and Undergraduate Students

The uOttawa students are given greater flexibility with respect to the expectations set for their bilingualism because according to the official regulation, "except in programs and courses for which language is a requirement, all students have the right to produce their written work and to answer examination questions in the official language of their choice, regardless of the course's language of instruction" (University of Ottawa, 2016).

This particular treatment gives the students a choice. They can decide to accept this regulation as an affordance encouraging them to improve their bilingual skills. They can also view it as a welcome compromise that will allow them to be exposed to academic content in their second language. It will spare them from being penalized and receive a lower grade due to their lower language proficiency in their L2 compared to their peers.

The JCRC caters specifically to students in the fields of linguistics and education in the University of Ottawa's Second Language Teaching (SLT) program who are studying to become certified teachers of French or English as a Second Language. These students are well regarded as future teachers and are offered special borrowing privileges, equivalent to the more experienced OLBI teachers. They are required, throughout the course of their program of study, to analyze textbooks and other teaching materials. A good number of them are active as volunteers in assisting international students to learn the intricacies of North American academia. Many of these students are also hired as second language monitors, assisting in the day-to-day functioning of the JCRC, as language workshop monitors or as student staff at the OLBI reception desk or with the Language Assessment sector.

Thus, the service provided to these groups, undergraduate and graduate students, implies bringing all members of the community on board. It is first done through a variety of programs and activities putting additional focus on this lived experience of everyday bilingualism. Then, it is put forward through the creation of communities of practice where the graduate students in OLBI's Master's program take full part in various faculty projects on linguistic policies, immersion, or evaluation and assessment (CCERBAL, 2020), thus bringing fresh insight into the field of research on bilingualism.

These graduate students also gain invaluable professional experience as Teaching Assistants (TAs), allowing them to establish links between the theoretical knowledge and insights gained through their research and its practical application in the classroom. The JCRC works closely with the instructors and TAs to foster student autonomy and enhance students' independence by encouraging them to improve their skills outside of the classroom:

In addition to classroom instruction, learners must also gain awareness of and draw on outside resources. To this end, for instructors this may include directing students to online resources or resource centres, or seeking to help them engage in real-life interactions beyond the walls of the language classroom. (Slavkov & Séror, 2019, p. 257)

Such real-life interactions that students can engage in come in many different formats. Some instructors are doing it through instruction offered in a hybrid format, where part of the course is taking place in the physical classroom, while the other part is taking place in a synchronous or asynchronous format online. Other instructors promote an experiential learning model through their courses, whereby students are required to attend a play, an exhibition, or watch a movie in their second language, all the while reflecting on their experiences through a journal or a portfolio. Yet another option for the students enrolled in our more advanced courses is to become involved in the local community in their second language and find a placement as volunteers with a Francophone or an Anglophone organization in the region. Then they report to their FSL or ESL class the experiences and professional and linguistic knowledge acquired through this community engagement. This approach is known as Community-Based Experiential Learning and can be defined as a "teaching and learning strategy which integrates meaningful, sustained and structured community service with reflective components that are able to enhance students' learning experience, social awareness and community connectedness" (Harfitt & Chow, 2020, p. 4).

4.3 International Students

As Yaden (2018) pointed out, "if students can walk in and experience the LRC in person one time, they are more likely to see the benefits of the resources and return for support" (p. 96). The English and French intensive, pre-university programs offered through the CLL serve as gateways for integrating those students into the uOttawa academic community through the classroom and the JCRC. They are also engaged in a variety of extracurricular activities (outings, social events, and academic workshops) that introduce them to the Canadian culture and its institutions in the National Capital. On a local level, students gain firsthand insight into the complexities of a city and a university striving to bring together two cultures, foster better mutual understanding, and overcome ongoing challenges that ensue from the various levels of government not always sharing the same vision.

These new students at the University of Ottawa, unfamiliar with the university environment and its structures, come to the JCRC prior to every term. The JCRC staff prepares an orientation session to show them the resources and tools, explain the functioning of the resource center, and introduce them to a number of other services on campus relevant for FSL or ESL learners.

4.4 JCRC Staffing and the Role of Technology

The majority of staffing needs on campus are met through hiring students, and it is crucial that they receive appropriate training and support as they juggle their academic priorities with their personal and professional ones. In terms of JCRC staffing, the students hired best represent the values of professionalism, friendliness, politeness, and overall knowledge of the local environment and available resources. My experience with respect to the relationship with the student staff, in fact, quite closely echoes Yaden's (2018) description:

> I am flexible with my staff, knowing that their priorities are first and foremost as a student. ... Our student consultants are the eyes and ears of the center. They interact with the patrons, they are language students themselves, and they know what is happening regularly in the center. I ask my student staff for suggestions in improving the services we provide. (p. 17)

As the "age of technology" (Chapelle, 2006, p. 5) advances, we are more and more aware of the vast possibilities it offers both in terms of its increasing ease of use and its adaptability to a variety of formats and devices. Moreover, we are just as aware of its drawbacks when it comes to protecting our data and the illusion it creates (and the pressure that comes with it) of constant availability and infinite potential. With the mobile applications and social media use in education, harnessing this potential and providing guidance to our patrons has fundamentally changed any remaining hierarchies, as we have come to realize that the traditional teacher and student roles as they pertain to technology have considerably shifted.

When it comes to the latest technologies and its use in education and learning, the students are taking on the role of "the student expert, or expert-novice" (Kang et al., 2018, p. 370). As Kang and her colleagues noted with respect to the language center's leading role in expertise in technology, "the pace of mobile app development has turned this paradigm on its head. The experts in emerging technology have become the students" (p. 370). In the case of the JCRC, some of the SLT students hired are in an even more advantageous position. Through their program of study, they are provided from the very beginning with the practical and theoretical basis to apply the tools at their disposal judiciously while putting to use the pedagogical knowledge they acquire. As student staff and after the initial training, such students are very quickly able to provide extremely useful assistance to their peers and the faculty looking for resources.

5. JCRC: Serving the uOttawa Community and Beyond

This section presents some of the partnerships in place meant to support students in their academic success at an institution where the official bilingualism and fluency in both official languages is the desired outcome. There is a potential risk of getting disoriented among all the units and services offering assistance, and units sometimes fail to reach their audiences due to insufficiently clear communications. It is therefore of utmost importance for the management of any organization to provide clear messaging, ideally in both languages.

5.1 OLBI's CLL and CCERBAL

The JCRC coordinates its activities with other centers and services both internally and externally. Within the structure of the Institute, the Centre's staff work with the CLL through providing technological support and resources for the teachers and teaching assistants. The JCRC also hosts various clubs designed to boost the international students' motivation, such as the Conversation Club, the Game Club, and the Book Club, all run by some of the teachers already in charge of the intensive courses.

The Centre also supports OLBI's research sector, CCERBAL, through initiatives and tools such as the Linguistic Risk-Taking Passport (Slavkov, 2015), which promotes a learner's sense of initiative and autonomy to create awareness "of their feelings of fear and anxiety and transform them into something positive and liberating, a sense of fulfilment and achievement, related to the institution's bilingual values and mission" (Slavkov & Séror, 2019, p. 260). This passport is used in different ways in various ESL or FSL courses, but it seems to be at its most effective in cases where the teachers are directly rewarding the students engaged in this initiative through a portion of their overall grade. These students actively go about "collecting" various linguistic risks, such as ordering their meal at the campus cafeteria or purchasing textbooks and school materials at the campus bookstore in their other official language. Once they have undertaken a number of these linguistic risks, students bring back their passports to have them stamped by their instructor. As a pedagogical tool used in the OLBI second language courses to further enhance task-based or project-based learning, the passport has enjoyed great success and attracted attention both from the Canadian federal government and other institutions locally and internationally throughout the network of OLBI partnerships.

5.2 Conversation Workshops

JCRC staff, usually students from the SLT program, facilitate French and English conversation workshops (different than the Conversation Club offered through the CLL, which is only offered to students in its pre-university intensive courses). These workshops are geared primarily toward the students in regular university ESL and FSL credit courses and most recently also toward uOttawa faculty and staff. They are structured according to the learners' language fluency level (beginner to advanced) and are limited to five students per group. Offered throughout the academic year, between September and April, they are primarily but not exclusively meant as additional language support for those enrolled in language courses. Students from other faculties and programs not taking any language courses with OLBI are welcome to participate and benefit from the opportunity to engage their peers and interact in their second language. Starting in the summer of 2020, the JCRC has started offering these workshops throughout the summer in an exclusively online format, first through MS Teams and then through Zoom.

As an alternative to OLBI workshops, the JCRC staff inform all those not enrolled in OLBI language courses about a similar type of program organized by the Bilingualism Centre, a service run by the uOttawa student union that provides further assistance to all members of the uOttawa student community regardless of their faculty affiliation.

5.3 Mentoring Centers

Each Faculty organizes Mentoring Centers that provide students assistance with their academic study skills. The Mentoring Center staff at the Faculty of Arts regularly take part in the events organized at the JCRC, such as Open House days when prospective students with their family and friends are invited to visit the University and learn about the requirements for specific programs and resources available.

5.4 Immersion Club

Yet another important service the JCRC works closely with is the Immersion Club that offers language support to the students enrolled in the FIS and organizes social and cultural activities for their members to learn about the French culture in this bilingual region and beyond. These students also actively participate in the conversation workshops offered at the JCRC.

5.5 The Academic Writing Help Centre

The JCRC collaborates with the Academic Writing Help Centre (AWHC) at the University of Ottawa, quite akin to the partnership established and maintained at Pacific Lutheran University (Yaden, 2018). The Centre's staff direct students coming to the JCRC with questions about structuring and conceptualizing their writing assignments to take advantage of this particular service. Similarly, the AWHC refers back to the JCRC all students looking to engage their peers in conversation workshops or to find appropriate second language learning materials.

5.6 Ottawa Public Library

In a city like Ottawa, where both official languages are strongly represented due to the seat of the federal government and the presence of significant French-speaking minorities (about 15% based on the latest official census data; Statistics Canada, 2016), the services available for its residents, whether they are students or new immigrants, are in many ways also relevant to the university community. The JCRC therefore also nurtures a partnership with the Ottawa Public Library (OPL).

While OPL services are not primarily geared toward the academic community, they provide another set of tools and additional support for their patrons who are sometimes also university students. It is also a very important source of information for some of the JCRC patrons, international students, and many TAs, who are quite often graduate students with teaching experience but without much first-hand knowledge of the city. The public library brings added value to the local integration and benefits especially those looking for involvement in the community, immigration services, or resources beyond the campus.

5.7 Partnerships with ESL and FSL Publishers

Because all ESL and FSL courses are the OLBI's responsibility, the Centre actively pursues and maintains professional relationships with the major publishers and distributors in the fields of English as a Second Language, English for Specific Purposes, English for Academic Purposes, and French as a Second Language in Canada or Français langue étrangère (French as a foreign language) internationally.

These informal partnerships with the main ESL and FSL textbook publishers enable the Centre to continuously develop its collection and ensure that it responds to its patrons' needs. New acquisitions for the JCRC feature prominently as a "showcase" within the University and allow its instructors to evaluate and potentially adopt pedagogical materials best suited for a wide variety of programs and courses offered to the uOttawa community.

The JCRC staff regularly organizes book displays or professional teacher development workshops at the center, where publishers' representatives are invited to present and interact with OLBI instructors. Such events, organized at least a few times every session, represent opportunities to learn firsthand about the latest publications relevant to OLBI language courses. They also serve to introduce JCRC patrons, both instructors and students, to the relevant technological trends, pedagogical platforms, and latest research as it pertains to international students and their experiences and the challenges facing students trying to thrive at a bilingual university.

6. Looking Ahead: Challenges

In 2013, the JCRC moved from a location on the edge of campus to its current one at the Faculty of Arts, on the ground floor of the building that houses all of the departments dealing with language teaching and learning. With its new, central location, the Centre has been able to welcome a greater number of patrons as it continues to foster partnerships and collaborations with other services. Along with the initial positive growth and the increasing number of visitors, the JCRC has been facing increasing competition for space and accommodation. The current challenges can be summarized as physical and virtual.

The main challenge in terms of physical spaces and their utilization was the addition in recent years of new infrastructure and the renovation of the existing one across the uOttawa campus. As a result, we have seen many new study and collaborative spaces being added for the constantly growing student population. Students were therefore actively encouraged to spend more time outside of their classes using campus facilities, thus reducing what could be called the "commuter-campus" effect of attending classes and not engaging with the university community.

The JCRC's ongoing virtual challenge in this sense has been to reach out beyond its own immediate community of learners and inform the students in other faculties and departments of its programming and resources. This challenge is closely related to the exponentially faster rate of growth in mobile technology and the availability of a host of cloud-based tools and learning resources. Such an information overload creates a need for constant mediation and a carefully targeted social media presence, while also providing traditional access to pedagogical materials.

In this technology-driven context, it has also been of vital importance to maintain best practices in terms of fostering and maintaining partnerships with language publishers and their constantly evolving platforms and tools. Such partnerships represent an attempt to reconcile the conflicting realities of achieving business objectives and reducing the financial burden of tuition and textbook fees. Libraries and language (or resource) centers are in this context perfectly positioned as intermediaries trying to find common ground between the publishers and the users. The JCRC has been able to keep its collection and resources relevant and up-to-date through its partnerships with publishers, thus successfully engaging with the constant influx of international students walking through its doors. It has also provided specialized academic or professional assistance to the faculty and employees requiring linguistic support, either individually or in groups, as an addition to the instruction they receive through the regular university courses offered at OLBI.

Another virtual challenge faced on a daily basis is a matter of sustaining a distinct and recognizable voice within a broader structure. For the Centre, being part of a bilingual institution where so many services and units contribute to the overall mission means constantly looking for opportunities to promote its services and programs. It also means going beyond the official message and finding ways of fostering bilingualism in a plurilingual environment. It is an issue directly related to the notion of official bilingualism. As such, it has played a very specific role in shaping the Canadian identity for at least the last 50 years, but in reality since the creation of the new nation. In an increasingly plurilingual society and with rising awareness of the First Nations and minority issues, the notion of "official bilingualism" will most likely be put to the test and possibly reconsidered as with any other "imagined community" (Anderson, 1983).

Lamoureux (2018) emphasized the importance of this challenge when she pointed out that "despite more than 40 years of teaching programs in the other official language to the English-speaking majority, few Canadians have attained functional official bilingualism" (p. 101). The main issue therefore seems to be one of leadership, for as Lamoureux further points out,

> It is crucial that decision-makers, whether government school boards and schools, universities and colleges, have high expectations of official bilingualism and that they be fully aware of its importance as an essential component of Canadian identity, of Canadian politics, as the key to understanding the country. (p. 100)

It is thus imperative to put together a concerted effort from all levels of governance if any minority rights, including the linguistic ones, are to be sustained on a more long-term basis. With the most recent creation of the Université de l'Ontario français (UOF), set to open its doors to students in Fall 2021 (Université de l'Ontario français, 2020), the University of Ottawa, as an institution welcoming and offering support to a large number of Franco-Ontarian students, will most likely be seeing a drop in enrollment for this segment of its community. At this point, however, only time will tell how the creation of Canada's first solely Francophone university outside of Quebec will impact the other higher education institutions in Ontario. Ultimately, the UOF's reputation and its ability to attract students, faculty, and staff will depend primarily on the quality and variety of its programs.

Along with these challenges come small and greater successes that are embodied on an individual level in taking the time to truly appreciate every learner's needs, regardless of their status. The relationships created through this personalized approach and commitment are the ones that remain and create long-standing bonds lasting well beyond the classroom or the time of language instruction.

7. Conclusion

This chapter offered an overview of the role of a very particular language resource center that is intricately linked to the overarching structure of the Official Languages and Bilingualism Institute at the University of Ottawa. As a reflection of an increasingly diverse Canadian society, OLBI is deeply invested in the overall mission of advancing official bilingualism through language teaching, post-secondary immersion courses, and advanced research in the fields of second language acquisition, linguistic management, and technology in education.

As its integral part, the JCRC offers a range of services directly related to language instruction in both Canadian official languages. It also supports and promotes through its partnerships with multiple other services across campus the minority language and cultural rights of the Canadian French-speaking minority in general, and of the Franco-Ontarian minority in particular.

In many ways, services and partnerships similar to the ones fostered at the University of Ottawa are offered through language centers across the world, but what makes the JCRC and the University of Ottawa stand out is the constitutional framework that has been in place in Canada for the last 50 years. This framework provides financial and political support to the long-standing institutional structure established at this particular university from the very beginning, albeit in different ways and with its programs and services constantly evolving and adapting to its socioeconomic and cultural environment.

In many ways, this institutional complexity lends itself quite well to what van Lier (1997) called the "ecological perspective on language learning" (p. 783) in as much as the various structures or elements that are brought together are "no longer separate components [since] they cannot be retrieved in their initial state" (Piccardo & North, 2019, p. 89). In fact, as Piccardo and North laid out the theoretical and practical underpinnings of an action-oriented approach to second language education, they also provided us with a conceptual and pedagogical framework for a better understanding of the complex network of pedagogical activities, learner-oriented services, and partnerships that is put in place at the University of Ottawa. As part of this network, the JCRC finds itself fully engaged in support of a variety of its French or English learner groups through affordances offered by means of real-life course-related tasks or projects and experiential learning activities via student engagement in campus, community, or city-at-large organizations.

The "uOttawa experience" therefore is a unique one, owing its existence to its geographical location and its historical and cultural dimensions and the most recent globalization/student mobility trends. The partnerships established and the services put in place, however, can certainly be used as examples in other contexts and adapted to other bilingual or multilingual regions or communities, with the appropriate political support and strategic vision in terms of its goals and objectives.

Despite the Centre's unique situation, the JCRC's experiences can be translated to other environments. The partnerships, formal or informal, established with nonacademic institutions such as the Ottawa Public Library, may at first seem counterintuitive. However, a public or municipal library serves a very important purpose in many bi-/multilingual communities with a large percentage of international or out-of-town residents. Not only does it bring newcomers together, it also provides through free membership easy access to literacy, educational, and linguistic resources along with additional support for local integration. For the JCRC staff, introducing international students to the public library as an integral part of their new environment beyond the immediate academic community has been a very rewarding and enriching experience.

A close collaboration with publishers and/or companies involved in educational technology is yet another way of keeping any language center's collection relevant and up-to-date as it fosters pedagogical exchanges and collaboration, whether through hosting external representatives' presentations or through internal, departmental, or campus-wide brown-bag lunches, lectures, or conversations. This type of collaboration also further underlines the importance of language centers as crucial intermediaries that bring together students, faculty, and publishers' representatives around common goals of providing truly relevant educational resources.

In this era of seemingly perpetual changes, radical shifts in the students' perceptions of authority, intellectual freedom of expression, and cultural norms, the language center ultimately remains a vibrant space moved by a centripetal force that constantly brings in new patrons and creates new experiences and exchanges around a shared objective of attaining bi-/multilingualism and educating global citizens. It is undoubtedly this singular and very specific focus that distinguishes language centers from the more generalized or academic libraries. It is also what makes them stand out, allows them to truly enrich their patrons' experiences, and ultimately make a difference.

References

Albero, B., & Poteaux, N. (Eds.). (2010). *Enjeux et dilemmes de l'autonomie: Une expérience d'autoformation à l'université - étude de cas.* Paris, France: Maison des sciences de l'homme. https://books.openedition.org/editionsmsh/189

Anderson, B. (1983). *Imagined communities: Reflections on the origin and spread of nationalism.* London, UK: Verso Editions and NLB.

Beillard, J.-M. (2000). Bilingualism in a Canadian context: The case of the University of Ottawa. *Higher Education in Europe, 25*(4), 469–476. https://doi.org/10.1080/03797720120037804

Brubacher, L., & Evershed, J. (2018). Managing media materials. In E. Lavolette & E. F. Simon (Eds.), *Language center handbook* (pp. 261–291). Auburn, AL: International Association for Language Learning Technology.

Burger, S., Weinberg, A., & Wesche, M. (2013). Immersion studies at the University of Ottawa: From the 1980s to the present. *OLBI Working Papers, 6*, 21–43. https://doi.org/10.18192/olbiwp.v6i0.1130

The Canadian Encyclopedia. (2013). *Quiet revolution*. https://www.thecanadianencyclopedia.ca/en/article/quiet-revolution

Canadian Centre for Studies and Research on Bilingualism and Language Planning (CCERBAL). (2020). *Research areas*. https://ccerbal.uottawa.ca/en

Chapelle, C. (2006), CALICO at center stage: Our emerging rights and responsibilities. *CALICO Journal, 23*(1), 5–15. https://dx.doi.org/10.1558/cj.v23i1.5-15

Clément, R., & Foucher, P. (2014). *Fifty years of official bilingualism: Challenges, analyses and testimonies*. Ottawa, ON: Invenire.

Collecto. (2020). *Des services et des solutions pour le réseau de l'éducation*. https://collecto.ca/a-propos/qui-nous-sommes

Courchêne, R., Burger, S., Cornaire, C., LeBlanc, R., Paribakht, S., & Séguin, H. (Eds.). (1995). *Twenty-five years of second language teaching at the University of Ottawa / Vingt-cinq ans d'enseignement des langues secondes à l'Université d'Ottawa*. Ottawa, ON: Institut des langues secondes / Second Language Institute.

Curzi, P. (2014). French, the common language of Quebec. In R. Clément & P. Foucher (Eds.), *Fifty years of official bilingualism: Challenges, analyses and testimonies* (pp. 15–19). Ottawa, ON: Invenire.

Garcia, O., & Kleyn, T. (Eds.). (2016). *Translanguaging with multilingual students: Learning from classroom moments*. New York, NY: Routledge.

Grosjean, F. (1989). Neurologists, beware! The bilingual is not two monolinguals in one person. *Brain and Language, 36*(1), 3–15. https://doi.org/10.1016/0093-934x(89)90048-5

Guindon, R. (1998). *La dualité linguistique à l'Université d'Ottawa: Coexistence équitable, volume 4: depuis 1965*. Ottawa, ON: Presses de l'Université d'Ottawa.

Harfitt, G., & Chow, J. M. L. (2020). *Employing community-based experiential learning in teacher education*. Singapore, Singapore: Springer. https://doi.org/10.1007/978-981-15-6003-3

Kang, H., Oglesbee, L. J., Ayo, D. A., Castellano, J., & Ó Conchubhair, B. (2018). From lab, to center, to hub: Evolution through technology and outreach. In E. Lavolette & E. F. Simon (Eds.), *Language center handbook* (pp. 363–380). Auburn, AL: International Association for Language Learning Technology.

Knoerr, H., Weinberg, A., & Gohard-Radenkovic, A. (2016). *L'immersion française à l'université: Politiques et pédagogies*. Ottawa, ON: Les Presses de l'Université d'Ottawa.

Kronenberg, F. A. (Ed.). (2017). *From language lab to language center and beyond: The past, present, and future of language center design*. Auburn, AL: International Association for Language Learning Technology.

Kronenberg, F. A., & Lahaie, U. (2011). *Language center design*. Auburn, AL: International Association for Language Learning Technology.

Labrie, N., Lamoureux, S., & Wilson, D. (2009). *L'accès des francophones aux études postsecondaires en Ontario: Le choix des jeunes*. Toronto, ON: Centre de recherches en éducation franco-ontarienne de l'Université de Toronto.

Lamoureux, S. A. (2018). Political issues and the politics of French immersion issues in universities. In H. Knoerr, A. Weinberg, & C. E. Buchanan (Eds.), *Current issues in university immersion* (pp. 89–106). Ottawa, ON: University of Ottawa Press.

Lavolette, E., & Simon, E. F. (Eds.). (2018). *Language center handbook*. Auburn, AL: International Association for Language Learning Technology.

Mazak, C. M., & Carroll, K. S. (Eds.). (2016). *Translanguaging in higher education: Beyond monolingual ideologies*. Bristol, UK: Multilingual Matters.

Official Languages and Bilingualism Institute (OLBI). (2021). *Our Mission, Our Values*. https://olbi.uottawa.ca/about/mission-values

Paulsrud, B., Rosen, J., Straszer, B., & Wedin, A. (Eds.). (2017). *New perspectives on translanguaging and education*. Bristol, UK: Multilingual Matters.

Piccardo, E., & North, B. (2019). *The action-oriented approach: A dynamic vision of language education*. Bristol, UK: Channel View Publications.

Prévost, M. (2008). *L'Université d'Ottawa depuis 1848 = The University of Ottawa since 1848*. Ottawa, ON: Université d'Ottawa / University of Ottawa.

Ruane, M. (2003). Language centres in higher education: Facing the challenge. *ASp*, *41–42*, 5–20. https://doi.org/10.4000/asp.1127

Slavkov, N. (2015). Introduction: Literacies and autonomy of the advanced language learner. *The OLBI Journal*, *7*, xiii–xvi. https://doi.org/10.18192/olbiwp.v7i0.1355

Slavkov, N., & Séror, J. (2019). The development of the linguistic risk-taking initiative at the University of Ottawa. *The Canadian Modern Language Review / La revue canadienne des langues vivantes*, *75*(3), 254–271. https://doi.org/10.3138/cmlr.2018-0202

Statistics Canada. (2016). *Census data 2016*. https://www12.statcan.gc.ca/census-recensement/2016/dp-pd/prof/details/page.cfm

Times Higher Education. (2019). *World university rankings 2019*. https://www.timeshighereducation.com/world-university-rankings/2019/world-ranking

Université de l'Ontario français. (2020, January 16). *L'université de l'Ontario français sur les rails!* Cision. https://www.newswire.ca/fr/news-releases/l-universite-de-l-ontario-francais-sur-les-rails--875151778.html

University of Ottawa. (2005). *Vision 2010: Academic strategic plan*. http://web5.uottawa.ca/vision2010/pdf/strategic_plan.pdf

University of Ottawa. (2007). *Administration and governance: State of affairs*. https://www.uottawa.ca/administration-and-governance/sites/www.uottawa.ca.administration-and-governance/files/volume_ii_-_state_of_affairs_anglais_final_24_aout_2007.pdf

University of Ottawa. (2016). *Administration and governance: Bilingualism*. https://www.uottawa.ca/administration-and-governance/academic-regulation-2-bilingualism

University of Ottawa. (2021). *French immersion stream*. https://immersion.uottawa.ca/en

van Lier, L. (1997). Approaches to observation in classroom research: Observation from an ecological perspective. *TESOL Quarterly*, *31*(4), 783–787. https://doi.org/10.2307/3587762

Yaden, B. E. (2018). Supporting the LRC mission through collaborative partnerships across campus and beyond. In E. Lavolette & E. F. Simon (Eds.), *Language center handbook* (pp. 91–103). Auburn, AL: International Association for Language Learning Technology.

Author Notes

Paco Lalovic (MA, MIS) is a Documentalist at the University of Ottawa's Official Languages and Bilingualism Institute where he is in charge of the Julien Couture Resource Centre (JCRC), a language resource centre specialized in second language acquisition, French, and English as a Second Language teaching and learning tools and materials. He received his BA in French Language and Literature from the University of Belgrade, his MA in French Literature from the University of Toronto, and his MIS (Information Studies) from the University of Ottawa. Paco has been managing the JCRC for more than a decade and has overseen its relocation across campus and its development into an academic and professional hub for all French and English as a Second Language learners at the University of Ottawa. His current research projects focus on developing smartphone applications for L2 learners and adapting Open Educational Resources to support language instructors and students with affordable alternatives.

Correspondence concerning this chapter should be addressed to Paco Lalovic (blalovic@uottawa.ca).

Chapter 8

Language Centers as Complex Dynamic Systems: A Case Study of Co-Adaptation in Japan

Branden Kirchmeyer, Sojo University, Japan

Abstract

Complex dynamic systems theory (CDST) offers a modern perspective of the language center (LC) as a system which affects and is affected by stakeholders and the environment, a process referred to as co-adaptation (Larsen-Freeman & Cameron, 2008). This chapter examines co-adaptation occurring in and around a LC at a university in Japan as the center was rebuilt after a series of devastating earthquakes. Redesign was focused on forging and sustaining dynamic connections between interrelated systems including stakeholders, curricula, and social activity within and around the center. Administrators leveraged existing and developing technologies to both ensure and bolster the legitimacy of the center for all stakeholders. Building upon a brief overview of CDST and key tenets, examples illustrate how new and existing technologies were leveraged to simultaneously support classroom tasks, self-access learning, and professional learning communities. Special attention is given to the ongoing co-adaptation between technologies, tasks, the taught curriculum, learners, teachers, and the center itself during and following the redesign process. Influential over a greater timescale, the effects of these examples are also considered in the LC's response to the COVID-19 pandemic. The chapter concludes by acknowledging anticipated challenges and suggesting that administrators prepare for them by considering LCs as complex systems.

Modern language centers (LCs) have continued to demonstrate adaptability as directors and their colleagues work to meet the needs of new generations of language learners in an interdependent and interconnected world. As LCs have proliferated worldwide, they have evolved from equipment-focused language laboratories influenced by technocentric mentalities popular during the Cold War (Hagen, 2017) into social hubs that facilitate global communities of practice (Frances, 2018), collaborative learning environments (Castaldi & Markley, 2018), and community development (Gossett, 2018). The present volume and its predecessors (Kronenberg, 2017b; Lavolette & Simon, 2018) provide evidence of a robust global community of LCs that routinely adapt to environmental changes, including and alongside the dizzying pace of technological advances in society.

Kronenberg (2017a) identified trends in modern language centers that involve continual evolution and adaptation, exemplified by the imagery provided by Brudermann, Grosbois, and Sarré (2017), who referred to their LC in France as "a constellation of interrelated components allowing for a flexible response to change" (p. 111). The change-oriented terminology employed by these and other authors (Jeanneau, 2017; Yaden & Evans, 2017) resonates with a burgeoning approach in applied linguistics: complex dynamic systems theory (CDST). In CDST, the world is perceived to consist of interrelated systems of varying degrees of complexity that are constantly changing and adapting to maintain relative stability. Society, communities, individual humans, language, traffic signals, and plant cells all function as interrelated systems in continuous motion. Over the last three decades, CDST has found growing application in the field of applied linguistics (see Hiver & Al-Hoorie, 2019; Larsen-Freeman & Cameron, 2008) and has more recently been used to describe both physical (Matthews, 2019) and social (Murray, 2017, 2018) dimensions of language learning spaces.

A CDST approach allows us to advance the metaphor of a LC as a technology-enhanced physical and social hub that provides context for language development and to consider it as a dynamic system that influences both its internal components and interrelated systems. This is a valuable perspective for any LC director looking to validate the central and active role their LC plays in the development of its users and local environment, and this approach can be especially useful for LC stakeholders in largely monolinguistic regions where cultural chasms may undermine LC aims and objectives. In Japan, for instance, many university-based LCs are confronted with the challenge of supporting and engaging language development in a largely monolinguistic environment often characterized by high levels of demotivation (Kikuchi & Sakai, 2009; Nakata, 2006) and ambiguity regarding the purpose of language learning (McVeigh, 2002). Applying a CDST approach to LC design and redesign may in this and similar contexts help identify and substantiate the full extent of a LC's influence on its users and environment.

This chapter has two aims: 1) to illustrate the role and function of a LC as a complex dynamic system, and 2) to more practically illustrate how new and existing technologies were leveraged to adapt to drastic changes in one LC's environment. Beginning with an overview of some of the essential tenets of CDST, the Sojo International Learning Center (SILC) in southern Japan is presented as a complex dynamic system that, after a series of devastating earthquakes, was able to maintain dynamic stability through co-adaptation of its components. Specifically, the leveraging of two technologies is detailed: Moodle (a learning management system) and Microsoft Teams (a collaboration platform). By this chapter's conclusion, wherein co-adaptation in response to the current global pandemic is considered, I hope that the reader will understand how a CDST approach might benefit the process of designing and redesigning a language center.

1. The Role of Context in Complex Dynamic Systems

Larsen-Freeman and Cameron (2008) defined complex systems as having "different types of elements, usually in large numbers, which connect and interact in different and changing ways" (p. 26). These systems compose the physical world in which we live over a wide range of scales, from planetary orbits and global ecosystems to community organizations and individual organisms, all the way down to microscopic plant cells and chemical reactions. Systems can describe organic (e.g., animals), inorganic (e.g., computers), temporal (e.g., conversations), or abstract (e.g., cultures) organizations of components, which can be animate agents (e.g., humans) or inanimate elements (e.g., electrical circuitry). Language development—on scales ranging from the individual to society—is thus considered a complex dynamic system that is constantly evolving.

According to Larsen-Freeman and Cameron (2008), "a key feature of complexity theory is that context is seen as an intrinsic part of a system, not as a background against which action takes place" (p. 16). They assert that contextual factors influencing a system might be appropriately incorporated as part of the system itself, and "if we can find ways to work with complex systems *in all their complexity*, we may produce better (i.e. more accurate and more useful) descriptions and explanations" (p. 40). This approach has already begun to inform research on language learning spaces in Japan. In reviewing their own five-year ethnographic study of a LC in Okayama, Japan, Murray and Fujishima (2016) wrote of their gradual shift toward adopting a complexity perspective: "We now see places, including learning environments, as emergent phenomena, the product of something new – something greater than the sum of its parts" (p. 8). *Emergent phenomena* in CDST describe new patterns of stable behavior in systems resulting from *self-organization*, the characteristic ability of a system to stabilize itself owing to its own dynamic properties.

The SILC in Kumamoto, Japan, is one such system, open to influence from external systems, yet able to maintain dynamic stability through adaptation of its subsystems and components. In the SILC, students, staff, and faculty (*agents*) are continually entering and leaving the program, bringing and creating new needs and affordances as they interact with each other and other system components in a technology-enhanced learning environment. As agents exert influence on the SILC system and vice-versa, both change in a mutual process known as *co-adaptation*. Remembering this is important to keep from slipping into the notion that the SILC is unchanging—a fixed building or department that remains relatively unchanged and free from the influence of its stakeholders. The next section details the SILC as it existed before the 2016 Kumamoto Earthquakes, providing a foundation for understanding how its components co-adapted in the face of extreme challenges.

2. The Sojo International Learning Center

The SILC was founded in 2005 at Sojo University, a private institution in southern Japan offering programs in fields of sciences, technology, engineering, and art. As a joint venture established with the External Language Consultancy Centre based at Kanda University of International Studies in Chiba, Japan, five mandates were adapted from an existing LC model to meet anticipated needs at Sojo University: 1) promote the use of English on a university-wide basis, 2) provide specialist teaching and advising expertise to students undertaking English proficiency courses, 3) promote a research-based curriculum of English proficiency courses and design and develop instructional materials for use in such courses, 4) promote the development of independent learning skills, and 5) provide research and professional development opportunities that will attract high caliber teachers to the center. As with many other university-housed language centers in Japan, the SILC was charged with providing communication-focused English language education to all first- and second-year students, regardless of their selected courses of study or their English language abilities or interests.

In the SILC program, new students took four semesters of classroom instruction in semi-standardized courses titled English Communication (EC1 through EC4). A communicative language teaching (CLT) approach was adopted to inform curriculum design and a variety of the center's other operations, including social events hosted in the SILC and a range of student support services provided throughout the center. This approach, as reported by the SILC director (Rowberry, 2010), was intended to promote the development of students' interpersonal skills and active participation in communicative class activities. Technology-enhanced learning was also a focal point, and teachers were encouraged to create learning opportunities within a Moodle learning management system. In 2010, each of the six classrooms, called Blended Learning Spaces, was equipped with a class set of laptops (about 26), and in 2015 university administrators approved the purchasing of 150 tablet PCs, replacing the already ageing laptops.

In addition to adopting a CLT approach to course design, strong emphasis was placed on promoting and facilitating independent learning (Mandate 4). This was expected to "encourage students to become more autonomous learners in all aspects of university life" (Rowberry, 2010, p. 60), which would in turn help students transition into graduate and postgraduate studies and enhance their future employment prospects. A self-access learning center, called simply "the SALC," was established within the SILC to help facilitate independent learning. It featured a wide range of language learning materials such as books, magazines, newspapers, CDs, DVDs, and computers, and a variety of resources including a staffed conversation lounge for naturalistic English discussions, skill-focused tutoring services with SILC faculty, and learning advisory services provided by trained learning advisors. Extracurricular events including parties, movie nights, and discussions were also scheduled to provide social contexts for English practice.

Self-access centers such as this have been on the rise in Japan, partly due to their ability to support the needs of language learners who have experienced language education in traditional, teacher-centered approaches (Thornton, 2016). One of about 51 registered self-access centers in the country (Japan Association for Self-Access Learning, 2020), the SALC at Sojo University was intended to help the SILC achieve all its mandates by acting as a resource not only for students enrolled in English courses, but also for students who had graduated from the SILC program and for other departments' faculty and staff. To promote its usefulness to students, the SILC curriculum often contained units that featured materials and resources offered in the SALC. Moreover, additional course credit was offered to students who completed predesigned independent learning tasks called *SALC Activities*, which were provided in the SALC. All Sojo students, faculty, and staff were kept informed of new materials and resources, social events, and policy updates via a seasonal newsletter published by the SALC and distributed across campus.

SILC/SALC integration was also manifested in the diverse team that managed it, which included two full-time and one part-time staff members, three faculty members, and several students in part-time positions with a range of responsibilities including material management, student support, and event organization. To various degrees, this team was responsible for ensuring that the SALC provided English language learning resources for the entire university. The relationships between stakeholders within the SILC system are depicted in Figure 1 with a concept map (for the construction and use of concept maps, see Novak & Cañas, 2006).

Figure 1

Concept Map of Agents in the SILC System

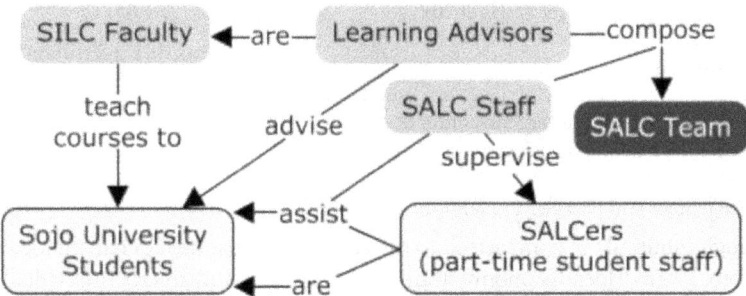

Architecturally speaking, the original three-storied SILC building held teacher offices and an open area for students to use freely (first floor), the SALC (second floor), and six classrooms, designated as blended learning spaces (one on the first floor, five on the third floor). All three floors of the building were occupied by the SILC, which contributed to a "home base" atmosphere. From the time it was established, the SILC had benefitted from a supportive administration and dedicated teachers who were committed to improving the SILC as a learning environment. In its first decade of operation, the SILC had evolved from a burgeoning support center for language education to a central hub for language and social learning on campus.

2.1 The 2016 Kumamoto Earthquakes: Change in an Open System

One condition of open systems is that they are subject to external influence, and in the case of the SILC this became hauntingly real between April 14 and 16, 2016 when seven earthquakes registering in the 6–7 band of the *shindo* seismic scale struck Kumamoto City and threatened the stability of the entire area and all local complex systems. As described by the Japan Meterological Agency (2009), during earthquakes of this magnitude, "It is impossible to remain standing or move without crawling. People may be thrown through the air. ... Wall tiles and windows are even more likely to break and fall. Reinforced concrete-block walls may collapse." Over 3,000 individual observations of related seismic activity (i.e., aftershocks) would be recorded within two weeks of the initial foreshock, a number that would rise to 4,298 in the year that followed (Japan Meterological Agency, 2018). On their own, data are grossly insufficient in portraying the full effect of any disaster; however, they can serve to provide a measure of appreciation, as Table 1 aims to do.

Table 1

2016 Kumamoto Earthquakes in Numbers

Deaths[a]	272
Related injuries[a]	2,735
Fully destroyed, partially destroyed, and damaged dwellings (reported)[a]	198,202
Peak displaced persons[b]	47,800
Currently displaced persons (May 31, 2020)[c]	1,631
Estimated cost of damages[d]	approx. JPY 3.8 trillion (USD 35 billion)

[a] Crisis Management and Disaster Prevention Section (2020)
[b] Department of Health and Social Services (2020b)
[c] Department of Health and Social Services (2020a)
[d] Crisis Management and Disaster Prevention Section (2017)

Although miniscule in comparison to the effect these earthquakes had on local systems both macro (local economy, transportation, etc.) and micro (individual lives), the effect of this disaster on the SILC system was dramatic. For safety reasons, Sojo University was forced to close its doors to students for a period of 32 days while the staff and administration worked fervently to salvage the semester and reestablish order among the turmoil. The SILC building was structurally assessed and condemned because the entire foundation had shifted enough to tilt the building off an even plane. Eager to maintain stability and characteristic of its commitment to the language program, the university administration quickly decided to rebuild the SILC, a process that would last two years.

For many who had survived the brief but dangerous ordeal, this marked the beginning of a long period of tension and frustration. Interim teaching situations posed many challenges, for example, teaching separate classes in close proximity simultaneously in an open space of the main library, where noise levels often clashed with library policy. Others found themselves competing with jackhammers as broken tiles were stripped away from the facade of the building just outside the classroom wall. Outside class time, communication between teachers and SALC staff suffered because the SALC was now far removed from both teacher offices and most classrooms.

For two years, the SILC system persisted in a precarious state, as a large number of subsystems and agents grappled with fluctuating and often adverse environmental conditions. However, except for a month of suspended operations, overall patterns of behavior within the SILC system did not change drastically, despite significant changes within and around the system. In the next section, I return to CDST for explanations as to how dynamic stability was maintained.

2.2 Rebuilding: Maintaining Dynamic Stability Through Co-Adaptation

A new SILC building would be erected in 2018, but in the meantime, remnant components of the formerly localized and stable system were distributed across campus. Unused office space in an old building was repurposed as temporary teacher offices. Classes were held among four different buildings on campus, some of which completely lacked digital resources. An interim SALC was established on the first floor of the main library, far removed from the daily student traffic it had previously enjoyed. While most of the materials from the original SALC were salvaged and transferred to the temporary location, some were damaged or lost. Despite the apparent chaos, almost all of the services and resources available to students in the former SILC were roughly realized in new locations. But would preservation of resources be enough to keep the center alive?

Complex systems like the SILC will often self-organize as they become increasingly affected by certain configurations of external conditions, settling into a preferred mode of behavior called an "attractor state" (Thelen & Smith, 1994, p. 56). Adapting Thelen and Smith's use of metaphor to illustrate this abstract construct, imagine that the entire SILC system could be measured by two observable components throughout a semester: class attendance trends and the number of language learning materials borrowed by students, whose possible values are depicted on a two-dimensional space in Figure 2. In this simplified model, the SILC's state space—all possible states of the system— are contained within the shaded regions A through D (students cannot have negative attendance or borrow negative materials). Attractor state A, in which class attendance is high and many materials are borrowed, describes the SILC system operating in normal, "healthy" conditions that are indicative of the LC fulfilling its mandates. The system can remain stable despite variable fluctuations of the two components within this attractor state, thus it is said to possess dynamic stability. Should conditions cause the SILC system to shift to a new attractor state (B, C, or D), the LC would no longer be fulfilling all its mandates. If, for example, students were to go on strike and stop attending classes but continued to borrow learning materials, the system would shift to attractor state B and continue to function as an altered system.

Figure 2

Hypothetical State Space of the SILC System

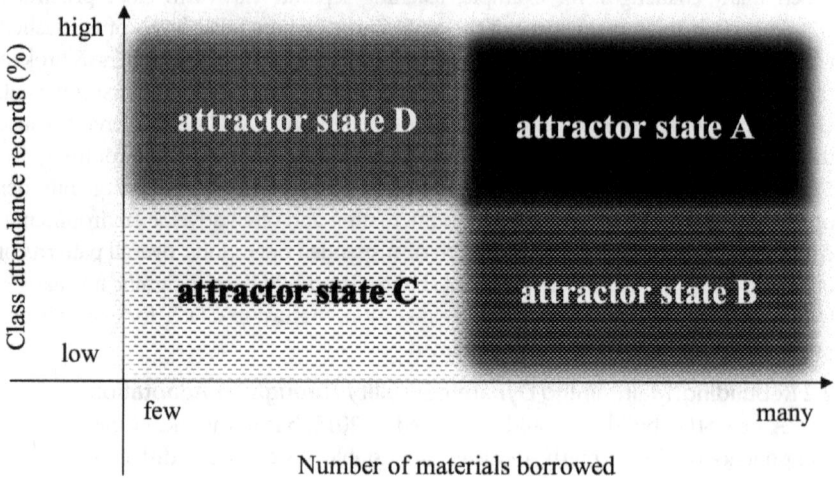

This simplified depiction of the SILC system's possible attractor states illustrates the capacity for a system to move between all possible states in the state space based on the dynamic relationships it has with internal and external elements. As noted by Hensley (2010) "a complex adaptive system's component subsystems will most often adapt to the change by entering a new attractor state while the overall system ecology remains relatively stable" (p. 86). In the case of the SILC, it is both interesting and insightful to consider that in all their terrible violence, the earthquakes did not cause the system to shift to an entirely new attractor state—students continued to attend and participate in classes, curricula groups continued to meet and develop new resources, the SALC staff continued to facilitate student access and use of materials, and the usual lineup of workshops and social events endured. Dynamic stability in complex systems is achieved in part through co-adaptation, and the SILC system had several contextual affordances—physical refuge space, sufficient time and human resources, and a supportive administration—which facilitated co-adaptation and dynamic stability within the system's state space.

After the earthquakes, co-adaptation occurred on different scales and among different system elements both within and around the SILC system. In one example, architects and contractors adapted their plans and timescales in relation to specific requests made by SILC faculty and staff members regarding the layout and features of the new building. Following the university administration's willingness to take faculty opinions into consideration, the SALC staff also solicited opinions and ideas from students who were "heavy users" of the original SALC, hoping to recapture and bolster the community of learners that had been nurtured in the original design. Through processes like these, a new building began to take form that incorporated the needs and desires of multiple stakeholders. However, before this new SILC was constructed, faculty and staff needed to find ways to quickly adapt to their new environments.

3. Leveraging Technology

By investigating co-adaptation between technological affordances and agents operating within the SILC system around the 2016 earthquakes, we may begin to visualize a more robust model of how language centers and their stakeholders evolve in relation to each other. The following sections outline two such subsystems and how they co-adapted in a manner that helped maintain overall stability within the SILC system.

3.1 Moodle: Co-Adaptation via Existing Affordances

Although the learning management system Moodle had been used to support SILC curricula since 2005, the SALC staff had not used it for any purpose. Three key affordances provided by Moodle made it an attractive solution to new challenges resulting from the earthquakes. First, in the year before the earthquakes, an app version of Moodle (Moodle Mobile 2.0) was released and made certain curricular resources and activities more attractive and accessible. Students were now able to access content on their personal devices from any location, using a clean and intuitive user interface. Second, Moodle served as a platform for providing digital and interactive content that could be used to convey SALC-related information in more meaningful and memorable ways (see Section 3.1.1). Third, information regarding student activity could be automatically summarized and passed back to faculty and staff with the purpose of analyzing trends and refining content, rather than having to be managed manually by SALC staff. Building on these affordances, the SALC staff leveraged Moodle to maintain and strengthen ties between students, the SILC curriculum, and the SALC in its new environment. Three examples of Moodle-driven solutions illustrate how SILC subsystems co-adapted in a changing environment.

3.1.1 A Self-Guided SALC Tour

First, a self-guided tour of the new interim SALC space was developed to introduce students to the physical layout of the makeshift center. In the former building, the SALC team (learning advisors and SALC staff members) conducted introductory tours of the SALC during scheduled class times of the first-year curriculum to ensure that all students were properly introduced to the available resources. However, library noise policy and space limitations made these types of group tours impossible in the new location, and the SALC team reasoned that a self-guided tour conducted via a mobile device could be used to circumnavigate these challenges and increase student engagement in the tour itself. Assigned by SILC faculty as homework in English classes, the tour was completed at a time convenient to each individual student.

The tour was relatively simple: Waypoints at key locations in the interim SALC were marked with easily identifiable signs that displayed important information about materials, services, and usage policies. Upon entering the interim SALC, students accessed an interactive lesson via their personal or borrowed mobile device and were then directed to these waypoints. The online tour activity displayed detail-oriented questions (e.g., "What can you do in the Conversation Lounge?")

that prompted students to read the physical signs for specific information. Students received immediate feedback depending on the answers they selected or provided. By monitoring activity data in Moodle such as question statistics, student responses, and access time, the SALC team was able to make real-time changes to the tour activity itself and pass along pertinent information to faculty regarding individual students and class trends. In this manner, the SALC team was also able to rely on data reports to determine if certain information was unclear to students. For instance, a high percentage of incorrect answers reported on subsequent attempts (after an initial incorrect response) for one multiple-choice question led the SALC team to rewrite and publish a less confusing set of answers before most of the students started the tour (Kirchmeyer, 2017).

Taking a CDST perspective, this example is illustrative of co-adaptation between several SILC subsystems. Changes in the methods employed by the SALC team (i.e., development and implementation of the self-guided tour) affected the behavior of students (i.e., mimicking self-access behaviors in a self-guided tour), which in turn affected administrative decisions made by the SALC team as tour activity data became available (i.e., making waypoint information clearer in response to a high proportion of incorrect answers). It should be noted that this is a simplification of complex dynamic relations, and these systems were also open to external influence as they adapted. For example, university scheduling affected students' ability to access the interim SALC, while software updates to students' mobile devices affected the tour user interface. Openness to external influence is a key feature of complex systems and contributes to the nonlinearity of change (Juarrero, 1999).

3.1.2 SALC Activities

In a second example of co-adaptation via Moodle, the SALC team digitally reproduced paper-based independent learning activities, called SALC Activities, in the same Moodle course that students used to access the tour. These short activities served to simultaneously introduce students to concepts of self-directed learning (e.g., goal setting and reflection) and facilitate awareness of SALC resources. They were available to all students, though they were incentivized for students enrolled in English classes with credit toward their class grades. In the original building, the former SALC was conveniently located on the floor directly below most classrooms, and students often completed these activities immediately before or after class. When the SALC was moved to its interim location in the main library, the SALC team anticipated that student use of the SALC would decrease, and efforts were particularly focused on providing first-year students with adequate experience with the interim SALC and its affordances. Reproduced digitally on Moodle, SALC Activities became accessible anywhere, allowing teachers to easily introduce and demonstrate them in classrooms across campus. In addition, integrating multimedia allowed students to visualize physical resources and preview activity tasks prior to visiting the interim SALC.

Co-adaptation between systems occurred over time as students interacted with the online SALC Activities. The provision of new (digital) means affected the ways in which students engaged in SALC Activities, and new capabilities affected the types of tasks the SALC team was able to create. The SALC team had reasoned that digital formats would allow for more appealing and effective means to present information within SALC Activities. However, student survey data collected at the end of the semester indicated a lingering preference for paper-based activities, which shaped future iterations. According to one administrative report, "students quickly learned how to do the activities using the app and according to the student feedback survey about 70% found the app convenient to use. However, 40% disagreed that 'doing activities on screen is better than paper'" (Rowberry & Horai, 2017, p. 19). The SALC team responded to these data by designing and offering hybrid SALC Activities that allowed students to complete tasks on paper, but still collected and reported data via Moodle. Whereas student behavior indirectly instigated change in the tour activity, this example illustrates how students were more actively involved in shaping their learning environment.

3.1.3 The SALC Series

Finally, a third example describes a program that was initiated with the intention of opening more pathways to autonomous learning behaviors by bolstering the relationship that existed between the SILC curriculum and SALC resources. Called *The SALC Series*, Moodle-based learning modules (*episodes*) were designed to present a sequence of independent and social learning tasks that were completed by students during class sessions. In each episode, students considered strategies for independent learning and were presented with information about relevant SALC resources. In contrast to the SALC Activities, which were presented as optional extensions to be attempted in students' free time, these episodes were integrated as part of the standard curriculum. Development of the SALC Series can be viewed as a product of co-adaptation: Over time, the continually changing nature of elements within the SILC system affected those very same elements and produced an entirely new subsystem, that is, the SALC Series. In the second semester after the new SILC building opened, during which the SALC Series was first implemented, the SALC saw both a 120% increase in foot traffic within the SALC and a 100% increase in the number of students using SALC services (Kirchmeyer, 2019).

Leveraging the Moodle learning management system to maintain stability was an adaptive behavior that resulted in other interconnected systems making their own adjustments. The three examples in this section illustrate a dynamic relationship between agents operating in the SILC system and how *existing* technology was used as an affordance of the system to ensure its own dynamic stability. The next section describes new patterns of behavior emerging among system agents as a result of *new* technological affordances being introduced to the system.

3.2 Microsoft Teams: Co-Adaptation Through New Affordances

While the SALC team was finding ways to maintain stability using Moodle, SILC faculty were also discovering new ways to communicate and collaborate effectively. Before the earthquakes, proximity allowed SILC faculty and SALC staff members to easily communicate face-to-face, and digital methods of communication included telephone, email, and instant messaging via services such as LINE and Facebook Messenger. Collaborative materials development for SILC curricula was supported through a local area network that housed public, private, and shared-access folders. Prior to the earthquakes, the university had invested in a license for Microsoft Office 365 that provided faculty, staff, and students with access to productivity software including Outlook, OneDrive, Word, PowerPoint, SharePoint, and more. It was through this license that the SILC faculty were able to use Teams when it was released in 2017.

Microsoft Teams is a communication and collaboration platform that allows users to organize chats, video meetings, and file storage according to the needs of a group. Individual users may belong to multiple groups (called *teams*) in which virtual spaces (called *channels*) can be created to compartmentalize communication and collaboration. The desktop user interface is shown in Figure 3. In this window, the user's team memberships are listed on the left, and a dropdown list of channels is displayed directly beneath the currently open "SILC Tech Team." The majority of screen space in this example is dedicated to instant messaging between team members in a channel regarding classroom projectors (labeled "Posts" above the discussion). The view can be quickly switched to display a shared file storage space (labeled "Files") or a collaborative notebook (labeled "Notes") on the same topic.

Figure 3

Desktop User Interface of Microsoft Teams

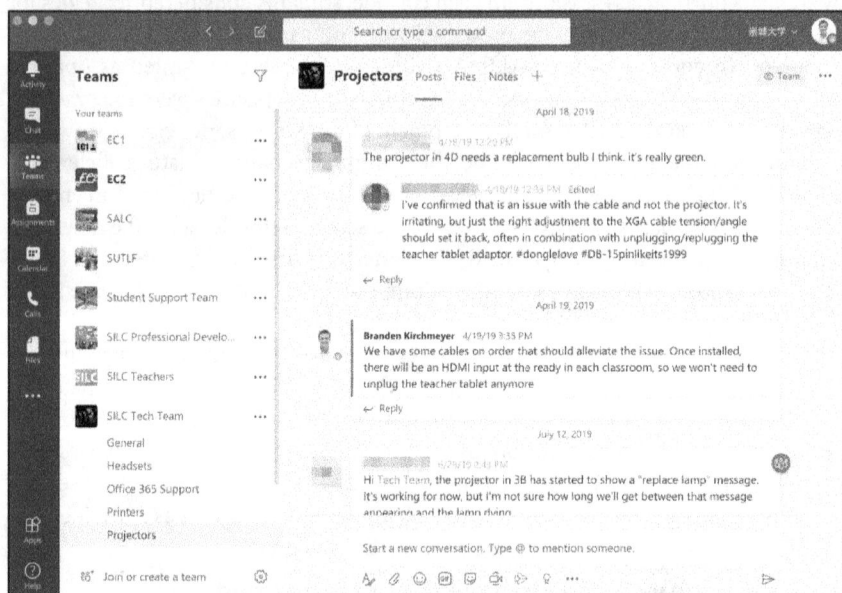

Microsoft Teams was introduced to the SILC by a small group of faculty who had been exploring new affordances in Office 365 immediately following the earthquakes. As the potential for its use to help maintain clear communication and collaboration between colleagues across campus became evident, it was adopted by more faculty and staff members until its use became ubiquitous in the SILC. The successful uptake of Teams was due in part to several affordances it provided, including integration with other Microsoft Office programs. The most impactful affordance was users' ability to compartmentalize topics into channels that allow working groups to maintain focused discussions asynchronously. This was particularly useful, for instance, to the eight faculty members who composed the first-year curriculum group who, just before the earthquakes, had begun the process of overhauling their courses English Communication 1 and 2. Within these teams ("EC1" and "EC2" in Figure 3), channels were created for different features of the courses that required collaborative revisions such as lesson plans, activity materials, vocabulary sets, and assessments. Rather than using multiple email threads or scheduling frequent face-to-face meetings, this group was able to adapt their communication and collaboration methods for a more efficient workflow, which allowed the group to create new course material at a much faster rate. Microsoft Teams was not only used to revamp the curriculum. As represented in the "Teams" column in Figure 3, teams and channels were created and deleted as needs arose and dissipated in areas of student services (SALC, Student Support Team), professional development (SILC Professional Development), and administration (SILC Teachers, SILC Tech Team). In fact, Teams was so influential in changing the way the faculty and staff communicated that it was acknowledged in research conducted on communities of practice within the SILC as a positive influence on "coordination and synergy" among members of a group (Barington & Xethakis, 2018).

The adoption of Microsoft Teams as a new method of communication within the SILC illustrates certain features of complex dynamic systems. First, the transition into Teams was demonstrative of *self-organization*, as the system of communication between the SILC faculty and SALC staff shifted into a new pattern of stable behavior due to elements within the system, not outside it. Both the earthquakes and the public release of Teams certainly played influential roles, but the faculty and staff orchestrated the transition from trial to full adoption. Second, new patterns of behavior *emerged* from this self-organization and resulted in something qualitatively different than what previously existed. For example, the group of tech-savvy faculty members who serves as unofficial tech support for the SILC was only formed during the transition into Teams and did not previously exist as a cohesive group. In a process called *reciprocal causality*, formation of the group within Teams affected the system in different directions. Tech problems could be reported and addressed more efficiently and publicly, and the SILC Tech Team was shaped into channels based on faculty reporting trends. Other language centers have taken deliberate steps to facilitate communities of practice (Scott & Hughes, 2017), and this CDST-based example illustrates an alternative, organic assemblage of individuals.

Communication and collaboration between the SILC faculty and SALC staff *co-adapted* with the affordances provided by Microsoft Teams, leading to an emergence of new patterns of behavior. These changes were non-linear in that faculty began using Teams in response to physical dispersion, but the result changed the way the department communicated and continued to shape communications once everybody was back in the same building. The emergence and organization of new teams, projects, workflows, and communicative behaviors within the SILC that resulted in part from the uptake of new and existing technology fits the model of emergent systems and co-adaptation. As an illustration of how these examples of co-adaptation have played out over time, the next section provides an extended timescale and considers system responses to a new, global crisis.

4. Dynamic Stability in a New Crisis: COVID-19

Shortly after the first draft of this chapter was submitted for review, news reports began surfacing of a highly contagious novel coronavirus that had been identified in China. Japan's first confirmed case of COVID-19 was reported on January 16, 2020 (World Health Organization, 2020), and three months later, prime minister Shinzo Abe declared a country-wide state of emergency ("Japan to Declare," 2020). Prior to the prime minister's announcement, administrators at Sojo University once again made the decision to close, restricting student access to campus and rolling back the start of the new academic year, which had been scheduled, as usual, for early April. Eager to begin providing classes and services for students—many of whom had already moved to Kumamoto from their hometowns—but leery of the consequences of opening too soon, the university administration subsequently released a series of weekly announcements of tentative start dates and lesson delivery methods. Ultimately, classes in the SILC began fully online on May 11, 2020, and the SILC building finally opened for blended online and socially distanced face-to-face classes on June 8.

The challenges posed by this new crisis have been quite different from those encountered after the 2016 Kumamoto Earthquakes. Physical elements of the SILC system have been relatively unaffected by COVID-19, though access restrictions and social distancing measures have reduced student use of classrooms and language learning materials. Using the metaphor in Figure 2, it could be said that the SILC has recently shifted to attractor state (D); attendance rates in a mix of face-to-face and online English classes have remained high, but borrowing trends have dropped significantly due to access restrictions placed on the SALC. Students, staff, and faculty have had to cope with many personal and professional challenges. Technological affordances within the SILC system, particularly Moodle and Teams, have proven invaluable in the current response to change. As such, they are briefly expanded upon in this section to demonstrate dynamic stability over time and the outward influence the SILC has had on interrelated systems.

When Sojo University, like many others, finally made the decision to offer online classes, SILC faculty were burdened with the task of creating an entirely new curriculum in a few short weeks. Due to the same affordances discussed in this chapter, Moodle and Teams once again played important roles in helping the system maintain stability. Because faculty and staff experience with Moodle and Teams had grown significantly in response to the earthquakes, use of these elements in response to lockdown measures occurred naturally. Moreover, as faculty and staff competence with these tools grew, the SILC's ability to achieve dynamic stability also improved. For instance, the SILC faculty and SALC staff used video conferencing in Teams to communicate and collaborate while certain members were under quarantine. Curriculum teams, intermittently required to work from home, were able to collaborate on content creation via Teams and Moodle and were thus able to create an extensive online learning program in a matter of weeks.

Although this chapter has primarily focused on co-adaptation of elements within the SILC system in response to the 2016 earthquakes, extending the analysis to include system responses to COVID-19 helps illustrate how long-term effects of co-adaptation within the system have in part affected the relationships it has with external interrelated systems (i.e., the organizational faculty in which the SILC is situated and the university at large). When administrative working groups gathered at Sojo University to consider their collective response to COVID-19, a different learning management system (WebClass) emerged as the preferred choice for most departments. The SILC, however, was allowed to continue using Moodle, due in part to its proven success, extensive integration with the English curriculum, and student and faculty familiarity and competency with the platform. In this case, the demonstrable stability of the SILC system itself guarded against further change caused by external influences.

5. Looking Ahead

The major claim of this chapter, based on the complexity perspective of the SILC as a complex dynamic system, is that language centers can remain stable despite the introduction of chaotic influences. If the SILC were simply a physical hub within which language development occurred, the destruction of the original building would have certainly meant the end of the center's existence, at least until a new space was constructed. When viewed as a system, however, we can point to the adaptability of system components as contributors to the center's overall stability. In the SILC, technologies new and old were leveraged to allow various components to co-adapt. Specifically, an online learning management system was adapted to suit new learning environments, which changed behaviors of students, and new forms of communication were adopted, which formed new organizational networks and behavior among faculty.

While this chapter has highlighted relatively successful initiatives, we must also acknowledge anticipated challenges and inevitable changes to current systems. Difficult as it is to make predictions about the future of complex systems and nonlinear relationships, CDST would be an insufficient approach if it could not help us prepare for the future. For the SILC, two immediate challenges are anticipated. First, the devices used in the SILC are currently approaching their seventh year of service and are showing signs of aging. Students commonly experience technical failures during lessons, and this often causes frustrations that interrupt learning. Although students are now required to provide their own devices for face-to-face lessons, many personal devices do not have the adequate processing power and memory to handle digitally-supplemented lesson activities. As mentioned in Section 3.2, there is no dedicated technical support position in the SILC, and all technical issues are handled by a team of volunteers with varying areas and levels of expertise. The absence of a certified professional with explicit tech-support responsibilities is an issue that can potentially influence the

LC system at every level, so the lack of dedicated tech support and the aging of equipment should be considered when investing in new hardware. However, these challenges can be mitigated with focused working groups, as demonstrated in the SILC.

Another important consideration is more humancentric and concerns the competence and willingness of SILC stakeholders to use technology appropriately. Generally, faculty and staff have embraced the initiatives detailed in this chapter, but individuals will not always be equally eager to learn and adopt new systems. If the current culture of continuous professional development and adaptability can be maintained as the SILC system progresses into a state of relative stability, then new technological affordances may be more easily introduced and appropriately used. However, if development stagnates and SILC professionals do not continue to develop as users and managers of these technologies, the co-adaptative relationships between faculty, staff, and students will become unbalanced. Care should be taken in any LC to nurture a culture of continual development to avoid this.

In sum, language centers can and should be considered as complex dynamic systems that shape and are shaped by agents and elements operating within the system and by external, interrelated complex systems. Progressive views have allowed us to move away from tech-focused labs and into social-oriented hubs, and this approach can provide directors with a more nuanced perspective of how different components may affect each other and the system as a whole. As individuals and institutions worldwide have relied on technological solutions to adapt to the COVID-19 crisis, administrators may be able to actively facilitate dynamic stability in their LCs by investing in flexible resources that allow faculty and staff to co-adapt to unforeseen circumstances. The future may be uncertain, but if we can identify and support those processes that allow us to adapt, we can better ensure the dynamic stability of our LCs.

References

Barington, R., & Xethakis, L. (2018). *Learning together & working together: Aspects of teacher collaboration.* Paper presented at the JASAL 2018 X SUTLF 5 Conference, Kumamoto, Japan.

Brudermann, C., Grosbois, M., & Sarré, C. (2017). Design and deployment of a language center in French higher education: A complexity and quality assurance approach. In F. A. Kronenberg (Ed.), *From language lab to language center and beyond: The past, present, and future of language center design* (pp. 110–126). Auburn, AL: International Association for Language Learning Technology.

Castaldi, P., & Markley, L. (2018). From lab to collaborative hub: Making the language center relevant. In E. Lavolette & E. F. Simon (Eds.), *Language center handbook* (pp. 319–339). Auburn, AL: International Association for Language Learning Technology.

Crisis Management and Disaster Prevention Section. (2017). 地震の概要と被害
状況 [Outline of earthquake and damage status]. https://www.city.kumamoto.
jp/common/UploadFileDsp.aspx?c_id=5&id=18725&sub_id=1&flid=133185

Crisis Management and Disaster Prevention Section. (2020). 平成 28（2016）年熊
本地震等に係る被害状況について［第304報］[About the damage situation
related to the Kumamoto earthquake [the 304th report]]. https://www.pref.
kumamoto.jp/uploaded/attachment/113406.pdf

Department of Health and Social Services. (2020a, May 31). 応急仮設住宅等の入
居状況（5月31日現在） [Occupancy status of temporary housing (as of May
31)]. https://www.pref.kumamoto.jp/kiji_33536.html

Department of Health and Social Services. (2020b, May 31). 応急仮設住宅等の
入居状況の推移 [Changes in the occupancy status of temporary housing].
https://www.pref.kumamoto.jp/kiji_33536.html

Frances, C. (2018). The language center: A hub for global communities of practice.
In E. Lavolette & E. F. Simon (Eds.), *Language center handbook* (pp. 295–317).
Auburn, AL: International Association for Language Learning Technology.

Gossett, N. S. (2018). Evolving the language center: Moving past the physical space.
In E. Lavolette & E. F. Simon (Eds.), *Language center handbook* (pp. 341–362).
Auburn, AL: International Association for Language Learning Technology.

Hagen, L. K. (2017). Kaputnik: Lessons from the life and death of the language lab.
In F. A. Kronenberg (Ed.), *From language lab to language center and beyond:
The past, present, and future of language center design* (pp. 13–27). Auburn, AL:
International Association for Language Learning Technology.

Hensley, J. (2010). A brief introduction and overview of complex systems in applied
linguistics. *Journal of the Faculty of Global Communication, 11*, 83–95.

Hiver, P., & Al-Hoorie, A. H. (2019). *Research methods for complexity theory in
applied linguistics*. Bristol, UK: Multilingual Matters.

Japan Association for Self-Access Learning. (2020). *The Japan language learning
spaces registry*. https://jasalorg.com/lls-registry/

Japan Meterological Agency. (2009, June 18). *Tables explaining the JMA seismic
intensity scale*. https://www.jma.go.jp/jma/en/Activities/inttable.html

Japan Meterological Agency. (2018, March 22). 「平成28年（2016年）熊本地震」
の震度１以上の最大震度別地震回数表 [Seismic frequency table by seismic
intensity of 1 or more for the "2016 Kumamoto Earthquake"]. https://www.data.
jma.go.jp/svd/eqev/data/2016_04_14_kumamoto/kumamoto_over1.pdf

Japan to declare nationwide state of emergency amid virus spread. (2020, April
16). *The Mainichi*. http://mainichi.jp/english/

Jeanneau, C. (2017). Redefining language centers as intercultural hubs for social and
collaborative learning. In F. A. Kronenberg (Ed.), *From language labs to language
centers and beyond: The past, present, and future of language center design* (pp. 61–
82). Auburn, AL: International Association for Language Learning Technology.

Juarrero, A. (1999). *Dynamics in action: Intentional behavior as a complex system*.
Cambridge, MA: Harvard University Press.

Kikuchi, K., & Sakai, H. (2009). Japanese learners' demotivation to study English:
A survey study. *JALT Journal, 31*(2), 183–204.

Kirchmeyer, B. (2017). *Promoting self-access centers with Moodle*. Paper presented at JALTCALL2017, Shikoku, Japan. https://researchmap.jp/kirchmeyer/presentations/15992685

Kirchmeyer, B. (2019). *The SALC Series: Promoting independent learning*. Paper presented at PanSIG 2019, Kobe, Japan.

Kronenberg, F. A. (2017a). Conclusion - From language centers to language learning spaces. In F. A. Kronenberg (Ed.), *From language labs to language centers and beyond: The past, present, and future of language center design* (pp. 161–165). Auburn, AL: International Association for Language Learning Technology.

Kronenberg, F. A. (Ed.) (2017b). *From language lab to language center and beyond: The past, present, and future of language center design*. Auburn, AL: International Association for Language Learning Technology.

Larsen-Freeman, D., & Cameron, L. (2008). *Complex systems and applied linguistics*. Oxford, UK: Oxford University Press.

Lavolette, E., & Simon, E. F. (Eds.). (2018). *Language center handbook*. Auburn, AL: International Association for Language Learning Technology.

Matthews, B. (2019). Assemblage theory: Coping with complexity in technology enhanced language learning. In F. Meunier, J. Van de Vyver, L. Bradley, & S. Thouësny (Eds.), *CALL and complexity - short papers from EUROCALL 2019* (pp. 280–284). Research-publishing.net. http://dx.doi.org/10.14705/rpnet.2019.38.1023

McVeigh, B. J. (2002). *Japanese higher education as myth*. Armonk, NY: M.E. Sharpe.

Murray, G. (2017). Autonomy in the time of complexity. *Studies in Self-Access Learning Journal, 8*(2), 116–134.

Murray, G. (2018). Self-access environments as self-enriching complex dynamic ecosocial systems. *Studies in Self-Access Learning Journal, 9*(2), 102–115.

Murray, G., & Fujishima, N. (2016). Exploring a social space for language learning. In G. Murray & N. Fujishima (Eds.), *Social spaces for language learning: Stories from the L-café* (pp. 1–12). Basingstoke, UK: Palgrave Macmillan.

Nakata, Y. (2006). *Motivation and experience in foreign language learning*. Bern, Switzerland: Peter Lang.

Novak, J. D., & Cañas, A. J. (2006). *The theory underlying concept maps and how to construct and use them*. https://cmap.ihmc.us/docs/theory-of-concept-maps

Rowberry, J. (2010). A new member of the family: The Sojo International Learning Center. *Studies in Self-Access Learning Journal, 1*(1), 59–64.

Rowberry, J., & Horai, K. (2017). *Sojo International Learning Center Annual Management Report 2016-7*. Kumamoto, Japan: SILC.

Scott, V. M., & Hughes, T. F. (2017). From consoles and cubicles to coding and collaboration. In F. A. Kronenberg (Ed.), *From language lab to language center and beyond: The past, present, and future of language center design* (pp. 28–43). Auburn, AL: International Association for Language Learning Technology.

Thelen, E., & Smith, L. B. (1994). *A dynamic systems approach to the development of cognition and action*. Cambridge, MA: The MIT Press.

Thornton, K. (2016). Promoting engagement with language learning spaces: How to attract users and create a community of practice. *Studies in Self-Access Learning Journal, 7*(3), 297–300.

World Health Organization. (2020, January 16). *Novel Coronavirus - Japan (ex-China)*. https://www.who.int/csr/don/16-january-2020-novel-coronavirus-japan-ex-china/en/

Yaden, B., & Evans, C. (2017). Envisioning new spaces - The human element. In F. A. Kronenberg (Ed.), *From language lab to language center and beyond: The past, present, and future of language center design* (pp. 83–98). Auburn, AL: International Association for Language Learning Technology.

Author Notes

Branden Kirchmeyer (EdM, University at Buffalo) is a Senior Assistant Professor in the Sojo International Learning Center, a department of the Center for Education and Innovation at Sojo University in Kumamoto, Japan. He has served the Japan Association for Language Teaching (JALT) in numerous capacities including Chapter President (Southern Kyushu), and he currently serves as Treasurer for the Japan Association for Self-Access Learning (JASAL). His research and professional interests include blended and project-based learning, intercultural communication, feedback and formative assessment strategies, and professional development of in-service teachers. He is currently engaged as the principal investigator of a three-year grant project, funded by the Japan Society for the Promotion of Science (JSPS), to develop and test an online group oral test targeted at improving the spoken English fluency of Japanese university students.

Correspondence concerning this chapter should be addressed to Branden Kirchmeyer (brandenk@m.sojo-u.ac.jp).

Chapter 9
Building for Sustainable Change: Co-Designing Language Centers in Germany and the United States

Felix A. Kronenberg, Michigan State University, USA
Klaus Schwienhorst, Leibniz Universität Hannover, Germany

Abstract

This chapter describes the co-design processes at two institutions: the redesign of the University Language Centre (ULC) at the Leibniz University in Hannover, Germany and the first stages of the transformation of the labs at the Center for Language Teaching Advancement (CeLTA) at Michigan State University. We describe the approaches involving multiple stakeholders in a carefully planned process, while also emphasizing the importance of prototyping, a term more often connected with software engineering. Throughout our design processes, we favored a view that process has precedence over product. Finding the perfect design, the perfect fit, is difficult to achieve in one go. In this chapter, we propose an evolutionary model where designing a language center and its services involves regular evaluation and adjustment in an iterative design process.

A co-design process (also called a participatory design process) includes all stakeholders throughout the whole process. It is inclusive, permeable, situated, and organic. It can also lead to continuous development of a space after it is constructed. As such, it can make the space more sustainable and resilient to becoming underutilized, avoided, or even obsolete. The participatory design process can be used as a placemaking approach. Design processes executed exclusively by professionals and experts are more likely to be perceived as imposed upon or top-down. Co-design can increase the sense of ownership and belonging because it is more attuned to local cultures, diversity, and social needs. In this chapter, we formulate best practices in a stakeholder-focused process and make recommendations for administrators and language center directors.

In this chapter, we describe the co-design processes at two institutions: The redesign of the Leibniz Language Centre (LLC) at Leibniz University in Hannover, Germany, and the iterative changes at the labs and office space at the Center for Language Teaching Advancement (CeLTA) at Michigan State University (MSU). We describe the approaches involving multiple stakeholders in a carefully planned process, while also emphasizing the importance of prototyping, a term more often connected with software engineering. Throughout our design processes, we favored a view that process has precedence over product. Finding the perfect design, the perfect fit, is difficult to achieve in one go. In this chapter, we propose an evolutionary model for language center (LC) design that involves regular evaluation and adjustment in an iterative and sustainable design process.

At the heart of our developments lies an understanding of co-design as described by Whitham et al. (2019):

> We understand collaborative design research practice as seeking new ways of connecting people to shared and individual futures, unlocking, amplifying and catalysing individual creative potential, and contributing to broader, systematic shifts in governance, politics, and social practice. This expansion of design intent away from its well-defined and well-equipped pathways of products and projects, service provision, briefs and stakeholders, criteria and critique offers a new landscape of possibilities for the designer. This work is frequently underpinned by a recognition of the complexity and diversity of challenges that the world faces, the entanglements of knowledge and technology needed to address such challenges, and the heterogeneous perspectives of individuals implicated in them. (p. 3)

Central to this view are notions of "complexity and diversity," "entanglements of knowledge and technology," and "heterogeneous perspectives of individuals." We recognize that these challenges need to be addressed by various top-down and bottom-up processes, which we describe in this chapter.

1. Evolutionary Design Model

We set out to propose an evolutionary model for LC design that involves regular evaluation and adjustment in an iterative and sustainable design process. Based on the Continuous Design Thinking Model (Reynard, 2017), we created the i7 Evolutionary Design Model (Fig. 1, next page).

Inspire. Creating awareness, aligning with vision and mission, relating to pedagogical models, prototyping. The design process should be based on a clear mission statement which in turn needs to follow the university's language policy and internationalization strategy (what services are being offered to whom and why?). This is first and foremost a leadership issue concerning the language center director and the university leadership, but also comprising input from staff members. A pedagogical model (how, in what form should we be offering these services?) is then also necessary for the design process.

Figure 1

Evolutionary Design Model

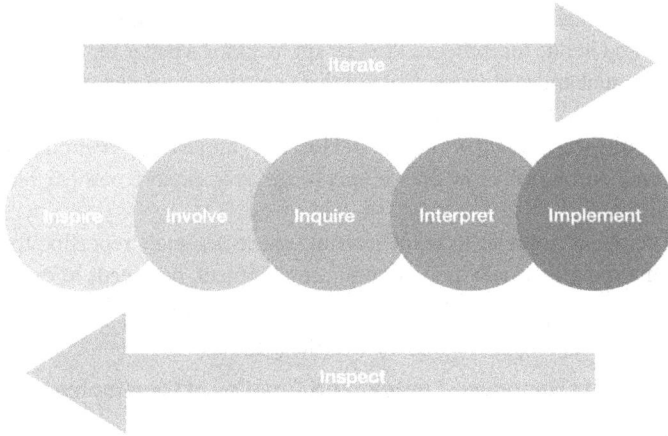

Involve. Involving various agents (disabilities representative, learning spaces advisors, student health management, student focus groups, sustainability office, staff, etc.), co-designing. Involving as many agents and perspectives as possible on building a language center is vital; however, it is important to distinguish between needs and wants. Learners and teaching staff may "want" to stay with what they know, they may "want" to sit in rows on uncomfortable chairs. Real needs may, however, be different and require a readjustment, a deeper involvement, and reflection on what we know about how learning works. The stakeholders we involved were always grateful for being asked; on the whole, an approach that valued expertise and different perspectives was welcomed. In some cases, positions such as sustainability officers or learning spaces advisors are not yet long-term positions, so for them to be involved in such projects underlines the importance of their work and strengthens their position within the university.

Inquire. Research and inquiry, needs analysis, catalog of specs. What we mean here by inquiry is that the involvement of agents needs to be carried out through systematic inquiry, through formalized tools such as semi-structured interviews, needs analyses, questionnaires, on-site visits, protocolled reports, etc.

Interpret. Context dependent: language specific, communicative, interactive. We then interpret the results of our inquiry and carefully consider all arguments before condensing them into a coherent argument.

Implement. Building prototypes and producing small changes. The implementation involves the realization of a radically new learning space concept, as exploratory prototyping, that differs as much as possible, in as many aspects as possible, from the status quo. In that way, learning space design directly impacts the many hidden assumptions about learning and teaching. For example, round tables mean that either a teacher needs to move around the space so that everybody can see them, or that learners need to shift their chairs to see them. Soon, both agents may come to a point where they ask themselves: "Is it important that we have eye contact all the time? What does this say about our teaching-learning relationship?" This exploratory prototyping precedes the implementation proper, which may involve the whole LC. Implementation, in our view, should not try to create the perfect fit in one go, but inspect and iterate this process, thereby approaching a better fit.

Inspect. Assessment and evaluation. We feel that prototyping needs to be closely monitored and evaluated. Which aspects of the learning environment are useful and are to be kept? Which aspects should be modified? How does the learning environment impact how we teach and learn? How does it encourage us to explore new teaching and learning strategies?

Iterate. By "iteration," we refer to many learning space designers reporting that designing a learning space is usually not a one-off development, but needs to evolve over time though iteration and inspection. At every point, we inspect what we have achieved and then reiterate the process for our next design phase.

2. Leibniz University Hannover: Context and Timeline of Development

Leibniz University Hannover (Germany) is a university with approximately 30,000 students, about 15% of whom are international students, mainly coming from China, Russia, and India (in order of percentage). As a member of the TU9 (nine main technical universities in Germany), it has a strong focus on engineering subjects, although humanities is still the biggest single faculty, and teacher education programs play an important part in the university's strategic goals. LCs at German universities usually offer language programs for all faculties, including services such as language learning counseling or testing (TOEFL, IELTS, and various German certificates), and, increasingly, counseling in academic writing. The design process of the new LC at Hannover began when it was decided that many engineering faculties would move from the vicinity of the main university building (the castle) to a new purpose-built engineering campus in a suburb of Hannover. Three floors of a 1960s five-story building then became available as the location of the new LC. The goal was to bring together all its staff members and seminar rooms in one building; due to the rapid growth from eight staff members in 2006 to almost 40 staff members in 2019, the center had been operating in three different locations. This move happened in May 2021. In the planning stages, the LC had to submit figures and projections on the number of staff members and the number of learners; standard seminar rooms were then calculated by building management to be able to host up to 25 learners. These figures were then connected to space (square meters per learner/staff) and provided an important starting point for planning. The framework of rules and regulations, including planning fire escapes and escape routes and other security measures, still leaves room for interpretation that we discussed with a number of stakeholders throughout the design process.

Our move coincided with several fortunate circumstances. First, in 2019, the university took over responsibility for commissioning building projects. This meant that more of the planning for building activities is now taking place "in-house;" this will speed up bureaucracy and changes in the building process. Second, it also meant that more building management staff were required and employed. Many of these new architects were highly motivated to build or rebuild exciting new learning spaces, while still keeping within the restrictive design framework of public sector buildings. Because private architects were also involved, our project had from the start a buzzing development team. Some of these architects were also teaching in the interior design faculty at the Hochschule Hannover University of Applied Sciences and Arts, and they used the new language center as a design project for their students to work on; we will return to this later. Third, 2019–2020 saw the consolidation of services and staff at the LLC. A university language policy had been published in 2018. This policy defines the way the university deals with languages, how it presents languages internally and externally (e.g., what languages are visible on campus? What languages are used in advertising?), how it appreciates languages, and how it encourages its members to learn languages. The same year saw an updated internationalization strategy, and many staff members had been made permanent or put on five-year instead of two-year contracts. We had also secured a solid revenue from third-party projects such as language certificates and German language foundation courses to contribute to the otherwise limited funding available for rebuilding. These four factors, (1) autonomy in design, (2) availability of a diverse and highly motivated design team, (3) a consolidation of strategies, services, and staff, and (4) a certain financial "cushion," no doubt opened up avenues for redesign that not all language centers can avail of. The development of the LLC can best be described in the timeline depicted in Figure 2.

Figure 2
Timeline of New LLC

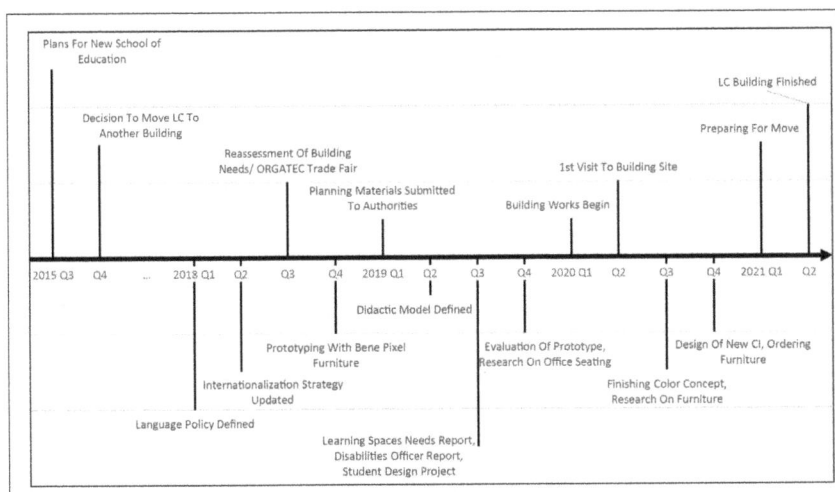

In the following sections, we describe our design process as it relates to the i7 evolutionary design model.

2.1 Inspire

The development of a new physical LC needs to start with a clear vision by the leadership of the LC, a definition of the tasks and services the LC is to perform, and a clear understanding of the didactic model of teaching and learning that should take place there. These three perspectives do not necessarily develop in that chronological order, and they should attempt to reinvent current services and frameworks provided. In the case of the LLC, our university went through an internationalization audit. The Audit Internationalization is an initiative by the German universities' rectors/presidents conference (the organization of German university rectors/presidents) that attempts to support universities in planning, implementing, and evaluating a strategy for internationalization. Subsequently, the university's vice president for international affairs assembled an "internationalization team," which combined representatives from various faculties and service facilities. The LC director had written a draft of a language policy document, which was then revised by the internationalization team. It was fortunate that the language policy document was discussed and published before the internationalization strategy was updated because it raised awareness of all issues of language use at the university, from signposting through displaying heritage languages by administrative staff through what languages should be used for instruction. The final document was specific enough that the university senate would check progress every two years while also offering avenues for the development of additional services in the years ahead. When the internationalization strategy was discussed, it was noticeable that many issues had been discussed already in the context of language policy. The LC director also had a clear vision of how the future LC should be developed and that we needed to radically question the structure of existing LCs in Germany, which were still largely technology-driven. The whole team of the LLC developed a pedagogical model, primarily based on language learner autonomy, a concept developed since the late 1970s by authors such as Holec (1979), Little (1991), and Little, Dam, and Legenhausen (2017). In this view, learner autonomy is not synonymous with self-access learning, but instead denotes three important principles of language learning. First, there is learner involvement, where learners become full agents in planning, implementing, monitoring, and evaluating learning; second, learner reflection, where learners engage reflectively with the process and content of their learning; and third, the exclusive use of the target language, whether for input, output, or reflective tasks. Together with the Common European Framework of Reference for Languages (Council of Europe, 2001; and its Companion Volume, Council of Europe, 2018) our model defined how we conceive of language learning and teaching, how we define the roles of learners and teachers, and what elements are important in the language learning environment.

2.2 Involve and Inquire

We noted in the previous section that while a clear vision or inspiration by the LC leadership is certainly required, the creation of a new LC needs to involve first and foremost the students and staff working there. The LC leadership needs to develop methods of inquiry so that all stakeholders would be heard and, where possible, involved. The process of involving our staff began much earlier during a team workshop that took place in 2015 on the topic of "what our ideal LC looks like." Staff members created a number of diagrams and drawings, collected pictures, and wrote down what they found important. Staff members also were able to take part in the language policy document and codeveloped the LLC's pedagogical model. The pedagogical model became particularly important to us because we wanted it to become visible as design choices in the finished building, in other words, become "built pedagogy" (Monahan, 2002). For example, a learner-centered classroom does not require a special teacher's desk with special lighting and presentation tools such as whiteboards mounted on walls; it may instead have desks with wheels, evenly distributed lighting and presentation tools with wheels. This would enable a lecturer to position herself anywhere in the room with flexible furniture/technology rather than including a huge teacher's desk up front. In this way, we developed the pedagogical model over several months, working with a coach external to the university.

It was comparably easy to find out by means of a questionnaire what office structures our staff members preferred. Overwhelmingly, they made a case for traditional (enclosed) offices. There was consensus among counseling, teaching, testing, and administrative personnel, both staff and students, that workspaces and consultation spaces needed to provide an atmosphere of confidentiality and privacy. For example, a learner writing a dissertation on a VW climate control component, funded by VW, may have signed a nondisclosure agreement where even coming in for a counseling session means taking a risk. We therefore opted for the rather traditional office structure of two staff members sharing an office. The broad corridor space enabled us to implement a small kitchen and lounge for staff and enclosed counseling/testing spaces. Room-in-rooms (Figs. 3 & 4) will be used for academic writing and tandem pair counseling. Tandem language learning is a method of language learning based on learner autonomy principles, where for example, a German student of Spanish is paired with a Mexican student learning German to learn both German and Spanish from each other. These tandem pairs need small, confidential spaces where they can learn together; as mentioned above, a confidential writing project may require the same environment; both learning settings require a sound-proof booth, a large screen to plug in, and a whiteboard. These room-in-rooms are therefore a good example of built pedagogy. A crucial part of this process of involvement is consultations with counselors to define learning goals and evaluate language learning and language learning strategies, materials, time frames, etc. (see Schwienhorst, 2007, pp. 37–40). We also need spaces for one-on-one testing scenarios that are required for some university entrance-level language exams. The availability of counseling/testing spaces together with the two-workspace-offices thus creates an additional confidential space: As one of the staff members enters the room-in-room, the other can have one-on-one consultations or tests in the office. The offices and consultation room-in-rooms are all located on one side of the building to give this space more privacy, whereas the seminar rooms and open learning spaces are all located on the other side of the building. The involvement of staff members continues throughout the building process.

Figure 3

Early Draft of Staff Offices and Consultation Room-in-Rooms (Gray) in the Corridor

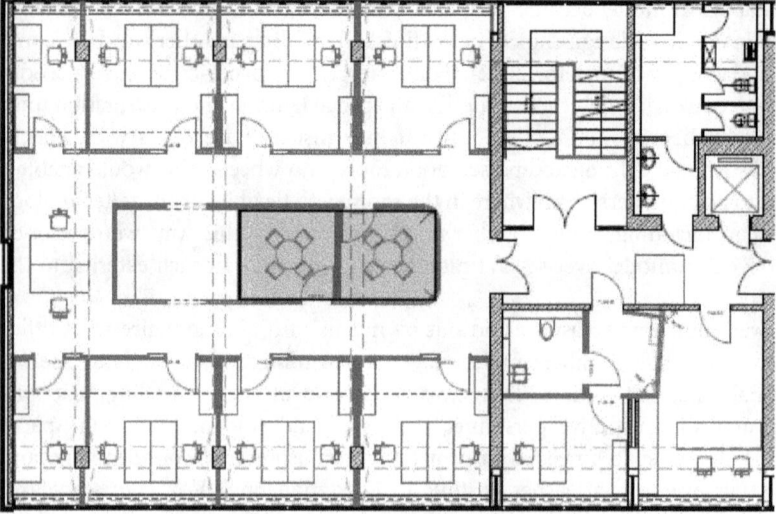

Note: Visualization used by permission, MOSAIK Architects ©.

Figure 4

Sample Room-in-Rooms (Picture Taken at the Booth of Carpetconcept, Orgatec Trade Fair 2018)

Note. In our case rooms are not only soundproof, but by using curtains, groups can work without others looking in. (Photograph © Klaus Schwienhorst)

Learning spaces advisors at our university then developed a method to involve students. They assembled focus groups and interviewed students from various faculties on their requirements for learning spaces and, more specifically, language learning spaces. Students reported, for example, that they needed height-adjustable tables/chairs and a mixture of single workplaces and group workplaces (2–4 people), if possible, as an alcove to enable a focus on work. Learners also liked the use of acoustic elements to create private spaces, vast collaboration spaces/whiteboards and interactive whiteboards, lockers, and coat hangers. Learnings spaces need to have sufficient power outlets and USB sockets because many learners regularly bring two or more mobile devices with them. Learners were skeptical about completely flexible furniture and seating without back support (also encountered in the design models by architectural students later on), and they did not like round tables. They were also opposed to "comfy" couch-type furniture with low tables; in their view, learning spaces should be "functional." Learners also frequently referred to sustainability, such as in the use of recycling bins, energy-saving building materials, and lighting and exterior blinds.

The learning spaces advisors also consulted with the disabilities officer to make sure that all learning spaces would be accessible to disabled students. The advisors prepared a short report following an on-site visit.

We also consulted with the student health officer who pointed out some important ergonomics studies and reemphasized the point that we needed adjustable tables and/or seating or tables at different heights. Learners should be invited to change their work position regularly and switch between sitting, standing, half-sitting, and moving around. For example, some of our discussions focused on whether back support and traditional classroom chairs were essential for all seating or whether active seating using ergonomic and sometimes unstable stools was healthier (see, for example, a discussion in Faulk et.al., 2019). These discussions are ongoing, we can see from student reactions to our prototype that there is little awareness among students on the ergonomic workplace, at least in our environment at Leibniz University. For example, many students expressed a desire for traditional chairs and tables rather than stools encouraging active seating and adjustable tables. Here, conflicting data sources need to be interpreted carefully so as not to confuse learner "wants" with learner "needs."

During this phase, the architects, who also had links with the Hochschule Hannover University of Applied Sciences and Arts, offered to present our building plans to final-year interior architecture students to develop a "short-term design project." Over the course of six weeks, students then developed various designs for our building, focusing on the open learning spaces. We began with an on-site visit and ended with an official presentation of their concepts. Because this was the first time we had seen a visualization of our new learning spaces, these concepts were particularly exciting to us. The students got the added bonus of developing a realistic project for a real customer and presenting it.

Finally, our studies did not ignore the existing literature, whether on language center and learning space design (e.g., Harvey & Kenyon, 2013; Kronenberg, 2017; Kronenberg & Lahaie, 2011; Oblinger, 2006) or on office and classroom ergonomics (e.g., McKeown, 2008; Smith, 2007). Several staff members visited recently designed language centers and libraries, office furniture companies and distributors and their web presences, and important office trade fairs (such as Orgatec Cologne, https://www.orgatec.com/).

2.3 Interpret

When involving as many perspectives and inspecting as many sources as we did, using a multitude of methods, it is to be expected that the results need to be balanced and seen in context with the "inspirational" documents in Section 1.1. Where contradictions arise, for example, between student "wants" and ergonomic "needs," LC directors or steering committees need to take responsibility and make decisions. In our case, all the data we collected were condensed into a profile of requirements, which we submitted to the architects to hear their view and to see what was possible within the constraints of the budget and the materials and structures of the building Our next step is to discuss specific furniture set-ups, adopting many ideas from the interior architecture students. We mentioned that staff members had very clear ideas on the office structure and the room-in-rooms (see Figure 2), so at this point we only need to clarify details because most staff members have received new ergonomic furniture over the past few years. The seminar rooms and open learning spaces, however, are not so clear. Because the financial budget is as yet unclear, we are considering using high quality but second-hand office furniture, also reemphasizing the sustainability theme. We also have existing (traditional) seminar room furniture, which we will use and gradually replace over the next few years, as we collect more data on learner and teacher use.

2.4 Implement

Just as interpretation of data continues, implementation as a process is still ongoing. In the case of the LLC, it was twofold. We could see Sections 2.1–2.3 as a standard procedure when we plan a new LC. After interpreting the data, we would simply build what was required, with the exception of a few contradictions that require decision-making. When we looked at the data, however, we were left dissatisfied. Not only were most of the results at best representative of a particular group, but even a full-scale involvement of all participants would not show us how stakeholders would react to a radical redesign of the learning spaces. Involving a large number of people and perspectives does not create the perfect workplace nor the perfect learning environment; neither does inquiry, where we used needs analysis and co-design to create a catalog of specifications for our learning spaces. We found that we needed an inspiration to set in motion reflective processes on learning spaces. Our inspiration was prototyping. We conceive of prototypes in Stappers's sense as "things we make to find out things" (2013, p. 85). The advantage of exploratory prototyping lies in its effort to understand problems, not to develop something that resembles the final product. The prototype allows the main players (here: learners and lecturers) to experience learning spaces. As both learners and lecturers are literally thrown into the experience, the prototype may provoke strong and often emotional reactions. The prototype is thus not a means to pursue the ideal product, but an ongoing process, "suggesting an erosion of the boundary between prototype and final object" (Kimbell & Bailey, 2017, p. 218; see also Floyd, 1984).

In our case, we replaced, almost overnight, the traditional furniture in an existing seminar room with modular office furniture called PIXEL by the Austrian company Bene (Fig. 5); we informed all teaching personnel by sending pictures and announced that we would evaluate this at the end of our half-year term. A recipe for disaster? Yes and no. The confrontation with very new furniture concepts overwhelmed most of our teachers and learners who are used to rows of seating and teacher-fronted classrooms. Reactions were as radical as the room transformation, but we also quickly discovered how deeply ingrained concepts of "spaces where learning happens" are and how these are linked to perceptions of what should happen in a language learning course, and thus to pedagogical concepts. We also discovered what features of a learning environment were well received and which did not seem to work. In that sense, prototyping with a radically new environment will get teachers and learners alike to lay their cards on the table: What is the basis of my teaching? What are my assumptions and conceptions about learning, and what is the best environment for me to learn? The confrontation with radical learning environments makes avoidance strategies difficult. Our starting point here was to implement a radically new learning environment, then closely monitor and evaluate how its users reacted.

Figure 5
A Refurnished Seminar Room Using Bene PIXEL

We gained some important insights, which were similar to those analyzed by Ramos-Gonzalez (2019):

- Learners were open to new learning environments.
- Learners appreciated ergonomic seating and flexible workspaces.
- Learners reported that the furniture allowed for different learning scenarios.
- Learning methods did not match the new furniture.
- Learners appreciated the flexibility, aesthetics, and ease-of-use of the furniture, but did not find it ergonomic nor comfortable.
- While some learners preferred to have chairs with backs to lean on, other learners preferred workspaces where they could change position or needed to move around.
- Learners appreciated the opportunity to work at low and high tables, but preferred height-adjustable stools/chairs, which allow their feet to touch the ground.
- Feedback from teaching staff was mixed: about 50% would call their teaching traditional or frontal. Most participants found the design aesthetic, flexible, and easy-to-use, but the teaching staff missed the teacher's desk up front.

Between the lines, we saw that the new environment also questioned traditional teaching assumptions. Why does the teacher or the teacher's desk need to be at the center? Why do learners need to see the teacher at all times? How can we teach when there is so much flexibility? How can we organize teaching when there is no obvious front, middle, and back of the room?

We are certain that less radical propositions would have received less criticism or enthusiasm, and we would have learned less about underlying learning and teaching concepts and the question of what constitutes a useful learning environment. We received many detailed remarks that show that many learners really want to help create new learning spaces. Our planning does not envisage technology-driven learning spaces nor comfortable lounge zones where learners relax. We will not implement new ideas in all learning spaces, but start with one, then evaluate the reactions by teaching staff and learners, then continue with the next space, etc.

We have confined built-in technology to a strong wireless LAN and a large number of power outlets in our planning, both normal and USB, for charging the devices users bring. Possibly we will offer laptops to learners; group workspaces will have larger monitors to enable collaboration. LED lighting will be installed in all rooms, but we made sure that the space where the teacher traditionally sits does not receive extra lighting to enable more flexible furniture constellations and avoid frontal teaching scenarios. There will likely be at least one interactive whiteboard in every seminar room (and possibly also in the open learning spaces) and large walls with whiteboard paint in every seminar room and learning space.

The open learning spaces require very careful planning because these present the "face" of our language center, and we know that more permanent design decisions concerning all three floors have to be made. At this stage, it is clear that these rooms will have a high degree of flexibility but that they also require "anchors" or focus points. In other words, they need fixed furniture installations that provide a sense of familiarity, a fact that was emphasized by the architecture students and the architects. The open learning space on the second floor, near the front office, will have a curtain surrounding a seminar room space (Fig. 6). Around this space are self-access areas with single and group workspaces. All three floors will have different color schemes to demonstrate decreasing noise levels (the top floor is planned to be the "quiet" learning space).

Figure 6

Concept of 2ⁿᵈ Floor Learning Space

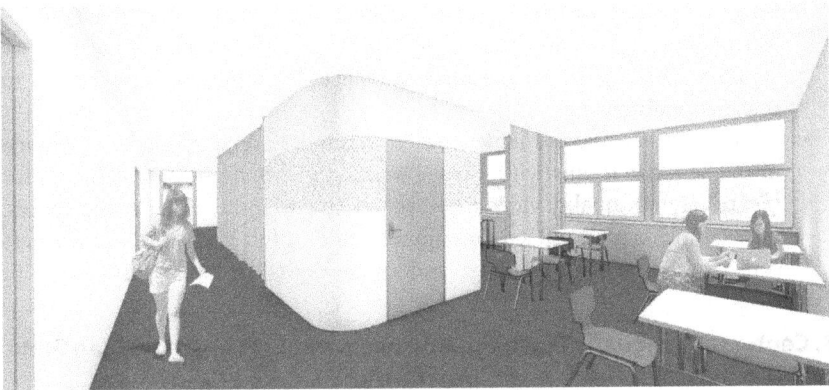

Note. Visualization used by permission, MOSAIK architects ©.

2.5 Inspect and Iterate

Our design for the three floors is incomplete, and we do not intend to fill all learning environments with new furniture when we move in. Rather, we will evaluate carefully how teaching staff and students experience the new opportunities. Just as we cannot expect teaching staff to "know" how to cope with the new learning affordances and restrictions of "built pedagogy," we cannot expect learners to break out from well-tried learning routines. In that sense, we will inspect and iterate, carefully analyze the use of our learning environments, and apply these insights to new learning spaces. This transformation extends not only to learning spaces, but more importantly to the bigger questions of a LC's activities: Are we continuing the format of 25-learner course structures, or are we moving toward an open learning center that largely depends on one-on-one counselling (see Edlin & Imamura, 2018; Mynard, 2016). Based on our mission statement and pedagogical model, we are planning to put in place the following:

- A teaching development program. In the absence of a full degree program on language learning in higher education (which is desperately needed in Germany), we will provide teacher training on all relevant aspects of language learning in higher education, such as language learner autonomy, curriculum design, testing and certification, and languages for specific purposes.
- A peer tutoring program. We already use student tutors in a variety of ways: as language assistants in class, as tandem tutors, as writing tutors, and as peer tutors in learning spaces. We intend to offer a program for peer tutors that results in a certificate because we recognize that individual learning scenarios will become more and more important in higher education.

- License management of online learning resources. While many language centers in Germany rely on media libraries and computer pools with complex language learning software installations, we will try to rely solely on internet resources, streaming services, and learning management and portfolio systems to manage and reflect on language learning.
- Event and showcase planning. In addition to language courses and open learning spaces, we are planning to host a constant series of language-learning related events. These could provide a showcase for the way we support learning or exceptional language learning projects related to internationalization.
- Studio-like settings and makerspaces. While we are planning to equip one of the seminar rooms with a one-button-studio and green-screen area for recording high-quality videos, we are working to install other makerspaces, for example, a makerspace for engineering or a full kitchen where learners can experiment with language and create digital or analog artifacts with language.

3. Center for Language Teaching Advancement (CeLTA) at Michigan State University

In the early 2010s, the language laboratory was merged with the newly established Center for Language Teaching Advancement (CeLTA) at Michigan State University. The department-level center houses a number of programs and services, for example, the Community Language School (CLS), which offers non-credit language courses and camps to learners of all ages; the fully online Master of Arts in Foreign Language Teaching (MAFLT) program; research and grant projects, such as the current focus on less commonly taught languages and Indigenous languages; student and faculty support; outreach and enrichment programs; and professional development. Recent new projects include the Online Language Teaching program and a consulting service for language departments.

CeLTA's vision is "to transform language education." There are several initiatives in the center's portfolio that provide models for meaningful change: a large-scale language survey initiative, language for specific purpose initiatives, technology-enhanced and hybrid language instruction, and a $2.5M grant from The Andrew W. Mellon Foundation to support further development in the research, teaching, strategic coordination, and creation of curricular models in the area of less commonly taught languages, which now includes an emphasis on Indigenous languages.

Currently, CeLTA employs 10 full-time staff and faculty members, 5 graduate assistants, multiple undergraduate student employees and interns, and multiple language teachers and volunteers. CeLTA is located on the ground floor of a new addition to Wells Hall on the main MSU campus.

What became known as the "CeLTA Labs" (270 square meters) was built next to CeLTA but separated through a corridor, with separate entrances, separate front desk personnel, and without visual permeability. The CeLTA Labs were based on the language lab model, consisting mostly of rows of moveable desktop computers and an observation room in between the two rooms of the labs (Fig. 7). Initially, usage was strong but declined over the years as computing became ubiquitous and the need for massive computer installations became less important. This is in line with changing usage patterns at other language centers as well. The rooms are now rarely used for drop-in purposes, and only a few classes are held in the windowless rooms per week.

Figure 7

One of the Underutilized CeLTA Labs Rooms With Traditional Lab Set-Up With Dividers

Some important usage scenarios continue, for example, large-scale proficiency and placement testing a few times per year and occasional specialized research and teaching. Furthermore, the CourseShare initiative, in which peer campuses of the Big 10 Academic Alliance share courses in Less Commonly Taught Language (LCTLs) through hybrid video conferencing sessions, uses the CeLTA Labs for its courses. While these are certainly important, they are not enough to justify largely empty rooms with expensive hardware and student worker support. Our data suggest that each room is only used about 2–3 times per day during the semester. As institutions continue to seek more sustainable spaces, they need to continuously examine usage patterns and increase capacity utilization.

Ironically, two of CeLTA's strongest programs, the Community Language School (CLS) and the Master of Arts in Foreign Language Teaching (MAFLT) program cannot make use of the space because of its current state. The CLS offers a variety of programs for children as young as 3 years, youth, and adults. The non-credit courses and camps are engaging experiences that do not follow a traditional language curriculum. As nontraditional offerings, they are innovative and highly communicative. The current lab space, with its vinyl flooring, bare walls, harsh lights, lack of windows, and rows of computers is not an ideal learning environment for the CLS, especially for the younger children. Therefore, the CLS uses other, generic classrooms elsewhere in the building. A more configurable setup that is suitable for learners of all age groups would allow CLS serve its patrons better. Because the CLS has moved its classes online and will continue to offer these both virtually and face-to-face after the pandemic, a more flexible format will be more conducive to teaching in multiple modalities. The growing MAFLT program would also greatly benefit from such capabilities.

3.1 Inspire

Currently, CeLTA does not have the capacity to conduct language education research that deals with physical space. However, in the future, we envision building a prototype space that can be modified to enable forward-looking space-driven research. Questions we seek to answer include how teachers and students perceive different spaces, the impact of space configurations and parameters on learning outcomes, design implications for phygital (a neologism combining the terms "physical" and "digital"—see Gaggioli, 2017, p. 774) spaces, and usage, movement, and communication patterns. Because MSU prepares prospective language teachers, the space could also function as a training and professional development environment. The redesign would be another element that would help CeLTA achieve the goals outlined in its mission statement: "As a locally grounded and internationally minded hub for language education transformation, our mission is to empower language educators, engage language learners, and enhance language learning and teaching practices through innovation, research, advocacy, and professional development." Furthermore, it would manifest CeLTA's values, which are to connect, to innovate, and to transform.

If we follow Monahan (2002) and view our spaces as an outward expression of our educational philosophies, or what he refers to as "built pedagogy," we must find better ways to align our learning spaces with our philosophies through a creative, inclusive, iterative, and well-structured process.

3.2 Involve

A co-design process includes all stakeholders throughout the whole process. We perceive it as inclusive, participatory, permeable, situated, and organic. It can also lead to continuous development of a space after it is constructed. As such, it can make the space more sustainable and resilient to becoming underutilized, avoided, or even obsolete. The co-design process can be used as a placemaking approach. Design processes executed exclusively by professionals and experts are more likely to be perceived as imposed or top-down. Co-design can increase the sense of ownership and belonging because it is more attuned to local cultures, diversity, and social needs (Zamenopoulos & Alexiou, 2018).

To make the Labs more usable and sustainable, CeLTA initiated a co-design process in 2019. We collected past usage statistics and had initial conversations with current stakeholders. In October of 2019, a comprehensive survey was sent to all language faculty and teaching staff, including teaching assistants. Of those who completed the survey, 43.75% answered the question "Would you be interested to be included in a focus group that is tasked with reimagining the CeLTA Labs?" with "Yes." The survey data suggest that there is considerable interest in providing input to create a more meaningful and usable space.

The goals of the co-design process include decreasing initial costs and enhancing sustainability (fiscally and environmentally), raising awareness of the impact of physical space on learning and teaching with an eye beyond the wow-factor, researching the process, sharpening CeLTA's profile, providing feasible models for other institutions (including primary and secondary educational institutions), capturing the process and iterations of the redesign, and fostering place-making and a sense of belonging. We also aim to provide a concrete example of the inclusive, values-based approach, known as the Culture of Care Initiative, practiced at the College of Arts & Letters (CAL) at MSU:

- To create a culture that is transparent, open, trusting, and safe
- To cultivate caring and accountable leadership
- To empower everyone to be engaged in a community that is inclusive and equitable (MSU Deans Values, 2019)

The inspiration for the co-design process at CeLTA came from a nine-year action research co-design project at the Language Learning Center at Rhodes College in Memphis, TN. But because the process and its findings were not captured in a systematic way, we decided to more deliberately study the CeLTA co-design project.

Traditional design processes merely survey stakeholders, especially at the beginning of the process: design professionals, experts, and/or those in power solicit input from all stakeholders using specific measurement tools and then analyze the responses. Based on those data, the space is designed with minimal further broad input. After completion, usually there is no post-occupancy assessment of the success of the design. In most cases at higher education institutions, the spaces will exist "as is" for the next decades. Retroactive work is usually only done when new technologies need to be installed or malfunctions occur. These adjustments are usually initiated and implemented in a top-down fashion by an infrastructure or physical plant office, not students, staff, or faculty.

Co-design differs from more traditional design processes in that it includes stakeholders throughout, as real partners. The benefits were outlined by Zamenopoulos and Alexiou (2018):

> Co-design activity produces new knowledge as people develop and experiment with (new) ideas around a matter of concern and as they engage in negotiations around the development of these ideas. Co-design is becoming important in the face of complex social, political, environmental, educational and technological issues, where no one person has the knowledge and skills to understand and solve them, and where a different approach is needed to empower people to participate and take control of their own life and environment. (p. 10)

Anyone who has an interest in making the Labs a better space is able to join the co-design team, including faculty, staff, students, parents (of our Community Language School students), and those who maintain, clean, or work in the space. We follow Sanders and Stappers's (2008) view of co-design "in a broader sense to refer to the creativity of designers and people not trained in design working together in the design development process" (p. 6).

The commitment to the team was initially for one semester. The team decided on the length of subsequent appointments. Figure 8 shows the participants at the first co-design session. Co-designers were expected to commit to some agreed-upon expectations in addition to those that the team set itself:

- Meet with the group for one hour per month until the end of Spring 2020.
- Fill out occasional questionnaires or surveys.
- Commit to a short interview once per semester.
- Come with an open mind and respect others' opinions.

While being a part of the team is not a paid position, participants can nonetheless benefit from the experience by working in a highly creative, diverse, and interdisciplinary team, being change agents, and supporting sustainability and cutting-edge research in higher education. They will also be able to see the learning spaces change over time and create tangible, real impact, help with creating models for other educational institutions in the US and beyond, and learn more about the emerging field of learning space design.

Figure 8

First Co-Design Session

3.3 Inquire

The multiyear co-design activities are chosen to create a sustainable, iterative, and slow process that avoids complete redesigns and capital-intensive work. The process is based on the goal of "underdesign" (Rapoport, 1990, p. 22), which leaves room for future developments and possibilities. Underdesign means that the space does not need to be completely finished, but rather allows for iterative, incremental improvements.

The activities are designed to hone in on more specific goals and can sometimes be described as ambiguous or "fuzzy" (Sanders & Stappers, 2008, p. 7). There are a number of possible co-design activities, such as doodling or group sketching, role play, design charrettes (collaborative design sessions, which often involve work of subgroups), a job description activity (described below), prototyping, structured discussions, reflections, brainstorming, external inspiration, and local field trips (to other learning spaces nearby).

For the co-design project at CeLTA, we chose to use and analyze the three following:

- Learning space job description activity
- Group sketching
- Prototyping.

The learning space job description activity tasks participants with the following: "In a group of about three people, discuss the current learning space you are in for a few minutes. Note some major features. Then, write about the space as if it were a job description. Include common elements, such as required and desired qualifications, education, duties, benefits, working times, etc." They may choose between two options: "1. Choose the space as it is currently set up and designed" or "2. Choose a possible or envisioned space in the current location."

For the group sketching activity, participants receive copies of a modified blueprint of the space (Fig. 9, next page). It only consists of the loadbearing walls and features that cannot be removed. The activity allows lay designers to externalize their thoughts, find a common mode of communication and idea sharing, and wrestle with dimensions and constraints. The finished sketches are presented to the group and later scanned for further analysis.

The third activity, prototyping, can take on different forms. For the project at CeLTA, we envisioned a two-pronged approach, manipulating the physical layout—literally moving chairs, tables, devices, etc. around—and utilizing newer augmented reality technologies. Using the LF2 from Lightform, we planned to create different setups along one blank wall and create varied scenes with assorted multimedia and physical elements. Because of the Covid-19 pandemic, we were not able to complete this phase and must wait until we are cleared to come back to campus.

3.4 Interpret and Implement

The co-design team was assembled in January of 2020. Eleven volunteers, including faculty, graduate students, academic staff, and one parent of a CLS student gathered for the first meeting in February of 2020. The first small changes were expected to happen during the spring. For example, only removing two tables and two computers and rearranging the tables might be a realistic goal for the physical changes but would yield tangible spatial and financial benefits because we would remove two computers as well. We also expected to generate a list of desirables and potential functions of the room. These are merely speculations because the nature of the co-design process is to not steer the process top-down.

Figure 9

Blank Group Sketching Activity Sheet

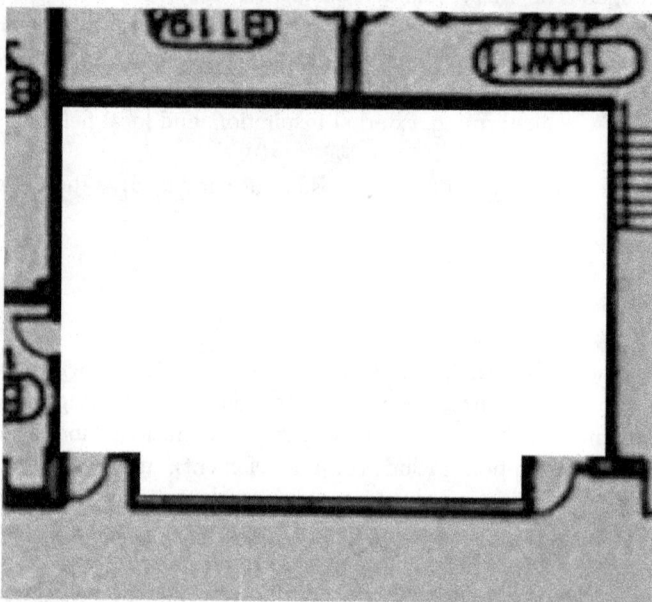

The project was interrupted by the novel coronavirus crisis. MSU went into lockdown in mid-March 2020 and, as of this writing, the Center continues to function remotely. Because the situation has changed profoundly, including a sharp decrease in the budget, a reenvisioning of the Labs will be more important than ever. As of May 2021, the project started again virtually with a listening session. At the time of publication, we are waiting for the results of a Qualtrics survey. The plan is to remove the computers from B125 completely and offer a clean slate for the fall semester of 2021. We will offer a faculty learning community on learning space design for 2021–22 and, if the pandemic allows, we will resume the co-design project. Much of this depends on the general health situation as well as federal, state, local, and MSU guidelines.

3.5 Inspect and Iterate

The values that were underlying the project continue to guide it even during these times of disruption: inclusivity, transparency, sustainability, flexibility, and resiliency. Continuous, iterative inspection and evaluation of the ongoing design will be a key to keeping the space relevant even as times change. Because we cannot predict future developments—something the pandemic made all too clear—this process will continue.

Spaces are not empty, static containers but rather are continually produced by people: "space is always changing as conceptions, perceptions, and lived experiences change" (Milgrom, 2008, p. 270). Because the changes are difficult, if not impossible, to predict, it is important to stay flexible and open to new developments. Therefore, values can be guides during shifting reinterpretations and redesigns of spaces.

Inspecting the space then means taking stock of how changes are experienced and perceived by stakeholders and measuring if the space delivers the intended outcomes. This kind of post-occupancy assessment can be done by regular observations, surveys, opportunities for feedback or focus groups. More information about the ongoing project can be found on the initiative's website: https://celta.msu.edu/co-design/.

4. Conclusion

The two examples we present in this chapter come from two quite different higher education systems. In Germany, LCs at universities act as service facilities, either attached to a literature/linguistics department or acting directly under the supervision of a vice president for international affairs. They usually offer all language teaching for all disciplines, in some cases, even for the literature/linguistics departments, and sometimes also catering to administrative and teaching staff.

LCs in the US have different missions that can range from supporting language teaching technologies to professional development, from conducting research to providing physical teaching and/or social spaces (Kronenberg, 2017; Lavolette & Simon, 2018). Many LCs support courses but do not offer them, although some centers do provide direct instruction.

In spite of the different contexts, we have tried to show that our approach to the design of language-learning spaces has been similar. It starts with a vision, an inspiration. As we showed in our German example, a language policy, together with an internationalization strategy and a pedagogical model of language teaching and learning, can send a clear message: this is what we do, this is why we are offering these services, and this is how we understand learning and teaching languages. We then involve a large number of stakeholders (staff members, students, architects, health officers, learning space advisors, disability officers, etc.) and inquire with various methods what their perspectives are. We continue by interpreting the data, condensing and balancing the results, then implementing exploratory prototypes. We repeat a new circle of developments through inspection and iteration. Our goal is not to find the perfect fit in one go, but to slowly and patiently identify more and more elements that work.

In summary, we can say that the co-design process is usefully based on both top-down and bottom-up processes that allow for utmost flexibility. Although it appears to be impossible to predict user behavior or the ideal learning environment, a thorough investigation into the needs and requirements of the users within the educational context is necessary. This process should be accompanied by (even radical) exploratory prototyping to provoke (similarly radical) reactions, followed by a thorough evaluation. We emphasized throughout that designing a LC is a complex task, touching on pedagogical assumptions and visions, learning experiences, ergonomics, a balance of flexibility and stability, and the structuring of space, to name but a few aspects. Designing a LC is not about the product; it is an iterative process. As we have learned from the decline of the language lab era, we cannot accept the status quo in space design as the world around us is changing at an ever-faster pace.

References

Council of Europe. (2001). *Common European framework of reference for languages: Learning, teaching, assessment.* Cambridge, UK: Cambridge University Press.

Council of Europe. (2018). *Common European framework of reference for languages: Learning, teaching, assessment. Companion volume with new descriptors.* Strasbourg, France: Council of Europe. https://rm.coe.int/cefr-companion-volume-with-new-descriptors-2018/1680787989

Edlin, C., & Imamura, Y. (2018). Resource coordination in the Self-Access Learning Center at Kanda University of International Studies for the 2017–2018 academic year: Activity, concept, and expanding definitions. *Relay Journal, 1*(1), 178–196. https://kuis.kandagaigo.ac.jp/relayjournal/wp-content/uploads/2018/03/Edlin-Imamura-Relay-Journal-178-196.pdf

Faulk, J. D., McKee C. C., Bazille, H., Brigham, M., Daniel, J., Jaffe, J. G., Lee, J., Sabinson, E., Zhou, Y., Zhu, Y., Chung, Y., & Hedge, A. (2019). Performance, movement, posture, and perceived discomfort in active vs. static seating. *Proceedings of the Human Factors and Ergonomics Society Annual Meeting, 63*(1), 1154–1158.

Floyd, C. (1984). A systematic look at prototyping. In R. Budde, K. Kuhlenkamp, L. Mathiassen, & H. Züllighoven (Eds.), *Approaches to prototyping* (pp. 1–18). Berlin, Germany: Springer.

Gaggioli, A. (2017). Phygital spaces: When atoms meet bits. *Cyberpsychology, Behavior, and Social Networking, 20*(12), 774.

Harvey, E. J., & Kenyon, M. C. (2013). Classroom seating considerations for 21st century students and faculty. *Journal of Learning Spaces, 2*(1), 1–13. http://libjournal.uncg.edu/jls/article/view/578

Holec, H. (1979). *Autonomy in Foreign Language Learning.* Strasbourg: Council of Europe.

Kimbell, L., & Bailey, J. (2017). Prototyping and the new spirit of policy-making. *CoDesign, 13*(3), 214–226. https://doi.org/10.1080/15710882.2017.1355003

Kronenberg, F. A. (Ed.). (2017). *From language lab to language center and beyond: The past, present, and future of language center design.* Auburn, AL: International Association for Language Learning Technology.

Kronenberg, F. A., & Lahaie, U. S. (2011). *Language center design.* Moorhead, MN: The International Association for Language Learning Technology.

Lavolette, E., & Simon, E. F. (2018). *Language center handbook*. Auburn, AL: International Association for Language Learning Technology.

Little, D. (1991). *Learner autonomy 1: Definitions, issues and problems*. Dublin, Ireland: Authentik Language Learning Resources. http://www.worldcat.org/oclc/29385807

Little, D., Dam, L., & Legenhausen, L. (2017). *Language learner autonomy: Theory, practice and research*. Bristol, UK: Multilingual Matters.

McKeown, C. (2008). *Office ergonomics: Practical applications*. Boca Raton, FL: CRC Press.

Milgrom, R. (2008). Lucien Kroll: Design, difference, everyday life. In H. Lefebvre & K. Goonewardena, *Space, difference, everyday life: Reading Henri Lefebvre* (pp. 264–281). New York & London: Routledge.

Monahan, T. (2002). Flexible space & built pedagogy: Emerging IT embodiments. *Inventio, 4*(1).

MSU deans values. (2019, January 24). https://cplong.org/msu-deans-values/

Mynard, J. (2016). Looking backwards and forwards: Evaluating a 15-year-old SALC for continued growth. *Studies in Self-Access Learning Journal, 7*(4), 427–436.

Oblinger, D. (Ed.). (2006). *Learning spaces*. Boulder, CO: EDUCAUSE.

Ramos-Gonzalez, J. (2019, September). *Introducing dynamic furniture into the language learning classroom* [Conference session]. Learner autonomy SIG of IATEFL, Braunschweig, Germany. https://www.tu-braunschweig.de/anglistik/seminar/esud/lasig2019/programme

Rapoport, A. (1990). *The meaning of the built environment: A nonverbal communication approach*. Tucson, AZ: University of Arizona Press.

Reynard, R. (2017, January 17). Continuous design thinking: Our process for staying human-centered, no matter what! *Medium*. https://medium.com/sap-tools/continuous-design-thinking-9a7c2530f6e0

Sanders, E. B.-N., & Stappers, P. J. (2008). Co-creation and the new landscapes of design. *CoDesign, 4*(1), 5–18. https://doi.org/10.1080/15710880701875068

Schwienhorst, K. (2007). *Learner autonomy and CALL environments*. New York, NY: Routledge.

Smith, T. J. (2007). The ergonomics of learning: Educational design and learning performance. *Ergonomics, 50*(10), 1530–1546.

Stappers, P. J. (2013). Prototypes as a central vein for knowledge development. In L. Valentine (Ed.), *Prototype: Design and craft in the 21st century* (pp. 85–98). London, UK: Bloomsbury.

Whitham, R., Moreton, S., Bowen, S., Speed, C., & Durrant, A. (2019). Understanding, capturing, and assessing value in collaborative design research. *CoDesign, 15*(1), 1–7. https://doi.org/10.1080/15710882.2018.1563194

Zamenopoulos, T., & Alexiou, K. (2018). *Co-design as collaborative research*. Bristol, UK: Bristol University/AHRC Connected Communities Programme. http://oro.open.ac.uk/58301/

Author Notes

Felix Kronenberg is the Director of the Center for Language Teaching Advancement (CeLTA) and an Associate Professor of German in the Department of Linguistics & Germanic, Slavic, Asian and African Languages at Michigan State University. His main research is about physical, virtual, and hybrid (language) learning spaces. Dr. Kronenberg is the immediate past-president of the International Association for Language Learning Technology and an advisory board member of the Learning Spaces Collaboratory. He has served as the president of the SouthWest Association for Language Learning Technology, has been a fellow for the National Institute for Technology in Liberal Education, and has been a learning spaces and language center design consultant for various colleges and universities.

Klaus Schwienhorst is the Director of the Leibniz Language Centre at Leibniz University, Hannover, Germany. His research focuses on learner autonomy, language learning spaces, and virtual environments for language learning. He has been a member of the standing committee of the Arbeitskreis der Sprachenzentren Deutschlands e.V. (AKS, Working group of German language centers) and has been a digital and language center design consultant for various universities and companies.

Correspondence concerning this chapter should be addressed to Felix Kronenberg (kronenb6@msu.edu).

Technologies

for Language Spaces

Chapter 10

Digital Media Management, Archiving, and Production:
How Language Centers Can Find More Ways to Support Learning via Media

Robert Majors, Russell Hugo, and Paul Aoki, University of Washington, USA

Abstract

The need for media conversion, curation, preservation, and creation will likely not diminish and is something that language centers (LCs) with the appropriate resources can actively assist with. There is a clear trend whereby media storage and delivery are being migrated from standard physical proprietary media formats (such as open reels or DVDs in the past) to intangible cloud or web-based models. Thus, LCs seem at first glance to have limited need for physical media collections and legacy hardware. However, we believe that LCs will have an important role in digital media management and production for years to come. First, there is a need to convert media resources from deprecated formats to modern standard digital formats. Archiving support is also needed for certain language communities and language faculty projects. LCs can leverage legacy equipment to support the wider learning community. This chapter outlines some of the challenges and workflows for media conversion for in-class use and archival purposes. It also discusses the ongoing need for digital media production support.

Digital media management and production continue to be important areas where language centers (LCs) can assist language instruction on and off campus. There are many challenges and opportunities ahead in the near future, but the need for support is unlikely to go away any time soon. In this chapter, we propose some concrete ideas, provide specific examples, and explain more abstract needs and possibilities. We also include some technical information, specific methods, and systems related to the topics of media acquisition and distribution. We try to provide a broad roadmap of technical hardware, software, and workflows. However, due to the ever-evolving nature of technology and the fact that every institution has different challenges and needs, we prioritize concepts that are, based on our experience and communication with other LC managers, the most common and useful steps.

The intended readership of this volume spans a great spectrum of technical knowledge. Therefore, this chapter offers some general contextual information and examples that a general audience can appreciate. We also provide some technical details where appropriate to more fully and accurately explore our context and our technical approaches, challenges, and solutions. Many of these contexts and challenges are relevant to many LCs, but not all will be, because each LC's situation is unique. We try to use generally understood terminology for these concepts. However, having the more technical (and accurate) terminology will be helpful for those looking to explore particular concepts further. We hope that some of these concepts may be inspirational for LCs to consider as they evolve in how they serve their communities. One goal of this chapter is to show some of the new ways that LCs can provide unique support for their institution and larger community in the present and near future.

This chapter builds upon the excellent work of Brubacher and Evershed (2018), published in an earlier IALLT volume, which provides a thorough overview of the acquisition and distribution of media for course use. We strongly recommend that if you are primarily interested in delivering media (physical and streaming) to students, that you read their chapter before this one.

The current chapter is structured so that each section begins by discussing the broader, and arguably less technical, system-based concerns and becomes more narrowly focused and technical as it progresses. We begin with a short history of the University of Washington's (UW) Language Learning Center (LLC) as a way to better illustrate how the following examples are situated. Section 2 provides an overview of basic digital media management and distribution for LCs. Section 3 explores the intake procedure for media resources and how they can be processed and organized and addresses how LCs can play an important role in supporting larger archiving needs. A brief example of an Indigenous language archive is included to explore the issues discussed in the section more fully. Section 4 is concerned with the process of analog-to-digital conversion and legacy equipment. Section 5 focuses on media production and the role that LCs can play at their institutions and in their communities. The last section provides concluding remarks and offers suggestions for next steps.

1. Brief History of the UW LLC

As background, our Language Learning Center is housed in the College of Arts and Sciences at the University of Washington. The earliest known reference to the UW LLC was in an issue of the University of Washington's student newspaper, *The Daily*, in 1947. According to *The Daily*, some surplus open-reel tape recorders from the end of World War II likely came to the University of Washington's Psychology Department. The recorders may have been used to experiment with B.F. Skinner's Behaviorist model using tape recorder technology for stimulus (native speaker model) and response (student's rendition of native speaker's model) for language learning. The UW LLC, like many others, has seen a shift in the technology it deals with regularly—multiple times since its creation—in part in concert with evolving pedagogical approaches. The rapid shift from physical to digital resources has provided some incredible challenges and opportunities. Only about 10 years ago, there was still a demand for physical media duplication and distribution (audio CDs, primarily), but now, online media streaming is the de facto method. We have a dedicated cloud-based server to host and stream the majority of our digital content to learners. However, a one-size-fits-all model is not always best for language instruction, and especially for less commonly taught or resource impoverished languages.

2. Working with Digital Media

2.1 Storing and Organizing the Media

Some of the first questions to consider with respect to digital media is how it will be stored, where it will be stored, and how it will be organized. Brubacher and Evershed (2018) discussed the use of Integrated Library Systems (ILSs) in a LC. An ILS is a web-based interface commonly used by libraries that indexes the inventory and allows visitors to search and browse the records. As Brubacher and Evershed said, "Not every LC will have the need or resources for a sophisticated ILS… However, some sort of relational database that allows information to be updated and accessed in a centralized manner is very helpful" (p. 277).

While an LC's primary collection may be best served by a general ILS, a specialized repository may be needed for separate collections. For example, the UW LLC manages two isolated online collections of media for different Indigenous languages. In addition, we support multiple websites with media for less commonly taught languages, including media for dictionaries or textbooks. In all of these cases, the resources to support such projects for the longer term are not available elsewhere. Most departments do not have the technical resources or staff with the necessary skill sets. Also, the larger computing services department at our institution is not scaled to support smaller projects like this.

In these cases, we needed solutions that were as streamlined as possible for the target audience and context, stable, and requiring as little maintenance as possible. Someone looking to access media from one of our Indigenous language archives needs a top page that is oriented to and organized for that content. In other words, a centralized and public-facing ILS that houses the Indigenous language collection might not be ideal for the community's needs, because the collection is only accessed by limited audiences who require specific user experiences in terms of quality and ease of access.

The value of a centralized ILS or a relational database is not diminished by the benefits of specialized repositories. Even if it is primarily for internal use, an ILS or a relational database of some sort is vital for any LC that has a substantial collection of media resources. There are many open-source options for ILS software, but only a fraction meet the requirements of being truly open source, having a healthy development community, and having robust functionality (Müller, 2011). A well-supported open-source system is usually best because you are not beholden to a private company for support or renewal costs and can retain complete ownership of your project. Also, most open-source systems prioritize methods for exporting and importing data so that your content is less likely to be trapped in a proprietary format. The three application options that Müller highlighted in 2011 (Evergreen, Koha, and PMB) continue to be supported and developed, and so continue to be ideal options.

Some ILSs may be overcomplicated for the needs of some LCs. So, some LCs might not require a full ILS, but could thrive with a simple relational database, or with a minimally modified content management system (CMS). A well-supported, standard CMS (e.g., WordPress) might be a more feasible installation and management option for LCs with limited technical support and resources. However, this would not be appropriate if the LC has an extensive and complicated media collection that they wish to make publicly searchable, like a standard library website. Or, like Brubacher and Evershed (2018) argue, if a goal is to transfer the content to a larger library system, the choice of the system should be dictated by the library's system and structure.

2.2 Streaming Media as the New Standard

Once a storage and organization system has been established, it is worth considering how the media will be made accessible to learners, instructors, and researchers. As Brubacher and Evershed (2018) noted, media distribution is rapidly shifting from physical media to streaming. In this section, we discuss the key complications related to the ongoing shift to streaming media and then briefly explore some technical and format complications and the increased presence of externally managed video streaming services that can be used for education (e.g., Kanopy).

In recent years, the UW LLC only distributes physical media to students or faculty in very rare circumstances. Instead, the great majority of media is distributed via a streaming server that we manage. Streaming media is delivered over the internet in small amounts at a time, so it is (intended to be) transmitted in an ephemeral way such that the main media file is not transferred as a complete file to the viewer's device. While a viewer can almost always capture content in some way, streaming media does improve security and reduce the ease of piracy, compared to having viewers download files. Streaming media also allows the content to be "throttled," so that people with slower connections will get less data (i.e., more compressed data) than people with faster connections. While the quality of the media might change, the goal is that the media will not be interrupted (as much) by poor data transmission rates. In other words, the software on a streaming media server can down-sample (i.e., reduce the quality of) the media files to deliver a stream that is more appropriate for the target device. For example, a mobile device that is on a slow cell connection would get a lower bit rate than a large desktop with a fast ethernet connection.

Not every LC may need to manage their own streaming media distribution server, but it is still useful to be aware of the technology and the various benefits and limitations. Most ILSs, including the one we use in the UW LLC, have no dedicated streaming media functionality. Some may, like many CMSs, allow downloading of smaller audio files (e.g., MP3 formatted files), sometimes in the form of progressive downloading (files are downloaded, but users can watch/listen before the entire file is downloaded). Using true streaming media software on a server allows files to be watched/heard with little delay, from the beginning of the file, and when playing from another location in the file; it also prevents files from being wholesale downloaded (packets of audio/video are temporarily stored in a user's computer's cache, then automatically deleted after being consumed), which is significant in helping to defer copyright infringement. Still, larger video files could present a considerable challenge because they cannot be efficiently streamed without specialized software. An existing streaming media service, like YouTube or Vimeo, might be leveraged in some circumstances, but issues related to rights, access, and content protection (especially for sensitive content, such as Indigenous language media) are all potentially limiting or problematic.

The UW LLC has deployed a cloud-based server with streaming software (Wowza and JW Player web frontend, adding Wirecast for live video streaming) to provide this service to language learners and instructors in our community. However, a similar system may not be feasible for many LCs depending on the available resources and expertise.

However, those who currently manage or are considering managing their own streaming media server need to consider the balance between the quality of the media (e.g., resolution and framerate), file storage costs, other functions like subtitle support, and the throughput rate (how much data can be successfully delivered across the network between server and end user). A data flow rate that exceeds the throughput rate can result in choppy video and audio, although some systems can adapt, to a degree, to the user's bandwidth using adaptive bit rate technology (e.g., MPEG-DASH).

Yet, we have found that in some instances the automatic downsampling (i.e., reduction in bit rate) is not sufficient. For example, for media that is being accessed overseas, and particularly in regions with poor internet speeds compared to US servers (e.g., regions of Bangladesh, Italy), our standard streaming media settings were too high quality, and students in those countries were unable to play any media. Therefore, we provided alternative streaming files of much smaller sizes and of lower quality compared to our default compression settings for resources that are often accessed by people in places with poor internet connections. A Bangla textbook we support is an example of a resource with an audience that is overseas and has limited internet access. With a five-year grant from the US Department of

Education, we developed a comprehensive Bangla textbook (Salomon, Abedin, & Brandl, 2011) and workbook (Bhaduri, 2011) with extensive multimedia resources that encompass the two primary cultures and dialects of Bangla. We continue to support the needs of students and teachers in Bangladesh in accessing and using the media resources from the books. Students often need to access such media resources during study abroad. In addition, at the time of writing this chapter, we have many students at our institution who are overseas due to the COVID-19 pandemic and need to access media for classes.

Finally, if a LC is interested in providing full-length films for language students and classes, services such as Kanopy and Swank can provide both licensing and distribution. These services are often managed via the libraries at many institutions and might not be a good fit for LC oversight. Other websites, such as Berkeley's Lumière, offers shorter clips from films that are specifically oriented to support language education. These trends arguably mean that a LC's role in copyrighted film distribution will continue to decline until it is solely managed by a central library system, perhaps with LCs acting in a support capacity by providing media that is specially encoded or modified for language instruction (similar to what Lumière is doing). Where then, does this leave LCs in relation to media processing, collecting, and distributing? In the following section, we recommend that LCs can, at the very least, be valuable allies for media archiving efforts.

3. Processing and Archiving

A LC can fill an important niche role for most institutions and surrounding communities by acting as an intermediate processor of specialized content. In a recent survey of archivists, when asked what their greatest challenge was, the most common response was "resources," followed by "communication" and "archival competencies" (Buchanan et al., 2017, pp. 279). The following quote was cited by the authors of the survey as being representative of the issue: "Too much material to care for (physically & electronically) without enough staff, supplies, or equipment to do the job well" (p. 279).

Crucially, as the quote notes, and as the third most selected challenge ("archival competencies") implies, the job needs to be done "well." This means that a LC that decides to take on this role should take care to become familiar with the field of archiving and establish a relationship with the most appropriate nearby long-term archive. Competency and training are, like in many professions, unequal amongst practitioners, and continuing professional development is strongly needed to make sure standards and practices are as efficient and consistent as possible (Irons Walch et al., 2006).

3.1 Temporary and Intermediary Archiving

Being a temporary and/or intermediary archive is an important role a LC can fill in the coming decades. Most LCs do not have the resources to be a long-term (or permanent) archive. These terms refer to an established archive that has the resources and intention to preserve materials in perpetuity, such as a dedicated archive that is part of a library. To claim the status of a long-term archive would require ample funding and evidence for substantial longevity. While a LC might have the intention to preserve their materials for the long-term (i.e., as permanently as possible), no guarantees should be made to faculty or community members with whom we collaborate. If a LC does any archiving, we can think of it as being a temporary and/or intermediary archive. To clarify, a temporary archive could last for hundreds of years, but it does not have the structure and resources to guarantee such a length of time from the outset. An intermediary archive, on the other hand, is a temporary archive that will be eventually transferred to a permanent archive, usually after a certain amount of processing and annotating has been completed.

A LC can offer support as an intermediary archive by doing the following: First, we can collect the content and process it, which may involve digitizing or conversion. Second, the materials can be annotated and, if appropriate, made available to the public or communities. Finally, a LC can act as a temporary archive and store the content until a long-term archive is ready to accept it. Alternatively, if there are no long-term archives that would be appropriate homes for it, the LC is better than no archive, and the situation regarding the availability of long-term archives may change over time.

That said, any institution may shut down in the future, including libraries and archives. That is why some people prefer the term *long-term* instead of *permanent* archive for an archive that is intended (and currently resourced) to be permanent. In theory, there should always be plans for transferring content to new homes if such a change occurs. Yet, if a LC has a particularly valuable set of resources, it may be prudent to keep a copy in the LC in addition to the external archive. Even in a worst-case scenario in which the entire institution shuts down, the LC would at least be in a better position to make sure those resources are preserved.

For example, a neighboring institution to the UW ended its American Sign Language (ASL) program, which had an extensive library of rare materials (mostly VHS cassettes). At that point, the head of our institution's ASL program worked to make sure that the materials were not lost and accepted them, even though the resources (e.g., space, time, equipment) were not available. Rights and access issues have prevented the materials from finding a permanent home, but we are working with the program to develop an intermediary archive where the materials can be digitized and backed up for safekeeping until the situation is resolved. In the end, the closing of the neighboring institution's ASL program illustrates the need for active planning, proper organization, and contingency plans. It also reinforces the value of digitizing materials now because transferring large amounts of physical materials may not always be feasible if time is limited and hands are tied. Also, analog materials (e.g., video cassettes, DVDs) can degrade over time. As soon as materials are received and digitized, it is important to append any information that might dictate future use (e.g., copyright, other rights, understandings, agreements) and enter metadata on the individual files into the ILS or database.

3.2 Improving Access

Making content more accessible is an important goal even if the content is going to be, or has already been, donated to a long-term archive. This is another benefit of intermediary archiving. Compared to most larger archives, a LC can provide more immediate access to the target community and arguably, a more user-friendly experience when accessing the materials. This could be as simple as providing a dedicated website for a specific collection of content (e.g., media for a dictionary) to make it more easily and efficiently accessed.

Also, some Indigenous communities have laws or customs that govern access to certain resources, and it is vital that they are respected. If the content belongs to an Indigenous community, whether materially or through cultural heritage, access restrictions must be put in place. Even if you do not have a larger public-facing system like an ILS, this information can be added to the metadata for the resources.

3.3 Expertise

Another benefit of acting as an intermediary archive for language-related content is that a LC can provide expertise on the possible value of a language resource and prioritize its processing accordingly. When evaluating resources, a wide scope of what qualifies as valuable language resources should be considered. For example, a series of recordings to accompany a French textbook recorded in 1960 may not be used in a modern French class, but it does not mean that the resources have no value. Future historical and applied linguists might find it very useful (e.g., for future diachronic or dialectal research). An example of a resource in our inventory that has a potentially high value is recordings made by a faculty member for Tamil, which were recorded sometime in the 1970s on reel-to-reel and likely do not exist anywhere else. Of these two examples, we would prioritize the processing of the Tamil recordings because they are rarer and more likely to degrade in quality over time.

3.4 Auditing and Quality Control

On numerous occasions, especially for less commonly taught languages, the UW LLC has been contacted by students using an older textbook who are seeking the accompanying media resources. Occasionally, we have learned that the publisher no longer has the old files or that the publisher no longer exists and traditional libraries do not offer access to the files. In these cases, the audio was originally supplied on legacy formats such as open reel or cassette. When those materials were still retained by our LC, they could be digitized and made available via streaming.

For some materials of higher value (e.g., materials that have greater demand and/or rarity), even if there are copies elsewhere, the possible variability in quality should be considered. Many formats can degrade with age and use, and if you have good quality copies of a valuable resource, it might be worth inquiring about the quality of other existing digitized copies, especially if it is not clear who processed it (e.g., the original publisher or a private instructor) and how it was done (e.g., what equipment, compression settings).

On more than one occasion, a faculty member brought us a noncommercial, nonprofessional CD of recordings they created in the 1980s or earlier, prior to the existence of digital audio recording technology. In one situation, the quality seemed unusually poor and seemed to have digital compression distortion. We asked them about the original masters, which were on audio cassette. Through the process, we learned that the cassettes were digitized in the early 2000s and saved as 128kbps MP3s, which were then burnt to an audio CD for storage. Because the faculty member had the source cassettes in their office, we were able to re-digitize them at much higher quality.

Another example involved audio files that were digitized from an audio cassette by a faculty member and saved uncompressed in a waveform audio file format (WAV). Nevertheless, listening to the recordings revealed clear signs of overmodulation and related distortion, which became even more apparent when the waveforms and spectrograms of the audio were viewed (see Section 4.4.3). Therefore, when the faculty member originally digitized the content, they likely turned the input level up too high. In this case, too, the faculty member had the source cassettes, and we were able to re-digitize them. These anecdotes illustrate the importance of understanding the quality of the resources you have compared to other copies in existence, and they highlight the value in supporting faculty by offering to help with the process or to train them on best practices.

The UW LLC has an extensive catalog of physical media collected over almost seven decades, representing over 100 languages, that requires organizing, digitization, and possible archiving. Some LCs are in a similar situation, while others may not have any media that was not created by a corporation (e.g., studio films, media accompanying existing textbooks from large publishers), and so may not have media on hand that would be appropriate for the processes described above. In this context, there are a few options to offer media support. The first is to reach out to faculty and offer services for digitization and/or archiving of their self-created or collected language materials. For example, we have been contacted by faculty who have a substantial collection of physical media in their offices that has not been digitized. We have been given some incredible collections of language documentation audio and video, recordings of lectures, and recordings of native speakers reading pedagogical dialogs, for example. These materials might not have a readily apparent long-term archive home, or they might not be appropriate for one at this time. However, digitizing analog content like this will preserve it in the best quality possible for when the time comes to make such a decision. If faculty are not concerned with maintaining sole control of the content, a LC can maintain content created by an instructor for long after they have retired, acting as a temporary archive. Most language instructors and their departments, in our experience, do not have the time, expertise, and resources to do so. The need is substantial for accessible collections of historical language and language learning content at larger institutions; however, in our experience, the digitization of content and sharing between instructors or with departments at large is not nearly as common as it should be.

3.5 Intermediary Archive Case Study

In this subsection, we will describe an intermediary archive project to better illustrate the ideas discussed above. The UW LLC hosts a large collection of language learning materials for a local Indigenous language that, while the LLC was in the process of annotation and transcription, were made available to that community. Many Indigenous communities throughout the world, and in particular our local communities, have a strong history of needing to keep cultural resources securely restricted to the citizens (or accepted and enrolled members) of the respective nation (or tribe, community).

A needs analysis that was conducted in the community about the particular Indigenous language collection found concerns about access, especially about the content being hidden in an archive with no access via the internet, or it only being accessible through an opaque and confusing internet ILS, or it being stuck in limbo waiting until the archive has the resources to process the content (Hugo, 2015). These concerns were coming from an Indigenous community with legitimate historical concerns for trusting academic institutional control of Indigenous intellectual content, which made it even more important to make the processes of archiving and the methods of access as transparent as possible. In addition, the content needed to be as accessible as possible, limited by the necessary access controls to secure sensitive content. Some of the materials are of more concern (e.g., cultural knowledge, legends, stories) than others (e.g., the alphabet, basic phrases), so at least three levels of access control were needed. The Indigenous community's feedback was a primary motivation in developing a separate website to host the collection and building a system with a relatively restricted feature set compared to most ILSs.

The materials were also donated to a long-term archive, which is part of our institution's library, but that archive did not have the means to process the content or provide access to the target community in the near future in a manner that would be most useful to them. This is because, for example, community members do not possess the necessary institutional login credentials, or they are geographically too distant to make in-person access practical.

The website for the temporary archive was launched shortly after the digitization of the media was completed. As content was assigned basic metadata and uniform resource identifiers (URIs), it was immediately added to the online archive. Once this phase was completed and all resources were made available to the community online, the physical materials were delivered to the permanent archive along with digital copies with respective metadata and URIs.

The process of transcribing and annotating the materials is ongoing and could take a few more years. Throughout this process, the UW LLC regularly provides updates to the data set to the long-term archive. The results are that the community can access the latest versions of the content immediately, the long-term archive is burdened with minimal labor, the level of annotation and transcription will likely exceed any best-case scenario that the long-term archive could have hoped to do in the next few decades, and the content is secured for the foreseeable future.

Returning to the issues of strong assumptions about long-term archives, the collection was originally intended to be housed at a different archive (not necessarily long-term either) at another smaller university (Heritage University) that is on the land of the Indigenous Nation (whose language is represented in the collection), although the Nation does not officially control the university. A few years after the collection was first offered to that university's library, no progress was made, even though a dean of the institution was actively in support of it. At the time, there were severe resource limitations with respect to available server space and staff to accept, initially process, and manage the content. Unfortunately, it has been almost five years since the original offer, and still no progress has been made. Instead, the collection is hosted by the UW LLC and archived by the UW's archive, while the UW LLC continues to act as an intermediary and temporary archive for the other institution as well. When they are ready, and if the Indigenous Nation continues to support the idea, we can transfer it.

If the UW LLC had not hosted the public facing site, the great majority, if not all of the materials, would likely not be accessible online to the community. We have been fortunate for the responsive support from our institution's library in preserving the physical materials, but that may not always be the case. As this case study demonstrated, LCs can be an extra line of defense when local libraries and archives do not have the resources to accept and process intake materials, even digital ones, in the foreseeable future.

The sections above have been concerned primarily with work involving digitized resources. In the next section, we will review some challenges, promises, and recommendations for digitizing analog media assets so that they can be preserved and used.

4. Digitization and Conversion

Another role a LC can fill in an institution is providing the tools for migrating media content from defunct technology to current digital files. This can prevent physical media from degrading in quality, reduce the risk of loss, and clear up physical space. In this section, we primarily use the term "digitize" to describe the process of converting analog information stored on legacy physical media to a current digital format. Digital files can also be transcoded from one digital format to a more compatible one for archiving and subsequent re-encoding for streaming, etc. To serve this effort of digitizing, some legacy technological equipment is required. At first glance, there could be concerns of turning a LC into an equipment museum or hoarding space, or that the costs of acquiring and maintaining such equipment will be considerable. In our experience, a core set of equipment is needed for this purpose, and both the required physical storage space and the financial investment are fairly reasonable. A LC does not need to acquire any equipment until there is a need, such as a faculty member's collection of microcassettes that need to be digitized. The majority of our tasks have been accomplished using a relatively basic PC workstation equipped with an analog-to-digital video converter and an analog-to-digital audio converter. In the following subsections, we explore some of the common equipment that is needed, the basic processes, and relevant terminology.

4.1 Digitizing Audio

There are several choices to be made regarding the digitization of audio files. Unless otherwise mentioned, we discuss concepts and workflows related to creating "master versions" of files. A master version is the highest quality version of a file, which you would use for archiving. You would not use a master version of a file for students to access for general consumption (e.g., streaming) for several reasons. Providing the master version would result in little perceptible quality gain, and it would typically require progressive downloading, where the file is actually downloaded to the end user's device. This could cause delays in playback, and the end user might be able to retain the file (a potential rights issue). In addition, storage requirements would be significantly increased. When digitizing or transcoding materials, the primary things to consider are the audio file compression (codec), sample rate, and bit depth, because each of these affects the quality, accuracy, compatibility (e.g., with applications, hardware, and throughput), and file size for the audio files. We will define and explain each of these terms in order.

4.1.1 Audio File Compression

Compression is commonly used to reduce file sizes (e.g., ZIP or RAR files), and audio files are often compressed, too. Specific formats (i.e., codecs) for audio files can make the file sizes smaller, with or without reducing the quality of the audio. MP3 is a common codec that reduces the quality of the audio (called "lossy" compression) but also greatly reduces the file size. FLAC (Free Lossless Audio Codec) is a common codec that does not reduce the quality of the audio (called "lossless" compression) but still reduces the file size somewhat. There are also audio file formats that have no codecs or compression, such as WAV (Waveform Audio File Format) and AIFF (Audio Interface File Format).

We recommend recording and digitizing audio with no (lossy audio signal) compression. In other words, never use the MP3 format to record or archive audio. Instead, use uncompressed encoding methods (like Pulse Code Modulation [PCM]), saved as BWF [Broadcast Wave Format], an extension of the WAV audio file format) or WAV files. PCM is a method for digitally representing sampled analog signals, where the analog signal is measured (sampled) at the given sample rate (e.g., 44.1 kHz, or 44,100 times per second). BWF files may be preferable to WAV files because they contain extended information (metadata) in the file header. We recommend a lossless compression codec, such as FLAC, which compresses the file size but does not "lose" any information. An audio file encoded in the FLAC format (which would look like "examplefilename.flac") allows for substantial metadata to be attached to the file (e.g., details about the production, copyright information, images).

The recommendations above are for the archival master versions of files. When you need to make audio available to students or other users, you will most likely make a copy of the file, converted to a lossy codec format (e.g., AAC [Advanced Audio Coding], MP3). For most cases, you can use the free software Audacity to convert and compress audio files, but a commercial application might improve your workflow and processing options. Some software (e.g., Adobe Audition, Foobar 2000) has some useful batch processing functions. For example, we often take a large group of FLAC master version files and convert them to MP3 in bulk, in a batch process.

4.1.2 Sample Rate and Bit Depth

The concepts of sample rate and bit depth are a bit technical. The sample rate is how often a sample of an audio signal is taken and recorded over time. If you imagine an analog waveform and zoom in, there is a nearly infinite level of complexity from one point to another. When we digitize an audio signal, the software "samples" the strength (level) of the analog audio signal (in both the positive and negative phase of the waveform) at regular points in time (based on the sample rate used, e.g., 44.1 kHz [44,100 times per second]), quantizes the level to the nearest bit value based on the bit depth (e.g., 24-bit audio has 16,777,216 discreet values measurable in each audio sample), and records that value, along with the time stamp of the sample, in the audio file.

A sampling rate of 44.1 kHz allows an upper frequency value of 20 kHz (the Nyquist Theorem states that analog signals must be sampled at a bit over two times the highest frequency you want to reproduce). The frequency range of (perfect) human hearing is considered to be 20 Hz–20 kHz (the upper limit, especially, lowers with age). Therefore, using a sample rate of 44.1 kHz or 48 kHz is highly recommended. (The upper frequency of the main energy of the human voice is often listed as up to 4 or 8 kHz, but there may be information such as overtones and other artifacts above those frequencies that is important to archive.) Very high sample rates (e.g., 88.2 kHz, 96 kHz) are unlikely to make your audio sound noticeably better than 44.1 kHz or 48 kHz. The higher the sample rate, the more information is produced, resulting in larger file sizes.

Depending on the context or who you ask, you will find differing information on recommended sample rates. The US National Archive provides a good guide for "Audio Maximum Capture" specs (National Archives and Records Administration, n.d.). They suggest a sample rate of 96 kHz, which is good quality, but likely excessive for most LC needs. 48 kHz (as referenced in their "Audio Limited Capture" spec) or 44.1 kHz is likely sufficient for most LC needs. Our general recommendations partially overlap with the remaining National Archive guidelines. In sum, we recommend that you record (and maintain master versions of) audio files at 44.1 kHz or higher, with 48 kHz as a reasonable quality upgrade if you are less concerned about storage space.

The sample rate, bit depth, and number of channels (mono = 1; stereo = 2) determine the size of a file (prior to compression). The higher the bit depth, the higher the maximum signal-to-noise ratio. The bit depth used for audio recordings is commonly 16, 24, or 32-bit floating point. Traditional audio CDs are encoded using a bit depth of 16. We recommend 24-bit or 32-bit (floating point), if your audio software supports it. These higher bit depths allows for better quality signal processing (equalization, noise reduction, etc.) because the extra resolution (vs. 16-bit) is significant for a more accurate representation of the waveform, allows for more headroom during recording (meaning you can record with the peaks, say, 6–12 dB below maximum—with a lower risk of distortion—and still have plenty of dynamic resolution), and creates higher quality digital signal processing (24-bit audio uses 16,777,216 discreet values for measurement, whereas 16-bit uses 65,536). According to the audio app Audacity, 32-bit (floating point), the default in the app, is said to preserve samples in excess of full scale. More information about 32-bit (floating point) can be found, among other places, at the Audio Hertz website (Silverstein, 2017).

To summarize, we recommend that your master version audio files (unless they are especially valuable resources) use the following specifications.

- Codec: FLAC
- Sample rate: 48 kHz
- Bit depth: 24

Your streaming media system will likely specify one or more audio formats that are able to be streamed by it. These files are compressed versions of the master files and can all have a variety of compression settings. If your streaming media system does not provide compression specifications for speech, we recommend the following. Note that a higher bit rate results in higher waveform accuracy (thus potentially better quality sound), but at the expense of a larger file size. For most speech, 128 kbps may be good enough, but for high quality recordings that need additional accuracy (e.g., pronunciation guides), 320 kbps is ideal.

- Codec: AAC or MP3, etc. (refer to the manual / website of the streaming software you are using)
- Bit rate: constant, at 128 or 320 kbps

4.2 Digitizing Video

Digitizing analog media requires connecting the analog playback unit to a video digitizer (external device, or a card in a computer) via cables (video and audio). Always use the highest quality video output of your playback device (e.g., S-VHS over composite) that is also available in your converter. At times, you may require an adapter, such as HDMI to composite. Note that the signal would be constrained to the composite quality in this case, and if you convert from composite to HDMI, the signal will be no higher quality than the composite source.

Digital video file formats, data rates, etc., is a deep and evolving topic. One useful resource is the Streaming Learning Center (2020), but using it requires some searching, reading, and learning. Unlike audio, digital video file sizes can be prohibitive, depending on your available storage space, so all digitized video will have to be compressed to some degree, using a lossy format. If you are archiving a large collection of video, we strongly recommended that you consult with an expert to establish a file specification template for you to maximize quality without multiplying storage costs unnecessarily.

The UW LLC regularly receives analog video resources that need to be digitized (e.g., VHS, Beta, PAL cassettes), as well as digital video resources (e.g., DVDs) that need to be converted to a computer-based file (e.g., MP4, AVI, MOV). As an example workflow, when we have a VHS cassette that needs to be converted, we use our highest quality VHS player as the playback unit. We then use the highest quality output option from the player. In our case, it is S-Video. We then use an analog-to-digital converter box (Elgato) that plugs into the S-Video from the playback unit, and then connects to the recording/capturing computer via USB.

4.3 Legacy Playback Equipment

The UW LLC most frequently uses the following legacy playback equipment to digitize older resources: an audio reel-to-reel player, a standard audio cassette player, a microcassette player, a 12" vinyl record player (with multiple playback speeds and support for 7" records), a VCR, and DVD player. We have three variations of VHS (Video Home System) videocassette players. One device can play PAL (Phase Alternating Line) media, which is used typically in Europe, Africa, and Asia. Another device can play NTSC (National Television System Committee) formatted cassettes. We also have a SECAM (Séquentiel couleur à mémoire) device, which was typically used in the former Soviet Union and Africa. Although the SECAM device does get used, it is only on very rare occasions. We recommend that you wait to acquire one until a specific need arises. However, the NTSC device is used fairly regularly, and the PAL device, while less frequently used, can be a valuable tool to have as they are rare in the US. Our LC also has three devices for DVD playback (Blu-ray, region free DVD, PAL DVD). Most DVDs can be transcoded using software (e.g., Handbrake) directly onto a computer from a DVD drive. However, some materials might need to be transferred using a real-time capture from an external DVD player. In total, the amount of equipment that we store takes up a very small footprint and is relatively manageable. We monitor surplus and interdepartmental giveaways and occasionally acquire potentially useful equipment at no or low cost. For example, a computer lab gave us two extra-large flatbed scanners that we use for digitizing large language posters, old language notebooks, or the covers of 12" vinyl records.

A related idea is that some LCs can offer the use of their legacy equipment to the larger community at their institution. This concept is somewhat similar to that of a tool library or makerspace. A LC might loan out equipment to faculty and provide some minimal training, allow them to use the equipment in house, or actually process the media for the faculty member. Having a LC that acts as a central hub or service for processing legacy media will arguably result in more efficient workflows, reduced costs, and final products of higher quality. It is inefficient to have faculty or departments purchase equipment to do the work themselves and then store or resell the equipment once it is no longer needed. A LC can purchase and maintain a minimal set of good-quality equipment, better justifying the expense if it is supporting multiple departments or the entire institution. If a LC has the resources (such as undergraduate student staff), having staff handle the digitization process relieves faculty of the need to be trained on best practices, allows them to focus on their other work instead, and produces a more predictable, quality result.

A variety of legacy formats may need digitization or conversion (Table 1, next page). It is also useful to have a database containing many of the details of owned hardware for clear reference for you and your staff to identify which hardware you own that can support the legacy media.

4.4 Basic Digitization Process Tips

In this section, we highlight some of the most important and commonly used processes, procedures, and settings for digitizing media. These can provide a good foundation for getting started with best practices in your LC, but they are, by no means, exhaustive. They may not cover all of your needs, and others may have slightly different opinions. Nevertheless, they are based on commonly utilized professional standards.

Table 1

Most Common Legacy Physical Media Formats for Language Resources (Oldest to Most Recent)

Analog audio	Digital audio
Wire	**Floppy disc** (Instavox)
Wax cylinders	**Optical compact disc** CD-ROM, CD-R, CD+R, CD+G
Open reel Mono, stereo Speeds in IPS (inches per second): 15/32, 15/16, 1-7/8, 3-3/4, 7-1/2, 15, 30, etc.	**Digital audio tape (DAT)**
Grooved disc ("Vinyl") Speeds in RPM (rotations per minute): 33 ⅓, 45, 78 Common sizes: 12", 10", 7"	
Cassette Common sizes: 8-track, standard, mini, micro	

Analog video	Digital video
Open reel Common sizes: 2", 1", ½", ¼"	**Cassette** Common formats: Betacam SX, Digital Betacam, HDCAM, DVCPro, DVCam, miniDV
Grooved disc Common format: Capacitance Electronic Disc	**Optical discs** Common formats: Video CD, LaserDisc (CLV and CAV), DVD, Blu-ray, HD-DVD
Cassette Common formats: U-matic (¾-inch), VHS, Betamax, Betacam, BetacamSP, Video8, Hi-8, Digital8	

4.4.1 Audio-to-Digital-Audio Converters

An Audio-to-Digital-Audio Converter (ADAC) is a hardware device that is used to capture an analog signal, convert it to a digital signal, and then output it so that another device (such as a PC) can capture it (and save it as a FLAC file). A two-channel ADAC will support mono and stereo sources and should be sufficient for most needs. Common input types found on an ADAC are XLR, 1/4" TRS (Tip Ring Sleeve), Neutrik combo (accepts both of the former), and sometimes RCA (phono). You will need cables to connect each playback device to the ADAC. If the playback device and ADAC both support balanced connectors, they should be used (refer to the owner's manual). The ADAC will send a digital signal to your PC, which will be captured by an audio recording/editing application, such as Audacity.

Audacity is available at no cost and is sufficient for most work. However, other applications (e.g., Adobe Audition) have arguably improved interfaces and more tools for doing precise cleanup of audio noise and unwanted artifacts (e.g., door slams or bird chirps in the background of language documentation recordings). We often use Audacity to capture audio. Because it is free and not resource intensive, we can run it on multiple computers at the same time at no additional cost to the center. Then, we have a few dedicated workstations with more powerful audio cleanup software, such as Adobe Audition, that we use to improve problematic (e.g., noisy) recordings, and Izotope RX Editor for more complex noise reduction. Note that it is beyond the scope of this chapter to cover software-based noise reduction; however, improper use can result in degraded audio, such as too much mid to higher frequency loss. The vendor sites of these software packages typically have good tutorials for avoiding this.

4.4.2 Open Reel Tracks and Channels

There are several tape track and channel formats, and they can affect how (and if) you can get a signal out of your open reel tape deck, with respect to the format in which the tape was recorded. Mark Harvey provides a particularly helpful guide for this (Harvey, n.d.).

Most spoken word recordings are mono, not stereo. In this case, the deck playing back a mono recording should only have one cable connected to the ADAC. For an optimal signal, and to avoid including audio that is played in reverse on the analog tape player (when certain tape formats are played back on certain decks), it may be necessary to move the cable from one output to the other. Stereo recordings should use two cables going directly from the output channel to the corresponding input channel on the ADAC. Whenever possible, use a single cable to connect devices (with the proper plugs on either end), rather than using adapters, which can slightly degrade the signal. Especially avoid passive transformers (simple mechanical devices) that convert balanced to unbalanced audio, or vice versa; instead, use a device with electronics (i.e., a matchbox). The article on *Balanced Audio* provides more information (Wikimedia Foundation, 2021).

4.4.3 Calibrating Gain (Signal Level) Structure

Every component in the audio signal chain has an optimal level. The "audio signal chain" is the "chain" of devices/applications that are connected and pass audio from one stage to the next. In other words, the playback reel-to-reel player sends a signal to the analog-to-digital converter box, which could come in the form of a mic preamp, voice processor, or mixer, which then sends the signal to the computer that is capturing the final signal.

All devices in the audio signal chain need to be "strong enough" but also not "too strong" or the recording will not sound good (i.e., digitally distorted). When a signal is not strong enough, extra noise is introduced when one stage of the signal path has to overamplify the signal to make up for a level sent too low from the previous stage. To ensure that audio is strong enough, the gain (signal level) must be properly set at each device. Think of "gain" as similar to the volume on a stereo when you play music. The louder the volume or "level" on the stereo, the louder the audio output will be. The difference is that "volume" is a more subjective and less precise term. "Gain" is a more exact measurement of the level of a sound signal.

By optimizing the gain of the devices in the audio signal chain, you can avoid digital distortion, which is one of the most common and disastrous problems with audio. Audio waveform samples are recorded as a number at every sample point, and if the analog waveform exceeds the capacity of the converter, the waveform will be recorded at the maximum digital level, resulting in a flat waveform for those samples, which is digital distortion.

To provide an example, we discuss how to set the audio signal chain properly when digitizing audio from a reel-to-reel. To calibrate the signal chain, use a "test tone" tape with a sine wave signal, typically 1 kHz recorded at 0 dBVU. A sine wave is the type of wave used by analog tape recorders and other analog equipment to calibrate the signal between devices. During playback on an open reel deck, turn the output levels of the deck so that the meters read 0 dBVU. When passing the signal through a mixer or other output devices, optimize them with the signal passed from the deck, using the owner's manual. Then set your audio ADAC to reflect 0 dBVU. The signal from the ADAC to your computer (via USB, etc.) is digital, so there is no input to control in your audio digitizing software (e.g., Audacity); you control the level through the ADAC. If you do not have an audio test tone tape, you can record one using a (physical) tone generator.

After calibrating the signal chain, and even if you do not have a test tone tape, play back your audio tape in several places to try to find representative high levels, and adjust the VU (volume unit) meter on the tape deck so that audio peaks hit about 0 dB or a little higher. Then adjust your ADAC input level to an optimal level; an ADAC typically has lights indicating when you are approaching distortion. For example, green indicates that the signal is not overdriven, and red means that distortion is approaching or has occurred. Increase the input level until the distortion light switches on, then decrease the level until the light switches off. Keep in mind that the distortion light switches on a level lower than distortion would be caused (this gap is called "headroom"). Note that on more than one occasion, we have found that the level of audio on a tape changed significantly from section to section because the level at the time of the recording was turned up or down. If it increases to the point of distortion in your recording, you will need to recalibrate based on the stronger level and start over. Later, when editing the audio, you may also want to adjust the volume of the recording to make the sections match in level.

It is extremely important to never overdrive the ADAC because it is one of the most common mistakes people make when digitizing media. Some digitizers will show the signal as green, and then red when the signal is approaching (or has reached) digital 0, which is the maximum the signal can be before digitally distorting. In practice, especially because many audio programs have quite a bit of dynamic variability, you should turn down the input on your ADAC so that the peaks shown in the digitizing software approach approximately -6 dBFS. That gives you about 6 dB of headroom. Unless you know the level of your material well, you may want to fast forward the recording and check whether the level increases greatly, which might cause distortion. Have your recording software in record-ready mode (or input monitoring) so that you can look for a proper signal. The software will often have a record of the strongest peak, and you can visually check for distortion by zooming into the waveform level of parts with a strong signal; many audio editing applications have a function to find the loudest peak. If the signal is distorted, the peaks will be partially flattened. In that case, decrease your level and redo.

If recording too strong of a signal risks causing distortion (from a loss of information), then why should you not be conservative and record a lower signal (i.e., a quieter output from the playback device and ADAC)? The problem is that the quieter the playback is (i.e., the lower the gain), the more you will lose information (i.e., dynamic resolution) because the lower amplitude portions of the waveform will be captured with less dynamic range (signal strength), resulting in a less accurate representation of the signal. If you capture a quiet signal on the computer, you can use software to normalize the gain to make the audio file louder, but the computer is only increasing the gain of what little information was captured there, and the original detail is lost. This is why you need to find a safe balance of "not too strong" and "not too weak." The higher the signal you can capture without distortion, the better. However, the value of maximizing the signal through testing has a limit. If you are not capturing highly valuable resources, you can record at a slightly more conservative level to save time on testing and needing to rerecord if the level peaks and causes distortion.

To recap, you want to optimize the output of the tape deck and the input of your ADAC, sending a strong enough (but not overdriven) level from the tape player to the ADAC and a strong enough (but not overdriven) level from the ADAC to the computer. Be sure to check the digital level and waveform in your audio software.

4.4.4 Working with Analog Tape

Audio cassettes, and some reel tapes, may be encoded with noise reduction. Tapes should be marked with the kind of noise reduction used, if any, but this is not always the case. If so, choose the appropriate setting on the deck as you work with analog tapes. If noise reduction was used, but not documented, you can play back with different noise reduction settings, including none, and choose the one that sounds best.

Regularly clean the tape heads and tape path of your deck to keep debris from interfering with tape-to-tape-head contact (and resulting in frequency loss) and to keep the rest of the path clean so that the tape travels across the tape heads straight. Periodically demagnetize the tape heads and tape path with a demagnetizer. Tape deck heads become magnetized when tapes are played, which can cause high frequency loss, and in some cases can cause partial erasure of tapes when played.

You can refer to your owner's manual, and the web has many excellent resources available to guide you. Other aspects of maintenance, such as tape head alignment, will most likely require a professional.

The current section offered a brief overview of the topic of media digitization. Not all LCs may need to digitize analog media, and as time progresses, the amount of undigitized analog content will decrease. A LC can assist its community in another way with respect to digital media: professional media production. In the next section, we argue that, even with the advent of accessible and affordable media creation tools, a clear need remains for quality media content creation, and LCs can be an ideal resource for it.

5. Media Production

The modern world has provided the average computer user the tools to create video or audio assets quickly and easily. For many language instructors, this has opened up new possibilities, particularly for hybrid or flipped instruction. While the increased access to these creative tools is clearly a benefit, it does not eliminate the need for quality media production. For example, while a basic webcam and USB microphone might be sufficient for a simple video that is meant to supplement a hybrid lesson, other projects might require professionally produced media.

For most language resources, the quality of the recording can affect its efficacy and longevity. Our institution has a for-hire professional central media production office, but it is cost-prohibitive for most language departments in nearly every case. Typically, the health sciences or science and engineering departments have the funding to cover the costs. A LC can fulfill the needs of language departments by providing support for media creation for their projects.

The UW LLC is fortunate to have a dedicated studio space that is acoustically designed and insulated/treated. Similarly, many LCs will have a space where they can control the environmental sound better than most faculty offices. A coatroom filled with coats or similar absorption materials can help keep reverb and echo under control; otherwise, the clarity of speech is reduced. Even if the LC does not have a clearly superior acoustic environment, it can provide high quality microphones with pop filters (often two layers of nylon stretched over either side of a six-inch ring, used to disperse plosives, such as "p" sounds, that might cause distortion) and analog-to-digital converters to produce better quality materials either in the center or on location. The core basic video equipment that the UW LLC has found very useful includes a good video camera, backdrops (e.g., black, white, green), lights, and mics (e.g., shotgun, lavalier).

The benefits that the LC provides are not simply the technology, but also the expertise to use it. Neither of these are something many faculty members have the time to acquire in a short time frame. Such support offered by a LC can result in faculty members being able to produce better learning resources and having more time for research and teaching. Often faculty members will inquire about a project and be unaware of what is feasible, so the LC staff can provide consultation and guidance for the production of the resources. As UW faculty become more aware of what is possible, we are approached by faculty members with additional interesting projects.

In fact, the demand for these services has continued to increase, even though lower quality resources (e.g., webcams) are more available and easier to use than ever.

As an example of a recent media production project, we recently worked with a faculty member on an online/print-on-demand textbook (with one of the Creative Commons licenses) to produce audio and video resources. Other examples of media production include recording lectures for online learning, interviews with invited guests, language documentation content, departmental podcasts, mini-documentaries about language experts and less commonly taught languages, and language class and study abroad promotional videos.

6. Conclusion

Although media technology is changing rapidly and the role that LCs served with physical media management has become less prevalent, LCs can support media-related projects in many valuable ways. There is a need for supporting media creation, processing, management, and distribution. If the recent past is any indication, the amount of data that will need filtering, processing, annotating, organizing, archiving, and distributing will only increase. Most language departments and faculty do not have the resources to keep up with this challenge. In fact, most archives do not have the resources. LCs can support more traditional archives by acting as an intermediary archive and by providing subject-matter expertise. For LCs with less demand for processing old media, new media is being created all the time. We have found a steady increase in demand over time for professional multimedia content development and expect this trend to continue. While this development is only part of the UW LLC's mission, there is probably enough work that we could dedicate all our time and resources to such projects for years to come. This is further evidence that although the role of LCs continues to change over time, they are a vital part of the present and future of language learning and language vitality (see UNESCO, 2017).

As a next step, it would be helpful to have data on the media production equipment and facilities LCs around the world have, the types of media they produce, and the perceived demand. It might also be beneficial to produce a more extensive guide for digitizing legacy media, with recommendations for equipment, setup, and settings.

References

Bhaduri, M. (2011). *Bangla across borders: Workbook*. Seattle, WA: University of Washington.

Brubacher, L., & Evershed, J. (2018). Managing media matters. In E. Lavolette & E. F. Simon (Eds.), *Language center handbook* (pp. 261–291). Auburn, AL: International Association for Language Learning Technology.

Buchanan, S., Gruning, J., Gursoy, A., & Barker, L. (2017). Surveying archivists and their work toward advocacy and management, or "enterprise archiving." *The American Archivist, 80*(2), 268–295.

Harvey, M. (n.d.). *Reel-to-reel, cassette and digital audio tape*. https://www.d.umn.edu/~mharvey/th1551reeltoreelcassetteda.html

Hugo, R. (2015). Constructing online language learning content archives for under resourced language communities. *University of Washington Working Papers in Linguistics*, *33*, 1–23.

Irons Walch, V., Beaumont, N., Yakel, E., Bastian, J., Zimmelman, N., Davis, S., & Diffendal, A. (2006). A* CENSUS (Archival census and education needs survey in the United States). *The American Archivist*, *69*(2), 291–419.

Müller, T. (2011). How to choose a free and open source integrated library system. *OCLC Systems & Services: International digital library perspectives*, *27*(1), 57–78.

National Archives and Records Administration. (n.d.). *Preservation. Audio recordings.* https://www.archives.gov/preservation/products/reformatting/audio.html

Salomon, C., Abedin, A., & Brandl, K. (2011). *Bangla across borders: An elementary language course.* Seattle, WA: University of Washington.

Silverstein, D. (2017, February 23). *What is 32 BIT FLOATING?* https://audiohertz.com/2017/02/23/what-the-fck-is-32-bit-floating/

Streaming Learning Center. (2020, November 22). https://streaminglearningcenter.com/

UNESCO. (2017). *A methodology for assessing language vitality and endangerment.* http://www.unesco.org/new/en/culture/themes/endangered-languages/language-vitality/

Wikimedia Foundation. (2021, February 2). *Balanced audio.* https://en.wikipedia.org/wiki/Balanced_audio

Author Notes

Robert Majors earned his BA in Electronic Media Communications from the Evergreen State College. Bob also completed the majority of course work for an MEd degree at the University of Washington, College of Education, with a focus on Curriculum and Instruction: Educational Technology. Bob has over four decades of professional audio experience (bridging the analog and digital worlds), including public radio, TV and radio commercials, documentaries, one Hollywood movie, learning product. He recorded world languages for Microsoft's Encarta and World Atlas products and has taught digital audio production. Bob has worked at the University of Washington Language Learning Center (LLC) for over 35 years and has managed the LLC's on-demand and live audio/video services for over 20 of those years (RealNetworks, QuickTime Streaming Server, QuickTime Broadcaster, Wowza Media Systems, Wirecast, and JW Player). Bob performs a variety of IT work for the LLC, including servers and databases.

Russell Hugo (PhD, University of Washington) is the Assistant Director of the Language Learning Center at the University of Washington. His academic interests are focused on Indigenous language vitalization, Computer Assisted Language Learning, and language attitudes in relation to language policy.

Paul Aoki (PhD, University of Washington) is the Director of the Language Learning Center at the University of Washington, a role he has held since 1988. He is active in developing digital media for language learning. He has also worked with Microsoft, Apple, Department of Defense, and others to develop digital language learning materials. He was Principal Investigator for many federal grants,

264

including STARTALK. His wide range of interests is reflected in his membership in several professional organizations, including being a long-time member of IALLT.

Correspondence concerning this chapter should be addressed to Robert Majors (majors@uw.edu).

Chapter 11

Enhancing the Telecollaboration Experience: Partnering with Language Centers Abroad to Cultivate Opportunities for Language Immersion and Practice

Anton T. Brinckwirth, Virginia Commonwealth University, USA
Martha Guadalupe Hernández Alvarado, Hilda Hidalgo Avilés, Norma Angélica Espinosa Butrón, and Isabel Alfaro Flores, Universidad Autónoma del Estado de Hidalgo, Mexico

Abstract

This chapter reports on four language exchange programs carried out between 2014 and 2019 at two large state universities, one in Mexico and the other in the US. The participating teachers and staff at both institutions collaborated through their respective school's language center (LC) to provide students from both countries with the opportunity to gain cultural and linguistic knowledge through student-centered and instructor-guided telecollaborative interactions.

Student groups consisted of general language learners, pre-service EFL teachers, and healthcare students with profession-related language needs. Each program provided language students with authentic immersion opportunities to enhance target language (L2) communicative skills and cultural learning in various contexts.

The teachers and staff employed action research strategies in iterative cycles to continually improve learning content, task design, partner-matching, level of engagement, program organization, and quality of implementation. They used mixed methods to collect, analyze, and interpret student evaluation questionnaires, written and voice-recorded student reflections, and the instructors' notes and observations.

The outcomes shed light on the pedagogical nuances and logistical necessities vital to successful implementation. Each program presented a unique set of objectives, but there were also common challenges. Students and faculty generally viewed telecollaboration as an effective means to enhance L2 engagement in courses with a language and cultural focus. The study shows how traditional centers can find renewed pedagogical purpose in connecting language students, teachers, and LC staff members with their respective peers abroad through structured telecollaboration partnerships. This chapter may be useful to language instructors considering telecollaboration to provide immersion opportunities for students and to LC directors planning to re-envision their center's mission and design.

This chapter reports on the English-Spanish telecollaboration programs that were jointly developed and implemented between 2014 and 2019 at two large state universities, one in Mexico and the other in the US. Both sites searched for reliable telecollaboration practitioners abroad interested in cooperating across a flexible, adaptable, and mutually beneficial partnership. The faculty members and language center (LC) staff from both universities shared the common goal of improving the services and support systems within their respective institutions regarding telecollaboration pedagogy and programming. They viewed the social interaction and negotiation aspects of telecollaboration as essential to improving language education in general. Moreover, they perceived its value in the development of intercultural and professional learning, too.

In 2015, the two groups began collaborating and conceptualizing how the exchanges could work. They formed a community of practice dedicated to exploring and improving the pedagogical and logistical procedures for the implementation of telecollaboration.

Although six programs were developed, only the four for which there were significant data will be reported in this chapter. As the practice of telecollaboration evolved, the directors and staff members at both LCs realized that it was necessary to look more closely at the pedagogy and logistics to improve telecollaboration in both areas to meet the needs of the various programs. The aims of the partnership were:

1. To use LCs as social and collaborative learning spaces where language students could have opportunities for language immersion and practice through dynamic and engaging interactions with native speakers,
2. To provide the appropriate support, training, and equipment needed to explore telecollaborative exchanges in-depth and routinely deliver high-impact sessions,
3. To assess the pedagogical value of telecollaboration and explore its full potential for language, cultural, and professional learning, and
4. To gain practical knowledge and experience in teletandem and identify ways to continually improve its efficacy.

The chapter is organized into four sections. Section 1 provides the theoretical framework for designing and implementing the various programs at both institutions. Section 2 presents the pedagogical and logistical strategies used to facilitate the exchanges. It outlines the methods used to collect and analyze the student evaluations and reflections and documents the instructors' perceptions of sessions. Section 3 reports findings from the analysis and interpretation of the data. Finally, Section 4 summarizes the lessons learned, describes the limitations, and offers future recommendations for the practice of telecollaboration.

1. Theoretical Framework for the Design and Implementation of Telecollaboration

1.1 Theoretical Foundation

Teletandem is a telecollaboration model (Telles & Vassallo, 2006) that evolved from face-to-face tandem learning, a situation in which two people with different native languages work together to learn from one another. This learning partnership provides students with opportunities to improve their communicative ability in their partner's native tongue, learn about their cultural background, and benefit from their partner's knowledge and experience in different areas (Brammerts, 2003). As new information and communication technologies emerged, it became possible for schools and institutions to organize and implement global telecollaborative exchanges and provide students with opportunities to have meaningful interactions with native speakers without the need for travel. Telles and Vassallo (2006) introduced the term "teletandem" to refer to the online language exchanges characterized by text, voice, and webcam video. We use the terms "teletandem" and "telecollaboration" interchangeably throughout the chapter to refer to the student interactions in the contexts of pedagogy, programming, and practice.

The effectiveness of teletandem may be inherently social, as evidence shows that collaboration fosters language learning and cognitive development (Lewis, 2003). In their review of more than 40 studies on the role of peer-to-peer dialog in second language acquisition, Swain, Brooks, and Tocalli-Beller (2002, as cited in Lewis, 2003) concluded that when language learners "encounter linguistic problems and attempt to solve them together in collaborative dialog, language is used both as a communicative and cognitive tool" (p. 16). Therefore, the dialogic nature of telecollaborative exchanges is deemed helpful for language and intercultural learning (Kinginger & Belz, 2005; Müller-Hartmann, 2000; O'Dowd, 2006; O'Rourke, 2005; Tian & Wang, 2010; Ware, 2005; Ware & O'Dowd, 2008).

1.2 Principles

According to Vassallo and Telles (2006), teletandem exchanges should be based on three principles:

1. Languages must not be mixed: Within a teletandem session, partners should devote equal time to each language's practice separately. That will allow them to gain proficiency in their target language and communicate in their native language when attaining challenging goals or completing demanding tasks.
2. Reciprocity: Learners should take turns in acting as students of the target language and as experts of their native language. As Brammerts and Calvert (2003) explained, teletandem is a free and mutual exchange of knowledge about language and culture, which should benefit both partners equally.
3. Autonomy: "Tandem partners are free to decide about what, when, where and how to study, and how long they wish to do it" (Vassallo & Telles, 2006, p. 88). The authors explained that the degree of autonomy learners have in their learning process depends on whether teletandem is carried out in an institutional context or an independent mutual agreement between individuals.

Brammerts (2003) pointed out the following:

Learning in tandem is learning by exchange: both partners want to learn from each other, and, to this end, each brings their skills and abilities, which the other wants to acquire, and the willingness to support a partner in their learning. (p. 31)

However, the learning partnership will only last if both partners benefit to the same extent, devote the same amount of time to practice, and equitably provide support. Once learners determine their own goals (with or without their teachers' guidance), students decide how they will reach them in collaboration with their partners. To support each other's learning, both students need to provide the assistance requested to the best of their ability. They can correct one another's mistakes, suggest alternative reformulations, explain meanings, and help with understanding texts (Brammerts, 2003).

1.3 Approaches and Settings

One of the main characteristics of teletandem is its flexibility. Vassallo and Telles (2006) stated that as a learning mode, teletandem could be conducted in many different ways depending on how, where, and by whom it is conceived and carried out. It can be implemented as a learning activity between individuals (independent teletandem) or as language practice organized in a school setting (institutional teletandem) inside or outside the curriculum.

Tardieu and Horgues (2020) pointed out that the choice of the most appropriate form of teletandem depends significantly on the learner's profile, goals, and learning context. They found that students who often participate in telecollaborative exchanges have multiple learning goals. Their priorities vary according to the individual, their linguistic and cultural biography, and academic institutional requirements. There is a wide range of teletandem learning objectives and configurations to address the variance in competencies and learning needs.

According to Tardieu and Horgues (2020), telecollaboration setups may include learners whose goals are:

- To improve their accuracy and fluency in the target language (L2) for academic purposes. In this setting, linguistic expertise is an essential criterion as participants benefit from their partners' corrections and explanations.
- To prioritize intercultural communication over language practice. In this case, telecollaboration partners mainly benefit from being exposed to language variation that will elicit language uses not restricted to the conventional standard forms usually found in the classroom.
- To rely on their plurilingual competence and develop a form of telecollaboration that prompts "linguistic hybridity" among multicompetent speakers (Belz, 2003, p. 92). Linguistic hybridity refers to using mixed languages, reflecting a natural and emerging state of multicompetence in the learner. This teletandem setup, according to Benoit and Lomicka (2020), helps participants build a translingual system (bilingual communication), acquire skills in negotiating cultural perspectives, and understand the cultural experience of others.
- To develop linguistic and intercultural skills and professional competence. Brammerts (1996, as cited in Tardieu & Horgues, 2020) emphasized the potential of this learning partnership for students who are members of the same professional group; they can learn more about their discipline and the language behavior in their partner's country as a result of the exchange.

For Bueno-Alastuey and Kleban (2016), the planning of a teletandem partnership may be pivotal to its success in terms of differing student goals. The objectives set at the beginning will help forecast the success of the collaboration and the students' involvement and participation. Pairing students according to their L2 proficiency, learning goals, age, gender, and interests, as suggested by Lewis (2005), can establish a long-lasting learning relationship in which both students are more engaged and motivated to learn and practice languages.

1.4 Strategies for Implementation

In his research on the integration of telecollaboration in European universities, O'Dowd (2013) disseminated a survey among experienced practitioners and identified reasons why telecollaboration can be challenging to integrate with universities. Among the reasons:

1. the time necessary to set up and run exchanges,
2. the complex nature of integration and assessment due to institutional requirements,
3. the lack of pedagogical knowledge about telecollaboration,
4. the lack of e-literacies, and
5. the difficulty finding appropriate partners.

To contribute to the integration of telecollaboration at universities, O'Dowd (2013) suggested the following strategies:

1. Building up reliable and steady institutional partnerships: Practitioners need to establish partnerships with colleagues who share the same visions, approaches, practices, and expectations. If the relationship between telecollaborative partners is reliable and stable, they may be more willing to make exchanges an integral part of their curricula and work practices.
2. Raising awareness and prestige of the telecollaborative exchange in the local institution and beyond: O'Dowd explained that telecollaborative exchanges can achieve greater integration and receive wider acceptance among colleagues and administrators when promoted in the local press and via campus communications.
3. Customizing telecollaboration to adapt to language needs in the curriculum, on campus, and in the local community.
4. Achieving credit or recognition for the students' telecollaborative work. O'Dowd believes this will automatically heighten the significance of telecollaboration for both students and teachers alike. It is also vital to implement assessment strategies tailored to the needs and realities of the institutions involved.
5. Linking telecollaboration to the broader international focus of the institution. O'Dowd recognized that there is a link between telecollaboration and campus internationalization and pointed out instances when administrators acknowledged the inherent value of telecollaboration in raising the institution's international profile.

1.5 Language Centers and Telecollaboration

According to Ruane (2003), the organization of LCs in higher education tends to reflect the environment, history, and context in which they have evolved. However, Ruane stated that innovation in pedagogy, institutional adaptability, and effective use of technology are qualities that have contributed to the successful development of LCs to date.

Using data from a 2013 survey of LC directors and members of the International Association for Language Learning and Technology (IALLT) and its regional groups, Kronenberg (2014) pointed out that most LCs are trying to keep up with disruptive technologies, new demands, and changing realities. Respondents agreed that one of their concerns was to remain relevant because most applications are now available on the web. Therefore, LCs need to redefine their focus while fulfilling their mission to support language teaching and learning with technology. For Kronenberg (2014), the LC mission is continuously shifting and changing as new technologies and pedagogies also demand new services and support systems.

Based on the 2013 survey and recent literature and research in the field, Kronenberg (2016) proposed five design criteria for reenvisioning brick-and-mortar LCs:

1. Flexibility and adaptability: LCs need to be conceptualized as spaces adaptable to various teaching and learning situations.
2. Mission-based design: It is essential to focus on the LC mission and role within the curriculum and institution more than on its architectural design or furniture.
3. Situatedness: A well-placed LC in an appealing and comfortable setting conveys to stakeholders that the institution values language learning and cares enough to provide quality support and fulfill its mission to world languages and cultures.
4. Social space and community design: Modern LCs have evolved into social and collaborative learning spaces. With this change, LCs could instill a sense of belonging to foster meaningful interaction, language engagement, and 21st-century teaching and learning communities.
5. Deemphasis of technology: Single technologies should not dictate LC designs because they become obsolete quickly. Instead, LCs should become learning spaces that promote and enhance social interaction and collaborative learning experiences.

Kronenberg (2016) suggested that these five criteria could offer a new path forward for LCs in the 21st-century. The participants of this study responded to the points raised by Kronenberg with the following questions:

1. Could well-organized and well-implemented teletandem programs transform LCs into more social and interactive learning spaces?
2. Would a teletandem-enriched language curriculum achieve the criteria and goals that Kronenberg outlined for the 21st-century LC?
3. Could teletandem programs allow LCs to adapt to the rapidly changing needs and new realities in language education?

The future of LCs should not focus entirely on technology, architecture, and furniture, but instead, on the mission to contribute to the teaching and learning of languages within the institution. As new technologies and pedagogies emerge, new demands arise for new services and support systems. The call to explore the vast possibilities for telecollaboration in the language curriculum is further justified by the surge of online learning during the COVID-19 pandemic in 2020–2021 and the unprecedented use of online videoconferencing applications. LCs need to continually evolve to meet the rapidly changing needs and realities in education. Telecollaboration provides a viable alternative for enhancing the pedagogical value of LCs in the ever-evolving contexts and spaces for teaching and learning languages in an interconnected world.

Telecollaboration programs can bring new immersive and intercultural learning experiences to traditional learning strategies. Like other forms of computer-mediated communication, telecollaborative exchanges can foster social interaction in language classrooms where learners have limited or minimal interaction with their instructors and peers (Cheon, 2008, as cited in Ross & Disalvo, 2020).

2. Methodology

This section describes the pedagogical, logistical, and research frameworks devised for the English-Spanish teletandem programs born out of the collaborations between the faculty and LC staff at the two sites. Although six programs are shown in Table 1 (pages 275–276), this chapter only reports on four based on their relevance, the data collected, and the impact on students' learning at both universities.

The methods used to observe, collect, analyze, and interpret data are outlined. Details are provided on how these processes were carried out between the two sites, particularly in areas where differences were noted.

2.1 Two LCs, One Telecollaboration Community: Pedagogical and Logistical Considerations

The primary objective at both sites was to bring mutually beneficial language immersion and intercultural learning opportunities to language students at both universities. A framework was created to establish the roles of the different participants involved, test the infrastructure needed to carry out the exchanges in campus labs and off campus, and continually improve telecollaboration quality and effectiveness. The protocols to implement the sessions and the criteria to evaluate them were also devised in the early planning stages.

2.1.1 The LC Partnership Roles

The LC staff and language teachers at both sites made optimal use of the partnership by working collaboratively and remotely to organize the exchanges, create new communication channels, and build new learning communities. The language instructors collaborated on each session's instructional design and learning goals, while LC staff members and teletandem facilitators at both sites assisted with implementing sessions.

LC staff members and student workers assisted with the scheduling of telecollaborative exchanges in campus labs. They set up the webcams and headsets before sessions. They seated students as lab sessions began and reseated students when technical problems surfaced. When repartnering was necessary due to

Table 1

Telecollaboration Program Summary

Group/ Program Prototype	MX student profile	Us student profile	Part of a course? Yes/no	Task design Structured/ unstructured	Location: LC labs/off-campus	Student pairing	Total n° sessions (per term)	Years	Program rating[1]
Group 1: Eng-Span Language Learners	EFL learners, L2 placement: A1–B1 CEFR	Enrolled in Spanish lang courses, L2 placement: novlow–intmid ACTFL	MX: no US: yes	Structured & unstructured	LC labs	Per L2 proficiency	2–4	5	MX: 4 US: 4
Group 2: Cinema & Social Justice	Pre-service EFL TEACHERS, L2 placement: B1–C1 CEFR	All majors, L2 placement: intmid–advlow ACTFL	MX: yes US: yes	Structured	LC labs & off-campus	Per L2 proficiency Profile, preferences	8–10	3	MX: 5 US: 5
Group 3: Healthcare Nursing Students	MX nursing students, L2 skills varied, volunteer	Us nursing students, L2 placement: novmid–advlow ACTFL	MX: no US: yes	Structured	LC labs & off-campus	Per L2 proficiency	10–12	1	MX: n/a US: 4
Group 4: Healthcare Medical Students	Mx medical students, L2 skills varied, volunteer	Us 4th-yr med students, L2 skills varied	MX: no US: yes	Structured	LC labs	Random	4–6	4	MX: 5 US: 5

Group 5: Language Partner Requests		Per request, L2 skills varied, volunteer	N/A	Unstructured	LC labs & off-campus	Per 12 proficiency	1–2	5	MX: 3 US: 3
Group 6: All- English Sessions	L2 placement: B2+ CEFR	Random	MX: no US: yes	Unstructured	LC labs	None	N/A	5	MX: n/a US: 3

Note. Instructors in Mexico used the Common European Framework (CEFR) to assess English proficiency. US instructors used the American Council on the Teaching of Foreign Languages (ACTFL) Proficiency Guidelines to assess Spanish proficiency.

[1] Program Rating: The authors, in collaboration with the instructors and LC staff at both sites, assessed each program with a performance rating that was calculated by averaging the following criteria: A) The student evaluation questionnaires, B) The degree to which instructional objectives were achieved, C) The level of planning and preparation, D) The ability to navigate the series of sessions and group, and the impact of technical and student-related problems. The performance rating used a 5-point scale: 5 (Excellent), 4 (Good), 3 (Satisfactory), 2 (Needs Improvement), and 1 (Unsatisfactory).

unexpected absences, the LC staff assisted with this critical function to ensure that sessions ran smoothly. Seating students within five minutes of a lab session's scheduled start time was vital to the success of session implementation. LC staff members and student workers also assisted with connectivity tests to ensure adequate bandwidth for audio and video clarity.

2.1.2 Infrastructure and Tools for Telecollaboration

Both LC sites relied on various adequately equipped computer labs for telecollaborative exchanges on campus. Before each lab session, the LC staff prepared and connected computers and made instructional materials available to students before they arrived for the session. This preparation ensured punctual start times, which proved to be vital to the success of telecollaboration.

Skype and Zoom were used to conduct the actual telecollaborative sessions. In some cases, instructors asked for additional browser tabs to be opened with glossaries, translators, and verb conjugation applications. Instructors provided students with this critical information before external sessions, too. They generally agreed that this was the optimal way to maximize telecollaboration opportunities and learn more about sessions delivered on campus in dedicated labs and off-campus, too.

All of the programs and applications used to power the LC partnership were virtually cost-free. Google Apps provided the tools needed to establish and maintain open communication lines, share documents, presentations, emails, and other file types in a shared Google Drive. The importance of having these bundled apps under the Google umbrella cannot be overstated. The sharing capabilities of Google Apps were essential to the partnership. Google tools were used in the process of pairing students, designing activities, and coordinating sessions. Because there was no official agreement between the two universities at the onset of the project, Google Apps provided much of the glue needed to bring organization and cohesion to the cooperation process. WhatsApp became the tool of choice for session facilitators to communicate with one another during the implementation of lab sessions. The LC staff at the US site used Sanako Study 1200, an IP-based digital language lab program installed on the teacher's main computer that showed a birds-eye view of the lab computers visually laid out in a grid. As shown in Figure 1 (next page), Sanako's "Thumbnail of a Group" function was particularly useful for assessing large groups of students, allowing instructors one-click access to each student session directly from the teacher's computer. Sanako Study 1200 allows for the instructor to enter an active session with or without the students' knowledge. Other lab management applications offer similar functionality, including free programs such as ClassDojo, Veyon, and Google Classroom.

2.1.3 Implementation Protocol

The participating LC directors, staff members, and teachers at both sites formed a cluster of telecollaboration practitioners. They created a workflow through cooperation and communication and generated language immersion opportunities in various instructional contexts. Telecollaboration programming can be delivered in multiple ways depending on the teacher and students' unique needs, goals, and contexts. The instructors' knowledge and understanding of telecollaboration came mainly through experience. The two groups maintained open lines of communication and shared a mutual desire to succeed. Table 2 (pages 279–281) illustrates the processes, contexts, and tools used to achieve a routine workflow and facilitate the cooperation, team-building, and practice required to realize the programs and prototypes discussed in the chapter.

Figure 1
Screen of Sanako Study 1200 IP-Based Language Lab

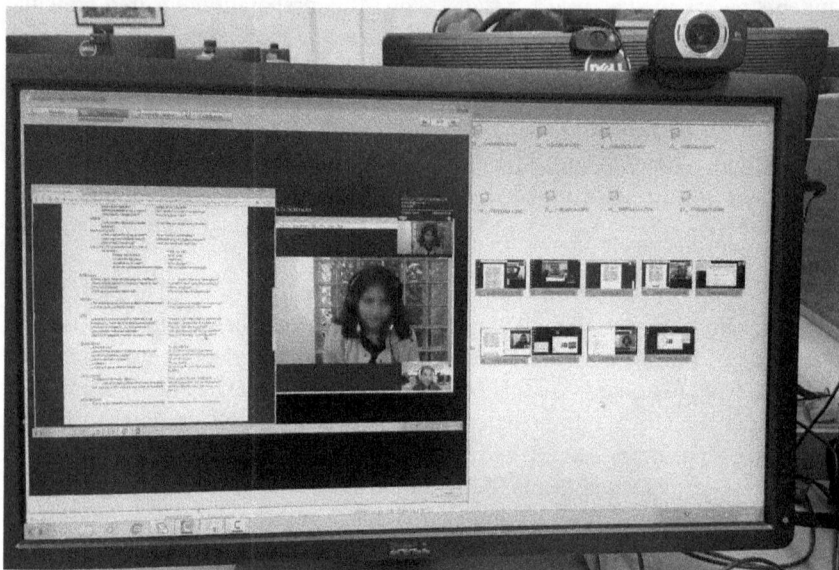

Note. The monitor in the picture shows the Sanako 1200 interface running in the background with the grid layout of the lab computers in thumbnail view to the right. Each icon represents a student desktop. On the left side of the monitor is an expanded view of one student's screen activity in a floating window. A teletandem role-play script appears on the left, and a Skype call window is open in the center, showing a pair of medical students interacting and completing telecollaboration tasks.

2.1.4 Evaluation of Telecollaboration

The instructors and LC staff members observed and evaluated sessions to shed light on factors that facilitate and hinder the quality and effectiveness of telecollaboration pedagogy and programming. Session facilitators used the following set of quality-control questions to identify and mitigate potential problems early and heighten the implementation rate of success in the school labs.

- Were students engaged within the first five minutes of the session?
- Did every student have a partner?
- Did students complete the assigned tasks?
- Did students change languages at the specified time?
- Were the instructional objectives carried out?

Table 2
Telecollaboration Programming and Workflow (2015–2019)

1. First steps: Initiated communication, organized strategic planning, held online meetings with LC staff members and language instructors.
   - Discussed the possibilities for joint development and delivery of telecollaborative exchanges.
   - Identified goals and areas of mutual interest.
   - Specified roles of key participants.
   - Specified potential dates and times for sessions.

2. Collaborated with LC staff members and instructors at partner LC site to develop a mutually beneficial telecollaboration program.
   - Analyzed the language learning goals for each course and the unique learning needs of students.
   - Set teaching objectives for the program.
   - Identified and aligned the learning needs, priorities, and goals for both groups.

3. Jointly created a viable implementation plan with partner LC and instructors.
   - Established a workflow for collaboration and cooperation.
   - Respected the policies, protocols, and priorities of the partner LC site and institution.
   - Created Google folders for file sharing.
   - Brainstormed ideas for session content and task-based activities.
   - Developed plans for student assessment and program evaluation.

4. Provided each student with a telecollaboration partner.
   - Established that a student's level of L2 proficiency is the primary criterion for assigning a suitable telecollaboration partner.
   - For enhanced pairing, instructors matched learners by academic major, career interests, and gender preference if one is given.
   - Created spreadsheets to consolidate lists of student pairs with names, contact info, and criteria.
   - Realigned partners per need or per request.
   - Attempted to pair groups and classes similar in size, made adjustments to pair different-sized groups (e.g., 30 learners in the first group paired with 15 learners in the second group resulted in two-on-one pairings.
   - Notified students about partner matches, provided contact emails, and checked partner activity status at the program's midpoint.
   - Developed a workflow to swiftly resolve partner problems and partner change requests when issues arose.

5. Negotiated a telecollaboration session schedule in cooperation with instructors and LC staff from partner sites.
   - Determined how many sessions were needed to achieve L2 immersion objectives for both student groups.
   - Determined the number of on-campus sessions realistically deliverable in the LC labs with dates and times.
   - Determined the number of off-campus sessions teachers would need to add to achieve objectives.
   - Selected dates and times for on-campus sessions and established due dates and date ranges for off-campus sessions.
   - Instructors generally preferred a hybrid program with x-number of sessions held in LC labs and the remainder held off-campus.
   - Created shared calendars showing all on-campus sessions in LC labs with details and instructor contact info.
   - Provided students with information about all sessions via LMS and syllabus (included sessions details and due dates).

6. Prepared the lab spaces and tested the equipment and bandwidth.
   - Verified bandwidth allocation for LC labs and tested signal strength.
   - Tested computers, headsets, webcams, and software in advance to ensure an optimal experience.
   - Equipped each student station with disposable hygienic earphone covers and antibacterial wipes.

7. Held telecollaboration orientation sessions for students and teachers.
   - Provided essential information to both groups about telecollaboration workflow, protocol, expectations, and etiquette.
   - Answered questions about telecollaboration-based L2 immersion and practice.

8. Created learning content and designed session tasks and activities.
   - Wrote a guide for each session with bilingual scripts, notes, and instructions to help students navigate tasks (see Appendix).
   - Developed supplemental content such as thematic bilingual vocabulary lists, scripts for role-play activities, and curated websites.
   - Added new bookmarks to the browser with links to custom content and tools requested by the instructors.
   - Assigned a final project to be completed collaboratively with various options for presentation.

9. Implemented the sessions per two implementation plans, both instructor-guided:
   - Plan 1 was for instructor-guided sessions held on campus in LC labs at specific dates and times with teachers on site.
   - Plan 2 was for off-campus sessions, instructor-guided, but held at times and dates of students' choosing without teachers present.
   - For Plan 1 sessions in labs, teachers attended, assisted LC staff, observed students, and retrieved files of recorded sessions (optional).
   - For Plan 2 off-campus sessions, teachers assigned reflection tasks, and students submitted time-stamped screenshots for full credit.

10. Created a process to provide students with opportunities to evaluate and reflect on each session.
    - The Mexican students submitted handwritten reflections to their instructor
    - The US students used the VoiceThread app to post comments about the sessions and a time-stamped screenshot for each session.

11. Ensured quality.
    - The instructors and LC staff of both groups held online meetings as needed to assess pedagogy, programming, and practice.
    - LC staff members at both sites ran connectivity tests to check systems and troubleshoot technical problems.
    - Resolved issues reported by students regarding partners and activities.
    - Identified administrative, instructional, and technical issues and made adjustments to enhance the telecollaboration experience.
    - Repeated these steps in iterative cycles to ensure continuous improvement of telecollaboration.

12. Conducted action research.
    - Observed sessions, documented nuances, identified problems, and collaborated with other instructors to improve telecollaboration.
    - Designed, disseminated, retrieved, and analyzed student evaluation questionnaires.
    - Analyzed data to report research in academic papers and to improve the implementation of future telecollaboration programs.

- Were there technical problems?
- Were there logistical problems?
- Were the issues isolated incidents or recurring problems?
- Were there issues with partners or activities?
- Were backup machines set up in case of technical issues?

The instructors and LC staff collaborated to design and coordinate sessions. They used shared Google folders to store and maintain instructional plans, spreadsheets of partner lists, evaluation questionnaires, and templates for task design and program evaluation. Shared content also included images, audio recordings, videos, and screen-captured sessions of each group. This information was handled with maximum security and discretion and shared only with teachers and LC staff to protect student identities.

2.2 Telecollaboration Programs, Group Profiles, and Learning Goals

The cooperation between the LC directors, staff, and language teachers at both universities contributed to a community of practice dedicated to improving telecollaboration pedagogy and practice. The LC staff members collaborated with the language instructors to develop tasks and activities aligned with each group's learning goals, course objectives, and profiles. They considered the language immersion and implementation needs of each group. Student pairs generally came from different academic majors and programs at the two universities. This was the case for all of the programs except for the nursing and medical students.

The partnership produced six distinct telecollaboration programs. Table 1 shows each program group and how they differed in pedagogical objectives and scope. Sections 2 and 3 of this chapter focus on four of the six program groups in detail. These groups were named Language Immersion for English and Spanish Language Learners, Cinema & Social Justice, Nursing Students, and Medical Students. As shown in Table 1, Groups 5 and 6, Language Partner Requests and All-English Exchanges, were inherently part of the initiative. However, their outcomes were less generalizable and less relevant to the topics addressed in this chapter. Therefore, they will not be discussed in detail.

2.2.1 Group 1: Language Immersion for English and Spanish Learners

The program group with the most students was Group 1, which consisted of English and Spanish language students, and each group had specific immersion needs and goals. The majority of US students who experienced teletandem first-hand through this initiative were enrolled in credit-bearing Spanish language courses from the standard lower-division sequence and had Novice-Low to Intermediate-Mid proficiency according to the American Council on the Teaching of Foreign Languages (ACTFL) proficiency guidelines. At the university in Mexico, students who were enrolled in degree or licensure programs with an English proficiency level between A1- and B1-level proficiency, based on Common European Framework of Reference for Languages (CEFR) standards, were eligible to participate. There were no special partner-matching efforts undertaken by instructors for this group beyond the one-directional ACTFL-CEFR alignment (ACTFL, 2016) for speaking and writing skills.

The majority of sessions for students in this group were planned as free-flowing interactions without task-based activities or specific communicative L2 goals. On occasion, the US instructors asked their students to integrate grammar topics learned in class into the teletandem conversation. For example, one teacher asked students to use the preterite and imperfect tenses to tell their partners about past experiences.

The teachers and LC directors at both sites used Google Forms to disseminate a 10-item Likert-scale evaluation to give students a voice in the action research process. The student perspective was highly valued at both sites. Large amounts of data were collected each term in the form of questionnaires, screen-captured and voice-recorded sessions, VoiceThread audio files, hand-written student reflections, and documented observations of lab sessions.

2.2.2 Group 2: Cinema & Social Justice

The programming for the Cinema & Social Justice group was highly developed. The paired learners came from credit-bearing courses at their respective universities. The US learners were enrolled in a Spanish conversation and film course for students with speaking and listening proficiency skills ranging from Intermediate-Mid to Advanced-Low (ACTFL). The Mexican students were pre-service English instructors with B1- to C1-level proficiency (CEFR), enrolled in a teacher preparation course called *Techniques and Strategies for Autonomous Learning*. The instructors connected Mexican pre-service EFL teachers with US Spanish language learners from different academic areas. The social justice-themed telecollaboration curriculum provided a forum for students to learn the L2 while addressing real world problems that impact the citizenries of the US and Mexico. Although the courses had different learning objectives, their common L2 immersion needs and mutual interest in the cinematic themes made the student groups a good match.

The instructors used a profile questionnaire to learn more about the students' L2 proficiency, academic major, career and personal interests, and partner gender preference. This profile information enabled the instructors to find the optimal partner matches for most students.

After pairing students, the instructors organized the exchanges as a series of ten 45-minute structured teletandem-based interactions within a 16-week academic term. Six of the ten sessions were scheduled in LC labs on campus, and four sessions were assigned as external activities to be initiated by students and held outside of class, most likely off-campus.

The teachers provided the students with a brief handout (one to two pages) for each session to summarize the learning content with bilingual Spanish-English instructions and specific tasks to be carried out with equal time allotted to both languages (see Appendix). The instructors encouraged learners to make cultural comparisons and express informed opinions about the social justice themes in the L2. Both groups were required to be engaged with their partners and provide assistance and feedback as needed.

The social justice topics included illegal immigration, government corruption, abuse of power, gender inequality, LGBTQ issues, and marginalization of

Indigenous peoples and people of color. Students were given thematic vocabulary lists that enabled them to articulate their ideas more thoughtfully.

Figure 2 shows two teletandem partners completing a task in the Cinema & Social Justice group. In this particular example, the students are using Google Maps and Images in conjunction with Skype's screen-sharing function to virtually visit locations in South America and collaboratively explore those communities' geographic, linguistic, and cultural identities.

Figure 2

Language Partners Working on a Telecollaboration Task in their LC Lab

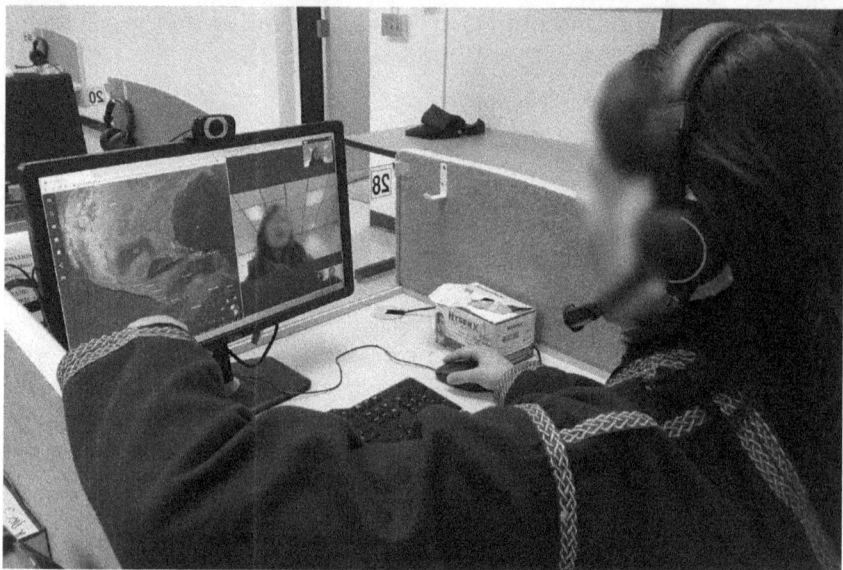

The lab sessions and tasks were mediated and assessed by instructors in both courses. Students were required to report their session tasks after every interaction, whether held in the LC or externally. The US Spanish language students were also tasked with making a two-minute voice-recorded reflection on their telecollaboration experiences using VoiceThread, an audio-based discussion board tool integrated into the LMS. The US instructor responded to each voice-recorded comment, creating a one-on-one line of audio-driven communication with each learner. The Mexican students were required to keep a teletandem learning portfolio to document their learning process. The portfolio consisted of three templates: a learning plan, a learning record, and a learning reflection. In the learning plan, students specified their learning objectives and the tasks for each session. In the learning record, students documented their experiences by writing down the language and cultural information learned in each session. In the learning reflection, students wrote about which factors had benefited or hindered their learning.

2.2.3 Group 3: Healthcare Nursing Students

At the US institution, an instructor of Spanish and healthcare professions deemed telecollaboration a viable strategy for connecting nursing and healthcare students from the US and Mexico to practice their L2 skills in their professions and apply newly learned medical terminology in simulated healthcare settings. The LC directors and staff at both institutions agreed to assist with the development and implementation of a telecollaboration program for a credit-bearing course at the US school called Spanish for Healthcare Professionals. They collaborated with a nurse practitioner/assistant professor, a Spanish language instructor, and the LC staff. Together, they customized a teletandem curriculum to meet the immersion needs of healthcare students with backgrounds in Spanish language who are called to serve predominantly Spanish-speaking communities. The nursing students in Mexico volunteered their time to meet with the US students. Their motivation was for personal and cultural enrichment. They did not receive academic credit for their participation. The session content was integrated and aligned with the healthcare topics covered in the course curriculum. The US nursing instructors sought to enhance their students' L2 communicative skills and develop linguistic and cultural sensitivities for interactions with Spanish-speaking patients with limited English.

The LCs provided implementation support for the sessions conducted in the labs. The instructors and LC staff had to find workarounds due to scheduling constraints and differences in the academic calendars. Eight sessions were developed for the labs. Four external sessions were added for a total of 12 one-hour sessions to be delivered within the 16-week academic term. Students were responsible for initiating and conducting the external sessions on their own.

An additional requirement for the US nursing group was to create a WordPress blog to:

1. Post written reflections of their teletandem interactions.
2. Develop a Spanish-English glossary on a healthcare area to be shared with other students.
3. Post the link to the final project, which was a collaborative external activity, presented as a video or slideshow presentation.

The tasks included role-play activities to simulate interactions between Spanish-speaking patients and English-speaking providers and vice-versa. The sessions also included project-based learning activities, which allowed each pair of L2 learners to collaborate over an extended period and explore healthcare topics in a global context. The final projects were presented by the US students on the final day of class and were embedded into the WordPress blogs.

2.2.4 Group 4: Healthcare Medical Students

In 2016, a task force at the US university explored the possibility of developing a telecollaboration component for 4th-year medical students enrolled in a medical Spanish enrichment block. The medical school faculty in Mexico responded favorably, and the LC staff organized meetings to connect the teachers at both sites to begin developing the content and tasks. The instructional goal was to provide medical students with opportunities to interact with peer medical students at universities in another country to develop L2 communicative proficiency and cultural competence through simulated doctor-patient interactions and bilingual medical case reviews.

The medical school faculty at the US institution designated a student teaching assistant to collaborate with LC staff and faculty in Mexico to create:

1. patient-doctor role-play activities,
2. bilingual discussions on relevant global healthcare topics, and
3. comparisons of healthcare practices in Mexico and the US.

Due to rigorous student schedules and misaligned academic calendars, sessions were scheduled within a one-month time frame. The LC directors and staff members provided support for scheduling and delivering sessions in the LC labs. Reflection activities were not required by the instructors, but the medical students generally evaluated the activities favorably and expressed appreciation and interest in meeting and collaborating with peer learners in another country. They were asked to evaluate the program and generally rated the experience as enriching and supported the continuation of the program.

2.3 Research Methods: Action Research and Ethnography

Both LC groups used action research methods to improve the quality of the telecollaboration programs. The research objectives never changed, but the initiative evolved significantly over the five-year partnership. Action research was the appropriate strategy for investigating the practice of telecollaboration for several reasons. First, it helped LC staff members and teachers to observe jointly implemented programming. Second, it enabled LC staff members and instructors from both sites to share findings and improve telecollaboration pedagogy and implementation at both sites.

The methods used to observe, collect, analyze, and interpret data from the partnership were quantitative and qualitative. They included student evaluation questionnaires, analyses of screen-recorded interactions, notes from teacher observations, and in some courses, written and voice-recorded reflections by students.

The LC staff and instructors created and maintained shared Google folders to archive and share instructional content, essential documents, and artifacts related to each program group. The folders included video and audio files of recorded sessions, lists of telecollaboration partners, evaluation questionnaire data, Skype and Zoom account information, and other administrative and instructional documents essential to the partnership, without compromising the security of sensitive student and institutional data.

The action research methods called for observation of program design, planning, and evaluation through iterative cycles to reveal best practices. This workflow enabled the instructors and staff at both sites to collaboratively troubleshoot problems and discuss ways to improve the processes, contexts, and tools used to design and deliver telecollaboration pedagogy and programming.

The LC staff and language teachers used ethnography to document their observations of the implemented sessions. According to Landri (2013), virtual learning environments "are fluid spaces of investigation that give ethnographers the opportunity to shape the field and the fieldwork in collaboration with those directly involved" (p. 252). Ethnography was a powerful research method for exploring telecollaboration because it enabled the researchers to provide descriptions of the learning environments from which participants' behavior patterns could be contextualized and predicted to enhance telecollaboration activities and task design.

All of the stakeholders who participated in the partnership—LC staff, teachers, and students—contributed significantly toward identifying areas needing improvement, providing unique perspectives, and sharing insights on pedagogy and programming, which led to enhanced telecollaboration quality. These points will be discussed in the next section.

3. Results and Analysis

The pedagogy and logistics developed for each group produced outcomes that contributed to a general understanding of telecollaboration. Participants focused on strategies to improve the design and delivery of jointly implemented pedagogy and programming across an international LC partnership. The overarching goal was to provide students with unprecedented opportunities for language immersion and practice with native speakers through dynamic and engaging learning tasks.

3.1 Language Immersion for English and Spanish Learners

The number of Mexican students needing English-speaking language partners far outnumbered the number of US students available for telecollaboration. This enabled the Spanish language instructors at the US school to implement as many sessions per term as they deemed necessary. Some instructors integrated one session per term. Other instructors implemented two or three sessions per term without planning.

Because the number of students in the Mexican groups was generally greater than the number of US learners, it was easier to find partners for US Spanish language students. When different-sized groups came together during the lab sessions, LC staff members used the class lists and partner-pairing spreadsheets, if available, to configure two-on-one and three-on-one pairings to accommodate all students. The problem of dealing with unexpected student absences was generally simple to resolve. Both LC sites maintained teletandem partnerships with other universities to fill gaps when necessary and make the process of providing language partners to students more consistent, fluid, reliable, and routine.

The initial exchanges lacked structure and pedagogical focus. At the onset of the partnership, there was a sense of achievement in developing the ability to align calendars, connect students in the labs, create content, and facilitate the student interactions. It did not take long for the language teachers and LC staff to realize that unstructured language exchanges are pedagogically limited. However, many students were able to find value in unscripted first-meeting encounters even without a guide or instructions to navigate the interaction, as the quotes below show. All comments in this section are from US Spanish language students' responses to the evaluation questionnaire in 2016, with the exception of one from 2017, as noted.

- "I had a lot of fun talking to my partner! ... I didn't feel pressured, which was nice."
- "I got to speak Spanish with a person who speaks it fluently and got feedback on how my speech could improve. It is always nice to practice Spanish with a native speaker."

- "My partner for the teletandem was very entertaining, and we had a great conversation in both Spanish and English. I really enjoyed the teletandem, and it made me feel a little more comfortable with speaking to native speakers."

With unstructured sessions, however, the outcomes can be unpredictable. The comments below are from students in the same group who had a different experience:

- "I think it was easier for the other folks to speak English which made it challenging at times. I also think preparation for the sessions was crucial to a successful session."
- "They had a difficult time coming up with questions to ask."

Learners quickly learned to enhance their interactions by using the text chat feature in Skype and Zoom and relying on translation tools and verb conjugation apps to communicate. Instructors observed students using hand gestures and positioning their mobile phone screens in front of the webcam to share images and clarify their thoughts and ideas:

- "Neither of us were that great at speaking the language, but being able to use google translate helped a lot."
- "We were forced to have an actual conversation, and it was extremely helpful."

Understanding the limitations of unstructured telecollaboration inspired the participating teachers and LC staff to create new telecollaboration pedagogy with structured tasks and goals, effective tools, detailed session instructions, and quality-control measures to ensure a superior telecollaboration experience on both sides.

The language instructors felt it was essential to harness the value of language exchange to establish a foundation in the first session that allowed the development of good camaraderie and rapport in subsequent sessions. This led to an interest in designing a whole series of sessions with specific learning tasks and goals for each encounter and building on the interaction and content from the previous meeting.

The outcomes for Group 1 varied because the sessions were spontaneous and students were coming from a broader population than the learners from the other groups. Still, there was an overwhelming consensus among students that even unstructured sessions are more valuable than learning in a static classroom environment and working through textbook activities and exercises.

- "I believe this should play a larger role in foreign language classes as most of us don't have anyone to speak with at home in our studied language." (2017)
- "This experience gave me more self-confidence in speaking the language and gave me more interest to learn the language beyond a basic conversation."
- "This opportunity has been valuable, with much consideration for engaging with varying worldviews, utilizing another language and way of thinking, and communicating with others among another culture."

3.2 Cinema & Social Justice

The instructors of Group 2, the Cinema & Social Justice program, achieved many pedagogical firsts for our programs in telecollaborative task design and implementation. The instructors increased the frequency of their collaborations to align the tasks and content of their jointly designed sessions to make the telecollaboration relevant to students. This program evolved naturally. The instructors continuously found more efficient ways of implementing sessions and tweaking the pedagogy. As a result of their persistence and rigorous cooperation efforts, the instructors showed how teachers from different countries teaching different academic courses can still find mutual areas of interest to create immersive language and cultural learning opportunities for their students. This enabled them to design and deliver relevant and meaningful telecollaborative exchanges for learners with L2 immersion needs, even when enrolled in distinct classes.

The telecollaboration evaluation survey and students' written and oral reflections confirmed that students perceived teletandem as a valuable learning mode that contributed to their language and cultural learning. There was an overwhelming consensus that the interactions helped to heighten their confidence when interacting with native speakers, improve their fluency, correct pronunciation mistakes, and practice language in a more authentic environment. Among the most illuminating comments were the following:

- "Teletandem made learning Spanish real and meaningful." (2017, US student)
- "My experience was very rewarding, I really liked having the opportunity to talk with a native, to practice my skills." (2019, Mexican student)
- "I would say that it was such an enriching experience... since we learned a lot of phrases commonly used in casual conversations between native speakers (which we are not used to use in an academic context, therefore we never could learn those at school) and natural/common language usage as some typical slang in some part of the United States." (2019, Mexican student)

Because the Mexican students were studying to become English teachers, they pointed out the value of teletandem for language learning and expressed interest in incorporating it as instructors:

- "... tandem was definitely a great experience and it is something that I, as a teacher, would apply to my students to motivate them and to know a little more about English language." (2019, Mexican student)

Students also highlighted the program's usefulness in contributing to their cultural learning and increasing their understanding and tolerance for other cultures. The following sampling of comments illustrates this point:

- "The teletandems helped me to gauge the reality of the vastness of the world, but also the proximate similarities between myself and peers who have been raised in completely different cultures and societies." (2017, US student)
- "Tandem helped me to learn more cultural aspects not only about the US but also about other cultures as my partner was well informed. I have to admit I had misconceptions about the US but my partner politely cleared them out for me. Hopefully, I was able to do the same about Mexico." (2019, Mexican student)

- "It fosters critical thinking, cultural awareness, language learning and autonomy's development, resulting in such an enriching experience." (2019, Mexican student)

Learners acknowledged the partner's role in supporting their learning process during the exchanges and in their final project. In this regard, they mentioned the following:

- "He helped me in my pronunciation; he gave me some pieces of advice about how I can improve my writing skill and how to organize my ideas correctly." (2019, Mexican student)

Finally, some of the recommendations to improve telecollaboration quality and effectiveness included suggestions to have fewer lab sessions and more opportunities for autonomous learning and to allow students to choose their topics and tasks for the exchanges:

- "I think that the objective of tandem would achieve its goal if only we had more questions or the liberty to talk of something more authentic." (2019, Mexican student)
- "What I would suggest to improve the implementation of tandem language learning in the B.A. is that it would be better if teachers let the students (either from Virginia or Mexico) choose the topics they would like to discuss in the sessions." (2019, Mexican student)

3.3 Healthcare Nursing Students

This group's outcomes provided insight into the development and implementation of telecollaboration modules designed as supplements for profession-themed language courses, in this case, for nursing and healthcare students. The same concept and structure could be applied to Spanish and engineering, business, social work, and information technology. The LC directors and language instructors who collaborated on this project reported significant advances in telecollaboration pedagogy and programming. In this case, a credit-bearing language course designed for nursing students included a module that afforded unprecedented opportunities for nursing students in the US and Mexico to explore healthcare themes and topics collaboratively through a series of Spanish-English exchanges. The nursing students were assigned a permanent partner, so they could develop a relationship. Students generally found that having the same partner was beneficial. The following comments come from evaluation questionnaires from US students in 2016.

- "I liked talking with the same student each time, it helped us improve with each session."
- "I particularly found the casual topics we discussed like the differences in our medical education and how the healthcare system worked in our countries useful because it helped me with my conversational Spanish. I also thought it was helpful to get feedback about my pronunciation from the Mexican students."

The program was delivered in the fall and spring semesters of the 2015–16 academic year. There were some implementation issues during the first term, mainly due to miscommunication and logistical errors. Still, in the second term, over 90% of the US students reported having a positive experience and recommended the course for healthcare students interested in serving predominantly Spanish-speaking communities, as evident in the following comments:

- "It was helpful when they [language partners] pointed out areas that we needed to work on."
- "I think it was helpful. I think I need to practice speaking, and it was helpful to talk to a native speaker."
- "The sessions provided practical experience and should be retained."

3.4 Healthcare Medical Students

The telecollaboration program for medical students ran seamlessly for four years. The outcomes were consistently positive for each term the program was offered. Approximately 80 medical students from the US university participated in a custom language exchange module integrated in a nonacademic enrichment block for 4th-year medical students. The medical student exchanges were implemented between 2016 and 2019, with an average of 10 students each semester. The number of students from the medical school in Mexico was slightly higher, although the numbers fluctuated during each term.

The program evaluations submitted by the US medical students revealed that they appreciated the opportunity to interact with peer learners from Mexico. The responses also indicated that medical students perceived pedagogical value in the doctor-patient role-play activities and translingual discussions about public health, community medicine, and national healthcare systems. The students seemed to be genuinely interested in medical practice and research in their partner's country. They were also curious about the differences in the medical schools. They discussed these topics during their conversations, as can be seen in these comments from evaluation questionnaires from US students in 2019:

- "Their medical education and health systems are totally different than ours and it was enlightening to learn more about their experience."
- "The roleplay activities were well-designed. The bilingual scripts helped me get through it without much difficulty. I also enjoyed the opportunity to have a conversation with a medical student from another country."
- "This is a groundbreaking way of learning foreign languages. I wish I had this when I was in high school."

Perhaps the most notable outcome of the teletandem program for medical students is that it became the only one of the telecollaboration prototypes that continues to run independently of the LC labs. All sessions scheduled before the COVID-19 pandemic were conducted in the LC labs. After the pandemic resulted in both university campuses being closed, the LC directors encouraged the medical school faculty members to continue working together and exploring ways to implement the programs virtually. Two suggestions for achieving this were (1) allowing the medical student teaching assistants to virtually preside over synchronous sessions of displaced students, or (2) pairing students in advance and allowing them to conduct the sessions independently. One of the LC staff members suggested that telecollaboration pedagogy, programming, and practice for students in graduate and preprofessional programs is worthy of further exploration.

4. Conclusion

The general consensus among instructors across the partnership was that telecollaboration, despite its challenges, had inherent educational value. The action research showed improvement in implementation, delivery, and practice through iterative cycles.

Vasallo and Telles (2006) affirmed that the pedagogical context of teletandem is richer and more complex than has been demonstrated in the literature. The LC partnership outcomes corroborated Vasallo and Telles' findings. Each program rendered unique results, and the cooperation and linkages realized through the LC connectivity enabled both groups to explore telecollaboration pedagogy and programming in depth. The teachers and staff at the participating LC sites identified mutually beneficial needs and goals, and their shared vision and fluid cooperation led to enhanced understanding, improved implementation, and in some cases, routinized practice of telecollaborative exchanges.

4.1 Lessons Learned

The student evaluation questionnaires consistently showed that most students overwhelmingly perceived telecollaborative exchanges as a viable modality for language practice and cultural learning. Students reported improvement in their L2 communicative skills due to the teletandem interactions. Some learners indicated that the exchanges enhanced their interest in the L2 and heightened their confidence when interacting with native speakers. Some students also expressed that the discussions enabled them to learn things about the language and culture that were not taught in traditional classroom settings.

Student feedback on the evaluation questionnaires was constructive for improving sessions. The instructors and LC staff at both sites made critical observations about pedagogy and programming that were consistent and generalizable across the various telecollaboration groups and prototypes. The most generalizable findings gleaned from the data and comments are outlined below.

1. **Every telecollaboration project, group, and paired interaction is unique.** When task design and session implementation are customized per student goals, needs, profiles, and practice contexts, the activities will generally be more engaging. The LC staff members and instructors at both sites established a workflow to improve the coordination and delivery of custom pedagogy and programming. The enhanced cooperation heightened the possibilities for dynamic and creative instructional design, cohesive tasks, and potentially transformative outcomes.

2. **Learner autonomy is a central tenet of telecollaboration.** However, according to Little (2003), autonomy is an ability that does not emerge suddenly; instead, it is built into the learning process. As learners become more familiar with the practice

of telecollaboration, they develop the capacity to manage their learning, navigate the tasks, and make the most of their opportunities. This autonomy will allow them to be more successful in making decisions about their education based on their goals and needs. When teletandem is implemented in accordance with the principles of autonomy, reciprocity, and separation of languages (Vassallo & Telles, 2006), students should feel empowered to make such decisions.

3. Instructor input, guidance, and evaluation are essential. Whether sessions were conducted in the campus labs or off campus, it was vital for instructors to guide learners through their telecollaboration journey and teach them to self-regulate their learning, communicate more effectively with their partners, and manage tasks more efficiently. When scheduling constraints limited the number of possible lab sessions per academic term, some instructors deemed external sessions necessary. There are advantages and disadvantages to both scenarios. The Cinema & Social Justice instructors implemented the most sessions per term and were able to compare student groups in both contexts. After three years of programming, the instructors concluded that external sessions were viable with integrated guidance and close monitoring of student activity by the instructors at both sites.

The qualitative data from the various groups indicated that exchanges were generally more effective when an instructional plan was implemented with clear learning objectives. Comprehensive task design should incorporate communicative goals and a guide for the language (grammar and vocabulary) used to achieve those goals. Vasallo and Telles (2006) expressed that the pedagogical flexibility of language exchanges provides adequate contexts for learners to "freely explore their creativity" (pp. 89–90).

4. It is helpful to partner with instructors, schools, and LC sites that share the same vision and mutual areas of interest. The criteria for establishing a telecollaboration partnership with language teachers, telecollaboration practitioners, and LCs abroad should be determined by the extent to which they share the same vision, function, priorities, needs, and expectations for telecollaboration programming, thus increasing the likelihood of a more reliable, successful, and long-lasting partnership (O'Dowd, 2013). Lewis (2005) concluded that language partners who are paired by common goals and interests are more likely to have an impactful experience than partners who have nothing in common.

5. Understanding the learner's experience helps instructors identify areas where adjustments are needed in the pedagogy, programming, and practice of telecollaboration. The instructors and other practitioners quickly learned that bandwidth strength and quality of audio and video streams were critical to the student experience. Therefore, teachers and facilitators should develop a preemptive strategy to identify and resolve or mitigate related problems during sessions conducted in the LC labs.

4.2 Limitations of the Programs

The qualitative data collected in the evaluation questionnaires for the four telecollaboration groups were used to better understand how to improve and harness the potential of telecollaborative exchanges. Some of the limitations identified in the programs include:

1. Technical issues: problems with the webcams, headsets, bandwidth, and/or lack of proper equipment.
2. Lack of support for students throughout the implementation of the teletandem programs.
3. Lack of experience by some teachers/LC staff to implement teletandem optimally.
4. Lack of student training on autonomy and reciprocity principles.
5. Issues of inequity relating to needs, priorities, numbers, and equipment.
6. Incompatibility of academic calendars and time zone differences.

4.3 Future Recommendations

Twenty-first-century LC directors can find renewed purpose and opportunity in partnering with LC directors abroad. Through cooperation and joint development of telecollaboration programming, they can transform traditional language labs into high-impact telecollaboration spaces designed for language and cultural exchanges. LC partnerships can help language departments develop and deliver critically needed immersion programs at virtually no cost to the LC or institution.

The products born out of the LC collaborations in this partnership shed light on the workflow and processes of telecollaboration pedagogy, programming, and practice. Not all of the programs were equally successful, but each one enlightened the instructors and staff members of the partnered LC sites. The action research also showed that routine collaboration in areas of mutual interest allowed two distinct centers in different countries, with varying educational missions and structures, to organize a cohesive, dynamic, and industrious instructional partnership that directly impacted students' language and cultural learning.

Still, the findings indicate that further research in this field is needed to continue yielding new knowledge about international online language exchanges and their pedagogical value. Our recommendations for advancing the research, work, and practice of telecollaboration include:
1. Seeking new methods for optimizing pedagogy, policy, equipment, and workflow for enhancing the telecollaboration experience.
2. Finding ways to better align pedagogical objectives at both partner LC sites.
3. Exploring new scenarios for pairing students from different academic disciplines and programs.
4. Identifying new strategies to improve the quality and outcomes of telecollaboration pedagogy and programming.
5. Exploring the possibilities for integrating telecollaboration in service learning, community engagement, and study abroad activities.
6. Developing new methods and workflows that allow instructors to preside over exchanges conducted remotely for students in distributed virtual environments. The authors believe that such virtual exchanges comprise one of the critical next-steps in the evolution of telecollaboration development and practice.

As discussed throughout this chapter, telecollaboration offers unique opportunities for authentic, immersive, high-impact language and cultural learning experiences. However, as Castillo-Scott (2018) pointed out, the appropriateness and effectiveness depend on the extent to which instructors can integrate telecollaboration into the curriculum and learners are prepared before sessions take place.

In light of the recent closing of college and university campuses globally due to COVID-19 and the ubiquity of online learning, it may be a good time for LC directors to explore new collaborative language learning spaces in virtual contexts. Partnering with LCs abroad seems like a logical next step in this process because it could empower LCs to develop this powerful pedagogical structure and generate authentic language immersion opportunities for their students without incurring costs.

Finally, it may benefit LCs to reach out to instructors in secondary schools where world languages and global citizenship comprise an essential component of every students' core curriculum. There are few studies on virtual language and cultural exchanges in K–12 settings, where telecollaboration could potentially make its most significant impact.

References

American Council on the Teaching of Foreign Languages. (2016). *Assigning CEFR ratings to ACTFL assessments.* https://www.actfl.org/sites/default/files/reports/Assigning_CEFR_Ratings_To_ACTFL_Assessments.pdf

Belz, J. A. (2003). Linguistic perspectives on the development of intercultural competence in telecollaboration. *Language Learning & Technology, 7*(2), 68–117. https://www.lltjournal.org/item/2431

Benoit, S., & Lomicka, L. (2020). Reciprocal learning and intercultural exchange in a virtual environment. In C. Tardieu & C. Horgues (Eds.), *Redefining tandem language and culture learning in higher education* (pp. 79–94). New York, NY: Routledge. https://doi.org/10.4324/9780429505898

Brammerts, H. (2003). Autonomous language learning in tandem: The development of a concept. In T. Lewis & L. Walker (Eds.), *Autonomous language learning in tandem* (pp. 27–36). Sheffield, UK: Academy Electronic Publications Limited.

Brammerts, H., & Calvert, M. (2003). Learning by communicating in tandem. In T. Lewis & L. Walker (Eds.), *Autonomous language learning in tandem* (pp. 45–60). Sheffield, UK: Academy Electronic Publications Limited.

Bueno-Alastuey, M. C., & Kleban, M. (2016). Matching linguistic and pedagogical objectives in a telecollaboration project: A case study. *Computer Assisted Language Learning, 29*(1), 148–166. https://doi.org/10.1080/09588221.2014.904360

Castillo-Scott, A. (2018). Teaching social issues through cinema and Teletandem. *Revista do GEL, 15*(3), 257–278. https://doi.org/10.21165/gel.v15i3.2409

Kinginger, C., & Belz, J. (2005). Socio-cultural perspectives on pragmatic development in foreign language learning: Microgenetic and ontogenetic case studies from telecollaboration and study abroad. *Intercultural Pragmatics, 2*(4), 369–422.

Kronenberg, F. A. (2014). Language center design and management in the post-language laboratory era. *The IALLT Journal of Language Learning Technologies, 44*(1), 1–16.

Kronenberg, F. A. (2016). Curated language learning spaces: Design principles of physical 21st century language centers. *The IALLT Journal of Language Learning Technologies, 46*(1), 63–91.

Landri, P. (2013). Mobilising ethnographers investigating technologised learning. Ethnography and education. *Doing Educational Ethnography in an Online World: Methodological Challenges, Choices and Innovations, 8*(2), 239–254.

Lewis, T. (2003). The case for tandem learning. In T. Lewis & L. Walker (Eds.), *Autonomous language learning in tandem* (pp. 13–25). Sheffield, UK: Academy Electronic Publications Limited.

Lewis, T. (2005). The effective learning of languages in tandem. In J. Coleman & J. Kappler (Eds.), *Effective learning and teaching in modern languages* (pp. 165–172). London, UK: Routledge.

Little, D. (2003). Tandem language learning and learner autonomy. In T. Lewis & L. Walker (Eds.), *Autonomous language learning in tandem* (pp. 37–44). Sheffield, UK: Academy Electronic Publications Limited.

Müller-Hartmann, A. (2000). The role of tasks in promoting intercultural learning in electronic learning networks. *Language Learning & Technology, 4*(2), 129–147. http://llt.msu.edu/vol4num2/ muller/default.html

O'Dowd, R. (2006). *Telecollaboration and the development of intercultural communicative competence.* Munich, Germany: Langenscheidt.

O'Dowd, R. (2013). Telecollaborative networks in university higher education: Overcoming barriers to integration. *The Internet and Higher Education, 18,* 47–53. http://www.sciencedirect.com/science/article/pii/S1096751613000110

O'Rourke, B. (2005). Form-focused interaction in online tandem learning. *CALICO Journal, 22*(3), 433–466.

Ross, A. F., & DiSalvo, M. L. (2020). Negotiating displacement, regaining community: The Harvard Language Center's response to the COVID-19 crisis. *Foreign Language Annals, 53*(2), 371–379. https://doi.org/10.1111/flan.12463

Ruane, M. (2003). Language centres in higher education: Facing the challenge. *ASp* (Online), *41–42,* 5–20. https://doi.org/10.4000/asp.1127

Tardieu, C., & Horgues, C. (2020). Conclusion: Redefining tandem language and culture learning in higher education. In C. Tardieu & C. Horgues (Eds.), *Redefining tandem language and culture learning in higher education* (pp. 270–280). New York, NY: Routledge. https://doi.org/10.4324/9780429505898

Telles, J. A., & Vassallo, M. L. (2006). Foreign language learning in-tandem: Teletandem as an alternative proposal in Computer Assisted Language Learning and Teaching (CALLT). *The ESPecialist, 27*(2), 189–212.

Tian, J., & Wang, Y. (2010). Taking language learning outside the classroom: Learners' perspectives of eTandem learning via Skype. *Innovation in Language Learning and Teaching, 4*(3), 181–197. https://doi.org/10.1080/17501229.2010.513443

Vassallo, M. L., & Telles, J. A. (2006). Foreign language learning in-tandem: Theoretical principles and research perspectives. *The ESPecialist, 27*(1), 83–118.

https://www.researchgate.net/profile/Joao-Telles-4/publication/277054748_
Aprendizagem_de_Linguas_In-Tandem_Teletandem_como_uma_
Proposta_Alternativa_em_CALLT/links/55d390f908ae0a3417226ab5/
Aprendizagem-de-Linguas-In-Tandem-Teletandem-como-uma-Proposta-
Alternativa-em-CALLT.pdf

Ware, P. (2005). "Missed" communication in online communication: Tensions in a German-American telecollaboration. *Language Learning & Technology, 9*(2), 64–89. http://llt.msu.edu/vol9num2/ware/default.html

Ware, P., & O'Dowd, R. (2008). Peer feedback on language form in telecollaboration. *Language Learning & Technology, 12*(1), 43–63. http://llt.msu.edu/vol12num1/wareodowd/default.html

Appendix

Sample of a Telecollaboration Session Handout
Cinema and Social Justice Group (Spring 2019)

Teletandem Session 5 - Implementada fuera de la universidad, iniciada por los alumnos.

Para los alumnos de español (Largometraje: *También la lluvia*)

22 minutos en español

Temas: El maltrato, la explotación y la marginación de grupos indígenas, el imperialismo, la colonización, la expulsión de miles de nativos de sus tierras, las manifestaciones, las grandes compañías multinacionales, una película dentro de otra película, la religión, la creación artística, el choque cultural. TAREA 1ª: Haz a tu compañero las siguientes preguntas. Escucha sus respuestas y el vocabulario que utiliza para expresar sus ideas. Toma nota para poder recordar la información posteriormenteal grabar tus comentarios en VoiceThread.

1. ¿Hubo marginación y maltrato a los indígenas en México y en otros países de América Latina? ¿Cómo son percibidos los indígenas en la actualidad? ¿Tienen acceso a los mismos derechos y oportunidades que el resto de la población mexicana?
2. ¿Se han integrado en la sociedad mexicana los pueblos indígenas de México o viven aislados en sus propias comunidades?
3. ¿Hay racismo y discriminación contra los indígenas en México? ¿Han mejorado las condiciones de vida de los indígenas o aún existe la misma desigualdad?

TAREA 2ª: Con tu compañero, elige uno de los largometrajes de la lista en Blackboard para el proyecto final. Comunica tu decisión a los profesores a la brevedad posible.

Teletandem Session 5 (Scheduled as an off-campus session, student-initiated, conducted outside of class).

For Students of English as a Foreign Language (FILM: *Even the Rain*)
22 minutes in English

Themes: Mistreatment, exploitation, and marginalization of Indigenous peoples, imperialism, colonization, the expulsion of thousands of natives from their own lands, the demonstrations, the large multinational corporations, the film within a film, religion, artistic creation, culture shock.

TASK 1: Ask your partner the following questions in English, listen, and take notes if necessary.

1. How have Indigenous people been marginalized in the United States? Are they still discriminated against in the United States? Is this the same kind of discrimination and marginalization as in Mexico and Latin America? How is it different? How is it the same?
2. What do you think is the best way to prevent the discrimination of Indigenous people in your country?
3. What has the US government done to integrate/isolate Indigenous people from the rest of American society?

TASK 2: Select a film from the main list for the final project you will do with your partner. One film per pair, selections on a first-come basis. Notify instructors of your film selection as soon as possible.

Author Notes

Anton T. Brinckwirth is a postgraduate Master of Teaching student in the School of Education and Human Development at the University of Virginia. He holds an MA in Spanish from Saint Louis University, an Education Specialist degree in Educational Technology from University of Missouri-Columbia, and a PhD in Education from Virginia Commonwealth University.

Martha Guadalupe Hernández Alvarado is a doctoral student (ABD) in Applied Linguistics at the University of Southampton, UK, and a lecturer and researcher in the Linguistics Department at Universidad Autónoma del Estado de Hidalgo.

Hilda Hidalgo Avilés is Head of the Linguistics Department at Universidad Autónoma del Estado de Hidalgo. She holds a PhD in Applied Linguistics from Lancaster University, UK.

Norma Angélica Espinosa Butrón is Coordinator of the BA in Language Teaching at Universidad Autónoma del Estado de Hidalgo. She holds an MA in Education.

Isabel Alfaro Flores is an academic language advisor in the Dirección de Autoaprendizaje (language center) at Universidad Autónoma del Estado de Hidalgo. She holds an MA in Educational Technology.

Correspondence concerning this chapter should be addressed to Anton Brinckwirth (antonbrinckwirth@gmail.com).

Chapter 12
Language Centers
and Immersive Technologies

Hope Fitzgerald, University of Virginia, USA

Abstract

Although language labs and centers in higher education have often provided technologies and materials in support of language learning, the missions of 21st-century language centers (LCs) often extend far beyond technology access. Therefore, immersive technologies such as Virtual Reality may find a campus home in the LC. Through the example of immersive technology adoption and exploration at University of Virginia's Language Commons, I argue in this chapter that LCs can be campus innovators in the exploration and application of new immersive learning technologies. Immersive technologies appear to hold promise for motivating students and connecting them to engaging cultural and linguistic content and experiences. That said, considerable work remains to facilitate the application of these tools in service of effective, accessible language learning. This chapter introduces immersive language learning technologies, considers the role of LCs such as the UVA Language Commons in supporting the use of this technology, identifies affordances and persistent challenges, and offers preliminary conclusions on the role of LCs in facilitating immersive learning applications.

Language labs and centers have long been the front-line providers of technologies and materials in support of language learning in higher education. As language learning resources and technologies have become untethered from the physical space of traditional language labs, technology support has become less central to many language centers' (LCs') identities. At the same time, LCs continue to broaden their roles in areas such as outreach, extracurricular programming, learning space provision, and instructional design. Nevertheless, LCs remain key players in the exploration, deployment, and support of new technologies in service of language teaching and learning. Through the example of virtual reality adoption and exploration at University of Virginia's (UVA) Language Commons, I argue in this chapter that LCs can be campus innovators in thoughtful, intentional exploration and application of new learning technologies. The recent rise of immersive technologies for language learning provides an opportunity to explore these issues.

Section 1 of this chapter will introduce immersive technologies (immersives) and examine recent interest in their application to language learning. Section 2 briefly reviews the roles of LCs in facilitating technology exploration and use. Section 3 details the experience of the Language Commons staff in facilitating faculty and student use of immersives, including several ways in which immersives have been utilized in language courses. Section 4 offers early observations based on the experiences of Language Commons staff in supporting immersive technology use for language learning, and Section 5 outlines specific and persistent challenges identified. Section 6 identifies possible opportunities and outlines future plans for immersives in the Language Commons, and the chapter closes with preliminary conclusions on the role of LCs in facilitating immersive technology applications.

1. Immersive Technologies and Language Learning

1.1 What are Immersive Technologies?

Immersive technologies, or immersives, attempt to surround a user with a visual and auditory environment different from the one in which they are physically present. This sense of immersion in another reality is accomplished using peripherals, commonly including a headset and handheld controllers. Immersives fall under the broad umbrella of extended reality (XR), which includes virtual reality (VR), augmented reality (AR), and mixed or merged reality (MR) technologies that seek to "extend the reality we experience" through digital interventions (Marr, 2019, para. 1). VR headsets, in particular, have the potential to immerse the user in a new sensory environment by replacing visual and auditory cues from the physical environment. This chapter considers the experience of the Language Commons staff in facilitating language class use of VR headsets (Google Cardboard and Oculus Go) to access VR experiences and 360° images and videos, with and without target language audio.

1.2 Immersives for Language Teaching and Learning

The last few years have witnessed an explosion in interest in immersive technologies in world language teaching and learning. At the 2019 convention of the American Council on the Teaching of Foreign Languages, at least four presentations introduced classroom applications of virtual reality. At the International Association for Language Learning Technology (IALLT) 2019 conference, two workshops and multiple presentations explored aspects of immersive technology applications in the language classroom. Though the technology is relatively recent, several studies have already investigated applications of immersive technologies to world language learning. Legault et al. (2019) explored the potential for VR to positively influence second language (L2) vocabulary acquisition. Others have theorized on the possibility for VR and AR to foster cultural exploration and create augmented linguistic environments (Godwin-Jones, 2016; Sykes, 2018). Blyth (2018) discussed the possible application of immersive technologies to create "immersion" experiences in L2 learning environments. Berti (2019) explored student attitudes toward VR implementation in Italian language courses, and, importantly, documented the process of developing, hosting, and sharing open-access VR material for language class use.

One goal in adopting immersive technologies in educational settings is to engage and motivate learners, and several studies support VR's capacity to improve student motivation (Berti, 2019; Bowen, 2018; Liu et al., 2019; Xie, Ryder, & Chen, 2019). Other research has indicated the potential of immersive technologies to bring learners closer to, and help them empathize with, characters and situations experienced therein (Shashkevich, 2018). New VR headsets and 360° video technologies also have the potential to simulate common immersion experiences of travel abroad, such as exploring a street or visiting popular landmarks in distant cities. Immersives may make such environments more engaging by increasing the user's sense of *presence* or "feeling as if transported to a virtual environment" (Weech et al., 2019, p. 2).

While exploring these affordances of immersive technologies, it is important to note some of their limitations. One key consideration is the accessibility of immersive technologies. Many VR headsets come with cautionary messages warning users with certain health conditions, such as seizures, to refrain from use, making them inaccessible to some users and potentially creating inequitable learning environments for students. Cost is another important barrier to access, with even popular consumer-level VR headsets priced at hundreds of dollars. Section 5 of this chapter outlines additional limitations identified during use of VR in the Language Commons.

Another important limitation on some VR devices (and particularly the most cost-effective devices, such as Cardboard headsets) is that they are not designed to support synchronous interaction with other speakers of the target language. While some interactive options are available, particularly for those who can join interactive spaces via individual (i.e., not university-networked) VR devices, many entry-level VR devices appear better suited to user-to-content engagement, rather than user-to-user engagement. As a result, these entry-level technologies can provide individual user experiences of content that can then become rich fodder for engagement with other target language speakers *outside* of the VR headset.

2. Language Centers and the Changing Role of Learning Technology

Language labs, centers, and resource centers have long been learning technology hubs on university campuses. From their emergence in the late 1950s (Hagen, 2017), labs have existed to support the technology necessary to access language learning materials or otherwise support language course activities. While not designed to create immersive learning environments, early labs provided access to language input that was otherwise unavailable to many learners, short of traveling abroad. As technology, pedagogy, and learning needs changed throughout the 20th century, many LCs largely maintained a primary mission of providing access to learning technologies, adjusting their technology offerings to suit the needs of the times.

More recently, a pedagogical shift from a focus on individual language learning to prioritizing social interaction and community has led to a reimagining of language centers (Ledgerwood, 2017). Some LCs, such as the Language Learning Center at the University of New Mexico, have minimized the relative importance of technology provision in favor of spaces and programs that facilitate innovation and student interaction (Castaldi & Markley, 2018). Others have transformed the use of their technology resources, leveraging new learning technologies to support activities that immerse learners in the target language, as in the case of the teletandem program at Virginia Commonwealth University's World Studies Media Center (see Brinckwirth et al., this volume). Kronenberg (2017) described the LCs of today as "moving away from massive technology installations…. Technology is not necessarily the only focus of language centers, but rather one (albeit often very important) aspect" (p. 162) of their campus identity. With technology playing an important but less-existential role, LCs may now have an opportunity to be more flexible in meeting emerging needs and interests of the university's language community.

3. Immersive Technologies in the UVA Language Commons

3.1 The Language Commons as a Space for Emerging Language Learning Technologies

The Language Commons (hereafter, the Commons) at the University of Virginia is a provider of spaces, resources, and instructional design support for the world language programs of the College of Arts and Sciences (the College). The Commons opened in 2017 as a collection of spaces for curricular and extracurricular language and culture activities, replacing a large language lab with new spaces for interaction while maintaining a smaller language lab nearby (Giering & Fitzgerald, 2019). The Commons is charged with facilitating new technology use in language courses, supporting faculty curricular and instructional initiatives, and promoting language learning in the College through student- and faculty-facing initiatives. The replacement of the outdated language lab with the new Commons created space (both physical and metaphorical) for explorations of new tools to support language instruction and learning, including immersives.

3.2 Exploring Immersive Technologies for Language Learning

The Commons began experimenting with immersives in partnership with colleagues from our parent organization, A&S Learning Design and Technology, beginning in early 2018. Several factors led to these experiments, most notably, the increase in popular and scholarly attention to VR technology and the introduction of the Oculus Go VR headset at an accessible price point of under $300. Hoy's (2018) IALLT webinar on student-created VR content helped staff to imagine concrete uses of

VR in language learning. In 2018, using VR equipment already available through other venues on campus, staff explored possibilities for immersive technology applications in language teaching. Based on these experiences, we ultimately decided to undertake a concerted effort to support immersive technology use in language learning.

To continue our own exploration of VR equipment and to make it available to language faculty to begin their own explorations, Commons staff developed a plan to purchase several items, design introductory workshops for faculty, and create supporting documentation and resources. The goal of this acquisition plan was to create opportunities for faculty to explore immersive experiences so that they, in turn, could imagine the possibilities for their courses. Given budgetary considerations, we sought affordable, flexible tools that faculty could adopt with relative ease in a class of up to 20 students. We invested in the following:

- Thirty Google Cardboard headsets (relatively inexpensive VR headsets for viewing 360° content such as Google Street View, immersive videos, etc.; these headsets pair with students' own mobile phones; $25 for two sets)
- Six Oculus Go headsets (more expensive, stand-alone headsets with handheld controllers; $299 each at the time of purchase)
- Six ImmerseMe program licenses (cloud-based language learning program for use on desktop machines, providing semi-interactive listening, pronunciation, and cultural exploration in 360° settings)
- Two Ricoh Theta and Ricoh SC 360° cameras (for faculty development of 360° video and photographic content; approximately $300-$500 per camera at time of purchase)

Over the course of the 2018–19 academic year, Commons staff collaborated with A&S Learning Design and Technology, the Institute for World Languages (a campus organization for world language faculty research and support), and other campus partners to introduce interested faculty to immersive technologies. These workshops proved to be fruitful opportunities to brainstorm possible applications in language courses. Workshops included an introduction to immersive technologies, an examination of augmented reality tools, and hands-on trials of various immersive tools. Workshop attendance was strong, and early uptake by faculty in Chinese, French, and Spanish courses encouraged us to expand our offerings with the purchase of additional cameras and Cardboard headsets in 2019.

3.3 Supporting Use of Immersive Technologies

To minimize barriers to faculty exploring the affordances of immersives, Commons staff developed supporting materials to accompany each new hardware resource acquired. These materials include quick-start guides for headset users, sample class activity plans, a guide to editing 360° videos, and lists of available immersive equipment and experiences relevant to the languages taught at the university. Additional troubleshooting guides were created to be used by Commons staff in supporting users (accessible at https://languagecommons.as.virginia.edu/immersive-technology-and-language-learning-vr-ar).

Anticipating that the more advanced Oculus Go headsets might be especially popular among language faculty and students, Commons staff developed annotated guides to available apps that seemed relevant for language learning and cultural exploration. Given the ever-growing number of available apps, and the inability for any one staff member to evaluate content across multiple languages, these guides were an imperfect resource. Ultimately, we shifted to a more personalized approach of meeting interested faculty individually to understand their goals and invite them to borrow equipment for further exploration. Though this approach promoted faculty control of VR projects, it also necessitated additional coordination to ensure that an instructor's lesson plan could be supported. This was especially the case with activities using the Oculus Go headsets, which required more extensive setup in advance of class use and hands-on support during use.

3.4 Applications of Immersive Technologies in the Commons

In the Commons, interest in immersive technologies has been strongest among non-tenure track faculty and graduate student instructors teaching in the first four semesters of language courses. Faculty teaching first- and second-year language courses in the Spanish, Chinese, and French programs have been the primary users of these resources, with the Spanish program being the most common user. Not all of these faculty innovators describe themselves as being comfortable with new technologies, but during consultations with Commons staff, all expressed interest in developing engaging experiences for their students. Faculty expressed specific motivations behind their interest in using VR technologies. A Spanish faculty member, for example, sought to deepen students' exploration of Spain beyond traditional tourist destinations and associated tropes. A French instructor wanted to identify more exciting content to spark students' interpersonal conversations. Another instructor sought to connect campus students to the experiences of Chinese counterparts on a campus abroad to encourage cultural comparisons. Still others were intrigued by the new technology and eager to explore it with students and gauge their reactions to it. To date, faculty have employed the immersive technologies of the Commons to meet various goals, including the following:

- cultural exploration
- a change of pace
- content discovery to enrich classroom activities
- bringing students' lived experiences to the classroom.

Activities related to each of these goals are briefly described below.

3.4.1 Cultural Exploration Through VR

A faculty member used a 360° camera to create a multi-scene video of her small hometown abroad. Prior to watching the video, students conducted directed research about the town. In class, they then watched the instructor's 360° video via Cardboard headsets, connecting their research to an immersive visual tour.

3.4.2 A Change of Pace

The Commons and its resources are often used for a change of scenery and a break from classroom routines, and several faculty members have incorporated immersives for that purpose. In one course, using Oculus Go headsets, students spent the first half of their Spanish class in a high-stakes oral exam, and then took a break by navigating a Spanish-language experience related to the popular animated film Coco.

3.4.3 Content Discovery to Enrich Classroom Activities

Some faculty have elected to use 360° immersive videos and images to introduce students to relevant content, viewing it as a more engaging alternative to textbook content on similar topics. In one French course, students watched 360° videos of French professionals in their work settings and then participated in an in-class jigsaw activity to share and compare elements of their videos.

3.4.4 Bringing Students' Lived Experiences to the Classroom

In one course, students created their own 360° photographs during holidays and weekends. They brought these images to class and shared them with classmates, who viewed them via Cardboard headsets. In another course, 360° photographs of campus were developed into a tour for students to describe and annotate.

In addition to the activities described above, language instructors have also used the 360° cameras to develop content for their course activities. During summer and winter breaks, faculty have used cameras to film and photograph hometowns, tourist locations, and the university's overseas study abroad sites. Upon returning to the university, Commons staff and student workers have worked with these faculty members to edit their footage for classroom use.

4. Initial Observations from Immersive Technology Use in the Commons

Through our initial experiences of supporting immersive technology applications to language learning, Commons staff have developed competence in using and supporting immersive technologies and gained experience in introducing new, complex technologies into classroom settings. What follows are early observations from the Commons' immersives program.

4.1 Immersive Technologies Change Rapidly

Immersive technologies are changing very rapidly, making it difficult to anticipate challenges. Oculus Go headsets, for example, are no longer supported or produced (the Oculus Quest is their successor). In preparing to facilitate one class activity, Commons staff found that an update to a popular mobile phone operating system was going to leave many students' devices unable to access faculty-created 360° content as planned. Thankfully, faculty and staff had enough advance warning to identify alternative solutions that allowed students to access the content through a different application, after a considerable investment of staff time.

In another classroom application of VR, it was discovered that the instructor's selected 360° experience was not accessible via the Cardboard headsets that had been arranged for the class. Luckily, the experience was accessible via the Oculus Go headsets. Because there were only six Oculus Go headsets and 18 students, the instructor quickly adjusted the activity plan so that the students could work in shifts. For subsequent activities, Commons staff began to request more specific information about the required immersive content and to double-check the availability of content further in advance so as to better prepare and help faculty consider adjustments that might be needed. Given the fast-changing nature of immersive devices and programs, we have found that planning immersive activities well in advance is key. As is often the case in trials of new activities and technologies, however, extensive planning is not a guarantee of an activity's success.

4.2 Student and Faculty Expectations of Immersives Vary

Only a handful of student users noted previous use of virtual reality headsets, and their expectations of the technology appear to vary considerably. During immersive activities, Commons staff observed that some students appear thoroughly engaged by 360° environments, gasping and laughing as they acclimate to the feeling of losing presence in their real physical environment as they move into VR. Others appear underwhelmed and express that they were expecting a more interactive experience. Those who experienced technical difficulties also seemed more apt to disengage from the activity. Monitoring and anticipating student expectations of immersive activities will be important in helping faculty create engaging activities. Explicit instruction in the goals of using immersives— in addition to effective technical support—may also help students engage with the experience more fully.

4.3 A Combination of Resources and Hands-On Support Can Enhance Faculty and Student Experiences

Both faculty and student users of immersive technologies find themselves in unfamiliar terrain. Given the immersive nature of VR headsets, troubleshooting and guiding users can be challenging for even the most knowledgeable staff. Orienting users to an upcoming immersive experience is a particular challenge. While video orientations are available to introduce users to popular VR headsets, limited class time was available for student orientations. LC staff sometimes faced difficulties guiding users through the menus and settings of their headset to ensure that they arrived at the app needed. Commons staff have developed "casting" solutions to allow those outside of the VR headsets to see what the user sees, for use in a more thorough orientation for students. While navigating the technology is often best learned by doing, time lost on guiding students through immersive technologies can lead to frustration and to a (valid) sense that technology is standing in the way of language learning.W

4.4 A Team-Based Design Approach May Simplify Design and Implementation

The introduction of immersive technologies in the Language Commons has generated new opportunities for Commons staff to work with faculty. We have been able to partner with several instructors from the design phase through classroom implementation of their VR activities. In other cases, however, Commons staff largely played a technology support role, rather than partnering closely with faculty in the design process. Given the complexity and changeability of immersive tools, an intentionally team-based design approach (see Bass, 2012), in which instructional designers and/or other campus experts collaborate with faculty to share the design and delivery of course activities, may be an effective model for designing with a new and changing technology such as VR. A team-based design approach would see technology experts play a more active role in supporting faculty to think through the possibilities and limitations of the technology as it applies to their course goals. During classroom activities, a team-based approach would also provide students more support in navigating immersive technology tools from staff members, leaving the instructor more able to focus on their planned activities in the target language.

5. Challenges

5.1 Unforeseen Limitations of Students' Devices

Providing students with the tools needed to create their own immersive content is, potentially, very powerful. Technical challenges abound, however, when students are tasked with exploring a new technology outside of class time via their own smartphones or other devices. In one project, students used freely available apps downloaded to their own phones to create 180° and 360° images. While some students completed this assignment successfully, others reported that they lacked the space on their phones for downloading new apps or storing new photos for the exercise. Others reported having trouble using the apps, and instead took standard photographs. In class, some students' phones were physically a bit too large for the Cardboard headsets.

5.2 Cybersickness

Anecdotal student feedback indicates that many experienced some physical discomfort while using the VR headsets. Students using Cardboard headsets and viewing lower-resolution images, in particular, reported headaches and nausea akin to motion sickness. This feedback is in line with widely studied "cybersickness" among some users of VR technologies (see, for example, Dennison, Wisti, & D'Zuma, 2016). Users might be able to lessen these effects, to some extent, by slowing down their head movements and/or remaining seated while using the headsets, though research indicates that the design of virtual reality interfaces and experiences may play a large role in this issue (Weech et al., 2019). Any pre-immersion introduction for student users ought to include warnings of possible physical effects.

5.3 Accessibility

A larger issue in the use of immersives for class activities is that inaccessible technologies may lead to inequitable access to learning. VR headsets may be inaccessible to students with visual impairment or limited range of motion, to those who experience strong motion sickness, or for those with conditions that can be triggered by immersive technologies (seizures, as an example). Following the principles of Universal Design for Learning (CAST, 2018), activities that use immersive content should be designed, at minimum, to include high-quality alternative plans, such as navigating a 360° image on a computer screen rather than through a headset. Even such planning, however, may not ensure equitable learning experiences. Designers of immersive technologies may need to more thoroughly address accessibility concerns for these technologies to be more widely adopted for higher education environments.

5.4 The Lack of Interactivity with Interlocutors

When first presented with immersives, some language faculty were quick to point out their limitations for supporting interactivity. The immersive tools available in the Commons, and indeed most immersives that are likely to be accessible to LC budgets, offer few opportunities for spontaneous interaction with the target language. This can be surprising for many users. Indeed, given popular images of artificial intelligence and VR, many users—faculty and students alike—may have expectations that the current technology cannot meet. Current technologies that are inexpensive enough for classroom use do not support the interactivity that might make them more applicable for conversational practice.

With an understanding of these limitations, though, faculty can design interactive classroom activities that draw on the content and experiences gleaned through use of immersives in ways that enrich student-to-student interaction. For example, a French course used a 'jigsaw' exercise to encourage interpersonal communication around immersive content. Using VR headsets, each student explored one of several French workplaces via 360° videos selected by the instructor. After exploring, they formed groups to describe and compare the content they had experienced in VR. Combining engaging immersive content with interactive class activities may meet the dual goals of motivating students and fostering interaction among them. Managing student and faculty expectations of immersive interaction will be important to the planning of such activities.

6. Looking Ahead: Areas for Further Exploration

6.1 Immersives in the Commons in the Age of COVID-19

In March 2020, use of the Commons' VR technologies immediately ceased when learning activities shifted online because of the COVID-19 pandemic. Even after students were welcomed back to the campus for some Fall 2020 courses, the Commons remained closed, with some of its spaces temporarily repurposed. We are unlikely to return to the practice of sharing handheld and worn immersive technologies, such as headsets, for some time. Moreover, tighter budgets in the near-term may impede the replacement or acquisition of new equipment to replace aging VR devices. On a more hopeful note, new interactive immersive tools may emerge from the COVID-19-era needs for meaningful communication among individuals unable to travel and meet in person.

6.2 Positioning Immersive Activities in the Curriculum

With a few important exceptions, applications of immersives in language classes in the Commons have been isolated activities that deviate from, rather than integrate with, the established curriculum. An exciting challenge for LCs, moving forward, will be to facilitate faculty efforts to position these activities more meaningfully within the target language curriculum. Developing sample lessons and content units that use immersives effectively, as opposed to discrete activity plans that are disconnected from a curriculum, may help spark further innovation in this area.

6.3 Immersive Content Development

Our preliminary experiences with immersive technologies relied primarily on already-available content, such as 360° videos shared openly online or developer-created apps on the Oculus Go. However, faculty interest in using 360° cameras to capture footage indicates that many faculty members are eager to develop their own content and to engage their students in content development.

Language Centers may have an important role to play in facilitating these efforts, perhaps in collaboration with other campus media and technology centers. LC staff might provide pedagogical and instructional design resources to inform the work of instructional technologists doing the technical development of new VR experiences.

6.4 Streamlining Processes Through Collaboration

Given the positive outcomes of early research on immersive technologies in language learning (see Section 1.2), continued exploration of immersive technology application in the language classroom is certainly warranted. That said, the Commons' experience indicates that the necessary investment in design, development, and implementation is considerable, both in terms of faculty and staff time and LC resources. Professional and student staff members worked with three to five VR projects each semester and spent approximately five hours per project in meeting with faculty, identifying material, offering feedback on lesson plans, and supporting activities during class (to say nothing of faculty time invested). For projects in which faculty or students create their own immersive environments (such as VR apps or 360° videos), the investment was well over 10 hours of staff time per project. Developing structures and processes to streamline the development of both content and activities will be important for the sustainability of immersive technology use in language learning. As more university language centers begin working with immersive technologies for language learning, it will be helpful to build networks of knowledge and technology. Efforts in this area are already underway, as can be seen in the Computer Assisted Language Instruction Consortium's recent launch of an immersive realities special interest group for practitioners interested in applications of VR, AR, and virtual worlds in language learning (https://calico.org/sigs/virtual-worlds/). Such networks may help LCs share relevant information and experiences and develop best practices for supporting classroom applications.

7. Concluding Thoughts: Designing for Immersive Language Learning in the LC

Though 21st century language centers are no longer limited by a singular mission to provide technology access, immersive technologies and other emerging tools may in fact find a home in the LC. The arrival of immersive technologies on campus may present an opportunity for LCs to take on a new role, as a hub for immersive language learning design. Immersive technologies appear to hold tremendous possibilities for connecting students to engaging cultural and linguistic content and experiences. That said, considerable work remains to facilitate the application of these tools in service of our core goal of supporting effective language learning. LCs are well positioned to play an important role in helping faculty design engaging learning experiences using immersive tools by combining technological resources with pedagogical expertise in language teaching and learning.

References

Bass, R. (2012). Disrupting ourselves: The problem of learning in higher education. *Educause Review*, *47*(2), 23–33. https://er.educause.edu/articles/2012/3/disrupting-ourselves-the-problem-of-learning-in-higher-education

Berti, M. (2019). Italian Open Education: Virtual reality immersions for the language classroom. In A. Comas-Quinn, A. Beaven & B. Sawhill (Eds.), *New case studies of openness in and beyond the language classroom* (pp. 37–47). Research-publishing.net. https://doi.org/10.14705/rpnet.2019.37.965

Blyth, C. (2018). Immersive technologies and language learning. *Foreign Language Annals*, *51*(1), 225–232. https://doi.org/10.1111/flan.12327

Bowen, M. M. (2018). *Effect of virtual reality on motivation and achievement of middle-school students* (Doctoral dissertation). Retrieved from *ProQuest LLC.* (Document ID 2050000008)

CAST. (2018). *Universal Design for Learning Guidelines, version 2.2.* https://udlguidelines.cast.org/

Castaldi, P., & Markley, L. (2018). From lab to collaborative hub: Making the language center relevant. In E. Lavolette & E. F. Simon (Eds.), *Language Center Handbook* (pp. 319–339). Auburn, AL: International Association for Language Learning Technology.

Dennison, M., Wisti, A., & D'Zmura, M. (2016). Use of physiological signals to predict cybersickness. *Displays*, *44*, 42–52. https://doi.org/10.1016/j.displa.2016.07.002

Giering, J., & Fitzgerald, H. (2019). The Language Commons: An innovative space supporting second language acquisition. *Journal of Teaching and Learning with Technology*, *8*(1), 33–41. https://doi.org/10.14434/jotlt.v8i1.26741

Godwin-Jones, R. (2016). Augmented reality and language learning: From annotated vocabulary to place-based mobile games. *Language Learning & Technology*, *20*(3), 9–19. http://dx.doi.org/10125/44475

Hagen, L. K. (2017). Kaputnik: Lessons from the life and death of the language lab. In F. A. Kronenberg (Ed.), *From language lab to language center and beyond: The past, present, and future of language center design* (pp. 13–27). Auburn, AL: International Association for Language Learning Technology.

Hoy, T. (2018, Aug. 17). *Virtual reality in the language classroom: Student-created VR panoramas* [Webinar]. International Association for Language Learning Technology. https://iallt.org/webinars/8-17-18/

Ledgerwood, M. (2017). Foreword, or musings on over fifty years of using technology for language learning. In F. A. Kronenberg (Ed.), *From language lab to language center and beyond: The past, present, and future of language center design* (pp. 6–12). Auburn, AL: International Association for Language Learning Technology.

Legault, J., Zhao, J., Chi, Y.-A., Chen, W., Klippel, A., & Li, P. (2019). Immersive virtual reality as an effective tool for second language vocabulary learning. *Languages*, *4*(1), 13. https://doi.org/10.3390/languages4010013

Liu, W., Zeng, N., Pope, Z. C., McDonough, D. J., & Gao, Z. (2019). Acute effects of immersive virtual reality exercise on young adults' situational motivation. *Journal of Clinical Medicine*, *8*(11), 1947. https://doi.org/10.3390/jcm8111947

Marr, B. (2019, August 12). What is extended reality? A simple explanation for anyone. *Forbes.* https://www.forbes.com/sites/bernardmarr/2019/08/12/what-is-extended-reality-technology-a-simple-explanation-for-anyone

Shashkevich, A. (2018, October 17). Virtual reality can help make people more compassionate compared to other media, new Stanford study finds. *Stanford News.*https://news.stanford.edu/2018/10/17/virtual-reality-can-help-make-people-empathetic/

Sykes, J. (2018). Digital games and language teaching and learning. *Foreign Language Annals, 51*(1), 219–224. https://doi.org/10.1111/flan.12325

Weech, S., Kenny, S., & Barnett-Cowan, M. (2019). Presence and cybersickness in virtual reality are negatively related: A review. *Frontiers in Psychology, 10*(158), 1–19. https://doi.org/10.3389/fpsyg.2019.00158

Xie, Y., Ryder, L. & Chen, Y. (2019. Using interactive virtual reality tools in an advanced Chinese language class: A case study. *TechTrends 63*(2), 251–259. https://doi-org.proxy01.its.virginia.edu/10.1007/s11528-019-00389-z

Author Notes

Hope Fitzgerald oversees the Language Commons at the University of Virginia, where she serves as an Instructional Designer and Foreign Language Consultant. She works closely with world language faculty to facilitate thoughtful integrations of technology in language teaching and learning. She earned MA degrees in Foreign Language Education and Geography from the University of Texas in Austin, and was an Arabic language lecturer and administrator in the US, Qatar, and Jordan prior to joining the University of Virginia. Her research interests include online learning of less commonly taught languages, technology and language teaching, and second language listening.

Correspondence concerning this chapter should be addressed to Hope Fitzgerald (hf6v@virginia.edu).

Marr, B. (2019, August 12). What is extended reality? A simple explanation for anyone. Forbes. https://www.forbes.com/sites/bernardmarr/2019/08/12/what-is-extended-reality-technology-a-simple-explanation-for-anyone

Shankar, A. (2018, October 12). Virtual reality can help make people more compassionate compared to other media, new Stanford study finds. Stanford News. https://news.stanford.edu/2018/10/17/virtual-reality-can-help-make-people-empathetic/

Sykes, E. (2019). High games and the co-creation of learning environments. Argos, 57(1), 219–228. https://doi.org/10.1111/1741-6248

Yee, N., Ratan, R., & Bailenson, J. N. (2019). Does using avatars create virtual reality-related... relationship. Cyberpsychology, Behavior, In. 11(1), 1–19. https://doi.org/10.1089/cyber.2019.00152

Xie, Y., Ryder, L., & Chen, Y. (2019). Using interactive virtual reality tools in an advanced Chinese language class: A case study. TechTrends, 63(3), 251–259. http://doi.org/10.1007/s11528-019-00389-z

Author Notes

Elena Stapponi oversees the Language Commons at the University of Maryland. She serves as an Instructional Designer and Foreign Language Specialist. She works closely with world language faculty to facilitate the ethical integration of technology in language teaching and learning. She earned a BA degree in Foreign Language Edu... and Geography from the University of... as an Indiana Purdue and Public language lecturer and administrator in the U.S. and abroad. In her prior life as the Director of English He... her research interests include nature, history of the acquisition, reading and language acquisition in... children, reading and world languages learning.

Chapter 13

The Smart Language Lab: Building and Integrating Emerging Technology into Language Programs

Elizabeth Enkin and Eric Kirschling, University of Nebraska–Lincoln, USA

Abstract

In this chapter, we introduce the concept of a "smart language lab," which reflects the move from Web 2.0 to Web 3.0 and associated emerging technologies. Web 3.0 can be thought of as the spatial web, providing access to immersive experiences within 3D virtual environments. Immersive experiences, such as immersive virtual reality (VR), hold significant implications for language programs because they offer a level of presence, contextualization, and engagement that is not possible through traditional instruction, thereby providing rich opportunities for task-based and project-based activities for language learners. This chapter describes three immersive VR-based projects that were conducted in the smart language lab and discusses their design, results, and implications. Moreover, each of these projects focuses on one of ACTFL's communication modes, thereby further framing the potential of emerging technology. Throughout this chapter we also provide additional ideas for integrating emerging technologies into language programs, as well as a discussion of the expertise needed to build a smart language lab. We hope that this chapter will be useful to LCs in keeping pace with rapidly evolving emerging technologies and the integration of these technologies into language programs.

In the 38th volume of the *IALLT Journal of Language Learning Technologies*, Wang (2006) discussed the changing role of language centers (LCs) in universities, for example, that they provide pedagogical and technical support, create opportunities for learner autonomy, provide a comfortable learning space, and recognize the need for and implement changes to keep pace with newer technologies that will "make our centers more indispensable" (p. 64). Over a decade after Wang's article was written, technology has continued to move rapidly, and students have noted that anytime/anywhere technology, such as smartphones, are convenient and useful when it comes to learning (see, e.g., Ducate & Lomicka, 2013; Godwin-Jones, 2017; Steel, 2012). Hence, LCs have had an important place in language programs when it comes to providing support for language learning apps and resources that are available on these anytime/anywhere devices.

Currently, however, one of the challenges for language labs and LCs is that easy access to widespread technology may render them obsolete, which is precisely the issue that we were facing at our institution. For example, our lab at the University of Nebraska–Lincoln houses iPad Airs and desktop/laptop computers intended for student use; however, many learners already have personal devices with access to the same applications that are on the lab's devices. Moreover, most classrooms now have desktop computers available for use by the instructor during class time. We therefore thought that the integration of emerging technologies might provide a renewed purpose for our language lab (and other similar types of labs) because these technologies are currently not as widely available as iPads, for instance. Emerging technology refers to technological tools that are novel and have yet to be fully implemented into teaching contexts (see Kessler, 2018). They might, therefore, provide new and exciting opportunities for both students and instructors. The 2020 Horizon Report (EDUCAUSE, 2020) also discusses the importance of emerging technologies for education and identifies technologies that have strong potential for instructional use; these include extended reality (XR), machine learning, artificial intelligence, and open educational resources (OERs).

This increased focus on emerging technologies in our language lab parallels the global move toward Web 3.0, the latest generation of the world wide web. Because we are still moving toward Web 3.0, no concrete or official definition exists of it yet; however, and most relevant for our language lab, it can be thought of as the "spatial web" in comparison to the Web 2.0-based "flat (screen) web." The spatial web provides access to immersive experiences that occur in three-dimensional (3D) virtual environments. These environments, which are commonly referred to as XR environments, include both immersive augmented reality (AR) and immersive virtual reality (VR). While immersive AR spatially recognizes and overlays virtual content onto the user's physical world, immersive VR allows users to step into simulations of virtual environments, where they can interact with the virtual world and with others (Lloyd, Rogerson, & Stead, 2017; Radianti et al., 2020). Thus, in line with our focus on emerging technologies, we saw a need to keep pace with this move to Web 3.0 by changing the focus of the language lab from Web 2.0-centered, where content creation and computer-mediated communication through a flat screen is the norm (see, e.g., Sykes, Holden, & Knight, 2019), to Web 3.0-centered.

Web 3.0-based immersive experiences are accessible on the web via a URL and can be built using an XR creation platform. For instance, the Amazon Sumerian platform can be used to create a web-based immersive VR experience in which users can engage in activities and tasks and interact with intelligent voice assistants that appear as 3D avatars. These avatars provide the same interaction as voice assistants, such as Siri or Alexa (see Vieira Monteiro & Pfeiffer, 2020, for a discussion of a project that used Amazon Sumerian to teach English for a specific purpose). Hence, this exemplifies a Web 3.0, or spatial web, experience. This experience is composed of different web-based emerging technologies (immersive VR and intelligent voice assistants), which function together to serve as a comprehensive Web 3.0 experience for the user.

This chapter is largely devoted to discussing three immersive VR-based projects that have been piloted in the innovation workroom space of our smart language lab (see Section 2 for a discussion of the spaces in the lab). These projects serve as proof of concept for the integration of this technology into language curricula. We believed that focusing our efforts first on immersive VR (as opposed to other emerging technologies) would not only work to enrich the curriculum but could also provide a foundation for other teaching-based projects in Web 3.0 (e.g., using immersive AR, using voice assistants, creating novel OERs), thereby potentially fostering future lab-based action research (see Van Deusen-Scholl & Young, 2017, for a discussion of this use of the language lab).

We offer a brief literature review of the emerging field of immersive VR, which is then followed by an overview of our language lab, and how we have structured it to keep pace with Web 3.0 technology. We then move to the main focus of this chapter and discuss each of the three immersive VR projects in depth. This discussion includes the context of the project, the main takeaways for language program integration, and extension/similar types of activities that could be carried out. Each of our projects also models how immersive VR can be used to facilitate the three communication modes outlined by the ACTFL World-Readiness Standards for Learning Languages (National Standards Collaborative Board, 2015). Thus, each project addresses one of the three communication modes: interpretive (one-way receptive), presentational (one-way productive), or interpersonal (two-way interactive) communication. Finally, a brief section at the end of this chapter looks to the future of the smart language lab and discusses some uses of the emerging technology other than immersive VR. The main goal of this chapter is therefore to demonstrate some of the ways in which we have integrated and used Web 3.0 emerging technologies in our lab for our language department, with a specific focus on immersive VR. Because technology develops rapidly, we hope this chapter can be of use to other LCs that wish to stay ahead of the curve for the language programs they serve.

1. Immersive VR

As noted above, the Web 3.0 projects that are the focus of this chapter all use immersive VR. VR is a technology that enables users to step into alternate physical realities. It therefore embodies the spirit of Web 3.0 because it creates a different spatial reality for users. In other words, VR creates the feeling of presence, or the feeling that you are truly physically present in another place (Freina & Ott, 2015).

In their review of research, Jensen and Konradsen (2018) discussed the use and merits of VR head-mounted displays (HMDs) across various educational disciplines and settings, and in a recent article in the *EDUCAUSE Review*, Pomerantz and Rode (2020) reviewed XR projects in higher education and argued for the development of more educational XR apps. Lloyd et al. (2017) summarized how VR can provide critical learning experiences like never before specifically for language learners, for example, through increased opportunities for supplemental speaking practice (that mimics real life) for all learners in a class, increased learner motivation and engagement specifically for storytelling and writing, and increased contextualization through virtual field trips to target culture locations. VR can also enhance task-based activities that promote effective collaboration and can facilitate engagement in social experiences through social VR apps where a sense of presence facilitates natural oral conversation. Kessler (2018) noted VR's potential for experiential learning and for building cultural awareness. Other research has found that VR can assist with vocabulary learning (Legault et al., 2019) and can help increase the sense of presence when building cultural understanding (Cheng, Yang, & Andersen, 2017).

Interestingly, the 2020 Horizon Report also describes the rich learning experiences that XR can offer and notes how labs or centers in particular have often pioneered this technology through either makerspaces or new facilities that encourage collaboration (EDUCAUSE, 2020). In fact, federally funded National Foreign Language Resource Centers in the United States have also directed their attention to using XR. For example, the Center for Applied Second Language Studies and the Center for Open Educational Resources and Language Learning are exploring the use of virtual and augmented reality language training modules for language education.

2. Web 3.0 Technologies and Language Labs: Our "Smart Language Lab"

In keeping pace with Web 3.0 and associated emerging technologies, the term "language lab," which is the lab's official institutional name, seemed insufficient for our space; we therefore created a new (unofficial) term, the "smart language lab," which indicates the concept of a lab that is composed of many smart devices that can be used for language learning and instruction. We use the term "smart" broadly to indicate any device that is networked or connected in some way to other devices. Many Web 3.0-based apps are designed to run on a variety of these internet-connected smart devices. We therefore hoped that this new term could adequately capture the renewed focus of our language lab and what could be expected from it as Web 3.0 continues to develop (see Victor & Mohammed, 2016, for a discussion of the role of Web 3.0 in education). This would also address the needs of today's students, who "expect significantly increased learning options and far more educational services from their colleges and universities" (Koeller, 2012, p. 78).

A specific note regarding terminology is needed here. First, although the term "center" may be more widely used than "lab," we feel that adopting the "smart lab" term can bring a language lab's "techy" focus into the forefront and can highlight its ability to facilitate innovative teaching and related research-based projects in applied linguistics. We therefore use the term lab in this way throughout this chapter. Second, we use the term "lab manager" because we currently only have this staff position at our university. This position manages and runs the technology in the lab, recommends additional equipment, and facilitates technology-based instruction for faculty and graduate students. Language centers often employ a language center director with a background in applied linguistics, which is why our lab manager (the second author of the current chapter) and an applied linguist (the first author) often work together. Indeed, we recommend having two separate positions in a smart lab: a manager focused on technology and an applied linguist director focused on pedagogical implications.

Our lab, which has been part of our languages department (the Department of Modern Languages and Literatures) since 1976, was most recently renovated in 2013 with funding from our institution's College of Arts and Sciences and Academic Affairs. The lab has since consistently been updated by our languages department. The smart lab is composed of three rooms: a technology classroom, a language lounge, and an innovation workroom. Each room has, or includes a space with, acoustic panels that are color-matched to furniture and function to deaden ambient noise and improve sound quality. The technology classroom (Figure 1), which does not have any specific Web 3.0 features, was designed around video conferencing; it is therefore equipped with ceiling microphones, speakers, web

Figure 1
Technology Classroom from Four Viewpoints

cameras, a projector, dimmable lights, and two 70" screens. In addition to the equipment, the desks can be arranged in various ways to facilitate pair work, group work, or individual work. The lounge (Figure 2) is designed with an open floor plan, which, as Kronenberg (2017) discussed in a keynote address, is important for facilitating a learner-centered environment. The room contains comfortable furniture with large tables and chairs meant for group work and tutoring. It also has large screens and a Google Chromebox for presentations. Most of the furniture is movable and can be arranged in a multitude of ways depending on event/class/activity/student needs. It therefore works well as an event space where talks, conversation tables, coffee hours, and language club meetings are regularly held. Its open design can also facilitate projects using Web 3.0 apps and tools.

Figure 2

Language Lounge from Four Viewpoints

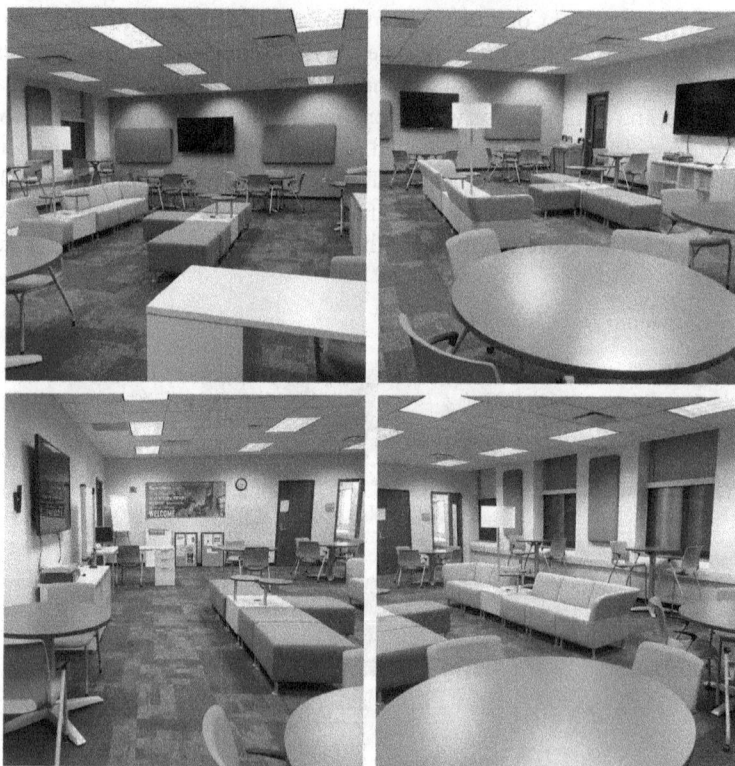

Lastly, the innovation workroom (Figure 3) was repurposed from an office space with the goal of expanding upon the use of emerging technologies in language learning. It is therefore the area in the lab where we piloted our three Web 3.0-based projects specifically designed to use immersive VR. The repurposing of this office space for emerging technologies is also in line with a recent call in an *EDUCAUSE Review* article (Craig & Georgieva, 2017) regarding the need to redesign learning spaces for immersive AR and VR. Two of our projects have targeted classes within our language programs to test the viability of the technology when integrated into a curriculum. Therefore, the workroom contains immersive VR equipment and accompanying technology: two desktop computers that are capable of rendering 360° videos and performing other processing-intensive jobs such as 3D modeling; two 70" 4K smart screens that are connected to the desktops; two Oculus Rift HMDs, which require the desktop computers to function; and several standalone HMDs (i.e., HMDs that do not need a separate computer to function), namely, two Oculus Quests and two Oculus Gos. All furniture in the innovation workroom is movable.

Figure 3
Innovation Workroom

Note. Top left: The main project-based learning space that contains a sound production platform (i.e., technology that was configured to enable direct line-in recording and editing) and a Raspberry Pi computer. Top right: One "XR space" containing an Oculus Rift. Bottom left: The second XR space that contains an Oculus Rift. Bottom right: A 3D printer.

The workroom contains additional technology that students can use for course projects. It can therefore be used effectively as a space for project-based learning and as an area that provides a full makerspace (see Gaugler, 2016, for a discussion regarding how technology can help support project-based learning). As Sheridan et al. (2014) illustrated, learners can use makerspaces to work with different types of media to engage in a process of "developing an idea and constructing it into some physical or digital form" (p. 507). Thus, and in addition to using immersive VR, students can make 3D scans of physical objects, create 3D models (which could be (re)created in immersive VR and used for other projects like XR web app development), and print 3D models (including cultural artifacts). Learners can also create audio files by connecting musical instruments or other sound-producing devices to a computer that we have configured for direct line-in recording, and those files can then be edited with audio editing software such as Audacity. In addition, the workroom contains a 360° 3D camera, which can be used in the lab and can also be signed out for use, and free access (via the Adobe Creative Campus program) to Adobe Premiere Pro and other relevant Adobe Creative Cloud apps. Thus, for example, students could use the camera inside the lab (in any of the rooms) for projects centering on video/image production, and/or learners could also work to produce their own target-culture 360° 3D video footage and images with raw footage that they capture with the camera while on education abroad or other immersion experiences. Although only some of these tools have been used and implemented in our language programs thus far, we envision an increase in the use of this newer technology as times goes on.

Finally, the workroom contains two devices that we are beginning to think about how to use for our language programs. The first device is an Amazon Echo smart speaker. We have chosen the Echo device because it is part of the Amazon ecosystem and uses the Alexa intelligent voice assistant service, which can also be accessed (via 3D avatars) from within the Amazon Sumerian platform (the rationale for using this particular ecosystem will be discussed in Sections 3 and 4). Thus, Alexa can be accessed in and affect both the physical and virtual realities. The second device is a Raspberry Pi computer, which has potential use within the lab, particularly when envisioning a makerspace (see Section 3.2).

The lab serves all eight undergraduate programs in the languages department (four with a major and minor, three with a minor only, and one that offers beginner through advanced coursework, though no major or minor). Only on occasion do other departments or the college ask to use the lounge for special events, and permission is granted on a case-by-case basis, prioritizing the space for our department. Each of the lab rooms can be reserved by language instructors (faculty and graduate teaching assistants) on a first-come, first-served basis for all students in a class at one time. However, if instructors want to reserve a room for all class sessions throughout the semester for one of their classes, they must reserve the technology classroom. This way, the workroom and lounge are still available to others during that timeframe. Note that all lab rooms (with the exception of walk-in lounge hours, see below) are kept locked 24/7, and instructors and staff can unlock these rooms via university-issued ID cards; they can therefore use the lab rooms at any time (individually or with their classes).

The lounge specifically is kept unlocked for student walk-ins for five hours each day (though if an event in the lounge is scheduled within the walk-in hours, a sign is posted on the lounge door indicating the time it will reopen). During normal business hours, students can also reserve any room within the lab with permission. During lounge walk-in hours, students often use the room as a study space, work together on class projects, or take advantage of the language tutoring offered by graduate teaching assistants and undergraduate students with advanced-level language skills. Tutors move to the other rooms of the lab when the lounge is reserved for a class or event. When we have carried out immersive VR-based projects with entire classes, students themselves from those classes have reserved the workroom to carry out the activity. As we work toward further integrating Web 3.0-based technology and activities into language programs, we envision students reserving lab time/space themselves as the norm. We also believe that as emerging technology becomes more and more saturated in the market and in our daily lives, students will become increasingly autonomous with the use of the equipment; this will necessitate less technical assistance from a lab manager, applied linguist, or instructor, thereby helping to further streamline the use of these technologies in language curricula.

3. Web 3.0 Projects in the Smart Language Lab

Our three immersive VR projects were carried out within two physical spaces in the innovation workroom (Figure 3), which we refer to as "XR spaces." These spaces can deliver VR experiences using the two Oculus Rift VR full 6DoF-head/6DoF-hand systems in the lab. DoF refers to degrees of freedom, or the predefined number of directions in which one can move. Six degrees of freedom allow rotational and positional movement, and three degrees allow only rotational movement. With full 6DoF systems (6DoF for both head and hands), users are free to move about a predefined "play space" while having their head and hands tracked; tracking hands through hand controllers provides more interactivity than head tracking alone. These types of systems are becoming increasingly affordable, especially since the acquisition of Oculus by Facebook in 2014. They are more advanced than other HMDs such as Google Cardboard, which is a less costly 3DoF HMD that only offers head tracking without any controllers. The use of controllers allows for a more real feel for users because they receive physical feedback through them (e.g., buzzes and vibrations), and they can manipulate objects. Moreover, full 6DoF systems enable controllers to be used more like hands; for example, a user can actually bend down and "pick up" an object.

As of the time of the writing of this chapter, standalone (wireless) systems that do not require a VR-ready computer to run have also recently been released onto the market, and many are full 6DoF systems. As noted earlier, we acquired several standalone HMDs and now have the Oculus Quest (a full 6DoF system) and Oculus Go (a 3DoF-head/3DoF-hand system) in the lab. Because we so recently acquired these, we have not yet used them with classes. Finally, and having spoken about the hardware associated with immersive VR, it is important to also discuss corresponding software that is currently available. Thus, we have included a helpful reference guide for some VR apps in the Appendix (several of which are also discussed in this chapter), which outlines useful information about each app, including price, category/function, devices it can be used with, and whether it is 6DoF or 3DoF capable.

Keeping in mind the benefits of immersion and presence that VR can provide for language programs, which can lead to engaging, motivating, real-life, contextualized, and task-based/project-based activities (see Kessler, 2018; Lloyd et al., 2017), we carried out three projects in the language lab centering around our two Oculus Rifts. The overarching goal was to explore how a smart language lab could better serve today's students. Though we were aware that one common drawback of VR is dizziness (see Kwon, 2019, for a discussion), we did not find many issues related to physical discomfort: Only two students noted slight dizziness on occasion on a post-project questionnaire in the first project. This finding creates even more optimism concerning the use of this equipment in the lab.

3.1 Project 1. Interpersonal Communication: Social VR

As Lloyd et al. (2017) discussed, social VR apps stand out as an interesting use of VR technology for language learning because they enable the element of presence during oral interpersonal interaction with others across time and space within a shared 3D immersive environment. In 2018, an institutional instructional improvement fund grant enabled a pilot project examining how using social VR in the language lab could be implemented in a language (Spanish) curriculum. More specifically, by collecting and analyzing student perceptions, the study (Enkin, under review) examined the benefits of dialogs in social VR as compared to face-to-face (F2F) conversations.

Throughout one semester, 26 learners in one advanced Spanish course scheduled and completed six 5- to 8-minute F2F and social VR dialogs in the lab as homework assignments. The class was geared toward developing speaking proficiency for Spanish majors and minors, and course material was intended to help build vocabulary and grammatical understanding. For the social VR conversations, we used AltspaceVR, which is a well-known social VR app owned by Microsoft. In this app, users can create private spaces to chat (which is what the learners were instructed to do), and each space represents a different environment. We chose three separate spaces for the VR dialogs in this project, which all students experienced (a house party, a pirate cove, and an outer space environment). Furthermore, because we were using full 6DoF equipment, learners were introduced to various interactable objects (e.g., fireworks, basketballs) throughout their dialogs.

In total, learners carried out three sets of conversations centering around course content, with different partners from within their class for each set. Using a counterbalanced design, each dialog set consisted of one dialog in VR and one F2F, thereby totaling six dialogs. The F2F dialogs occurred in one space in the workroom, whereas the VR conversations occurred in our two XR spaces that were each equipped with an Oculus Rift and accompanying noise-canceling headphones that streamed sound from the app for a more immersive feel. All dialogs were recorded and then uploaded to the Canvas learning management system for the instructor. The F2F dialogs were recorded using a Logitech webcam, whereas the

VR dialogs were recorded using a screen recorder that captured a third-person view of both learners, who appeared as avatars, using a camera object in the app. This experimental design created similar conversation conditions in both F2F and VR, since in both cases students would need to stay within a stationary camera's viewpoint (which is how recorded conversation assignments are often completed). In this way, the impact of an immersive space on conversations could be further examined since variables between the two environments (F2F and VR) were limited.

Twenty-one students from the class completed an end-of-project survey. The survey contained both quantitative and qualitative questions regarding student experiences with social VR dialogs as compared to the counterpart F2F dialogs. The quantitative results showed that learners enjoyed using VR and thought it was very helpful for practicing speaking; they also reported fewer feelings of self-consciousness when speaking in VR and that VR was more enjoyable than speaking F2F (the latter two results were statistically significant findings; see Table 1 for a summary of these findings). Their open-ended responses echoed the quantitative findings and illuminated themes related to the impact of presence in VR. Specifically, these themes highlighted that students felt less stress (e.g., less nervousness and less awkwardness) when speaking through a VR avatar, that conversations in the lifelike VR settings were freer and more fun, that manipulating objects in VR enriched their conversations, and that they were more engaged with the speaking task when in VR. They also suggested that the virtual environments should be better integrated with the conversation topics and that they needed sufficient time for acclimating to the VR equipment and to complete the activity.

Table 1

Wilcoxon-Pratt Signed-Rank Tests (Within-Subjects Tests) for Student Perceptions of F2F and VR Conversation Experiences

Speaking practice in F2F and VR: Question topic*	F2F mean rating	VR mean rating	Corresponding Z value; p value, effect size (r)
Enjoyment	3.5	4.5	$Z = -3.2$ $p < 0.001, r = 0.5$
Feelings of self-consciousness	3.2	2.0	$Z = 3.5$ $p < 0.001, r = 0.5$

* *Note.* Likert rating scale range: 1 (Not at all) to 5 (Extremely).

When it comes to implementing social VR specifically in a lab, some takeaways from this first study are helpful to discuss further, especially given that some of the emerging themes highlighted improvements for curricular integration. To start, learners would have liked an opportunity to make better use of their immersive settings and connect them more clearly to the conversations. Teachers should therefore plan to better match the virtual environment to conversation topics such that learners can make full use of the lifelike spaces and interactable objects. In addition, rather than using the app's camera object, which was necessary in the study to keep conditions between the F2F and VR dialogs as similar as possible, the first-person view within the app (which shows what an avatar sees through their "eyes") could be recorded (using a screen recorder). This way, learners would not have to keep their avatars within the camera object's view while recording their dialog, which would allow for more freedom to move about and explore their environments while recording. Another important point is that because students wanted to make better use of their VR environments, social VR activities in the lab may also be extremely useful for autonomous learning through informal speaking practice, especially because there will be fewer preplanned discussion topics in those cases. As an added benefit, when using the equipment for autonomous learning, students can take as much time as they would like to learn and become comfortable with the equipment/activity, which was a need that learners pointed to. However, as with any new technology, students learned using the equipment at various speeds, with some learning quite quickly.

On a related note, even though the dialogs themselves were short, we structured the VR sessions such that they took up to an hour at a time in some instances. This was due to the way that we scaffolded the learning of the equipment/app. The first session included a separate VR orientation to acclimate students to the equipment (students completed the Oculus First Contact tutorial) and an introduction to the social VR app, including the creation of students' VR avatars. During subsequent sessions, students were introduced to other features of the app (e.g., interactable items). Furthermore, throughout the sessions, because we wanted to keep to a one-hour limit to respect students' time, we helped guide them as needed with aspects related to activity setup (e.g., creating rooms and meeting their partners in those spaces) to speed up the process. Because we were using Oculus Rifts, which are connected via wires to a PC, we could easily see where learners were looking and what buttons they would need to press. However, one could also use the Oculus Quest standalone HMD (which is wireless) in the same way because it features the ability to cast to a mobile device or onto a screen via a Google Chromecast device.

With all of this said, there is no way to know for sure how much time each individual student will want for a given social VR assignment. Though this can also be true for regular F2F collaborative activities, estimates of time may be even more difficult for social VR activities given their novelty. Thus, when social VR is integrated into a curriculum, we suggest limiting the number of dialogs students need to complete in the lab or working this type of assignment into a hybrid course structure, where some class time is replaced with lab time. Another possibility is to create a single social VR assignment as either a final project or capstone experience that students could look forward to completing. Finally, advances in technology itself might help streamline the use of social VR (and of VR in general). For example, the Oculus Quest has recently released hand-tracking technology that does not use controllers; ultimately, users will not need to learn how to use hand controllers, which could substantially cut down on learning time.

Other social VR apps that are similar to AltspaceVR (e.g., VRChat) can also be used by instructors in the future. However, an exciting newer area that holds potential for teaching is the merging of video conferencing and social VR, as exemplified by the ENGAGE educational VR platform for example. With this platform, teachers can carry out tasks as they would through Zoom for example, but they have the additional advantage of creating a more present feel for learners because they are virtually embodied in an avatar; they can therefore carry out tasks such as virtually meeting one-on-one with students (e.g., for office hours), holding entire classes, and using tools such as a whiteboard and their PowerPoint presentations while in VR. As we move further into Web 3.0, social VR will only continue to develop, and this project has helped provide suggestions for its implementation within language labs.

3.2 Project 2. Presentational Communication: The Art Makerspace

The second project used the smart language lab as a makerspace for cultural and language learning (see Enkin, Tytarenko, & Kirschling, 2021). An advanced Russian cultural studies course used the space for a multipart final course project. This project required outside-of-class lab activities throughout the semester and focused on developing course concepts through presentational/narration-based speaking in the form of both preplanned and spontaneous speech monologs (filmed for the instructor and lasting 3–5 minutes). The course was designed for Russian majors and minors and specifically focused on learning Russian culture and advanced Russian vocabulary through art. The class's content therefore included the study of various Russian masterpieces, genres of art, artistic movements, and artists.

Before starting the project, all students became familiar with the VR equipment by completing an orientation session in the lab; as in the social VR project, students completed the Oculus First Contact tutorial. After the orientation session, each part of the project was completed during lab sessions that spanned 1–2 days per part, and each lab session took the place of a class meeting during that week. Nine students completed all parts of the final project, and seven of those students completed an end-of-project survey about their experiences, which included quantitative and qualitative data.

To start the project, and before any lab sessions, students first used a web browser on a PC and visited the 360Cities website (https://www.360cities.net/) to view a 360° image of a room (in this case, the "Large Italian Skylight Room") within the Hermitage Museum in St. Petersburg, Russia. Each student chose two pieces of artwork (paintings/sculptures) within that room and prepared a monolog about them. Students were also required to research and read about their chosen art pieces. Students then came in for their first lab session to view the same 360° image of the room using an Oculus Rift HMD. To do this, they used a web browser on the Rift-connected PC to visit the 360Cities website so that they could then view the same "Large Italian Skylight Room" image. Students then clicked on a button on the website labeled "Watch in VR," and the image was displayed using the Rift. While using the Rift, students delivered monologs in the target language about their chosen art pieces.

During that same lab session, students also used the Rift to view a 360° image of a room within the Sampilov Museum of Fine Arts located in Ulan-Ude, Russia. They described the paintings within that room in a spontaneous speech format. This image was extracted from video footage brought back by a graduate student assistant who had travelled to Russia the previous summer, captured using the lab's 360° 3D camera. We used the still frame image for the spontaneous speech component of the project because we thought that the use of our own in-house created OER materials would speak to the spirit of a makerspace.

In the process of extracting the still frame, we discovered that any image taken from the raw video footage would require additional processing to make it viewable using the Rift. We therefore designed a workflow that extracts an image from raw footage and prepares it for viewing using the Rift. The workflow is applicable to any HMD and is briefly outlined as follows: First, stitch lines from the raw video footage were blended using the Humaneyes VR Studio software that came with the camera. (A non-camera-specific app, such as Adobe After Effects, could also be used for this step.) Next, Adobe Premiere Pro was used to (i) format the video footage to make it viewable using an HMD and (ii) extract and save a still frame as an image file from the formatted footage. Students then used the Oculus 360 Photos app to view the image using the Rift. Interestingly, not only did this process of creating materials speak to the makerspace feel of the project, but it was also a pilot test of one role we envisioned for undergraduate/graduate assistants in the smart lab; that is, they capture images such as these and make them available as OERs for learners.

The final lab session of this project used the lab as a VR-enhanced makerspace. Students used the Oculus Medium digital sculpting VR app (which is now called Adobe Medium) on the Rift to sculpt artwork in VR. After completing their sculptures, which were based on artistic movements covered in class, students discussed them using a preplanned monolog while using the Rift. As an added bonus, students' sculptures were exported as 3D model files at the end of the project and were then 3D printed in the lab. Students were free to decorate or paint these sculptures if they wanted. Given that there was only one sculpting session, we gave students the option of starting their sculptures from a blank 3D model of a Russian nesting doll, which they could use as a base to sculpt anything from. We would guide instructors who were interested in using free 3D models (i.e., those under the Creative Commons 0 [CC0] license) for their activities to explore 3D model repositories such as Sketchfab and Thingiverse.

Students' perceptions about this makerspace project indicated that they enjoyed its learning-by-doing element and thought it facilitated a creative and exciting way to learn and speak about culture. Learners also noted that VR sculpting fostered motivation and a focus on a task that other types of activities do not create, and they enjoyed having a 3D model of their artwork at the end. (If teachers are interested in learning-by-doing activities in VR other than sculpting, we direct them to Google Tilt Brush, which enables learners to engage in VR painting.) Although students believed that presentational speaking was fostered through this project, they also noted that more interpersonal speaking could be a goal of future projects that use VR. Therefore, an app like SculptrVR, for example, which merges social VR and sculpting by allowing users to enter a space and create objects with each other, could serve as a similar activity that directly incorporates two-way communication. Furthermore, some social VR apps (e.g., AltspaceVR) also allow 3D models to be imported into them, which can help teachers develop interaction-based extension activities.

Another interesting way to facilitate interaction among learners while they are creating a product might be to structure a group activity around a VR app that is single-user (or that can be used in single-user mode), such as Flipside Studio. This is a 3D storytelling/animation platform that allows users to create animations and import 3D models. Therefore, it could also be used as an extension activity to VR sculpting with Adobe Medium or SculptrVR. In a single-user VR app setup, one learner uses VR while the other students do not. By mirroring the HMD display onto a large screen, learners who are outside of VR can converse with the student who is in VR, thereby facilitating projects that require oral interaction. This type of learning activity is referred to as asynchronous or asymmetrical VR (see, e.g., Sra, Mottelson, & Maes, 2018). Asymmetrical VR is an important concept because it can solve the problem of not having HMDs for each student in a class, given that the acquisition of multiple room-scale VR devices may not always be possible financially. These activities can be easier to facilitate if a lab has standalone HMD equipment because these types of HMDs are more mobile than their wired counterparts and offer students a VR experience unencumbered by wires. In our lab, therefore, using the larger open-floor-plan environment of the lounge might be advantageous for asymmetrical VR-based activities. This would also be ecologically advantageous because the lounge can be easily divided into several XR spaces (generally a 2m x 2m open physical area is needed) for an activity if required, and the large space itself can be used to better facilitate group or whole-class activities.

One example of a whole-class VR language learning activity was recently designed by the MIT Media Lab (see Vázquez, 2018, for a discussion). This was a conversational and total physical response activity that used the Words in Motion full 6DoF VR app. This app was developed by Vázquez et al. (2018) and has been shown to facilitate effective vocabulary retention through kinesthetic learning. The whole-class activity discussed by Vázquez (2018) was designed around the use of a single VR HMD (an HTC Vive, a wired full 6DoF HMD) to address the reality that educational facilities often have budgetary constraints. In this activity, "observers" (students outside of VR) interacted with a "performer" (a student in VR) to help them carry out the correct sequence of actions in a virtual kitchen using virtual objects. On two external monitors, the observers see the performer's viewpoint along with the required path forward with instructions regarding which objects to use. The observers can therefore interact with the performer so that the task can be completed. Although this example did not use a standalone HMD, it provides a clear illustration of how lab-based asymmetrical VR could be carried out with a language class.

A final aspect to consider about makerspaces is their reciprocal nature: That is, they not only can provide project-based learning opportunities, but they can also be used as places where materials are developed for language program use. Thus, some students' work from makerspace projects could also potentially be used as OERs for classes in a language program or could be used by students autonomously within a lab. For example, in our makerspace project, the products that were created and that could be reused in a curriculum were the undergraduate students' 3D models and the graduate student's 360° 3D video footage. We further elaborate on how the smart language lab can be used as an OER development space in the following subsection (3.3).

On a related note, because the lab makerspace can be used to create products from projects, it also highlights how it can work to enhance both undergraduate and graduate students' skills in using, understanding, and applying emerging technologies. Thus, not only could the use of a lab makerspace for diverse projects have a profound impact on a language curriculum and the potential for project-based learning, but it can also assist learners in building transferrable skills for the workforce (see, e.g., Blikstein & Krannich, 2013). Indeed, the landmark 2007 Modern Language Association report, titled *Foreign Languages and Higher Education: New Structures for a Changed World* (Modern Language Association, 2007), highlighted the great need for professional development in teaching and technology for graduate students specifically, as has other research in the language teaching field (e.g., Angus, 2017; Enkin, 2015; Lord & Lomicka, 2004).

3.3 Project 3. Interpretive Communication: The Word Maze VR App

The creation of the makerspace catalyzes the notion that the lab could be used as an OER development space, which would enable the production of in-house OERs that are usable in a language department (and beyond). Thus, and inspired by the use of web apps in language education (see, e.g., Gunter et al., 2016), we decided to add web apps as one of the OERs that could be produced in the smart lab. Relevant to our notion that a smart lab contains many smart devices, web app development can be used to produce several types of apps (e.g., mobile apps, voice apps, XR apps) that are designed to function on either one specific device or on a multitude of devices (see Godwin-Jones, 2011, for a discussion regarding designing web apps for cross-platform use). Web-based apps are created using web application frameworks, and many of these frameworks exist. Hence, in our smart lab model, the lab manager in consultation with an applied linguist (who is also a language teacher [and could also be the lab director if both a lab manager and director position exist]) chooses the appropriate framework for a given project.

Depending on the needs of the project, a cloud computing platform such as Amazon Web Services (AWS) can be used effectively in conjunction with web app development. This is because many services offered through this platform are integrable into web apps (such as the Amazon Alexa Voice Service, discussed in Section 4), thereby adding enhanced functionality and increasing the efficiency of development. Thus, having a lab manager with a background in IT hardware and software support who has the skills to properly implement and use these tools is advantageous for moving a lab forward in the use of Web 3.0 technology in a curriculum and OER development for a language program.

Putting web app development and cloud computing to use, we have carried out one project that exemplifies the concept of a lab serving as the platform for the creation of Web 3.0-based OERs. In 2018, an institutional grant enabled us to develop the Word Maze VR (WMVR) app, which to our knowledge is the first spatial-web-based full 6DoF VR language learning app designed to work with the Oculus Rift. The app provides learners with primarily reading-based (interpretive communication) practice in their target language. Interestingly, not only is the app itself an example of an OER that can be created and used in a smart language lab, but it is also an example of how such an OER can contain other OERs within it (specifically, original sounds and 3D models, as discussed below). We will therefore delve further into the components of the app, how it was created using the smart lab's resources, and its origin and place in a language curriculum.

The WMVR app is based on the Spanish Language Maze (SLM) app, which is a web-based mobile iOS/Android app that was developed using the Ionic Framework for mobile web application development (https://ionicframework.com). The SLM app was the result of another institutional grant awarded in 2015 and was released in 2017, about one year prior to the smart lab being conceived. It is currently free to download from the Google Play Store and the Apple App Store, and we also have it installed on the lab's iPad Airs.

The SLM app is based on the maze task, which is an experimental technique used in psycholinguistics to measure reading processing in real time (Forster, 2010; Forster, Guerrera, & Elliot, 2009). The task is different from other types of psycholinguistic experimental tasks in that it forces an incremental processing mode that is rapid: After being presented with the first word of a sentence, readers progress through a sentence word by word as quickly as they can, thereby constructing the sentence by way of making grammatical decisions incrementally and intuitively. In other words, after the first word, readers must choose between two word alternatives at each stage of the sentence, and one word choice is the correct continuation of the sentence, while the other word is a distractor that could not possibly continue the sentence; this procedure continues until the end of the sentence has been reached (demo in English of the maze task: http://www.u.arizona.edu/~kforster/MAZE/index.htm).

Although the process of reading with the maze task is highly unnatural, Enkin and Forster (2014) and Enkin (2016) hypothesized that it was precisely the task's incremental and rapid nature (which makes it an unnatural way to read) that could aid in language learning. The researchers therefore examined the effects of using the maze task procedure for beginner-level Spanish language learning. In these experiments, the authors found that after a period of practice with the maze task on difficult-to-process sentence structures (i.e., those that were unlike the students' first language, English), students were faster to construct these types of sentences in a test session. Enkin (2016) took the maze task a step further and developed the story maze task, which had the added benefit of contextualization: Here, learners needed to construct entire stories (made up of four sentences) rather than disconnected sentences, and pictures introduced each sentence, thereby adding further contextualization.

The SLM app reimagines both the regular sentence maze and the story maze tasks into two separate games, thereby facilitating a game-based approach to language learning. It focuses on the key structures that were used in the maze task studies discussed above. The app contains pictures of sentences (stories) in the story maze game, and both games are based on timed responses of correctly completed sentences, thereby utilizing the innate design of the maze task as it is used in psycholinguistic experiments. Learners can try each sentence again if a mistake is made, and they are shown the sentence in full in the story maze game if they move on without completing it. Thus, the goal for learners is to try to beat their fastest time while making the fewest errors possible. The app can therefore be used in multiple ways: For example, students could use the story maze game to practice and then use the sentence maze game to test themselves on structures. Although the app was conceived as mainly an autonomous learning activity focusing on beginner-level Spanish structures, it could also be used with students in class as a fun pair activity (which has been done by some of our instructors), where learners team up to complete the maze together (by taking turns being the one actually tapping words on the screen) as quickly and as accurately as possible. One of the shortcomings of the SLM app to note, however, is that it has no external database. This means that new sentences/stories cannot be easily added to the preexisting material set, nor can user high scores be logged, for instance.

Returning to the WMVR app, a major difference between this app and the SLM mobile app version is the incorporation of an external database. We integrated a database because it creates a more comprehensive app with additional functionality, including, for example, the ability to incorporate other languages, add more materials (sentences), and record high scores. We decided to use the AWS DynamoDB database service because it is a part of the Amazon ecosystem, which we were already using.

As a way to enable instructors from around the world to use the app for their own classes and activities, we plan to implement a web form on an AWS-hosted website. This will enable instructors to submit their own sentences for any of the languages available in the app. Currently, the app supports English and Spanish, and we are working on adding support for French and Russian. In fact, one of our graduate students contributed materials for both of these languages. We also plan for the app to support other languages in the future and are presently working through programming challenges related to language character display within a VR environment.

As noted above, we envisioned the WMVR app as a spatial-web-based VR version of the SLM mobile app, and more specifically, a VR version of the story maze game component of the SLM. Hence, this app was developed using the A-Frame XR web application framework (https://aframe.io), which is used for creating spatial-web-based VR and AR apps and experiences. The WMVR app is web-based, which means that a user must navigate to the WMVR website and click a button to activate and display the app within the Oculus Rift. The user then dons the Rift and is transported into a VR experience where they find themselves in a virtual hedge maze. Floating in front of them at about eye level are two word choices, and the user must "grab" the correct choice using a button on a controller (instead of tapping on the correct word choice as one would in the SLM mobile app). The user must then place the word into a bucket below the floating words.

They can press another button on their controller at any time to view the sentence structure that is forming below the bucket and at the bottom of their field of view (this improvement of being able to view the sentence that is forming is due to student suggestions gathered from survey data on perceptions of the SLM). In this way, learners are moving as they are learning, thereby facilitating an element of kinesthetic learning, which is a way to learn successfully in VR, as shown by Vázquez et al. (2018). To provide more of a game feel and thus add to the enjoyment factor, we also have a "maze mole" for the task, which is a 3D model that appears at the end of each story and throws words at the user that they must physically dodge (or lose points if a word "hits" them).

Currently, the app is in beta form and is available for use in our language lab only, though we are working to make it available online so that others can access it (for free). Presently, the app contains the same Spanish sentences that appear in the story maze game of the SLM app. We have had several undergraduate students try the app in the lab, and we envision it being used mainly as an autonomous learning activity. However, it could be used for a whole-class lab activity using asymmetrical VR. In this way, one learner could be in the HMD while the display is mirrored onto a screen for the other students in the class to see. One possible activity, then, would be that students could interact with each other and act as "maze helpers" for the student in VR. Lastly, learners could be involved in the creation of additional sentence materials, fulfilling our desire to include students as much as possible in the app creation process. In fact, we had an undergraduate student create original sounds with a guitar for the app; these sounds were recorded in the lab via direct line-in recording and are available to be used as OERs.

We now turn our attention to some possible extension activities based around the use of 3D modeling, which is a component fundamental to the creation of the WMVR app. We focus on 3D modeling because it can be particularly useful when creating language- and cultural-based OERs that are usable in both a curriculum and in XR web app development. Thus, 3D modeling is a valuable skill to develop for both a lab manager and a language student. Though they are not cultural artifacts, the maze mole and the bucket in the WMVR app are examples of 3D models that were created by the lab manager in the Adobe Medium app for OER use. We are also currently looking into using the Tvori VR 3D animation app to animate the maze mole so that it can appear more lifelike when interacting with the learner in this game-like environment.

One example of the use of 3D modeling in a smart language lab is students creating a cultural artifact for a VR app, which is based on content learned in class. Moreover, because 3D models can be imported into various VR apps (e.g., Flipside Studio), students can use the models they create for an array of projects; and, when imported into a social VR app (e.g., AltspaceVR), numerous users can view or interact with the model while speaking to each other in the target language. One could also use a 3D scanner to scan a cultural artifact for use as a 3D model.

On a related note, students could engage in another type of activity that is an offshoot of 3D modeling: rendering 2D text into 3D text using the easy-to-use multi-channel signed distance (MSDF) font generator tool (available online for free). For example, learners could create a 3D version of a special character in their target language (a character that is not included in the American Standard Code for Information Interchange [ASCII] character set, such as a letter that contains a specific accent mark) for a VR app as part of a larger language-based activity. The reason that this could be useful when creating a language-based VR app or experience is because an app created with A-Frame, for instance, only displays characters that are contained in the ASCII character set as well as characters that have been converted into MSDF fonts. Overall, this activity would therefore provide students an opportunity to learn about the use of a specific special character they are assigned to create (such as a letter that contains the French acute accent mark) and to contribute a 3D asset as an OER to the department and greater language learning community.

In conclusion, because creating a web-based XR app has so many stages (from creating sounds and 3D models to developing the actual app and language materials), we believe that a smart lab can shine by involving students in various stages of the process. In this way, the smart lab has the potential to facilitate unique experiences that are impactful, interdisciplinary, and practical. Finally, we acknowledge that not every aspect of app creation will be directly related to language learning goals. However, we believe that fostering an overall environment of creation in a lab where emerging technology is used may be a way of raising language learning motivation levels for undergraduate students; it may also serve as an inspiration to try innovative teaching approaches for graduate students and faculty.

4. Beyond VR: Future Projects in the Smart Language Lab

We have not yet touched upon several other Web 3.0 technologies in this chapter. We mention two of these technologies here because we see them playing a future role in the smart lab and within language programs: voice user interfaces and machine learning. First, voice user interfaces (VUIs) enable users to use their voice to interact with a computer. Examples of VUIs include intelligent personal assistants, such as the Amazon Echo device, which uses the Alexa Voice Service (AVS), Amazon's cloud-based suite of services that enable the integration of intelligent voice control into a device or app. Second, machine learning (ML), a subfield of computer science, aims to train computers to recognize patterns on its own, which is done via repeated training through many exemplars.

With respect to the use of VUIs, we use Alexa for practical functions around the lab, such as turning lights on and off and setting the volume level on smart screens. Alexa now features a multilingual mode that enables seamless switching between English, Spanish, and French. As the technology develops, new languages will be added to this mode. In the future, we can therefore see how this type of technology can help support target language speaking practice (see Incerti, Franklin, & Kessler, 2017). For example, students who happen to be in the lab (e.g., when studying or using equipment on their own) could use Alexa for the practical functions mentioned above, and this might serve as an enjoyable way to practice speaking and pronunciation skills. Indeed, both speaking and pronunciation are skills that learners place a substantial emphasis on acquiring (Enkin & Correa, 2018). Moreover, several language learning Alexa Skills (i.e., voice-driven apps) are available on the Echo (or any device that uses the AVS); these Skills can be accessed in the lab and used for the purpose of autonomous language learning or for learning with friends.

VUIs are composed of two primary components: natural language understanding (NLU) and automatic speech recognition (ASR), which are both powered by ML technologies. While NLU refers to the technology that enables a machine to understand human language, ASR is the technology that processes human speech into text and has been found to help with pronunciation improvement and accuracy (see Golonka et al., 2014, for a review). Recently, McCrocklin (2016) found that ASR had a positive effect on learners' beliefs about autonomous pronunciation practice because it provided useful feedback, facilitated creativity, and created less anxiety around pronunciation.

With regard to ML, it could be used to create a variety of OERs in the smart lab. These could include, for example, learner support instruments (e.g., tutoring systems that help to develop listening, speaking, reading, and writing), web apps, and games (see Vajjala, 2018). TensorFlow.js and Amazon SageMaker are two platforms that are designed to integrate ML into web apps, thereby enabling a language lab manager with a web app development background to incorporate ML into a project or activity.

One potentially interesting makerspace project that we are envisioning for the future, which would incorporate both VUIs and ML, revolves around the use of the lab's Raspberry Pi computer as the basis for a robotic intelligent personal assistant device. This device could take any form (such as a cat, for instance) and would have the ability to move around the lab on its own for students to interact with and use. By integrating AWS Lex (a service for building conversational user interfaces that utilizes ASR and NLU) into the device, students could engage via voice in scripted target-language dialogs with it (since Lex supports a variety of world languages). These dialogs could be created in the lab by an instructor, for instance, and could then be entered into the Lex interface by the lab manager. Because the Lex service uses ML-powered technologies, it learns over time how to improve itself, thereby enabling more natural conversational experiences. Moreover, the integration of computer vision for facial detection could create a more lifelike experience because the device would then have the ability to turn toward students when they are interacting with it (note that facial detection, which can only detect the shape of a face, would alleviate any privacy concerns that arise with facial recognition). Intriguingly, one could also use the Amazon Sumerian platform to create a virtual version of this device in VR. Hence, this project demonstrates a comprehensive Web 3.0 experience in that it is composed of several integrated Web 3.0 technologies.

5. Conclusion

In this chapter, we have discussed a new way of viewing an outdated language lab as a smart language lab, which takes into account the burgeoning of Web

3.0. We have discussed one account of building and integrating newer emerging technologies into this type of lab, with a focus on how we have used immersive VR in three teaching-based pilot projects within our language programs. The discussion of these projects included outlining their methodology and outcomes, extension or similar types of activities, and the roles of teachers and students. Note that depending on the type of lab project (e.g., the extent of it, whether it is a research study, and the amount of technical support it requires), the help of the lab manager, the instructor, and/or an applied linguist may be needed. This should be kept in mind when planning lab projects. Furthermore, we have highlighted the role of a smart language lab manager and the essential technical skills they should possess. On a related note, lab projects that use emerging technology might require some additional training/professional development for the instructor. However, we believe that less training will be required as time goes on because the emerging technology of today inevitably becomes the common technology of tomorrow.

Broadly speaking, our projects have led us to envisioning a smart lab as a space for innovative student projects and class assignments. In turn, these can help bring students into labs more often, can facilitate increased student motivation levels, and may also inspire teachers to use labs as full technology-infused makerspaces. In addition, lab projects can result in the creation of in-house-developed OERs, which can then be used within (and beyond) language curricula. This general idea of making/creating is also important when thinking about the future and about how a smart lab can facilitate the acquisition of transferrable skills in using and understanding emerging technology. Taking this idea a step further, a lab makerspace can provide learners with an opportunity to build a portfolio of projects so that they can make themselves more marketable in various endeavors (see Hui & Gerber, 2017, for a discussion of how makerspaces can be used for entrepreneurial purposes).

Looking to the future, we believe that the concept of a smart lab will continue to proliferate, and language labs will thus increasingly become a space for innovative teaching that is essential for providing a quality and current curriculum for our students. As we have shown, emerging technology-based projects can be guided by research in applied linguistics that occurs in a smart lab, which will in turn guide the trajectory of novel approaches to instruction through needs analysis, outcomes-based learning, and opinion/perception studies. We also believe that as Web 3.0 develops, so too will the notion of emerging technology and its ability to facilitate self-regulated and self-guided project-based learning, whether it is a project that is part of a language course or a project that is done on one's own time. We therefore envision the lab becoming a place for self-exploration guided by language-based projects that are designed to work in conjunction with a student's various fields of interest (e.g., computer science, art, music, film, language). Furthermore, as new developments arise in emerging areas (e.g., machine learning and immersive augmented reality), so too will the number of projects that are possible in a lab. Therefore, we believe that reimagining the traditional language lab as a smart lab will help frame the newer needs of such a lab: that is, the equipment, teaching approaches, and blend of technology and applied linguistics expertise that is necessary to make the smart lab a reality. We hope that this chapter has illuminated these needs and that it has highlighted ideas for labs and centers as emerging technology continues to flourish.

Acknowledgments

The authors are grateful for several institutional grants from the College of Arts and Sciences and the Office of Research and Economic Development Research Council at the University of Nebraska–Lincoln, which helped support the projects/research discussed in this chapter: (i) Grant-in-Aid (awarded in 2015) for the project *The maze task: Developing a psycholinguistic experimental procedure into a language learning mobile device application*; (ii) ENHANCE award (awarded in 2018) for the project *Developing and assessing virtual reality for language learning and open education resources*; and (iii) Instructional Improvement Fund grant (awarded in 2018) for the project *Using and assessing educational technology in the "smart" language lab: Virtual reality dialogues for Spanish curriculum development*.

References

Angus, K. (2017). Learning "about" and learning "through" technology: An analysis of syllabi from foreign language teaching methods courses. *CALICO Journal, 34*(3), 317–335.

Blikstein, P., & Krannich, D. (2013). The makers' movement and FabLabs in education: Experiences, technologies, and research. In *IDC '13: Proceedings of the 12th international conference on interaction design and children* (pp. 613–616). New York, NY: Association for Computing Machinery.

Cheng, A., Yang, L., & Andersen, E. (2017). Teaching language and culture with a virtual reality game. In *CHI '17: Proceedings of the 2017 CHI conference on human factors in computing systems* (pp. 541–549). New York, NY: Association for Computing Machinery.

Craig, E., & Georgieva, M. (2017, October 31). VR and AR: Designing spaces for immersive learning. *EDUCAUSE Review*. https://er.educause.edu/blogs/2017/10/vr-and-ar-designing-spaces-for-immersive-learning

Ducate, L., & Lomicka, L. (2013). Going mobile: Language learning with an iPod Touch in intermediate French and German classes. *Foreign Language Annals, 46*(3), 445–468.

EDUCAUSE. (2020). *Horizon Report: Teaching and learning edition*. https://library.educause.edu/resources/2020/3/2020-educause-horizon-report-teaching-and-learning-edition

Enkin, E. (2015). Supporting the professional development of foreign language graduate students: A focus on course development and program direction. *Foreign Language Annals, 48*(2), 304–320.

Enkin, E. (2016). Second language learning with the story maze task: The training effect of weaving through stories. *Canadian Journal of Applied Linguistics/Revue canadienne de linguistique appliquée, 19*(1), 1–21.

Enkin, E. (under review). Comparing two worlds: Spanish learners' face-to-face and immersive social VR speaking experiences in Spanish.

Enkin, E., & Correa, M. (2018). Evaluating learner and teacher perceptions of program outcomes in the foreign language major. *Electronic Journal of Foreign Language Teaching, 15*(1), 66–80.

Enkin, E., & Forster, K. I. (2014). The maze task: Examining the training effect of using a psycholinguistic experimental technique for second language learning. *Journal of Linguistics and Language Teaching, 5*(2), 161–180.

Enkin, E., Tytarenko, O., & Kirschling, E. (2021). Integrating and assessing the use of a "makerspace" in a Russian cultural studies course: Utilizing immersive virtual reality and 3D printing for project-based learning. *CALICO Journal, 38*(1), 103–127.

Forster, K. I. (2010). Using a maze task to track lexical and sentence processing. *The Mental Lexicon, 5*(3), 347–357.

Forster, K. I., Guerrera, C., & Elliot, L. (2009). The maze task: Measuring forced incremental sentence processing time. *Behavior Research Methods, 41*(1), 163–171.

Freina, L., & Ott, M. (2015). A literature review on immersive virtual reality in education: State of the art and perspectives. In *Proceedings of the 11th international scientific conference on e-learning and software for education (eLSE): Rethinking education by leveraging the eLearning pillar of the digital agenda for Europe, vol. 1* (pp. 133–141). Bucharest, Romania: "Carol I" National Defence University Publishing House.

Gaugler, K. M. (2016). Technology and the 21st century language classroom. In J. L. Shrum & E. W. Glisan (Eds.), *Teacher's handbook: Contextualized language instruction* (pp. 409–434). Boston, MA: Cengage Learning.

Godwin-Jones, R. (2011). Emerging technologies: Mobile apps for language learning. *Language Learning & Technology, 15*(2), 2–11.

Godwin-Jones, R. (2017). Smartphones and language learning. *Language Learning & Technology, 21*(2), 3–17.

Golonka, E. M., Bowles, A. R., Frank, V. M., Richardson, D. L., & Freynik, S. (2014). Technologies for foreign language learning: A review of technology types and their effectiveness. *Computer Assisted Language Learning, 27*(1), 70–105.

Gunter, G. A., Campbell, L. O., Braga, J., Racilan, M., & Souza, V. V. S. (2016). Language learning apps or games: An investigation utilizing the RETAIN model. *Revista Brasileira de Linguística Aplicada, 16*(2), 209–235.

Hui, J. S., & Gerber, E. M. (2017). Developing makerspaces as sites of entrepreneurship. In *CSCW '17: Proceedings of the 2017 ACM conference on computer supported cooperative work and social computing* (pp. 2023–2038). New York, NY: Association for Computing Machinery.

Incerti, F., Franklin, T., & Kessler, G. (2017). Amazon Echo: Perceptions of an emerging technology for formal and informal learning. In Y. Baek (Ed.), *Game-based learning: Theory, strategies and performance outcomes* (pp. 25–44). Hauppauge, NY: Nova Science Publishers, Inc.

Jensen, L., & Konradsen, F. (2018). A review of the use of virtual reality head-mounted displays in education and training. *Education and Information Technologies, 23*(4), 1515–1529.

Kessler, G. (2018). Technology and the future of language teaching. *Foreign Language Annals, 51*(1), 205–218.

Koeller, M. (2012). From baby boomers to generation Y millennials: Ideas on how professors might structure classes for this media conscious generation. *Journal of Higher Education Theory and Practice, 12*(1), 77–82.

Kronenberg, F. A. (2017). From language lab to language center and beyond: The past, present, and future of language learning center design. *Alsic Journal, 20*(3). http://journals.openedition.org/alsic/3172

Kwon, C. (2019). Verification of the possibility and effectiveness of experiential learning using HMD-based immersive VR technologies. *Virtual Reality, 23*(1), 101–118.

Legault, J., Zhao, J., Chi, Y-A., Chen, W., Klippel, A., & Li, P. (2019). Immersive virtual reality as an effective tool for second language vocabulary learning. *Languages, 4*(1), 13.

Lloyd, A., Rogerson, S., & Stead, G. (2017). Imagining the potential for using virtual reality technologies in language learning. In M. Carrier, R. M. Damerow, & K. M. Bailey (Eds.), *Digital language learning and teaching: Research, theory, and practice* (pp. 222–234). New York, NY: Routledge.

Lord, G., & Lomicka, L. (2004). Developing collaborative cyber communities to prepare tomorrow's teachers. *Foreign Language Annals, 37*(3), 401–416.

McCrocklin, S. M. (2016). Pronunciation learner autonomy: The potential of Automatic Speech Recognition. *System, 57*, 25–42.

Modern Language Association Ad Hoc Committee on Foreign Languages. (2007). *Foreign languages and higher education: New structures for a changed world.* New York, NY: Modern Language Association of America.

The National Standards Collaborative Board. (2015). *World-readiness standards for learning languages.* 4th ed. Alexandria, VA: Author. https://www.actfl.org/resources/world-readiness-standards-learning-languages

Pomerantz, J., & Rode, R. (2020, June 29). Exploring the future of extended reality in higher education. *EDUCAUSE Review.* https://er.educause.edu/articles/2020/6/exploring-the-future-of-extended-reality-in-higher-education

Radianti, J., Majchrzak, T. A., Fromm, J., & Wohlgenannt, I. (2020). A systematic review of immersive virtual reality applications for higher education: Design elements, lessons learned, and research agenda. *Computers & Education, 147*, 103778.

Sheridan, K. M., Halverson, E. R., Litts, B. K., Brahms, L., Jacobs-Priebe, L., & Owens, T. (2014). Learning in the making: A comparative case study of three makerspaces. *Harvard Educational Review, 84*(4), 505–531.

Sra, M., Mottelson, A., & Maes, P. (2018). Your place and mine: Designing a shared VR experience for remotely located users. In *DIS '18: Proceedings of the 2018 designing interactive systems conference* (pp. 85–97). New York, NY: Association for Computing Machinery.

Steel, C. (2012). Fitting learning into life: Language students' perspectives on benefits of using mobile apps. In M. Brown, M. Hartnett, & T. Stewart (Eds.), *Future challenges, sustainable futures: Proceedings ASCILITE Wellington 2012* (pp. 875–880). Wellington, New Zealand: Australasian Society for Computers in Learning in Tertiary Education.

Sykes, J. M., Holden, C. L., & Knight, S. W. P. (2019). Communities: Exploring digital games and social networking. In N. Arnold & L. Ducate (Eds.), *Engaging language learners through CALL: From theory and research to informed practice* (pp. 353–389). Bristol, CT: Equinox.

Vajjala, S. (2018). Machine learning in applied linguistics. In C. A. Chapelle (Ed.), *The encyclopedia of applied linguistics* (pp. 1–8). Oxford, UK: Wiley.

Van Deusen-Scholl, N., & Young, S. (2017). The role of language centers in the professional development of non-tenure track language faculty. In F. A. Kronenberg (Ed.), *From language lab to language center and beyond: The past, present, and future of language center design* (pp. 46–60). Auburn, AL: International Association for Language Learning Technology.

Vázquez, C. D. (2018). Kinesthetic language learning in virtual reality: Tapping into the physicality of language to enhance the way we learn. *MIT Media Lab.* https://www.media.mit.edu/posts/kinesthetic-language-learning-in-virtual-reality/

Vázquez, C. D., Xia, L., Aikawa, T., & Maes, P. (2018). Words in motion: Kinesthetic language learning in virtual reality. In *Proceedings of the 2018 IEEE 18th international conference on advanced learning technologies (ICALT)* (pp. 272–276). New York, NY: Institute of Electrical and Electronics Engineers.

Victor, S. R., & Mohammed, A. A. (2016). Evolution of Web 3.0 technologies in the sector of education. *Indian Journal of Applied Research, 6*(8), 212–214.

Vieira Monteiro, A. M., & Pfeiffer, T. (2020). Virtual reality in second language acquisition research: A case on Amazon Sumerian. In P. Kommers, A. Backx Noronha Viana, T. Issa, & P. Isaías (Eds.), *Proceedings of the 7th international conference on educational technologies 2020 (ICEduTech 2020)* (pp. 125–128). São Paulo, Brazil: International Association for Development of the Information Society.

Wang, J. (2006). The changing roles of a language learning center at a residential liberal arts college in the midst of technological development. *IALLT Journal of Language Learning Technologies, 38*(1), 56–65.

Appendix

Apps for Language Learning with VR

Below is a reference guide to VR apps for language learning, some of which are mentioned in this chapter. These apps are currently available worldwide for student and instructor use.

Name of App	Category	Platform	Price
AltspaceVR	Social	VR (6DoF/3DoF), Mobile, Desktop	Free
VRChat	Social	VR (6DoF), Desktop	Free
Rec Room	Social	VR (6DoF), Mobile, Desktop	Free
Mozilla Hubs	Social	VR (6DoF/3DoF), Mobile, Desktop	Free
Facebook Horizon	Social	VR (6DoF)	Not applicable (beta release only; release date to be announced)
SPACES	Video Conferencing	VR (6DoF)	Free and Pro version with tiered subscription model
ENGAGE	Training and Education Platform	VR (6DoF), Mobile, Desktop	Tiered subscription model
Adobe Medium	Sculpting	VR (6DoF/requires PC)	$29.99/one-time price
Google Tilt Brush	Painting	VR (6DoF)	$19.99/one-time price
SculptrVR	Sculpting/Social	VR (6DoF)	$9.99/one-time price
Tvori	Storytelling/3D animation	VR (6DoF/requires PC)	Free and Pro version with tiered subscription model
Flipside Studio	Storytelling/3D animation	VR (6DoF/requires PC)	Free

Author Notes

Elizabeth Enkin (PhD, University of Arizona) is Associate Professor of Spanish Applied Linguistics in the Department of Modern Languages and Literatures at the University of Nebraska–Lincoln. Her research focuses on second language learning, with an emphasis on computer-assisted language learning, language learning with emerging technology, and curriculum design. Her recent work has centered on learning with immersive virtual reality, and she has also published articles in the areas of sentence processing, online learning and teaching, outcomes assessment, and graduate student professional development.

Eric Kirschling (BA, Westfield State University) is Language Lab Manager in the Department of Modern Languages and Literatures at the University of Nebraska–Lincoln. He works hand-in-hand with faculty and lends technology-related expertise and web app development skills to lab projects that are geared toward language learning and technology. He currently focuses on the integration of emerging technology into language programs. He also manages lab equipment and day-to-day operations.

Correspondence concerning this chapter should be addressed to Elizabeth Enkin (eenkin@unl.edu).

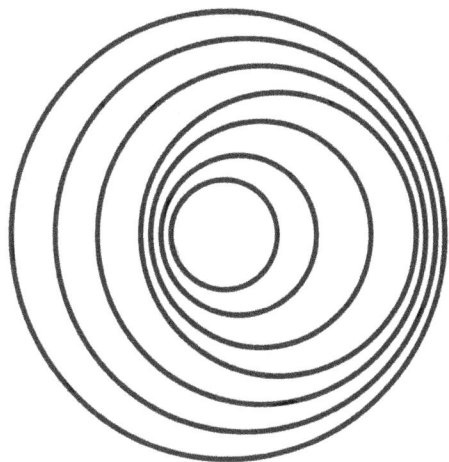

IALLT

WHERE TECHNOLOGY SPEAKS YOUR LANGUAGE

Mission Statement

The International Association for Language Learning Technology (IALLT) is a professional organization whose members provide leadership in the development, integration, evaluation, and management of instructional technology for the teaching and learning of language, literature, and culture. Its strong sense of community promotes the sharing of expertise in a variety of educational contexts. As a registered 501(c)3 not-for-profit professional organization, IALLT welcomes tax-deductible donations from individuals and businesses.

Who We Are

IALLT is a meeting ground for professionals with overlapping interests: language teachers, librarians, lawyers, architects, software developers, and others. We are a community of volunteers dedicated to providing students and teachers the best language methods and technologies possible.

History

The organization that became IALLT traces its history back to a period of great growth for the "language laboratory" and the need to share knowledge about how to run a lab effectively. In 1965, several university language lab directors, who had been meeting at the annual convention of the National Education Association (NEA) within the Department of Audio Visual Instruction, decided to create their own organization known as the National Association of Language Lab Directors (NALLD). For many years NALLD continued to meet as part of larger NEA and Association for Educational Communication and Technology (AECT) conferences. By 1981 the membership had grown well beyond the borders of the United States, and the organization renamed itself the International Association for Learning Laboratories (IALL) to coincide with its first international conference held in Tokyo in partnership with the Language Laboratory Association of Japan; this joint Foreign Language Education and Technology (FLEAT) conference now alternates between the US and Japan and held its seventh meeting again in Tokyo in 2019. In 1989, under the presidency of Ruth Trometer of the Massachusetts Institute of Technology, IALL began hosting independent, biennial meetings on the campuses of its members. In 1991, in recognition of the growing importance of new technologies in language learning, IALL changed its name to the International Association for Language Learning Technology (IALLT). In March of 2001 the organization was officially incorporated under this new name.

Throughout its evolution, the organization has emphasized the sharing of pedagogical and technical knowledge in an open community of like-minded professionals.